University of London Historical Studies

VII

UNIVERSITY OF LONDON HISTORICAL STUDIES

PERSIA AND THE
DEFENCE OF INDIA, 1884–1892

Persia and the Defence of India 1884-1892

A STUDY IN THE FOREIGN POLICY OF THE THIRD MARQUIS OF SALISBURY

by

ROSE LOUISE GREAVES

UNIVERSITY OF LONDON
THE ATHLONE PRESS
1959

Published by
THE ATHLONE PRESS
UNIVERSITY OF LONDON
at 2 *Gower Street, London* WC1

Distributed by Constable & Co. Ltd
12 *Orange Street, London* WC2

Canada
University of Toronto Press

U.S.A.
Essential Books Division
Oxford University Press Inc
New York

Printed in Great Britain by
WESTERN PRINTING SERVICES LTD
BRISTOL

IN
MEMORIAM

I.V.C.
L.A.C.

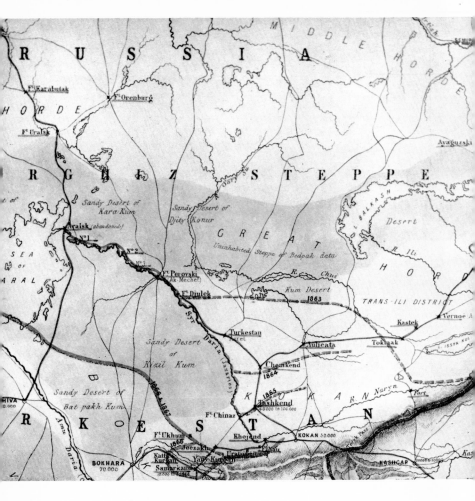

1. Part of a 'Map of Part of Central Asia, shewing the Russian Forts and Communications', prepared by the War Office.

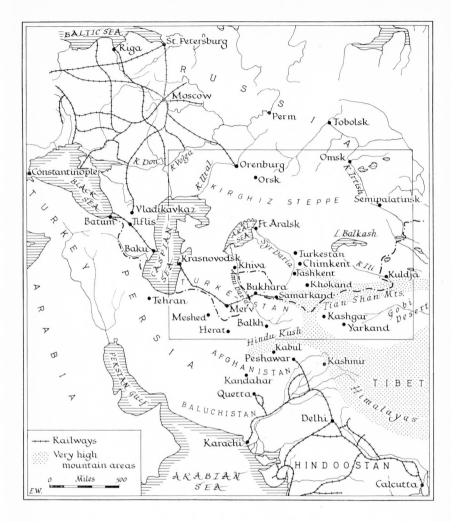

2. Successive Russian advances in Central Asia, and railways completed to 1890.

(*a*, above). General outline.

(*b*, opposite). Detail of central area.

3. Proposed British and Russian railways in Persia, 1889.

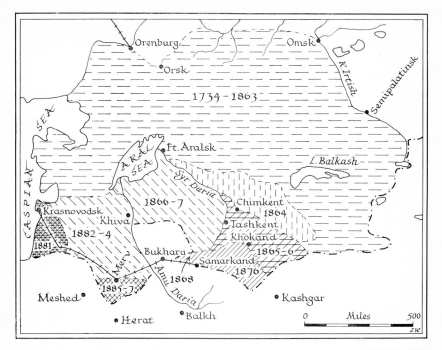

Orenburg

Orsk

Omsk

R. Irtish

Semipalatinsk

CASPIAN SEA

ARAL SEA

1734 – 1863

Ft. Aralsk

L. Balkash

Syr Daria

1866–7

Chimkent

1864

Krasnovodsk

Khiva

1882–4

Tashkent

Khokand

1881

Merv

Bukhara

Samarkand

1865–6

1876

Amu Daria

1868

1885

Meshed

Herat

Balkh

Kashgar

0   Miles   500

E.W.

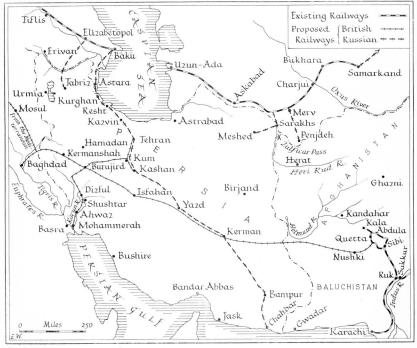

Tiflis

Elizabetopol

Erivan

Baku

CASPIAN SEA

Uzun-Ada

Bukhara

Samarkand

Askabad

Charjui

Oxus River

Tabriz

Astara

Urmia

Kurghan

Resht

Mosul

Kazvin

Astrabad

Merv

Sarakhs

Meshed

Penjdeh

Hamadan

Tehran

Zulficar Pass

Herat

AFGHANISTAN

Kermanshah

Kum

Heri Rud R.

Baghdad

Burujird

Kashan R.

From the Mole caravans

P

E

R

S

I

A

Ghazni

Euphrates R.

Tigris R.

Dizful

Shushtar

Isfahan

Birjand

Kandahar

Kala Abdula

Ahwaz

Yazd

Helmund R.

Quetta

Sibi

Basra

Mohammerah

Kerman

Nushki

Ruk

Sukkur

Bushire

PERSIAN GULF

Bandar Abbas

Bampur

BALUCHISTAN

Indus R.

Jask

Chahbar

Gwadar

Karachi

Existing Railways

Proposed { British
Railways { Russian

0   Miles   250

E.W.

4. Part of a map accompanying a memorandum by Lt.-Gen. Frederick
Roberts, 31 December 1883.

PREFACE

PERSIA IN THE latter part of the nineteenth century had a significant place in British policy. The position she occupied between the rapidly expanding Russian Empire on one side and Great Britain's Indian Empire on the other gave to her, like Afghanistan, her neighbour to the east, the political and strategic importance of a buffer state. She constituted a substantial outwork in Indian defence, and a barrier to the Russian southward drive. If Turkey was the pivot of what is commonly called the Eastern Question, Persia no less than Afghanistan may properly be regarded as a focal point of the Central Asian Question. As the first Lord Kimberley remarked: 'the decay of Persia touches us I think more nearly than that of Turkey, and the pressure of Russia in that quarter is strong and continuous'.

In this book I have tried to set forth as clearly as I can what British policy in Persia actually was, and to explain so far as is possible the reasons which lay behind it. This task has proved to be surprisingly complex. The Foreign Office, the India Office, and the War Office were all concerned, in London, with the affairs of Persia. Persia was inevitably a vital concern of the Government of India. In the hammering out of policy the voices of London and India had to be co-ordinated, and sometimes reconciled, while at the same time the recommendations made from Tehran and St. Petersburg had to be taken into account. This study is largely based on material in the British Museum, the Commonwealth Relations Office, the Public Record Office, and in private collections.

Oriental names have presented a problem. In the years with which this study deals the land of the Shah was known as Persia, not Īrān. I have, for the sake of continuity, used that form throughout. I have also retained the nineteenth-century style of transliteration for several words which occur frequently. In all quotations the spelling and punctuation have not been standardized, but appear as they are in the original document.

I have incurred many debts in the preparation of this book. First, I am grateful to my home university, the University of Kansas. I owe an especial debt to Professor Charles B. Realey. In his seminar in 1947 I first became interested in British activities in Persia.

Many other people have helped me. Mr. Richard Taylor, who was the Executive Secretary of the United States Educational Commission in the United Kingdom when I was a Fulbright scholar, gave much timely encouragement. Miss W. D. Coates and the late Mr. R. L. Atkinson, of the Historical Manuscripts Commission, were tireless in gaining access for me to collections of documents which otherwise could not have been consulted. The staff of the Public Record Office have gone to considerable trouble to meet my requests, and I thank them not only for what they have done but also for their patience and friendly helpfulness. I am particularly indebted to Mr. E. K. Timings.

I deeply appreciate the generosity of Lady Hermione Cobbold, the Earl of Kimberley, Earl St. Aldwyn, and the Marquis of Salisbury for allowing me to examine their family papers.

The papers of Lord Dufferin and Lord Lansdowne, in the India Office Libary, became available only after this book had gone to press.

This book has grown out of a thesis which was approved in July 1954 for the degree of Doctor of Philosophy in the University of London. I have to thank Professor Dame Lillian Penson under whose supervision my thesis was written, and I owe debts also to Professor C. H. Philips of the School of Oriental and African Studies and Dr. C. C. Davies of Balliol College, Oxford.

Finally I must thank my husband for his encouragement and helpful criticism.

R.L.G.

Bedford College, London

CONTENTS

MAPS

(between pages viii and ix)

1. Part of a 'Map of Part of Central Asia, shewing the Russian
    Forts and Communications', prepared by the War Office.

    Successive Russian boundaries are shown, 1863–8; forts are under-
    lined. From a copy in the Pte Kimberley Papers.

2. Successive Russian advances in Central Asia, and railways
    completed to 1890.

    (*a*) General outline: (*b*) Detail of central area. Based on a 'Skeleton
    Map shewing the Successive Russian acquisitions in Asia', prepared
    by the Intelligence Branch, War Office, October 1882 and revised,
    July 1890. From a copy in the Public Record Office (F.O. 65/1395).

3. Proposed British and Russian railways in Persia, 1889.

    Based on a map of 'Rival Projects of Railways in Persia', prepared
    by the Intelligence Branch, War Office, July 1889. From a copy in
    the Public Record Office (F.O. 65/1379).

4. Part of a 'Sketch Map shewing the position of Russia in Central
    Asia in 1863 and 1883', accompanying memorandum by Lt.-
    Gen. Frederick Roberts, 31 December 1883.

    From a copy in the Pte Kimberley Papers.

CHAPTER I

Introduction

'We certainly wish', declared Lord Salisbury in 1896, 'to be good friends with Germany: as good friends as we were in 1892.' He then explained to Sir Frank Lascelles, the newly appointed ambassador to Germany, that this meant a leaning to the Triple Alliance, without belonging to it. This policy, which Lord Salisbury had maintained from 1886 to 1892, was entirely consistent with his resolute avoidance of specific military undertakings.[1] His views were shared by other British statesmen and diplomatists, such as Lord Iddesleigh and Sir William White. They saw Germany and Austria as 'satisfied powers' who had with Great Britain a common interest in preserving the *status quo*. An active co-operation with the Central Powers was therefore possible, without the danger of being taken into their treaty system.

Set over against the 'satisfied powers' were the 'restless powers', as they were commonly regarded, that is France and Russia. They threatened the security of the British Empire, especially in Asia. As long ago as 1886, Lord Kimberley had pointed to the dangerous activities of the French. 'The French Government', he had then said, 'must I am sorry to say be counted as an adversary, seeking to do us harm in every part of the world. As far as it dares it plays into the hands of Russia.'[2] In the next year these fears were reflected in the official reports of the Director of Military Intelligence. 'The countries with which we are most liable to go to war are France and Russia, and

---

[1] Salisbury to Lascelles, private, 10 March 1896: bound volume, Germany, Pte Salisbury Papers.

[2] Kimberley to Dufferin, private, 25 August 1886: bound volume, Letters to the Earl of Dufferin, February 1886 to September 1886, Pte Kimberley Papers.

the worst combination we have any reason to dread is an alliance of France and Russia against us.'[1]

Although the Dual Alliance was not launched until the winter of 1893–4, the impact of Franco-Russian co-operation was strongly felt earlier. In 1889 Lord George Hamilton proposed the Naval Defence Bill, the leading idea of which was the two-power standard: the British fleet was to be at a minimum superior to the naval strength of any two other countries.[2] Then the most formidable combination was France and Italy, but the navy estimates for the decade 1889 to 1899 show that Great Britain built primarily against France and Russia, although she increasingly took into account such new factors as Japan, the United States, and Germany. As late as 1901 it was held that:

naval war with France, or with France and Russia, is less improbable than any other naval war which we can foresee, and I would point to the fact that France practically exclusively, and Russia largely, frames her naval policy with a view to a war with us. Russia, for the present, has to take Japan into her first consideration, but even so she never for a moment neglects to harmonize her naval policy with that of France.[3]

England's first line of defence was her fleet, just as it was the foundation of her strength and prestige, but it would be misleading to think that her army was negligible. The wide expanse of her Empire made it necessary for her to be a land power as well. In one part of the world, in the East, she ceased to be an insular and became a continental power with the obligations, responsibilities, and expenses incident thereto. This position was imposed upon her by Russia's advance through Central Asia which halted only at 'the very gates of Persia and Afghanistan'.[4] Lord Roberts explained the Anglo-Indian viewpoint as follows:

[1] Telegraphic Communications with Stations Abroad from the point of view of Imperial Defence, confidential, 2 April 1887: W.O. 33/47. See also second edition, revised and corrected to 31 May 1889: W.O. 33/49.

[2] The packet entitled 'Admiralty Memoranda for the Cabinet' and numbered PC/PP/74 is full and useful: Pte Hicks Beach Papers. The correspondence between Hicks Beach and Goschen is also of value.

[3] The Navy Estimates and the Chancellor of the Exchequer's Memorandum on the Growth of Expenditure, confidential, 16 November 1901: Pte Hicks Beach Papers.

[4] *The Parliamentary Debates (authorised edition)*, Fourth Series, Lords, 7 March 1898, liv, 795. Hereafter cited as *P.D.*

The two objectives of Russia are believed to be Constantinople and India. Her action in Europe and Asia Minor in connection with the first of these two is brought more prominently before the English public from being nearer to them, and were there no India in question, the insular military policy, which naturally finds favor amongst politicians and soldiers at home, would be the proper course for counteracting her advance. The possession of India, however, completely alters the situation, and makes it incumbent upon us to adopt what I have described as the continental policy. But, India is a long way off, and although the magnitude of interests at stake is fully admitted by the home authorities, the local conditions and requirements of the political and military situation out here are, perhaps, somewhat imperfectly realized.

So long as we retain our naval supremacy, the British Empire, except on the North-West frontier of India, is practically secure from attack. For India special arrangements must be made, and viewing England and Russia as continental powers in Central Asia . . . is regarded out here as essential to the maintenance of this great Empire.[1]

India's long land frontier extending from Tibet and Chinese Turkestan in the east to Afghanistan and Persia in the west was, of course, far removed from the sphere where naval superiority could be exerted with anything like its full weight. But for hundreds of miles along this frontier India was insulated geographically by the highest mountain barrier in the world. Only in the north-west was she really vulnerable. Even so, the danger was not acute so long as Persia, Afghanistan and the great deserts beyond separated the Russian Empire and British India. That safeguard was lost in 1884 when Russia finally succeeded in pushing her frontiers southwards until they were coterminous with Persia and Afghanistan. Then the British in India faced an entirely new problem—that of meeting an invasion from the front while at the same time providing means of controlling a possible rebellion in the rear. When the Queen asked for information on this subject she was told:

[1] Memorandum by Roberts on 'What part should India take in the event of a war between England and Russia?', strictly confidential, 22 August 1888: loose papers, Pte Salisbury Papers. Great Britain's military leaders disagreed fundamentally on how to meet a Russian advance. Lord Roberts favoured Afghanistan while Lord Wolseley maintained that meeting Russia there forfeited England's advantage in sea power. F. Maurice, *The Life of General Lord Rawlinson of Trent: From his Journals and Letters*, pp. 5, 19.

the new situation created by the approach of the Russians to the
Afghan frontier has in it many elements of anxiety. How can it be
otherwise? For the first time we are practically in immediate contact in India with a great European Power, and the effect must be to
create new complications and difficulties from which we have
hitherto been happily exempt.

I do not however at all fear a Russian invasion or direct attack
upon Herat. The danger will take another form, which I may term
'sap and mine.' . . .

If we had a quarrel with Russia, a direct advance of Russian
troops might be expected with a view to harass us, and prevent us
from acting efficiently in any other quarter.

But my own opinion is that Russia will use her position in Central
Asia rather as a means for bringing pressure to bear on us as regards
the affairs of the Turks, than with a view to any policy of conquest
in India. . . .

I have suggested *very confidentially* to Lord Ripon to have the whole
of our system of frontier defence carefully considered with a view to
plans being formed for perfecting our communications by road and
railway, such plans to be steadily pursued from year to year, until
the system is complete. Lord Napier of Magdala has given me some
valuable advice which I have made known to Lord Ripon with
whom I am in constant communication on the subject.[1]

Russia's rule over the Central Asian khanates and tribes induced the British not only to build roads, railways, and forts,
but also to investigate and to decide what were the political and
strategic bounds necessary for security. Afghanistan, Baluchistan, and Persia had long been regarded as part of India's
hinterland, but not until the last three decades of the nineteenth
century did the British establish some control over Baluchistan,
regularize their relations with the Amir, and take a systematic
interest in the affairs of Persia. In 1884 Lord Kimberley maintained that there 'would be only a remote possibility of differences between England and Russia were it not for India',[2]
and in the next year the American minister in Persia reported

[1] Kimberley to Ponsonby, private, 12 June 1884: loose papers, Pte Kimberley
Papers. Cp. Government of India, Foreign Department, to Secretary of State for
India, No. 25 of 1884, secret/frontier, 22 September 1884: Letters from India,
Political and Secret Department, vol. xli, India Office Records.

[2] Kimberley to Ripon, private, 16 October 1884: bound volume, Letters to the
Marquis of Ripon, January 1884 to November 1884, Pte Kimberley Papers.

that 'the growing importance of the question of India is gradually shifting the so-called Eastern question from Constantinople
to Teheran'.[1] Thus the geographical situation of Persia, and the
political considerations arising from its proximity to India, gave
to the kingdom of the Shah a significance far out of proportion
to its size, population, or wealth.

The Caspian Sea was once Persian. Much of the territory in
Russia's Caucasus provinces had also belonged to Persia. In
the north-east her boundaries had stretched to the Oxus river.
The Persia over which the Shah ruled from 1848 to 1896 was a
shrunken country. The Atrek river, which flows hundreds of
miles south and west of the yellow waters of the Oxus, formed
part of her north-eastern boundary after 1881. In the west the
Aras river, the Araxes of classical times, had from 1828 on-
wards separated the kingdom of the Shah from the empire of
the Czar.[2]

In spite of these territorial diminutions the country over
which the Shah ruled was very large in extent. Its 628,000
square miles exceeded the combined land area of the British
Isles, France, Switzerland, Belgium, Holland, and Germany.
The sparsity of its population was as striking as its size. When
Curzon travelled through Persia in 1890, he wrote:

As regards the population, which is estimated (not, however
upon any trustworthy basis of calculation) at from seven-and-a-
half to eight millions, the ruined cities and deserted towns show that
it must once have largely exceeded this total; while long lines of
choked up kanats [irrigation tunnels], and wide acres that have
relapsed into sand and stones, show the paralysis that has overtaken
the agricultural interest, and transformed the country from what

[1] Benjamin to Frelinghuysen, diplomatic series, strictly confidential, 2 February 1885: Persia, i, American Department of State.

[2] As early as 1869 the Russian Government had declared that the Atrek river
formed the north-eastern boundary of Persia, but the Persian Government did not
capitulate on this point until 1881. Memorandum by Hertslet on the Attrek, or
Northern, Frontier of Persia, printed for the use of the Foreign Office, confidential/
3325, September 1877: F.O. 65/991. The maps included in this historical survey
are particularly useful. The document bears the endorsements: 'This is one of Mr
Hertslet's exhaustive & lucid memoranda.' 'It is very well drawn. D.' Cp. Memorandum by Hertslet respecting the boundary between Persia and Russia; and the
Understanding between Great Britain and Russia as to the Maintenance of the
Independence and Integrity of Persia, printed for the use of the Foreign Office,
confidential, 22 April 1874: F.O. 251/57.

B

historians describe as a garden to what travellers denounce as a desert.[1]

Persia is dry as well as hot in the summer. Little rain falls over the plateau, and though it varies from place to place, it usually does not exceed fourteen inches per year. Snow falls during the wintertime on the mountains, and provides water for irrigation if properly handled when it melts. The Persians could not, as did the Romans, build open aqueducts since the hot sun and winds would soon evaporate the exposed water. Instead, long subterranean tunnels called qanats radiated out from the village to water pockets in the surrounding hills or mountains. The underground channels choked up easily, and without their reconstruction an entire settlement might disappear. Since many of Persia's people were agriculturists who lived in small villages of from fifteen to forty mud houses, a proper irrigation system was vitally important to the country. The nineteenth century found these works in a crumbling state. Water has undoubtedly been the country's most precious resource, and attention to the problem of supplying adequate amounts accounted for Persia's prosperity in the past.[2]

The most important river in Persia was the Karun in the south-west. Although it was the only navigable river in a country which had few roads, it was not used for commerce until 1888 when the Shah, at British instigation, opened it to the world as a trade route. Rising in the 'Yellow Mountains', it winds through the provinces of Luristan and Arabistan (Khuzistan), and belongs to the old fertile crescent area. Once this locality was the centre of a flourishing empire, but by the nineteenth century only the long-deteriorating ruins gave evidence of past wealth. Large mounds marked the site of former dwellings. Stone columns and broken pottery were met at every

[1] Special article in *The Times*, 31 January 1890.

[2] B. Fisher, 'Irrigation Systems of Persia', *Geographical Review*, xviii (1928), pp. 302–6. F. J. Goldsmid, *Eastern Persia: An Account of the Journeys of the Persian Boundary Commission 1870-71-72*, i, 7. C. E. Biddulph, *Four Months in Persia and a Visit to Trans-Caspia*, p. 65. In its original form this work was entitled 'Memorandum on Visit to Persia', 1891: F. O. 65/1416. It was circulated to the Intelligence Division of the War Office and was returned to Sir Thomas Sanderson by the Director of Military Intelligence with the recommendation that it 'might with advantage be printed', 16 October 1891: F.O. 60/529.

turn.[1] The great dams which had harnessed the river's water had been useless for centuries. Instead of thousands of acres under cultivation only a few settlements dotted the Karun's banks and for many years it had been used mainly by the nomadic Arabs, Lurs, and Bakhtiaris who paused briefly by its shores to water their flocks.[2] The regions which once were granaries had turned into wastelands, but many writers still hold that much of the land could be restored to productivity by an intensive irrigation and reclamation scheme.

Some parts, however, seem condemned to eternal desiccation. Persia has been described as 'a series of small deserts in a big desert'.[3] An examination of a map of the country reveals a glaring and imposing blank in the eastern and central sections. The words Dasht-i-Kavir and Dasht-i-Lut may well spread boldly across an otherwise vacant space. These are the great deserts—'the most remarkable physical feature of the high tableland of Îrân'.[4] They are estimated to account for between one-fourth to one-third of Persia's land area.

From the north-west near Tehran, the salt deserts stretch south-eastward for nearly eight hundred miles. The two are sometimes described as merging together, but a low range of hills along which runs the main caravan trail of the east central area separates the Kavir in the north from the Lut in the south at a point somewhere between the thirty-second and thirty-fourth parallels of latitude. Neither is inhabited, and they are rarely crossed. The Kavir apparently surpasses the Lut in its almost complete absence of vegetation. The latter does grudgingly give life to a few miserable shrubs and some poisonous snakes. The Kavir has the reputation of being, outside the ice packs around the poles, the largest 'absolutely barren' region on earth.[5] The former American financial adviser, Arthur Mills-

---

[1] Enclosure in Thomson to Granville and minute by Rawlinson, No. 18, commercial, 26 December 1882, printed for the use of the Foreign Office, 17 February 1883. Report by Nasr-ul-Mulk on the Karun: Home Correspondence, Political and Secret Department, vol. lv, India Office Records.

[2] W. Ainsworth, *The River Karun: An Opening to British Commerce.* G. N. Curzon, *Persia and the Persian Question,* ii, ch. xxv, pp. 330–87.

[3] V. Chirol, *The Middle Eastern Question or Some Political Problems of Indian Defence,* p. 129.

[4] G. le Strange, *The Lands of the Eastern Caliphate,* p. 6.

[5] W. Haas, *Iran,* p. 51. E. Groseclose, *Introduction to Iran,* pp. 4–5. C. E. Bid-

paugh, wrote of these salt deserts: 'This of all deserts in the world is probably the most lifeless, the most trackless, and the most hopeless.'[1]

The influence of the deserts is great. They reduce tremendously the useful land area. Like a great wedge they separate parts of eastern Persia from the rest of the country, and make effective control over the outlying portions very difficult. Rebellious chiefs and contenders for the throne have sought to escape in their vast expanses the consequences of defeat. The scorching heat in summer, bitter cold in winter, quicksands, moving hills and windstorms, and poisonous vermin took their toll of those who dared to enter—but some survived to challenge authority another day. That the British took note of this geographical feature is illustrated by Curzon's observation:

Should it ever be the fate of Persia to submit to territorial and political partition, nature has, in this part at any rate, saved the contracting or conflicting parties the expense and trouble of a Boundary Commission.[2]

Other regions are more pleasant. In the provinces around the Caspian enough rain falls to cover part of the Elburz mountains with dense forests and luxuriant vegetation. Here the climate is humid, and conditions so different that Gilan, Mazandaran, and Azerbaijan have been described as the 'alien Caspian province . . . alien in scenery, in climate, in history'.[3]

Azerbaijan, bordering Russia in the extreme north-west, had long been the richest and most densely populated of the Shah's provinces. Its people lived mainly in the valleys of the Aras, the Kizil Uzun, and the Safid Rud rivers, and south and west of Lake Rezaieh (formerly Lake Urmia). Nevertheless, a noma-

dulph, 'A March through the Great Persian Desert', *Asiatic Quarterly Review*, second series, ii (1891), 234–42.

[1] A. Millspaugh, *Americans in Persia*, p. 4.

[2] Curzon, *Persia and the Persian Question*, ii, 246–52; quotation from p. 251. For an historical account of the influence of the deserts see Le Strange, *op. cit.*, pp. 322–8.

[3] Quotation from L. Lyde, *The Continent of Asia*, p. 338. S. G. W. Benjamin, *Persia and the Persians*, pp. 46–7, 110–11. L. S. Fortescue, 'The Western Elburz and Persian Azerbaijan', *Geographical Journal*, lxiii (1924), 302–6. J. B. L. Noel, 'A Reconnaissance in the Caspian Provinces of Persia', *Geographical Journal*, lvii (1921), 401–5, 414. Report on the Agricultural Resources of Azerbaijan by William Abbott, 25 August 1889: F.O. 60/505.

dic element, principally Kurdish, ranged over the uplands there as in some other parts of Persia. The capital of the province, Tabriz, was the Tauris of classical times. In the nineteenth century it was the busiest commercial centre of the country. Traditionally, the Valiahd (Heir Apparent) governed this prize possession—a custom unfortunate for the British because of Russia's proximity and her entrenchment there. One of England's ablest ministers to Persia, Sir Arthur Hardinge, described Nasir ad-Din's son and successor as a 'weak, childish and ignorant puppet, brought up, whilst acting as nominal viceroy of Azerbaijan, in an atmosphere of subservience to Russia'.[1]

Such a combination of mountain and desert could support only a population of nomads, remote and difficult to control. All the tribal units had a marked spirit of independence, looked with contempt upon the peasant population, and were willing if provoked to defend what they regarded as their freedom by force. A Persian proverb summarized their outlook. 'I and my tribe against the nation. I and my cousins against the tribe. I and my brothers against my cousins. I against my brothers.'

The Bakhtiaris, Kurds, Lurs, as well as the Turkomans of Khorassan, produced fine warriors. Any government would have found them a challenge. To the Qajar Shah they presented an insuperable barrier to co-ordination. So long as properly organized and officered, the Persians have made good fighting material, but in the latter part of the nineteenth century their soldiers contributed little to the strength and prestige of their government. The army was described by one British observer as 'more terrible to their friends than their enemies',[2] and by another as 'probably, with the exception of the Chinese, the worst so-called standing army on anything like a large scale in the world'.[3]

[1] Quotation from A. H. Hardinge, *A Diplomatist in the East*, p. 269. See also Miscellaneous Papers, Rough Notes, etc., by Colonel Ardagh, confidential, cases entitled 'The Political Outlook in Persia and Afghanistan' and 'Persia. Reigning Family and Official Hierarchy': Pte Ardagh Papers, P.R.O. 30/40/12.

[2] Memorandum by Lieutenant-Colonel R. Murdoch Smith on the Persian Army, 29 March 1883: F.O. 60/458.

[3] Quotation from *The Times*, 11 February 1890. See also Curzon, *Persia and the Persian Question*, i, ch. xvii, pp. 571–612.

The most noteworthy military organization was the Cossack Brigade, which was established by contract with Russia in 1879. These troops kept order in Tehran and acted as the Shah's bodyguard, but their usefulness to the country as a whole was lessened by their foreign connection.[1] B. H. Sumner, writing from Russian sources, has described the Cossack Brigade as 'one of the main arms of Russian influence in Persia'.[2] Its commander did not take his orders from any Persian official or even from the Shah. He 'dealt directly with the Ministry of War in St. Petersburg'.[3] Although the British believed that the Persian army would have to be completely remodelled before it could become effective, they were far from dismissing it entirely. Towards the close of the century considerable attention was paid to the southern tribes and various projects were put forward for organizing units as a counterpoise to the Cossack Brigade. General Gordon wrote in 1891: 'The Lurs I met with on my journey had all the appearance of first-rate material for infantry as well as cavalry, and the Bakhtiari horse I saw at Kovnek impressed me as very serviceable, and capable of superior training.'[4]

Throughout the nineteenth century both Russia and England were interested in Persia. In the early years the Russians pushed down from the Caucasus and extracted substantial territorial cessions by treaties concluded in 1813 and 1828. By the latter part of the century the centre of pressure had moved from Azerbaijan in the west to Khorassan in the east. The Perso-Russian frontier stretched along a 1,200-mile line from Mount Ararat in Turkey to the Perso-Afghan village of Sarakhs.

One of the main problems underlying British policy in the

[1] Brackenbury to Currie, 1 January 1889: F.O. 60/506. Wolff to Salisbury, No. 253, very secret, 31 July 1890: F.O. 60/512.

[2] B. H. Sumner, *Russia and the Balkans, 1870–1880*, p. 514, n.

[3] B. H. Sumner, *Tsardom and Imperialism in the Far East and Middle East, 1880–1914*, pp. 52–3.

[4] Gordon to Foreign Office, 13 March 1891, enclosure 2, secret, Addendum to Report of Journey from Tehran to Mohamrah: F.O. 60/528. A memorandum following General Gordon's reports states: 'Lord Salisbury has now decided that Gl. Gordon's reports (Persian Army. Journey from Tehran to Ahwaz) are to be circulated to the Cabinet. . . . E.B. May 27/91.' See also Chapman to Gordon, confidential, 11 November 1891: Letterbook of General E. F. Chapman, D.M.I., 1891–93, W.O. 106/16. Sumner, *Russia and the Balkans*, p. 40.

Persian question was the difficulty in interpreting the motives of
Russia. Some observers believed that she hoped to obtain a port
on the Gulf. Others held that she aimed at incorporating the
four northern provinces in order to enhance her wealth—but
others again that the Shah's kingdom might be used as a convenient route for the eventual conquest of India. The last of
these speculations was frequently accompanied by a passage
from the apocryphal testament of Peter the Great:

We must progress as much as possible in the direction of Constantinople and India. He who can once get possession of these places
is the real ruler of the world. . . . Hasten the downfall of Persia, push
on into the Persian Gulf; if possible, re-establish the ancient commercial intercourse with the Levant through Syria, and force our
way into the Indies, which are the storehouses of the world.[1]

The British, however, based their analyses of the Russian
motives less on the spurious will than on the writings of Russian
generals, the facts connected with her expansion in Central
Asia, and the tenor of her important newspapers.

One of the most acute of the many interpretations of Russia's
possible aims is that advanced in 1885 by Sir Mountstuart
Elphinstone Grant-Duff, a moderate Russophil, whose opinions
were tempered by his experience as Under-Secretary of State
for India and as Governor of Madras. He reasoned that Russia's
vital interests demanded an outlet to the southern seas; that is
'unobstructed communication with the great ocean highways of
the world'. For this purpose Constantinople and the Dardanelles
were ideally suited, but between Russia and Constantinople
intervened the rival ambitions of several European states—
particularly Austria. Russia could deal, he thought, with the
other powers interested in Turkey 'were it not for England;
England, who the moment the question of Constantinople
passing to us [the Russians] is raised, trembles for her Indian
Empire, and is ready to pour out blood and treasure to thwart
our designs'. By pressing upon the Indian frontier Russia could
gain a substantial advantage because by moving a pawn in

---

[1] Testament reproduced in J. Abbott, *Narrative of a Journey from Heraut to Khiva,
Moscow, and St. Petersburgh, during the late Russian Invasion of Khiva*, ii. Appendix G.
pp. 326–39. L. Lockhart, 'The "Political Testament" of Peter the Great', *Slavonic
Review*, xiv (1936), pp. 438–41.

Central Asia England could be prevented, at some decisive moment, from moving a castle on the Bosphorus. The Central Asian empire was *l'orient de fantaisie*, while Turkey, and Turkey alone, remained *l'orient sérieux*. But the conquest of the desert and steppe land was, nevertheless, crucially important since 'England is so nervous about her Indian Empire that we [Russia] may very easily, by even seeming to threaten it, paralyse her opposition to us in Europe.'[1] This conclusion seems to be borne out by the writings of General Mikhail Skobeleff. In 1877 he said of Central Asia:

A knowledge of this region, and of its resources, leads inevitably to the conclusion that our presence in Turkestan, in pursuance of Russian interests, is justifiable solely on the ground of an endeavour to solve the Eastern question in our own favour from this quarter. Otherwise the hide is not worth the tanning, and all the money sunk in Turkestan is lost.[2]

Grant Duff dismissed the Russian menace lightly since he was certain that England possessed the power to drive her rival out of Central Asia whenever it suited her to do so. The real danger, as he perceived it, was 'that the aspirations of the growing class, known as the "educated natives", towards self-government may, before the first half of the next century is over, make it impossible for us to govern the country without measures so severe as to be unpalatable to the British electorate'. But, he continued, the nearer approach of Russia would act as a partial counter to this rising tide since the Indians must recognize the impossibility of defending themselves alone. From the threat on the north-west frontier, therefore, 'we may well pluck the flower of internal safety; for we may say to the Russians what Charles II said to his brother: "Depend upon it, they will never kill me to make you king!"'[3]

The presence of Russia on the outskirts of India added to the

[1] Confidential Memorandum by Grant Duff on the Russian Advance Towards India, enclosure in Secretary of State to Viceroy, secret, 11 June 1885: Pte Kimberley Papers.

[2] Quoted in H. S. Edwards, *Russian Projects against India: From the Czar Peter to General Skobeleff*, p. 285.

[3] Confidential Memorandum by Grant Duff on the Russian Advance Towards India, enclosure in Secretary of State to Viceroy, secret, 11 June 1885: Pte Kimberley Papers.

problems involved in governing that region. The financial strain imposed by the increasing defence burden made social and political progress more difficult.[1] Lord Dufferin, the Viceroy, telegraphed that in view of the military expenditure he must insist upon great reductions in all departments and especially in public works.[2] Lord Kimberley replied:

We cannot afford to burn the candle at all ends at once. Defence against our foreign enemy is more urgent even than 'protective' works designed to alleviate famines, important as the latter undoubtedly are.[3]

Exchanges of this sort were to become increasingly frequent.

The problem of the north-west frontier involved not only the hill tribes of those districts immediately beyond the provinces of Sind and the Punjab, but also the territories of Afghanistan, Baluchistan, and Persia. The British connection with Afghanistan was long-standing, and had tended to increase in significance and in complexity during the century. When Lord Lansdowne was Viceroy the Government of India maintained:

The most important State outside India with which the Foreign Department has intimate relations is Afghanistan, the affairs of which country are connected with Asiatic Russia, and with the tribal country on the northwest of India.[4]

In Baluchistan the influence of Great Britain was brought into prominence largely through the efforts of Sir Robert Sandeman, who has been described as the 'ruling spirit of the Western

[1] Kimberley to Grant Duff, private, 17 July 1885: loose papers, Pte Kimberley Papers.
[2] Dufferin to Kimberley, private telegram, 26 April 1885: bound volume, Telegrams to and from India, March 1885 to June 1885, Pte Kimberley Papers.
[3] Kimberley to Dufferin, private, 15 May 1885: bound volume, Letters to the Earl of Dufferin, November 1884 to July 1885, Pte Kimberley Papers. In his letter of 28 May 1885 Lord Kimberley wrote: 'It is sad that instead of devoting ourselves to internal improvement, we must give our principal thoughts to warlike preparations, but there is no help for it. Russia is not a Power to be lightly dealt with, and the only argument she pays attention to, is, unhappily, force.' Again, on 30 March 1893, he said: 'If your expenditure keeps growing, you will be face to face with financial difficulties more dangerous than the Russians.'
[4] Summary of the Principal Measures of the Viceroyalty of the Marquess of Lansdowne in the Foreign Department, secret, December 1888 to January 1894: Pte Ardagh Papers, P.R.O. 30/40/10.

Frontier of India',[1] and who was Agent to the Governor-General for Baluchistan from 1877 until his death in 1892. Thus the British were, in a sense, Persia's neighbours from Zulficar to Gwadar—a distance of approximately eight hundred miles.

The relationship of Persia to India was essentially affected by the temper of Anglo-Afghan affairs and by the advance of Russia upon the Oxus. The feelings of hostility which existed between Persia and Afghanistan were such that in those intervals when the Amir was thought reliable and when the outlook of British India and Afghanistan was identical a corresponding decline in Anglo-Persian relations ensued. The acquisition by Russia of the Central Asian territories was a still more powerful factor in determining British policy towards Persia. So long as Czarist armies kept to the north of the Jaxartes, and the khanates of Bukhara, Khokand, and Khiva remained an independent barrier between the two empires, the strength of Russian influence at Tehran did not matter vitally to India. But after those armies crossed the deserts and steppes and the great neutral zone disappeared it became quite as important for the British to maintain ascendancy in Persia as in Afghanistan. In 1891 Lord Salisbury wrote privately to Sir Frank Lascelles, who had recently been appointed minister to Tehran:

One of the most anxious cares of the Indian Gov[ernmen]t for at least two generations has been to provide against the possible danger of a Russian attack upon India. But, of late years at least, they seem to have confined their apprehension to dangers connected with Afghanistan. That Russia should seduce Afghanistan from her alliance, or that she should occupy one or more important positions in the country, & that she should, from these, operate upon the allegiance of the people of India, has been a danger ever present to the mind of the Indian Gov[ernmen]t, & all their precautions have been directed to avert it. But I do not think they have done wisely to neglect the Persian dangers to the extent to which they have done. The same circumstances & motives which might carry Russia into Afghanistan, might, if she finds it too dangerous a venture, carry her into Persia. A successful occupation of Persia, reducing it to Russian vassalage, using & improving all its vast resources, & preparing them from that base for a further move Eastward, would

[1] T. H. Thornton, *Colonel Sir Robert Sandeman: His Life and Work on our Indian Frontier*, p. 325. See below, Chapter XII.

be a policy that might attract a Russian Gov[ernmen]t, & might be very menacing to India. It can only really be frustrated by the construction of railways from the coast or the mountains, from Quetta, Kurrachi or Gwadeh, which should carry troops to within striking distance of Meshed. But to any policy of this kind the Indian Gov[ernmen]t is at present very averse, partly because it is at variance with recent traditions, partly because it involves financial burdens which at present they are in no condition to bear. I cannot but hope that they will see the mistake they are committing of neglecting this great danger, & the remedies which are required to meet it. But in the meantime we on our side must do what we can in a similar direction. . . .[1]

When Lord Salisbury wrote there seemed to be no grounds for believing that Russian expansion would cease. She had incorporated a liberal slice of Asia, but she had not yet reached what were thought to be her two goals—the Straits and India. The trans-Caspian railway line, based on Krasnovodsk and built along the northern frontier of Persia, brought the Russians to within striking distance of Persia, Afghanistan, and India. B. H. Sumner summarized the change made by the construction of this transportation line when he said: 'Whereas at the time of the Crimean war the Russian threat to India appeared solely as a lateral threat to British communications through command of the Straits or of the upper Euphrates and Tigris, twenty years later it figured prominently as a direct menace. During those twenty years Russian imperialism had swallowed the greater part of Central Asia.'[2] The Russian Foreign Minister, M. de Giers, declared that the possession of Central Asia gave to his country 'a basis of operations which, if required, can be offensive'.[3] Later Czar Nicholas II went even further:

I do like knowing that it lies solely with me [he wrote to his sister, 2 November 1899] in the last resort to change the course of the war in Africa. The means is very simple—telegraph an order for the whole Turkestan army to mobilize and march to the frontier. That's all. The strongest fleets in the world can't prevent us from settling

[1] Salisbury to Lascelles, private, 6 October 1891: bound volume, Persia, Pte Salisbury Papers.

[2] Sumner, *Russia and the Balkans*, p. 36.

[3] Giers to Mohrenheim, 6 August 1883: A. Meyendorff (ed.), *Correspondance diplomatique de M. de Staal*, i, 18.

our scores with England precisely at her most vulnerable point. But
. . . the time for this has not yet come; we are not sufficiently prepared for serious action, principally because Turkestan is not yet
linked up with the interior of Russia by a through railway line.[1]

Moreover, Russia's military power was consistently overrated,
and not by Great Britain alone. Prince Henry of Prussia told
Lord Charles Beresford: 'We Germans are considered as the
first military Power in the world, but . . . in all our calculations
we allow two Germans to one Russian.'[2] Not until the Japanese
war were Russia's weaknesses laid bare, and only then did
Great Britain's appraisal of the danger from the north undergo
a pronounced change.[3] Even in his last administration Lord
Salisbury pleaded for his Seistan railway in order to be sure that
British resistance to Russia could take place beyond the frontiers of India. On 8 June 1900 he wrote to the Governor of
Bombay:

There is another Indian policy or rather Indian neglect which
greatly afflicts me and on which I have preached in vain both to
Lansdowne and Curzon. I mean the want of the military railway
from Quetta to Seistan within the Belooch border. I acknowledge
that Curzon is exonerated by the terrible financial problems he has
had to meet. But our delay in making this railway may cause us
great embarrassment. It means that when Russia advances we shall
have to fight her on the Indian frontier. The strain of doing so will
be enormous: our defence will be a frontal attack on a mountain
barrier, which is not held by ourselves. Occasionally the defence will
fail for a time—and a spasm of sedition will shoot from one end of
India to the other. On the other hand if you had a railhead at
Seistan—connected with Quetta—or better still with the sea—
Russia could not advance Eastward without masking your force at
Seistan: an enormous effort. I am not so bent on this because I
believe Russia has any definite view of conquering India. But when
her Siberian railway is ready, she will want to be mistress of the
greater part of China: and if Afghanistan is unprotected she can
force us to give way in China by advancing upon India. She won't
try to conquer it. It will be enough for her if she can shatter our

---

[1] Extract reproduced in Sumner, *Tsardom and Imperialism*, pp. 29–30.
[2] Memorandum of Interview between Lord Charles Beresford and Prince Henry,
18 November 1898, private and confidential, printed for the use of the Cabinet,
10 January 1899: Pte Hicks Beach Papers.
[3] C. C. Davies, *The Problem of the North-West Frontier, 1890–1908*, pp. 171–2.

Government and reduce India to anarchy. These things will not concern me—but my successor of I know not what degree. But nevertheless the forecast is not pleasant. . . .[1]

Such a railway as Lord Salisbury described was a major desideratum for the British in Persia. If constructed, it would act as a counterpoise to the hitherto unanswerable menace of Russia's position along 1,200 miles of undefended frontier. However friendly the British might feel towards the Shah and his ministers, they could not escape the fact that in the event of Russian aggression material assistance simply could not be forthcoming.

Furthermore, the Seistan basin, on the Perso-Afghan border, was of real importance to the British since it commanded the valley of the Helmand and with it a route to India. Charles Christie had called attention to its latent possibilities in the early part of the nineteenth century, and from that time forward the question of Seistan, like that of Herat, persistently recurred.[2] 'It is, after all,' wrote Colonel Holdich, 'the highways of Herat and Seistan that form the only avenues for military approach to the Indian frontier that are not barred by difficulties of Nature's own providing, or commanded from the sea.'[3] Curzon emphasized the strategical worth of Seistan in one of his letters to *The Times*:

if Russia reaches Seistan before Great Britain, a more serious blow will have been dealt at British influence in the East, and even at British power in India, than would be involved in the capture of Balkh or the fall of Herat.[4]

Nearly a decade later, as Viceroy, he wrote officially in a special supplement to the Government of India's dispatch on Persia:

[1] Salisbury to Northcote, private, 8 June 1900: loose papers, Pte Salisbury Papers.

[2] Sir Alexander Burnes, Lieutenant Leech, Doctor Lord, and Lieutenant Wood, Employed on missions in the years 1835–1836–1837, in Scinde, Affghanisthan and Adjacent Countries, *Reports and Papers, Political, Geographical, and Commercial, Submitted to the Government* (Calcutta, 1839): No. VIII, *On Herat, With a Sketch of the State of Affairs in Surrounding Countries*, No. XIII, *A Description of the Country of Seisthan*.

[3] T. H. Holdich, *The Gates of India, being an Historical Narrative*, pp. 335–6, 525; quotation from p. 525.

[4] Special article in *The Times*, 21 December 1889.

Seistan is, by virtue of its position and its features, an object of much interest both to Russia and Great Britain. Situated at the point of junction of the frontiers of Persia, Afghanistan, and Baluchistan, its future affects the destinies of all three countries. Lying, as it does, almost midway between Meshed and the Persian Gulf, no advances can be made from Khorasan to the sea except through Seistan. Its position upon the exposed flank of Afghanistan would render its occupation of great value to any Power contemplating either a move against that country, or an advance upon Kandahar. Nor will it be denied that the Kandahar–Herat line could not be held with safety by India, nor the valley of the Helmand defended, were a hostile Power in possession of Seistan. Furthermore, the grain-producing capabilities of the district, to the bygone richness of which eloquent testimony is borne by the immense number of ruined cities encumbering the soil, and which could without serious difficulty be revived by scientific employment of the waters of the Helmand, render Seistan of much value, as a possible granary, either to a Power engaged upon a forward advance, or to a Power interested in commercial and industrial expansion.[1]

Seistan had from time to time been ruled by Persia, but in the nineteenth century the Shah's authority was vaguely felt in the area and much of it was either quasi-independent or under Afghan rule. The population was predominantly Persian, but geographically the region belonged to Afghanistan. The Amir's hold on the country during the nineteenth century was 'more spasmodic than sustained'. A British commission had, at the Shah's request, demarcated the boundary in 1872. Persia was awarded all 'Seistan Proper', but not all 'Outer Seistan'.[2]

The potentiality of this basin was not limited to its command of one of the gates to India. In earlier times it had been known as the granary of Asia, but the region had never recovered from Tamerlane's devastation. In the nineteenth century it barely supported 100,000 people, and Sir Alexander Burnes remarked that 'ancient forts are often laid bare by the blowing away of the sands, while modern ones are overwhelmed'.[3] Still, its rich

[1] Supplement to the Government of India, Foreign Department, to the Secretary of State for India, No. 175, dated 21 September 1899, secret/external, Minute by the Viceroy of 4 September 1899 on Seistan: F.O. 60/615.

[2] An account of the work of the boundary commission is given in Goldsmid, *op. cit.*, quotation from i, 410–11.

[3] Quotation from A. Burnes *et al.*, *Reports and Papers*, No. VIII, *On Herat, With*

alluvial soil was thought to be capable of great production if the waters of the Helmand were properly channelled. The British feared that the area might be occupied, developed by the Russians, and then used as a base for moving troops towards India or the sea. As Valentine Chirol put it:

Seistan alone, amidst the wildernesses of Eastern Persia, would afford her [Russia], in virtue of its natural resources and of its geographical position, a tempting field for economic and political expansion, as well as an admirable strategic base for future military operations. Seistan lies midway athwart the track of the shortest line which could be built to connect the Trans-Caspian Railway with the Indian Ocean.[1]

In the closing years of the nineteenth century Seistan became a scene of lively activity—the 'meeting point of the advanced pioneers of British and Russian influence'.[2]

Since the British had moved up to Persia's eastern frontier and since the navy maintained virtually unchallenged supremacy in the Gulf, England's dominance in those regions might seem to parallel that of Russia in the north; but the comparison is not valid. Persia's northern provinces bordered on both European and Asiatic Russia, and were made increasingly vulnerable by the rapid and constant development of an elaborate system of strategic railway lines. The Imperial Government could at any time order thousands of soldiers to march against the Shah's forces. An invasion could be undertaken by any one of several routes from Sarakhs on the Afghan border to Julfa near Turkey. There was practically no problem of supply. With such proximity and overwhelming military superiority, the Russians could speak persuasively at Tehran.[3]

The position of Great Britain in the east and south was by no

a Sketch of the State of Affairs in the Surrounding Countries, pp. 39–40. Le Strange, op. cit., pp. 334–51.

[1] Chirol, op. cit., p. 288.

[2] Government of India, Foreign Department, to the Secretary of State for India, No. 175, dated 21 September 1899, secret/external: F.O. 60/615. An extract from this document, known as the 'Curzon Despatch', is reproduced in G. P. Gooch and H. Temperley, assisted by Lillian M. Penson (eds.), British Documents on the Origins of the War (hereafter cited as B.D.), iv, 356–63.

[3] Enclosure by Major Wells in Wolff to Salisbury, No. 87, secret and confidential, 18 June 1888, Report on the Strategical Position of Tehran: F.O. 65/1350. Thomson to Salisbury, No. 3, commercial, 30 July 1879: F.O. 60/449.

means so advantageous. British control over Afghanistan was largely confined to keeping other powers out. The foundation of the Baluchistan Agency in 1877 established a closer relationship with the Indian Empire, but Baluchistan could offer no practicable route into Persia so long as roads and railways remained unbuilt. The alternative approach was by way of the Persian Gulf. This entailed an exhausting sea journey for the troops before they reached the country, hard marches into the interior over roads little better than caravan trails, and almost prohibitive supply lines. Moreover, the Persian Gulf was not necessarily a *mare clausum*, and hostile powers could menace the British troops *en route*.

It would be misleading to measure the danger to Persia simply in terms of the distances from the Russian frontier to the various objective points and the time required to cover them. The problem centred less in Russia's strength than in Persia's weakness. A British intelligence officer put it thus:

The real menace to the independence of Persia lies in the fact . . . that owing to the disorganization of her forces, and the supineness of her government, she is incapable of offering any resistance to a well-directed blow aimed at her integrity. Though mistress of a population the various elements of which . . . are well suited to the profession of arms, she does little or nothing to utilize their martial instincts. It is to the remedy of this neglect that our efforts, in the first instance, should be mainly directed, if any improvement in the situation is to be looked for.[1]

The task of the British in Persia was therefore to sponsor and to encourage those measures that might reasonably lead to improvements in government, in the army, and in the life of the people so that the Persians themselves would not welcome the Russians as deliverers, and so that, in addition, outside powers whose influence counted in St. Petersburg would become not only sympathetic but also helpful to Persia in her struggle to retain her independence.

The Russians imposed Persia's northern boundary upon her.

[1] Memorandum by Captain Wolfe Murray on report by Wells. 27 July 1888, endorsed 'Approved. H. Brackenbury, Lt. Gen., D.M.I. 3/8/88': F.O. 65/1352. The memoranda by Wells and Wolfe Murray should be read together with the War Office memorandum entitled *Russia's Power to Concentrate Troops in Central Asia*, secret, 4 May 1888: F.O. 65/1349.

British commissions supervised the delimitation of her frontiers with Afghanistan and Baluchistan. The British-controlled Arabian Sea and the Persian Gulf clearly marked her southern limits from Gwadar to the mouth of the Shatt al-'Arab—a distance of nearly nine hundred miles. Turkey on the west completed the encirclement. Persia's relations with both Afghanistan and Turkey were embittered by religious cleavages. The majority of Persians were Muslims belonging to the Shi'i sect, but the Afghans and Turks were Sunnis. Antagonism between these two branches of the Muslim religion reached fanatical heights, and often resulted in persecutions. Moreover, the Turkish possession of the sacred Shi'i shrines of Kerbela and Nadjaf rankled with the Persians as much as Afghan rule over Herat—a fortress over which the standard of the Lion and the Sun had often floated. Persia's relations with her neighbours to the east and to the west were far from friendly, but the real foreign impact came from the north and south—from the Russians and the British. The American minister in Tehran wrote: 'The Representatives of the other Powers including your own are merely lookers on and watchers of the game which the two great Powers above named, are playing.'[1]

[1] Winston to Bayard, diplomatic series, No. 14, 20 April 1886: Persia, ii, American Department of State.

C

CHAPTER II

Indian Interests and Military
Considerations in Persia

SITUATED as it was between the rapidly expanding Russian
Empire on one side and Great Britain's Indian Empire on
the other, Persia had a diplomatic importance which was
greater than that of other more powerful nations. Throughout
the nineteenth century Persia was a buffer state. It was the
'outer glacis of an extreme bastion'.[1] The Shah's domain and
that of his neighbour the Amir served as outworks in Indian
defence.

The Marquis Wellesley, by dispatching Mehdi Ali Khan on
a mission to Tehran in 1798, took the initial step in bringing
Persia into the orbit of Indian foreign policy.[2] His purpose was
to ascertain the Shah's attitude towards the aggressive Afghans
led by Zaman Shah. But the rumoured plans of Napoleon of
France and Paul of Russia soon became a subject of much
graver concern. In 1800 Captain John Malcolm was sent by
Lord Wellesley to represent the British Government at the
court of the Shah. His instructions were 'to establish with Persia
an intimate connection founded on durable and comprehensive
principles'. Lord Wellesley went on to explain to the Secret
Committee of the Court of Directors:

The policy which dictated my opinion, was calculated to provide
not only against the menaced invasion of Zemaun Shah, but also
against the views which other powers may entertain of attacking the
British possessions in India. This object is important in proportion to
the hazard to which the British interests would be exposed, by a con-

[1] Hamilton to Curzon, private, 26 January 1900: Private Correspondence, India,
part ii, vol. v, Pte Hamilton Papers, India Office Library.
[2] H. W. C. Davis, *The Great Game in Asia (1800–1844)*, pp. 4–6. W. H. Hutton,
The Marquess Wellesley, pp. 129–30.

nection between the Court of Persia, and those European powers, whose views have long been directed to this quarter of the British dominions.[1]

An Afghan invasion proved illusory and the French menace faded away. The Russians and the British emerged as the principal opponents in what came to be named by one of its participants 'the Great Game in Central Asia'.[2] The game lasted for more than a century and was played upon a field which extended north over the plateau of the Pamirs and east into Chinese Turkestan; it swept westward through the deserts and steppes of the Muslim khanates of Central Asia; it moved south over Afghanistan's Hindu Kush mountains, and it found its westward limits in the Iranian plateau.

Some of the ablest British administrators in India, while admitting that Russia's approach would be very serious if real, were slow to admit that it was sufficiently imminent to mould their policy. They pointed to the vast distances which had long separated the Russian possessions from India, the warlike and barbaric temperament of the populations of the intervening territories, the barrenness of much of the region, the physical obstacles, and the cost in men and money of any attempted conquest. Nevertheless, as early as 1800, the idea of an invasion of India, though not invasion by Russia, pervaded the writings of some officials responsible for the safety of India. In the January of that year General James Stuart wrote as follows:

The route by which Alexander, and other conquerors arrived in India, is still open, and the people whose ancestors composed their armies, possess at this moment perhaps an equal degree of courage and adventure as their forefathers. They require but an ambitious or enterprizing leader, to pour forth their uncivilized bands, and to overspread like a torrent, the fertile fields of Hindostan, which,

[1] The Marquess Wellesley to the Honourable the Secret Committee of the Honourable the Court of Directors, 'Persian embassy and Treaty, and advantages thus secured. Why an European ambassador, in state, was required', 28 September 1801. Reproduced in S. J. Owen, *A Selection from the Despatches, Treaties, and Other Papers of the Marquess Wellesley, during his Government of India*, pp. 607–8.

[2] J. W. Kaye in his *History of the War in Afghanistan* seems first to have popularized the expression 'Great Game in Central Asia' when he used it in his second chapter in volume ii. The phrase evidently originated with Arthur Conolly who, while an agent in the service of the Indian Government, was tortured and finally beheaded at Bukhara in 1842. Kaye, *op. cit.*, ii, 71; iii, 257–8.

aided by the remembrance of the exploits of their predecessors, holds
out a perpetual object of temptation.

But it is easier to resist the unregulated efforts of barbarians, than
the constant and systematic attempts of European nations. The
superiority which has always attended the people in possession of
the commerce, or power of this part of Asia, must ever excite
jealousy and raise up opponents. . . . No native state can ever be very
formidable without the assistance of an European ally; . . .

In a political light our intercourse with Persia deserves attention,
for it is in the power of the sovereigns of that country to repress or
assist the hosts of barbarians ready at all times to precipitate themselves on India as on a certain prey.[1]

Ever since that time Persia has entered into the calculations
of those who have planned the defence of India. Her rôle
changed radically according to the circumstances of the
moment—such as the proximity of Russian power and the state
of relations between England and Russia in Europe. It also
changed with the school of frontier policy in ascendancy.
Unless it is viewed against its Anglo-Russian background the
conduct of Britain in Persia presents a series of mystifying varia-
tions. The British emphasized commercial interests, then sacri-
ficed them; co-operated with the Shah as a friend and ally, then
made war on him; urged reforms for the improvement of the
country, then failed to encourage those reforms when they
appeared; blocked Russian advances into the Iranian area, then
co-operated in the promotion of Russia's 'natural interests'
there.[2] Yet all these apparent reversals and seeming incon-
sistencies become comprehensible when looked at from the
European and Asiatic, and not merely from the local point of
view. The course pursued in Persia had to be contingent upon
larger choices. Thus Lord Derby in 1877 asked the India Office
for its opinion on a question which had arisen in Persia, 'bear-

---

[1] Copy of a private paper written by General Stuart prior to his leaving India in
January 1800, and submitted to the Right Honourable Henry Dundas, on his
arrival in England, in July in that year. Owen, *op. cit.*, pp. 567-77; quotations from
pp. 569 and 576-7.

[2] The best published survey of Anglo-Persian relations from 1798 to 1875 is
given in the first two chapters of H. C. Rawlinson, *England and Russia in the East*.
See also his memorandum relative to the Appointment of British Officers to
organize the Persian Army, confidential, printed for the use of the Foreign Office,
6 August 1874: F.O. 60/368.

ing in mind the peculiar relations now existing between England and Russia'.[1]

Uneasiness characterized the spirit of Anglo-Russian relations. This dated at least from the treaty of Turkmanchai in 1828. Negotiations were conducted in an atmosphere of mutual distrust which sometimes flared into open hostility. Even Sir John Lawrence admitted that Russia's approach to India was 'fraught with future trouble and danger'.[2] Lord Roberts, 'through his Indian service, dispassionately and without panic, . . . assumed the certainty of a struggle in Asia with Russia'.[3] India lacked the military strength to deal with Russia alone, and in any serious conflict would depend upon reinforcements. Therefore, the War Office in London was directly concerned with Central Asian and Persian affairs.[4]

Great Britain's nineteenth-century interest in the Shah's kingdom was not confined merely to strategic nor to commercial interests. The primary consideration was always India. Lord Salisbury once declared: 'were it not for our possessing India, we should trouble ourselves but little about Persia'.[5] Over a decade later Lord George Hamilton reaffirmed that principle: 'the more you investigate the sources of our interest in Persia the clearer it becomes that they are almost exclusively Indian'.[6]

The conduct of the Legation at Tehran was under the jurisdiction of the India Office in 1858 and 1859. From 1860 onward the Foreign Office resumed control, but the Government of

[1] Undated minute by Derby on notes by Currie and Tenterden of 2 and 3 July 1877: F.O. 65/990.

[2] Memorandum by Lawrence on the Central Asian Question, 4 November 1874: F.O. 65/904.

[3] J. L. Morison, *From Alexander Burnes to Frederick Roberts. A Survey of Imperial Frontier Policy*, p. 27.

[4] Military Needs of the Empire in a War with France and Russia, secret, 1901: W.O. 106/48, E3/2. Secret memorandum by Brackenbury on the relations between the Intelligence Departments of the War Office, Admiralty, and India, 15 May 1890: W.O. 33/50.

[5] India Office to Foreign Office, 22 May 1889: F.O. 60/506. Indian contributions for China Establishments, East Indian Squadron, and Persian Mission respectively. Memorandum drawn up at the Treasury, recording the several Agreements made between the Secretaries of State for Foreign Affairs and India, the Chancellor of the Exchequer, and the First Lord of the Admiralty, at a Conference held in the Foreign Office, on 26 March 1890: F.O. 60/517.

[6] Hamilton to Curzon, private, 7 November 1901: Private Correspondence, India, part ii, vol. vi, Pte Hamilton Papers, India Office Library.

India continued to pay a substantial part (twelve-seventeenths after 1879) of the costs of British establishments in Persia.[1] That this arrangement did not give complete satisfaction is evident from Lord Salisbury's assertion in 1879 that 'the whole Legation ought to be handed over to India'.[2] In later years, while continuing to recognize the primacy of Indian interests, he believed that the transfer was impossible if for no other reason than the intractable attitude of the Shah who imagined that control from India relegated the affairs of his country to a lower level.

Persia's dual significance, her relationship to India and to Russia, rendered it inevitable that the formulation of policy towards her would be a slow and complex process. Its determination involved three departments in London, the Foreign Office, the India Office, and the War Office, and, in addition, the Government of India, the minister in Tehran, and the ambassador in St. Petersburg. Nevertheless, the Foreign Office bore by far the greatest responsibility.[3]

Both Lord Salisbury and Lord Rosebery appreciated India's vital concern, and reached their conclusions only after careful consultations with the India Office. On important issues, the opinions of the Government of India were weighed as well. During the years from 1885 to 1892 the tripartite control of the three major bodies—the Foreign Office, India Office, and Government of India—was characterized by essential harmony and unity of purpose. Occasionally, conflicting advice induced the Foreign Secretary to rely on the discretion of the British representative in Tehran. One of the most striking evidences is the following:

. . . under the circ[umstanc]es—considering that F.O.—I.O.—& I.G.—have all different views on the subject: & that Persia says one

[1] C. U. Aitchison (compiler), *A Collection of Treaties, Engagements, and Sanads Relating to India and the Neighbouring Countries*, xiii, *The Treaties . . . relating to Persia and Afghanistan*, p. 12. Note on British Mission at Tehran, confidential, 25 February 1887: Letters from India, Political Department, vol. xlix, India Office Records.

[2] Minute by Salisbury of 19 July on India Office to Foreign Office, 17 July 1879: F.O. 60/426.

[3] Indian contributions for China Establishments, East Indian Squadron, and Persian Mission, respectively. Memorandum drawn up, etc. . . ., 26 March 1890: F.O. 60/517.

thing here and another at Teheran—I think Nicolson ought to be allowed to act according to his own judgment. . . .[1]

The Russians set the tone of Anglo-Persian relations by their relentless advance through Central Asia in the latter part of the nineteenth century. Reactions to that southward drive occurred in Persia, in India, and in England. Nasir ad-Din remembered that his grandfather had once ruled Georgia, Daghistan, and Karabagh, and that his domain had also included the Caspian Sea. The loss of all these territories together with the recognition of Russia's exclusive rights over the Caspian was the price Fath 'Ali Shah paid for having the Czar as his neighbour in the north-west.[2] As Russian generals possessed with the 'K.C.B. mania'[3] pushed nearer to Persia along a line stretching for hundreds of miles east of the Caspian, Nasir ad-Din and his ministers became progressively more alarmed. They appealed to England for protection.

The Government of India, too, watched anxiously. No longer was Russia's approach regarded as a vague menace which might require attention some day. Lord Lytton described her encroachment upon India's frontiers as 'a very real, a very close, and a very ponderable, danger'.[4] Steps were taken to meet the challenge. Little could be accomplished without accurate information on Russian movements and apparent intentions. Therefore, a succession of officers of the Indian army proceeded to Khorassan and Baluchistan with orders to organize an intelligence service and to inject an element of stability into the border regions if possible.[5] The Government of India, prodded

[1] Minute by Salisbury of 4 October on Foreign Office memorandum on Afghan refugees, 3 October 1887: F.O. 65/1323.
[2] Aitchison, op. cit., p. 8; Appendix V, Translation of the treaty of Gulistan between Russia and Persia, 1813, pp. xv–xviii; Appendix VII, Translation of the treaty of Turcmanchai between Russia and Persia, 1828, pp. xxiii–xxxiv.
[3] Salisbury to Lytton, private, 2 June 1876: Letters from the Secretary of State, i, Pte Lytton Papers.
[4] Lytton to Salisbury, private and confidential, 16 July 1877: B.M. Add. MSS. 39164, vol. ccxxxiv, Pte Layard Papers.
[5] Foreign Office memorandum by E.B., 18 December 1882: F.O. 65/1153. Secret Report of Lieutenant-Colonel Charles Edward Stewart, Bengal Staff Corps, on Special Duty on the Perso-Afghan Frontier, 8 February 1883: F.O. 65/458; a copy is in the Pte Kimberley Papers. Foreign Secretary, Viceroy's Camp, Rangoon, to Colonel Charles S. Maclean, No. 7, secret telegram, 6 February 1886:

by Lord Roberts, also prepared for 'eventualities' by drawing
up elaborate defence plans. These were submitted to the Home
Government for revision.[1] In the field of frontier policy the
British sought to bolster the remaining buffer states and to
strengthen Britain's position in Afghanistan, Baluchistan, and
Persia. The methods adopted, in varying forms, for Afghan-
istan and Baluchistan were not, however, readily applicable to
Persia. For many years to come, able men, in London and in
India, grappled with the Persian question, but with such lack
of success that it almost seemed as if the fates had elected that
the Persian problem would remain unsolved and for ever, as
Grey put it in 1911, 'very tiresome and very serious'.[2]

The conquest of Khiva in 1873 induced the Shah to make
representations to England which brought the whole Persian
question into focus. The Government of India examined it carefully and submitted to London separate minutes by the Viceroy
and all the members of his Council.[3] These suggestions met with
little approval in the Foreign Office. As Lord Tenterden put it:
'what they [the Government of India] seem to me to be aiming
at is an English Protectorate over Persia'.[4] In reality, the
Viceroy, Lord Northbrook, did not advocate, as did Napier of
Magdala, a guarantee of territorial inviolability, but he emphasized Persia's importance to the Empire and put forward
several concrete proposals to be undertaken for mutual advantage—such as the improvement of communications between
the Gulf and the capital and the addition to the Legation at
Tehran of a military attaché from the Indian service.[5]

The India Office, as illustrated by Lord Salisbury's endorsement of the Viceroy's minute and by Sir Henry Rawlinson's
memoranda, advocated a milder course than a guarantee and

F.O. 65/1347. Secretary to the Government of India to Brigadier-General Charles S.
Maclean, No. 2005F, 6 October 1887: F.O. 248/450.

[1] Several of the important plans are summarized in an appendix to the following
document: Military Needs of the Empire in a War with France and Russia, secret,
1901: W.O. 106/48, E3/2.   [2] *B.D.*, x, part i, 813.

[3] Enclosures in Government of India, Foreign Department, to Secretary of State
for India, No. 123 of 1875, political, 7 June 1875: F.O. 60/377.

[4] Undated minute by Tenterden on India Office to Foreign Office, 17 August
1875: F.O. 60/377.

[5] Enclosures in Government of India, Foreign Department, to Secretary of State
or India, No. 123 of 1875, political, 7 June 1875: F.O. 60/377.

protectorate but deprecated the policy of drift. Lord Salisbury
reiterated the reasons for constructing roads and railways from
the Gulf towards the inland cities of central Persia and ultimately to the capital itself. He also favoured a more energetic
policy in Tehran.[1]

Rawlinson, drawing on his forty years of experience of the
East, perceived that a *juste milieu* had to be found between an
aggressive policy which might provoke a collision with Russia
and lethargic inaction which would inevitably end in Persia's
complete submission to her neighbour on the north.[2] Differences would undoubtedly arise over the suitability of the various
suggestions, but Rawlinson was convinced that at least one
point could not be doubted.

Some activity must be shown, some expense, some responsibility
must be incurred, if we are to arrest the downward course of events
which are rapidly converting Persia into an outlying Russian
dependency.[3]

The ensuing years saw no satiation of the Russian appetite
for land. Lord Salisbury wrote in 1877: 'The one absorbing
question is our policy towards Russia.'[4] As the generals carried
the double eagle nearer Merv, Persia attracted more attention
since the Shah claimed a vague suzerainty over the Turkoman
tribes of that area. The Viceroy and his Council again exhaustively reviewed the Russo-Persian situation with special reference to the fate of Merv, and sent a unanimous recommendation to London urging the utilization of Persia to stem Russia's
advance. The Government of India asked that 'no time . . . be
lost in making every possible effort to restore British influence
at Teheran', offered a number of suggestions for immediate
action, and even volunteered some 'pecuniary sacrifice' for the
attainment of their objectives.[5]

[1] India Office to Foreign Office, 6 August 1874: F.O. 60/406. Same to same,
17 August 1875: F.O. 60/377.
[2] Enclosures in India Office to Foreign Office, 13 October 1874, memoranda by
Rawlinson on the Persian Question, 5 and 12 October 1874: F.O. 60/368.
[3] Rawlinson, *England and Russia in the East*, p. 137.
[4] Salisbury to Lytton, private and confidential, 22 June 1877: B.M. Add. MSS.
39164, vol. ccxxxiv, Pte Layard Papers.
[5] Government of India, Foreign Department, to the Secretary of State for India,
No. 21 of 1877, secret, 2 July 1877: F.O. 65/992.

The Foreign Office was already aroused. The reconnaissances undertaken by General Lomakin in 1876 and 1877 from Krasnovodsk on the Caspian towards Kizil Arvat looked suspiciously as if they had Merv for their ultimate objective. The Foreign Office instructed the British ambassador in St. Petersburg to make clear the 'evil consequences' which would follow any such manœuvre.[1] At Lord Salisbury's suggestion the Russians were reminded of the assurances they had given and of their having denied 'any idea of occupying Merv'.[2] This firmness probably accounts, at least in part, for the postponement of the disappearance of the tribal territories surrounding the oasis as independent entities.

Neither the Foreign Office nor the India Office fully accepted the views of the Government of India. Indeed, the Foreign Office described the communication as that 'alarmist despatch from India'.[3] The India Office reply to the Viceroy has some traces of a cavalier tone. 'Merv would bring to Russia neither revenue, nor subjects, nor security. Save as a basis for a further advance towards India, the permanent occupation of Merv would be a needless and wanton waste both of money and of military force'—so the Viceroy was informed.[4] A year later Lord Lytton referred to the reception in London of his Merv dispatch.

We were then told that our warnings were witless; our anxieties, nightmares; our calculations, the crude excursions of an untutored fancy; our conclusions, airy fabrics raised by unreasonable fears from a foundation which, whilst we were building on it, had already vanished from the region of fact. High authorities at that time im-

---

[1] Foreign Office draft to Loftus, No. 244, 13 July 1877, endorsed 'Send Dft. to Ld. Salisbury': F.O. 65/990. The dispatch was in part revised by Salisbury and approved by Beaconsfield before it was sent. The territory from Khiva to the Atrek had already been annexed to Russia by a secret protocol signed by the Emperor in October 1874. See 'Protocol of Conference held at St. Petersburgh on the Affairs of Central Asia' in Memorandum by Hertslet on the Attrek, or Northern, Frontier of Persia, printed for the use of the Foreign Office, confidential/3325, September 1877: F.O. 65/991.

[2] India Office to Foreign Office, 6 June 1877: F.O. 65/990. Same to same, secret, 12 July 1877: F.O. 65/991.

[3] Minutes on India Office to Foreign Office, secret and immediate, 9 October 1877: F.O. 65/992.

[4] India Office to Government of India, No. 68, secret, 18 October 1877: F.O. 65/992.

pressed on me that 'the complete collapse of Russia as a great military Power' rendered practically impossible any serious danger to the land frontiers of India from that quarter.

I venture to think that our political foresight will stand comparison with that of our critics, and that subsequent events have better justified our alarm than their confidence. . . .[1]

Others, too, regretted that more of the proposals from the Government of India had not been adopted. Sir Owen Burne wrote to Lord Lytton: 'Do you ever read and re-read your Despatch of 2 July 1877? It gives me great satisfaction to do so.'[2]

Less than a decade later, the Turkomans of Merv and Penjdeh owed their allegiance to the Czar. The British considered the capitulation serious.[3] Sir Mortimer Durand, then Under-Secretary in the Indian Foreign Department, wrote in his diary: 'The Russian question has assumed an altogether new phase.'[4] One of the ramifications of this new phase in Anglo-Russian relations was a more energetic policy in Persia.

Between 1885 and 1892 three men held the post of Secretary of State for India—Lord Kimberley (1882–5, 1886, 1892–4), Lord Randolph Churchill (1885–6), and Lord Cross (1886–92). Lord Kimberley's numerous minutes and long private letters reveal a conscientious and assiduous minister who directed his department with penetrating insight and a steady hand. His attitude towards Russian expansion and its bearing upon India is set forth in a minute written in April 1885:

In two or three years at longest the Russian railway will be extended to Merv or perhaps nearer their new frontiers. The difficulties of transport etc. will then be greatly lessened. Further, I fully anticipate that ere long Khorassan will fall into the hands of Russia. A march to Herat will then be comparatively easy, and it can hardly be maintained that, when the Russians are firmly established in the Herat district, India will be inaccessible to them except by a

[1] Lytton to Cranbrook, private, 3 August 1878; quoted in Lady Betty Balfour, *Personal and Literary Letters of Robert First Earl of Lytton*, ii, 113–14.

[2] Burne to Lytton, private, 18 July 1879: Letters from England, viii, Pte Lytton Papers.

[3] Kimberley to Ripon, private, 22 February 1884: bound volume, Letters to the Marquis to Ripon, January 1884 to November 1884, Pte Kimberley Papers.

[4] Diary entry of 23 July 1884, quoted in P. M. Sykes, *The Right Honourable Sir Mortimer Durand*, p. 135.

'gigantic' effort. Russia, it must be recollected, has a very large army
composed of troops (putting aside her Central Asian irregulars),
more than a match for any but our best native troops (of whom we
have but a limited number). Poland and the Caucasus and the preservation of internal order in her vast and not very contented
Empire absorb, it is true, a great number of these troops: but still,
allowing for this, she has a powerful force at her disposal for a
foreign expedition, and her position on the Caspian, communicating
with the interior of her Empire and the Volga, and with the Black
Sea viâ Tiflis is very favourable for the movement of such a force
towards India.

Without pursuing the matter further I have said enough to show
why I am strongly of opinion that India should have a properly
armed frontier, such as exists between the great Continental States.

If we settle our present difference with Russia, we shall have an
interval which she will use to improve her means of aggression. If we
on our side use it diligently to put our frontier in a real state of
defence, we have no reason to dread the future, but on this condition only.[1]

In June of the same year, Lord Randolph Churchill succeeded Lord Kimberley. Writing to Lord Salisbury a decade
later, Sir Philip Currie's thoughts carried him back through the
years; he recalled: 'when you formed your Gov[ernment] in
[18]85 [and said] that the India Office would be a padded
room for that restless being'.[2] Restless Lord Randolph proved
to be. Communications between the India Office and the
Foreign Office increased in volume, and the Indian Secretary
pressed for vigorous action in Persia. Lord Randolph's plans
were bold, but they also appear to have been well conceived
and the product of careful thought. How much this activity
owed to Lord Randolph Churchill, however, is questionable.
His minutes were infrequent. Moreover, for several years the
permanent staff of the India Office had advocated a more forceful line against Russia, had called for a clarification of Persian
policy, and had writhed as their recommendations went

[1] Minute by Kimberley of 5 April 1885 on Government of India, Foreign
Department, to the Secretary of State for India, No. 38 of 1885, foreign/secret,
10 March 1885: Letters from India, Political and Secret Department, vol. xliii,
India Office Records.
[2] Currie to Salisbury, private, Constantinople, 30 January 1895: loose papers,
Special Letters, Pte Salisbury Papers.

unheeded.[1] Lord Randolph was no doubt greatly helped by his private secretary, A. W. Moore, whose knowledge of the affairs of Central Asia and of the work of the Political Department of the India Office was indeed remarkable. The Viceroy, Lord Dufferin, often wrote of Lord Randolph's consideration and of his exertions with his Council and his colleagues to champion proposals from India.

The policy, whether originated by the Secretary of State or his colleagues, was twofold. In a letter of 25 July 1885 the India Office recommended that the long-sought assurance of material support should be granted to the Shah to encourage him to resist inroads upon his territory, and that Prince Bismarck should be invited to join with England in sponsoring enterprises designed to rescue Persia from final subordination to Russia.[2] These two projects collapsed, but at the time the Government fell a more moderate scheme was being devised— a middle course between a pledge of direct military support and passive acquiescence in Persia's dismemberment.[3]

Lord Randolph had little time to develop a policy. The Liberals returned to power in February 1886, and the change brought Lord Kimberley back to the India Office. This government, however, was too short-lived to give him scope for originality. The next Secretary of State was Lord Cross, and he retained this office throughout the whole of Lord Salisbury's second administration. He was *persona grata* with the Queen, and he often discussed Indian frontier policy with her. Queen Victoria considered him admirably qualified with 'g[rea]t knowledge & insight' into the affairs of her vast Eastern empire.[4] The Queen's references to Persia became more frequent, and she remarked in a letter to Lord Salisbury: 'Lord

[1] Burne to Lytton, private, 14 November 1879: Letters from England, ix, Pte Lytton Papers. Same to same, private, 9 May 1880: Letters from England, x, Pte Lytton Papers.

[2] India Office to Foreign Office, secret and immediate, 25 July 1885: F.O. 65/1247. For the Bismarck episode see below, Chapter IV.

[3] India Office to Foreign Office, secret, 11 August 1885: F.O. 65/1248. Case 1255, Persia, India Office to Foreign Office, secret and immediate, 24 September 1885: Home Correspondence, Political and Secret Department, vol. lxxvii, India Office Records.

[4] The Queen to Salisbury, private, 13 November 1887: loose papers, Pte Salisbury Papers.

Cross was telling the Queen last night a good deal ab[ou]t
Persia & the intention of cultivating more friendly relations
with the Shah wh[ich] the Queen thinks very important.'[1]

During these years British officials in London and Simla
pulled together in an effort to checkmate Russia, and worked to
revive and strengthen British influence in Persia. Lord Cross
was 'most anxious' to place relations with Persia on a more
'satisfactory footing', a task whose magnitude he by no means
underestimated.[2] If Persia could not be kept intact, he wrote in
a letter to the Foreign Office, the effect on both Imperial and
Indian interests 'must be disastrous'.[3]

Like many of his predecessors he regarded Persia as important primarily because it was an 'outlying portion of the defences of India'.[4] By 1886, the time had come for prompt action,
and Russia's progress had to be stopped. Lord Cross's policy was
to consolidate Great Britain's position in southern Persia by
stationing an officer at Isfahan, promoting the Karun river and
railway schemes, encouraging trade, and cultivating the Zil es-
Sultan, who was the *de facto* ruler of southern Persia. He also
hoped to regain some of the lost ground by sending a man of
prestige and ability to Tehran as minister. Lord Salisbury
wrote that 'the suggestions seem to me generally good'.[5]

It was Persia in its Russo-Indian setting that absorbed attention, and occasionally the letters of Lord Cross betray an atmosphere of gloom over the respective positions of England and
her Asiatic rival. He once wrote:

... it is an undoubted fact that the Russian Empire is looked upon
in Central Asia as the growing and spreading power, and that the

[1] The Queen to Salisbury, private, 18 March 1887: loose papers, Pte Salisbury
Papers.
[2] Case 262, Persia: Future Policy towards, Draft of a letter from India Office to
Foreign Office, secret and immediate, 5 March 1887: Home Correspondence,
Political and Secret Department, vol. xcii, India Office Records.
[3] India Office to Foreign Office, secret and immediate, 5 March 1887: F.O.
60/490.
[4] Case 443, Persian Mission—Indian Contribution, Department minute on
secret letter from the Government of India, No. 51, 25 March 1891: Home Correspondence, Political and Secret Department, vol. cxxi, India Office Records.
[5] India Office to Foreign Office and minute by Salisbury, secret and immediate, 5 March 1887; same to same, 24 June 1887: F.O. 60/490. See also Foreign
Office draft to India Office, secret and immediate, 9 March 1887: F.O. 60/490.
Cross to Salisbury, private, 20 October 1888: loose papers, Pte Salisbury Papers.

British Empire is not so regarded. So people worship the rising sun.[1]

The India Office carefully reviewed the intelligence reports from the Government of India since its policy had to be based upon the solid ground of what could be done in the frontier regions. The possibility of a Russian advance was never far from mind, and officials in London and Simla systematically endeavoured to harmonize their viewpoints and to prepare for eventualities. Lord Cross inclined towards the views of General Sir Frederick Roberts, and some evidence indicates that Lord Salisbury also belonged to the Roberts school.[2]

Great Britain's soldiers have, throughout the course of their country's contact with Persia, demonstrated a lively interest in the Iranian area and have often advocated policies beyond the range of those the Foreign Office consented to undertake. Sir Henry Rawlinson summarized the value of Persia from the strategist's point of view:

. . . any serious Russian advance from the Caspian in the direction of Merv and Herát would be impossible, if the column were threatened on the flank from Persia; and they [the strategists] will further maintain that if we are to defend India from attack, it would be better to fight our intended invader in Persia than upon our own frontier, where any check would raise a host of enemies in our rear.[3]

When Persian policy had been exhaustively reviewed in 1875 by the Viceroy and his Council, the Commander-in-Chief, Napier of Magdala, had presented a very strong case for supporting the Shah. He had dwelt upon the Russian menace and pointed out that in the final analysis the defence of India depended upon 60,000 Europeans—a force that was expendable. In his view, the nearer approach of Russia had to be prevented, and for this objective Persia should receive the 'friendship she seeks'. In conclusion, he had recommended:

We should do all in our power to prevent Russia from working round our flanks. . . . We should immediately oppose any further

---

[1] Cross to Salisbury, private, 31 May 1887: loose papers, Pte Salisbury Papers.

[2] Cross to Salisbury, private, 6 October 1888; same to same, private, 27 October 1891: loose papers, Pte Salisbury Papers. Roberts to Salisbury, private, 4 July 1890: loose papers, Pte Salisbury Papers.

[3] Rawlinson, *England and Russia in the East*, p. 137.

encroachment on Persian territory. By increasing our diplomatic
influence in Persia, we shall best be able to prevent that country
from giving Russia cause for aggression, but should we be driven to
war, the people of Persia, supported by a British contingent and
aided by British arms, supplies and officers, would render the task
of conquering the country as difficult and exhaustive as the conquest
of the Spanish Peninsula was to France.[1]

In a memorandum written eight years later the master of
experts on frontier policy, Roberts, concurred with the above
and regretted that the proposals had not received favourable
endorsement. Russian progress in Central Asia might have been
checked, he maintained, if Persia's request for British army
officers had been granted and if real efforts had been made to
regain predominance at the Court in Tehran. By 1883, he
despaired of saving Merv, the surrounding Turkoman areas,
and even northern Persia itself. Merv will fall, he wrote, 'whenever it may suit Russia'.[2] It suited Russia less than a year
later.

The Merv crisis of 1884 precipitated a detailed examination
of Indian frontier policy and defence plans. General T. F.
Wilson, the Military Member of the Supreme Council, called
attention to the unfortunate tendencies towards retrogression
and bankruptcy in Persia, discussed Russia's entrenchment on
the Khorassan border and its implications, and emphasized the
need for counter-action since 'the integrity and political future
of Persia is important to English interests'.[3] In the following
year, when war seemed unavoidable, the military authorities
examined the possibilities offered by Persia as a means of

[1] Minute by Napier of Magdala of 4 May 1875, enclosure in Government of
India, Foreign Department, to Secretary of State for India, No. 123 of 1875,
political, 7 June 1875: F.O. 60/377.

[2] Confidential memorandum by Roberts, Is an Invasion of India by Russia
Possible?, 31 December 1883, enclosure in Ripon to Kimberley, private, 19 Feb-
ruary 1884: bound volume, Letters from the Marquis of Ripon, January 1884 to
December 1884, Pte Kimberley Papers.

[3] Minute by Lieutenant-General Thomas F. Wilson of 10 September 1884,
enclosure in Government of India, Foreign Department, to the Secretary of State
for India, No. 38 of 1885, secret/frontier, 10 March 1885: Letters from India,
Political and Secret Department, vol. xliii, India Office Records. See also Government of India to Secretary of State for India, No. 25 of 1884, secret/frontier, 22
September 1884: Letters from India, Political and Secret Department, vol. xli,
India Office Records.

reaching Russia.[1] After the emergency subsided, the strategists still were attracted by the potentialities of the Shah's kingdom. The Director of Military Intelligence, General Sir Henry Brackenbury, in his letter to Sir Julian Pauncefote enlarged upon the significance of a railway from the Persian Gulf to the capital city.

If we could regain our influence in Persia, we might laugh at Russian advances in Central Asia. A railway from the Gulf to Tehran would enable us to seize the throat of Russian communications on the Black Sea.[2]

The War Office continued to obtain information on Russian troop concentrations, military developments, and objectives. In the autumn of 1886 General Brackenbury wrote: 'The greatest interest for this country centres in the movements of Russia.' He maintained that Russian work on the defences of Batum and on the Turkish frontier, her railway construction in Caucasia and Central Asia, and her building of a powerful Black Sea fleet all pointed to a 'determination to obtain the command of the Black Sea, and to prosecute her designs in Asia'. He consistently asserted, however, that Russia's primary objective, though not necessarily first in time, was Constantinople. On the basis of recently acquired Russian documents, he attributed the activity in Central Asia to a desire to reach 'a position from which by threatening our East Indian possessions she can at the opportune moment influence the general policy of England'.[3] Lord Kimberley had perceived the danger two years previously. After a conversation with the Russian ambassador over Merv he disclosed his apprehensions to the Viceroy:

[1] Kimberley to Dufferin, private, 24 April 1885; same to same, private telegram, 25 April 1885; Dufferin to Kimberley, private telegram, 26 April 1885: bound volume, Telegrams to and from India, March 1885 to June 1885, Pte Kimberley Papers.

[2] Brackenbury to Pauncefote, Covering letter for memorandum on Railway from Tehran to Persian Gulf, 4 September 1886: F.O. 65/1291.

[3] General Sketch of the Situation Abroad and at Home from a Military Standpoint, secret, 3 August 1886: W.O. 33/46. General Brackenbury commented upon this paper in his memoirs. 'After seven months of study I had written a carefully prepared paper', a copy of which was at Lord Salisbury's direction given 'to every member of the Cabinet', *Some Memories of My Spare Time*, p. 352.

D

Russia, he [the Russian ambassador] said, had no designs on India, *but* of course if we quarrelled with her in other parts of the world, we must expect that she would use her position in Central Asia accordingly. This is exactly what we have to apprehend, and what makes her advances so significant.[1]

Russia's presence in the regions immediately beyond the shadows of the Hindu Kush induced soldiers both in India and in England to define the territories which were absolutely essential for Indian defence and to meet the question how further encroachments could be forestalled. The Government of India, War Office, India Office, and Foreign Office systematically exchanged information and tried to co-ordinate their policies. Defence proposals from the Government of India were reviewed by a joint committee of the India Office and War Office and then submitted to the Prime Minister or the Cabinet.[2] The Director of Military Intelligence consulted frequently with Foreign Office staff and forwarded copies of important War Office memoranda for consideration. He also kept in close touch with the India Office and received weekly from the Political and Secret Department the secret papers relating to India. General E. F. Chapman, Director of Military Intelligence from 1891 to 1893, said that he saw a great deal of Currie at the Foreign Office and Neil at the India Office.[3] One of Chapman's successors wrote: 'The most intimate confidential relations exist between the Foreign Office and the Intell[igence] Dep[artment]: even to the extent of matters which are secrets from the Head Quarters Staff of the Army.'[4]

After the demarcation of Afghanistan's northern boundary

[1] Kimberley to Ripon, private, 7 March 1884: bound volume, Letters to the Marquis of Ripon, January 1884 to November 1884, Pte Kimberley Papers.

[2] Government of India, Military Department, to the Secretary of State for India, No. 112 of 1885, confidential, 10 July 1885: W.O. 32/263, No. 40233/1. India Office to War Office, M5033, immediate, 6 August 1885: W.O. 32/263, No. 40233/1. Secret memorandum by Brackenbury on the relations between the Intelligence Departments and the War Office, Admiralty, and India, 15 May 1890: W.O. 33/50. War Office to India Office, secret, 15 March 1892: W.O. 32/264, Nos. 0149/1/564, 569, 571, 574, 575.

[3] Chapman to Brackenbury, secret, 8 September 1892: Letterbook of General E. F. Chapman, D.M.I., 1891–93, W.O. 106/16.

[4] Miscellaneous Papers, Rough Notes, etc., by Colonel Ardagh, confidential: Pte Ardagh Papers, P.R.O. 30/40/12. See also Brackenbury to Ardagh, 7 April 1896: Pte Ardagh Papers, P.R.O. 30/40/2.

by a joint Anglo-Russian commission in 1887, General Brackenbury in a long letter to the Foreign Office put forward the War
Office opinion that for the safety of India a line should be drawn
beyond which Russia must not be allowed to pass. He believed
that a small secret committee of the Government of India
should be appointed to consider their needs in the event of war,
the number of reinforcements expected from home, and the
tactics to be employed in meeting Russian forces.[1] But military
advisability and diplomatic practicability did not coincide.
Lord Salisbury stated:

This has just reached me.

As the F[oreign] O[ffice] are asked their opinion, I would say that
I concur in the proposal that the Indian Gov[ernmen]t should be
asked to refer this question as a whole to the strongest small Commission of military experts it can find. But I demur to laying down
beforehand that they are to trace a military frontier beyond which
Russia shall not be allowed to pass. 1st. Because it is impossible. It
implies a continuity of policy which our Gov[ernmen]t in recent
times has not shown & is not likely to show. 2d Because it is superfluous—because if Affghanistan is to be the only theatre of war the
point where Russia is to be checked must depend on the circ[um-
stanc]es of the moment. The memorandum shows that 'making war
with Russia all over the world' is an empty phrase unless we command the Turkish army: & I think it is as certain as any diplomatic forecast can be that we never shall have command of the
Turkish army. Lastly—but this is a military objection which I offer
with great diffidence—does not the idea of a military frontier line
ignore the character which our struggle must assume whenever it
comes? It will be a war not of battles but of devastation[:] our security
will be not to defeat them but to make it impossible for them to live
within reach of us. And that will imply not a frontier line but a
frontier region.[2]

For the next five years the military and diplomatic authorities in India and in England devoted much time to devising a

[1] Enclosure in War Office to Foreign Office, secret, 16 August 1887, Memorandum by Brackenbury, as to the determination of a Military Frontier Line for India,
7 August 1887: F.O. 65/1321. The opinions of the India Office are given in Case
899, England and Russia in Asia, September 1887: Home Correspondence, Political
and Secret Department, vol. xcvi, India Office Records.

[2] Minute of 19 August by Salisbury on Brackenbury's secret memorandum of
7 August 1887: F.O. 65/1321.

realistic Russo-Indian policy. Out of the masses of documents
and statements of conflicting views certain basic principles
finally emerged. Indian forces alone could not deal with Russia,
but in a serious emergency would depend upon reinforcements
from home. Final decisions about Russian policy, even in relation to Central Asia and to India, did not rest with the Government of India but with the Foreign Office in London.[1] The
incident most likely to cause a rupture between England and
Russia was the violation by Russia of Afghan territory.[2] If war
did break out the main theatre of operation would be somewhere in Central Asia, although simultaneously measures
against Russia would be taken in the Baltic, the Black Sea area,
and the Far East. In any such conflict, England would aim not
only at decisive military victories, but also at exhausting Russia
financially and thus forcing a favourable peace.[3]

In the Indian Mobilization Committee report of 1887, which
strongly urged meeting Russia in Afghanistan, it was pointed
out that other lines of operation were feasible. British forces
based on the Persian Gulf could advance to Russia either by
way of the Tigris and Euphrates valley or by way of Tehran.[4]
General Wolseley, Adjutant-General at the War Office from
1885 to 1890, in his comments on the various schemes, discussed
Persia:

... if an active alliance with Persia were possible, we should then be
in a position to strike at Russia in a very vital quarter. The materials
for the rank and file of a very powerful army exist in Persia; we could
supply the Officers ... from a strategical point of view a powerful
Persia would occupy the most important position in the settlement

[1] Memorandum by Lieutenant-General Brackenbury, Director of Military
Intelligence, War Office, and Major-General Newmarch, Military Secretary,
India Office, 19 August 1889: W.O. 33/49. War Office to India Office, secret,
15 March 1892: W.O. 32/264, Nos. 0149/1/564, 569, 571, 574, 575. Notes [mainly
printed] written for the information of His Excellency by Colonel Ardagh, Case
64 [1891]: P.R.O. 30/40/12.
[2] Report of the Conference on Question of Indian Reinforcements, secret, 19
December 1892: W.O. 32/218, No. 40116.
[3] Report of the Indian Mobilization Committee, 1887, summarized in W.O.
106/48, E3/2. The Military Resources of Russia, and Probable Method of their
Employment in a War between Russia and England, secret, 1902: W.O. 106/48,
E3/1.
[4] Report of Indian Mobilization Committee, 1887, summarized in W.O.
106/48, E3/2.

of this central Asian question. Is it possible to make Persia strong, and have her for an active ally?[1]

General Chapman's private letters, too, contain frequent references to Persia. He asked an officer in Persia for periodic confidential reports, and explained that he was most interested in the affairs of that country, 'especially so at this critical period'.[2] As a definite line of policy he advocated the consolidation of Britain's position in the southern provinces so that Russia might be kept out of the Gulf.[3]

Within a time span of twenty-five years England's military leaders had looked at Persia from several angles. Napier of Magdala's picture was of a strong ally and formidable bulwark. The War Office of the middle eighties saw in Persia a possible means of reaching the enemy and cutting her communication lines. By the close of the century, the strategic usefulness of the country was confined to the Gulf littoral and Seistan in the east.

To the military experts, concerned as they were exclusively with the strategic problems of Indian defence, Persia was a factor of uncertain and fluctuating significance. They sought to fit her into their Russo-Indian schemes, collected and sifted information, and offered advice about her potentialities, from a strictly military point of view. The diplomatic issues, such as the feasibility of an alliance with the Shah, or of seeking Turkish co-operation, were not their affair. Since the long-expected war in Central Asia did not occur, all arrangements for military action against Russia were destined to become nothing more than paper exercises and all plans passed into the limbo of the theoretical and the forgotten.

[1] Memorandum by Wolseley, 25 August 1889: W.O. 33/49. Although Wolseley believed that Great Britain would have to fight Russia over India, he strongly opposed the plan for meeting Russia in Afghanistan—a scheme which he said should be 'snuffed out by the Home Government in very decided terms'. His policy was to 'have our hands free all over the world to attack her wherever it may be thought most advisable to do so, by land or sea'. There was great rivalry between Roberts and Wolseley. Roberts wanted to be ready to fight in the East; Wolseley wanted to be ready to fight in the West. See, for example, Dufferin to Northbrook, private, 3 May 1888: India Office Library.

[2] Chapman to Wells, private and confidential, 17 November 1892: Letterbook of General E. F. Chapman, D.M.I., 1891–92, W.O. 106/16.

[3] Chapman to Gordon, private and confidential, 11 November 1891; Chapman to Elles, private and confidential, 19 May 1893: Letterbook of General E. F Chapman, D.M.I., 1891–92, W.O. 106/16.

CHAPTER III

The Beginnings of Lord Salisbury's Persian Policy

THE military interests of Great Britain in Persia seem intangible, but her Indian interests were real and vital. Lord George Hamilton asserted that 'if you exclude Indian interests from Persia, British interests in themselves are a very small quantity'.[1] But neither the India Office nor the Government of India enjoyed a commanding voice in the conduct of Anglo-Persian relations.

Two factors accounted for this anomaly. The impact of Russia upon Persia and upon Anglo-Persian affairs brought the Shah's kingdom into the vortex of European politics. The Duke of Argyll wrote:

Teheran is the Capital where Indian and European politics meet. But the centre of interest is European. Even as regards Indian questions, the methods of operating upon them in Persia, are essentially connected with the main currents of European diplomacy.[2]

Furthermore, the technological developments of the cable and the electric telegraph enabled the Home Government to maintain a closer contact with and to tighten its control over Indian officials. When Lord Curzon complained of the stringent supervision from London, he was informed that

the increased facilities of communication, and the much greater publicity that is given to everything the Government of India do, necessitate a much more frequent exchange of opinion than in the

[1] Hamilton to Curzon, private, 17 October 1901: Private Correspondence, India, part ii, vol. vi, Pte Hamilton Papers, India Office Library.
[2] The Duke of Argyll (G. D. Campbell), *The Eastern Question from the Treaty of Paris 1856 to the Treaty of Berlin 1878, and to the Second Afghan War*, ii, 368–9.

old days was necessary. And the advance of Russia, till her territories or protectorates border upon India, has made a number of questions which in the old days were purely Asiatic, now of European import.[1]

Thus the mastery over Persian affairs fell neither to the Indian officials nor to the soldiers, but to the diplomats. Whether it suited Anglo-Indians or not, and there is considerable evidence that it did not, they had to recognize this supremacy. Sir Henry Rawlinson acknowledged Foreign Office ascendancy in a letter to one of his colleagues in the India Office:

The real embarrassment seems to be how far we are competent to deal with such matters [Persian] at the India Office. The Foreign Office must decide, and we can only throw out hints in support of the interests of India.[2]

This trend culminated in 1907 when the Anglo-Russian Convention was concluded in spite of determined opposition from India. Sir Charles Hardinge wrote from the Foreign Office: 'Recently we have left the Gov[ernmen]t of India entirely out of our account.'[3]

From 1885 to 1892 the Foreign Office depended primarily upon Lord Salisbury's guidance. His concepts and experience, therefore, in dealing with India, Russia, and Persia are of fundamental importance. Twice Lord Salisbury's official headquarters were in the India Office as Secretary of State—for a brief interval in 1866 and again from 1874 to 1878. Unfortunately, his career as Secretary of State for India has not yet been studied. Lord George Hamilton, who worked closely with him during part of this time and who later held the post of Secretary of State for India for nearly a decade, emphasized Lord Salisbury's 'remarkable performance at the India Office' and alluded to his new principles in frontier policy.[4] In his reflections he

[1] Hamilton to Curzon, private, 1 October 1902: Private Correspondence, India, part ii, vol. vii, Pte Hamilton Papers, India Office Library.

[2] Case 630, Rawlinson to Sir Edward [Bradford], private, 26 May 1887: Home Correspondence, Political and Secret Department, vol. xcv, India Office Records.

[3] Hardinge to Nicolson, private, 10 July 1907: B.D., iv, 294.

[4] Hamilton to Lady St. Aldwyn, private, 3 February 1922: Pte Hicks Beach Papers.

paid tribute to his former chief's ability, noted particularly his accessibility, and praised his skill in drafting.[1]

Lord Salisbury's work at the India Office, his special mission to Constantinople in 1877, and his experience as Foreign Secretary from 1878 to 1880 trained him thoroughly in Russian politics and methods. He had no illusions about the character of Great Britain's Asiatic rival. 'It is an internal necessity to Russia to move on—Directly her frontier becomes fixed her political troubles begin', he wrote in 1876.[2] Fifteen years later, he said: 'They believe in Russia for the Russians, reserving to themselves the liberty of making Russia stand for as large a territory as they can manage.'[3]

Similarly, he relied not at all upon the 'talisman of diplomatic remonstrance'.[4] Little could be accomplished through protests at St. Petersburg, partly because of the Russian Government's control over its frontier officials was so shadowy,[5] but mainly because Russia knew herself to be virtually immune from attack, and so could afford to remain indifferent to British annoyance. She was bent on increasing her influence in the Black Sea area—which was, as Lord Salisbury said, 'the one thing we cannot willingly see her acquire'. Except in this one direction, England could neither smooth nor obstruct Russia's way in Europe. In Asia the picture changed:

Of course, an announcement of an intention to resist *in Asia*—whether it is made by you or us—is received with respect, & influences calculations: because it is a threat which has power behind it. But this is not pressure from home such as your colleagues are fond of suggesting. They seem to fancy that we can save them the trouble of parrying the Russian lunge by getting behind their

[1] Lord George Hamilton, *Parliamentary Reminiscences and Reflections, 1868 to 1906*, i, 73; ii, 252-3.

[2] Salisbury to Lytton, private and confidential, 10 March 1876: Letters from the Secretary of State, i, Pte Lytton Papers.

[3] Salisbury to Wolff, private, 22 June 1891: bound volume, Persia, Pte Salisbury Papers.

[4] Salisbury to Lytton, private, 22 June 1877: Letters from the Secretary of State, ii, Pte Lytton Papers.

[5] Salisbury to Lytton, private, 12 May 1876: Letters from the Secretary of State, i, Pte Lytton Papers. Undated minutes by Salisbury on India Office to Foreign Office, 5 July 1878: F.O. 65/1030. 'Whatever opposition we can make to Russia's advance by force may be effectual. But no other remonstrances will be of any use. For years to come they will do all they can to annoy us. S.'

opponent & holding his arm. And this is the difference between the older & the younger prophets of the Lawrentian school. The older men do not believe in the possibility of a Russian lunge at all: the younger, who are in India, cannot so far blind themselves: but they think it is our duty, not theirs, to repel it. Of course we shall do our best—as in the case of Kaufmann's letter: for which Schouvaloff shall be duly admonished. But his future abstinence from such a manœuvre depends on the skill with which you play your very difficult game of chess. Whatever you do protect Khelat—it is your Queen.[1]

The theme of Russia's invulnerability flowed through his letters to viceroys, ambassadors, and ministers, and to members of the Royal Family. With Turkey effete and questionably disposed to England, the only feasible meeting-point for Russian and British forces was in Central Asia. Hence, Lord Salisbury envisaged and pressed as persistently as he could for an elaborate system of railway construction—from India to Kandahar and on to Herat; from India to Quetta and thence to Nushki and Persia's Seistan province; from the Persian Gulf to the inland cities and finally to Tehran. Had these lines been completed, England could have met the enemy far from India's borders, threatened Russia's flank, and interrupted her transportation system. If a conflict broke out, Lord Salisbury expected to strike quickly at Russia's long communication lines. He tried to pursue a defensive policy diplomatically, but simultaneously he prepared for an offensive war.[2]

Throughout his career Lord Salisbury was intensely interested in Indian frontier defence. He closened the ties with Khelat and contributed to the establishment of British influence in Baluchistan. He promoted the organization of an effective intelligence service and encouraged the collection of accurate geographical information about the regions surrounding India. The exploration of the north-western frontier passes, a surveillance over Herat and Merv, and the examination of the ground around Seistan were the main objectives of many roving British

[1] Salisbury to Lytton, private, 16 August 1876: Letters from the Secretary of State, i, Pte Lytton Papers. See also Lady Gwendolen Cecil, *Life of Robert Marquis of Salisbury*, ii, 151 ff.

[2] Salisbury to Lytton, private, 22 June 1877; same to same, private, 13 July 1877: Letters from the Secretary of State, ii, Pte Lytton Papers.

officers.[1] No frontier can be impregnable, but India's natural
fortress was as strong as any could be. Lord Salisbury told
Lord Lytton: 'If . . . you can stop up that hole at Merve, &
prevent Affghanistan from becoming a Russian outpost I
believe you may sleep in peace.'[2] His active interest in Indian
defence continued after he had left the India Office. In 1887
Lord Dufferin, who was then nearing the close of his Viceroyalty, reported:

I have also noted your recommendations about the fortification of
our frontier. In reply I can give you the most positive assurance that
we are straining every nerve to carry out your wishes in this respect.
In fact the placing of India in a proper state of defence has been the
chief object of my solicitude since I came to the country. . . .[3]

On the other hand, Lord Salisbury always seemed unafraid
of Russia's power, and contemptuous of her diplomacy. He
thought her 'feeble',[4] and when she blustered for the establishment of a consulate at Meshed in 1888, he remarked that her
diplomacy was 'so bad that we have no cause to fear its extension'.[5] Her penniless exchequer provided him with an endless
source of comfort since any serious campaign against Great
Britain in Central Asia would be an expensive undertaking.[6]
Furthermore, the ever-increasing amount of equipment required for modern warfare was a deterrent to Russia. The
Asiatic conquerors of old had descended as ravaging hordes and
had carried most of their equipment on their backs. But im-

[1] Cecil, op. cit., ii, 73–5. Salisbury to Lytton, private, 5 May 1876; same to
same, private, 12 May 1876; same to same, private, 19 May 1876; same to same,
private, 26 May 1876; same to same, private, 2 June 1876; same to same, 16
August 1876: Letters from the Secretary of State, i, Pte Lytton Papers. Same to
same, private, 4 May 1877: Letters from the Secretary of State, ii, Pte Lytton
Papers.

[2] Salisbury to Lytton, private, 24 March 1876: Letters from the Secretary of
State, i, Pte Lytton Papers.

[3] Dufferin to Salisbury, private, 5 February 1888: loose papers, Pte Salisbury
Papers. See also minute by Dufferin, confidential, 8 December 1888: Pte Ardagh
Papers, P.R.O. 30/40/12, case no. 32.

[4] Salisbury to Lytton, private, 15 June 1877; quoted in Cecil, op. cit., ii, 145.
The original of this document is in the Pte Lytton Papers.

[5] Undated minute by Salisbury on Morier to Salisbury, No. 69, decypher
telegram, secret, 5 December 1888: F.O. 65/1334.

[6] Salisbury to Lytton, private, 24 March 1876: Letters from the Secretary of
State, i, Pte Lytton Papers. Same to same, private, 12 February 1877: Letters from
the Secretary of State, ii, Pte Lytton Papers.

pedimenta such as rifles, quantities of ammunition, and artillery made the piercing of the Hindu Kush a more formidable task.[1]

Lord Salisbury received Lord Lytton's dark forebodings and militant recommendations for counter-measures with a detachment bordering on philosophic unconcern. The reference he made in the House of Lords in June 1877 to 'large scale maps' indicated his conviction that the Russian menace was not immediately crucial.[2] He explained privately to the Viceroy, however, that 'sedatives' were needed before active measures on the Indian frontier would be accepted in England. Many influential writers and speakers had, in their youth, seen the 'Afghan ghost', and condemned any movement on the Indian frontier as a revival of Lord Auckland's policy.[3] Still, Lord Salisbury's task of soothing the opposition at home did not completely bridge the gap between his views and those of Lord Lytton on Russia in Central Asia. In answer to an anxious exposition on Merv, he argued: 'You foreshorten the vista of the future, and crowd up into the next few years, or less, events which will take a generation to complete.'[4] Merv capitulated in 1884—thus vindicating the judgment of the Viceroy and not that of his superior in London. But the Japanese proved that the Colossus did have but feet of clay, and the war between England and Russia in Asia did not come to pass.

It must not be supposed that because Lord Salisbury remained calm and refused to join those who prophesied the inevitable conflict between Cossack and Sepoy, he was on that account inattentive to Russia's advance in Central Asia. The number of drafts and minutes in his own hand in the Central Asian correspondence testify to the time which was consumed in grappling with the problem of Russia *vis-à-vis* India. Although he did not believe that a clash with Russia was unavoidable, he was far from discounting all possibility of war, or from treating as fantastic the idea of an expedition against

[1] Salisbury to Lytton, private, 24 March 1876: Letters from the Secretary of State, i, Pte Lytton Papers.   [2] Cecil, *op. cit.*, ii, 155–6.

[3] Salisbury to Lytton, private, 13 July 1877: Letters from the Secretary of State, ii, Pte Lytton Papers.

[4] Salisbury to Lytton, private, 22 June 1877: Letters from the Secretary of State, ii, Pte Lytton Papers. See also India Office to Government of India, No. 68, secret, 18 October 1877: F.O. 65/992.

India. Even in the year when the Russian danger had faded
into the 'shadow of a shade',[1] he admitted that Russia's
superiority in light cavalry constituted a potential threat.[2]

In the latter part of the seventies, Lord Salisbury acquired a
thorough knowledge of Persia and her problems. As Secretary
of State for India, he alone dealt with matters touching India's
frontier and her relations with neighbouring countries.[3] Sir
Owen Burne said that he kept 'all frontier information even
from the Political Committee'.[4]

Evidence that Lord Salisbury hoped to improve relations
with Persia can be found as early as 1876. He was dissatisfied
with the management of the Legation in Tehran and was in
favour of placing it under Indian supervision.[5] In 1879, being
now Foreign Secretary, he even proposed to Lord Cranbrook
to 'hand Persia back to the India Office', but the latter did not
welcome such an increase in responsibility.[6] Later he came to
believe that the transfer, although highly desirable on some
grounds, was not practicable. In a letter to Lord Lansdowne,
written in 1891, the affairs of Persia were described as 'strictly
a Foreign Office matter'.[7]

During the time that Lord Salisbury was Secretary of State
for India no real attempt was made to cultivate the friendship
of the Shah. He seemed, however, attracted by both the
potentialities of the Seistan basin and by the possibilities offered
by the opening of the Karun river to navigation.[8] One of his
minutes reveals the trend of his thought:

[1] Salisbury to Lytton, private, 21–22 September 1877: Letters from the Secretary
of State, ii, Pte Lytton Papers.
[2] Salisbury to Lytton, private, 27 April 1877: Letters from the Secretary of
State, ii, Pte Lytton Papers.
[3] Salisbury to Lytton, private, 4 May 1877: Letters from the Secretary of State,
ii, Pte Lytton Papers.
[4] Burne to Lytton, private, 24 May 1878: Letters from England, v, Pte Lytton
Papers.
[5] Salisbury to Lytton, private, 23 June 1876: Letters from the Secretary of State,
i, Pte Lytton Papers.
[6] Salisbury to Lytton, private, 23 May 1879: Letters from England, vii, Pte
Lytton Papers.
[7] Salisbury to Lansdowne, private, 21 October 1891: loose papers, 'Drafts,
Copies, Minutes, Memo[randa], etc., 1890–1892', Pte Salisbury Papers.
[8] Salisbury to Lytton, private, 2 June 1876: Letters from the Secretary of State,
i, Pte Lytton Papers.

In these questions [policy towards Persia] we must bear in mind the condition of the Russian Counsels. The peace party have the Emperor: the war party have the whole military strength & some influential members of the Imperial family. It appears certain that the Emperor holds his own with difficulty. We know the effect of Russian advances on the public mind in England & India. What will be the effect of English advances on the more impulsive, & more military public mind of Russia?

Of all alternatives I deprecate the most an incomplete & hesitating assistance to Persia. A *complete* assistance is an intelligible policy. If we took the matter entirely into our own hands, it is possible that we might successfully defend the Persian Frontier & even Merv. The demerit of such a policy would be its exceeding costliness; & that it would precipitate the conflict between ourselves & Russia upon a distant & ill-selected field. But at least it would for the purposes of that conflict place the resources of Persia at our disposal.

He greatly doubted whether even military help would keep the Shah faithful, whom he suspected of being ready to exploit either party as he thought profitable.[1]

In the years from 1878 to 1880, when Lord Salisbury was Foreign Secretary, a new policy was evolved for Persia. Interest there was stimulated by the breach which developed between England and the Amir of Afghanistan, Sher 'Ali. That ruler had ventured to trust his fate to Russian promises; to put his confidence in the 'mighty Russian Government which, wise as a serpent and harmless as the dove, understands what he cannot'. The dispute over the admission of Russian and the refusal of British missions to Kabul brought British troops into Afghanistan late in 1878.[2] The campaign was speedily successful since the Afghans, deserted by their Russian guardians, were left to fight alone. But all authority within Afghanistan had been undermined by the uncertainty of the past years. The new Amir, Yaqub Khan, who succeeded on the death of his father in 1879, was unable to control his people, and amid seeming calm

[1] Minute by Salisbury of 6 October 1874 on the question of providing British officers for the Persian army: Home Correspondence, Secret Department, vol. lxxxi, India Office Records.

[2] Précis of captured Russo-Afghan correspondence; Viceroy of India to the Secretary of State for India, No. 609, cypher telegram, 8 November 1879: bound volume entitled Attack on the British Embassy at Cabul, 1879, Pte Lytton Papers. Copies of this correspondence are in F.O. 65/1097.

all the members of the British mission in Kabul were suddenly massacred. Their deaths brought more British brigades into the country.[1]

Under the circumstances the picture of a united, strong, and friendly Afghanistan was difficult to conceive. Many of the most competent authorities on the spot believed the disintegration of the country to be inevitable. A dangerous political vacuum engulfed Herat and Seistan, and so Lord Salisbury turned to Persia. The more ambitious plans for that country were seconded by Sir Owen Burne, who had long preached alliance with the Shah.[2] Thus Lord Salisbury expressed to the British minister in Tehran the view that

the condition of Affghanistan raises again the question of the disposition of Herat. It may not be possible to unite all Affghanistan securely under one head; in that case it may be more prudent to entrust Herat to Persia under conditions than to leave it to the chance guardianship of some petty chief who may be accessible to Russian bribes. We have more control over Persia than we should have over such a chief.[3]

The aim of the negotiations of 1879 and 1880 was to make Persia instead of Afghanistan the main bulwark in Indian defence. Lord Salisbury carried the Cabinet with him and he kept the Queen informed, but he, practically alone, carried forward these tedious negotiations with the Shah. According to the terms which were offered to Nasir ad-Din, Persia would acquire the coveted Herat and Seistan territories, and would receive a subsidy, in return for which the Shah would permit British officers in Herat; he would place no obstacles in the way

[1] See for example W. K. Fraser-Tytler, *Afghanistan. A Study of Political Developments in Central Asia*, pp. 143–50. The volume in the Lytton papers entitled Attack on the British Embassy at Cabul, 1879, contains much interesting and valuable material.

[2] Burne to Lytton, private, 10 January 1879: Letters from England, vii, Pte Lytton Papers. Same to same, private, 18 July 1879: Letters from England, viii, Pte Lytton Papers. Burne did criticize Salisbury's negotiations with Persia—of which he approved in principle—on the ground that they were proceeding too rapidly. See for example Burne to Lytton, private, 14 November 1879: Letters from England, viii, Pte Lytton Papers.

[3] Salisbury to Thomson, No. 16, secret telegram, 22 October 1879, endorsed 'Lord Beaconsfield, copy sent to the Queen, C[hancellor] of Exchequer': F.O. 60/419.

of constructing a railroad from Kandahar to Herat, would resist
further Russian inroads, and would undertake, under British
supervision, projects for internal reform and for improving
transportation from the Gulf inland.[1] A letter to the Queen
explained the motives underlying this policy:

If . . . we admit Persia . . . we place Herat in the hands of a
responsible Power whom we can punish by operating on her sea-
board, as we did in 1857: and we give Persia a strong interest to
resist to the utmost of her power the further advance of Russia. This
appears to Your Majesty's advisers the best arrangement to make at
all events for the time. There is indeed no alternative between this,
and advancing ourselves to Herat in defiance both of Persia and
Russia. If we give Herat to Persia and she proves faithful we shall
escape the necessity of this dangerous advance for a long time. If
she is faithless, we may have to make the advance in a few years.
But by that time our railway will be made to Candahar, perhaps
further, and the supply of the troops operating on Herat will be very
much facilitated.[2]

The Shah, although obviously pleased with the offer, protracted the discussions and suspended them temporarily in
1880. Lord Salisbury continued to believe that a successful
conclusion would eventually be reached.[3] But in 1880 the
Liberals returned to power, and such an extension of responsibility seemed to them unthinkable. Thus, by his untimely
haggling, Nasir ad-Din passed by the opportunities for territorial aggrandizement and for British support which would not
come again.

In his Persian policy from 1885 to 1892, Lord Salisbury was
guided by two main principles. One was his concept of Persia
as a buffer state, and to him the words 'independence and
integrity of Persia' were more than an outworn and empty
phrase. He strove for the regeneration of that ancient land,

[1] The volumes in both the F.O. 60 and the F.O. 65 (Russia in Central Asia)
series contain quantities of material on these negotiations. There are numerous
red-ink drafts in Lord Salisbury's hand. For an outline of the terms see Draft
Convention between Her Majesty and the Shah of Persia, most secret, undated:
F.O. 65/1097.

[2] Salisbury to the Queen, private, 30 December 1879: bound volume, Drafts,
The Queen, 1878–1880, Pte Salisbury Papers.

[3] Cranbrook to Lytton, private, 13 March 1880: Letters from the Secretary of
State, v, Pte Lytton Papers. Cecil, *op. cit.*, ii, 374–8.

sponsored reform programmes, and refused to look exclusively to British interests in the south and east, until it became obvious that the Persians lacked not only the means but also the will to oppose Russia.[1]

Lord Salisbury's other principle was more practical and specific. It concerned the improvement of communications between the Gulf and Tehran. The finest fleet of ironclads could not save Khorassan. Thus for years he hammered incessantly, in conversations with Malkom Khan in London and in instructions sent to Tehran, on the theme of the absolute necessity of a railway from the Gulf inland. But the Qajar rulers refused to allow this innovation, and no such line was constructed until the twentieth century—by Persia's iron man and the founder of a new dynasty, Riza Shah Pahlavi.

[1] Contrast Salisbury's addition on draft dispatch to Thomson, No. 75A, 6 August 1885 (F.O. 65/1278) with his private letter to Morier, 10 May 1891: bound volume, Russia, Pte Salisbury Papers. See below, pp. 88 and 182.

CHAPTER IV

The Submission of Merv, 1884

EARLIER Muscovite rulers had inevitably manifested some interest in Central Asia, but Peter the Great was the first to undertake an expedition of serious military importance. In 1717 a detachment under the command of Prince Bekovitch Tcherkasky proceeded against Khiva and was completely destroyed. In spite of this reverse, Russian pressure in this direction was soon renewed, and was maintained almost unremittingly, and with deliberation, for the next century or more. In 1732 the khans of the Little Horde of the Kirghiz people submitted. During the next three decades the Russians built a line of fortifications which extended from the Ural river to Omsk and finally ended at Ust-Kamengorsk, over one hundred miles beyond the old Mongolian capital of Semipalatinsk on the Irtish river. Thus the Russian frontier abutted upon the whole extent of the Kirghiz steppe, to the north of Persia, Afghanistan, and Tibet. Both land and people proved hard to conquer. Between 1824 and 1838 the Russians entrenched themselves a stage further. They constructed a new series of military works some four hundred miles south of the Ural–Omsk–Irtish line. It was a fruit of this advanced base line that they were able to include the khanates of the Central and Great Hordes in the newly created West Siberian province. The year 1863 is usually given as the date of the final subjugation of the Kirghiz steppe, although records exist of later revolts. Once this almost impregnable natural barrier was crossed the Russians became the 'immediate neighbours of the Central Asian Mussulman rulers'.[1] They had already begun

---

[1] Case 866, Affairs in Turkestan, compiled by Colonel Belyavsky of the Russian General Staff, St. Petersburg, 23 November 1884: translated in the Intelligence Branch of the War Office, with a preface by Major-General H. Brackenbury,

E

operations for the next phase of the conquest of Central Asia by making substantial inroads on Khokand when they were deflected by the Crimean war.

The subjugation of the Kirghiz steppe was soon appreciated as of great strategic significance. It foreshadowed the complete Russian dominance of Central Asia. In 1868 Sir Henry Rawlinson was moved to compose his famous minute[1] which opened the whole Central Asian problem for the rulers of British India.

As long as the Kirghiz Steppe, which is a zone of almost uninhabited desert stretching 2000 miles from west to east, and nearly 1000 miles from north to south, intervened as a 'buffer' between the military colonies of the Orenburg and Siberian lines, and the swarming centres of Mohamedan population beyond the Aral, so long peace was possible in Central Asia; but when once the 'Debatable ground' was passed, and Russian garrisons jostled against Uzbeg posts upon the Jaxartes, there was no longer a possibility of quietude or amicable relations. No sooner was one portion of Uzbeg territory annexed than the Russian outposts came in collision with the tribes beyond. One extension begot another with the unerring certainty of a law of nature.[2]

Moreover, it is plain that this sequence of advances was neither casual nor unpremeditated, but was the working out of a long-term plan. The Russian officer Belyavsky, writing in 1884 about the affairs of Turkestan, set out in explicit terms

the conviction that, sooner or later, *we should be obliged* to unite our Orenburg and Siberian lines, thus reducing the length of our frontier; and the conviction that in the event of a European war, we, ruling in Khokand, would constantly menace the English possessions in India, and that *only* from there could we be dangerous to this our enemy; and also the various declarations of submission given by the Karatau Kirghiz during our reconnaissances of their country in 1863; and lastly, the hostile attitude assumed by England at the

London, printed at the War Office, 1886: Home Correspondence, Political and Secret Department, vol. lxxxvii, India Office Records. The Russians at this time referred to the Kazakhs as Kirghiz.

[1] Memorandum by Rawlinson on the Central Asian Question, 20 June 1868. Correspondence respecting the relations between the British Government and that of Afghanistan since the Accession of the Ameer Shere Ali Khan. [C.–2190], pp. 31–41. *Accounts and Papers*, vol. lvi (1878–9), pp. 405–15.

[2] Rawlinson, *England and Russia in the East*, p. 273.

time of the Polish Insurrection removed all doubts, and on the 20th December 1863, an Imperial Order was issued that the troops were 'to carry out in 1864 the union of the advanced lines of Siberia and Orenburg, occupying Suzak and Auli-ata, so as subsequently to carry the frontier to the River Arys, drawing the line from there through Tchimkent to Turkestan'. The means whereby this enterprise was to be carried out were left to the judgment of the Corps Commanders on the spot.[1]

The Kirghiz steppe being conquered, Russia's frontier in 1863 ran from the shores of the Sea of Aral along the Syr Daria or Jaxartes river to Julek; and then striking almost due east it followed the line of the Chu river to the Issik Kul lake. It was soon to change. General Tchernaieff occupied Chimkent in 1864. The Khan of Khokand petitioned to the Viceroy for assistance against Russia. This request was refused. Tashkent fell in 1865. The acquisitions of 1864 and 1865 alone brought 4,000 square miles and one million people into the Russian empire. General Kaufmann took over as Governor-General of the recently established province of Turkestan in 1867.

Khojand fell in 1866, and operations began against Bukhara. The Amir turned hopefully to the British in India for help. The torture and eventual execution of Charles Stoddart and Arthur Conolly there in 1842 had not been forgotten, and the Viceroy lost little time in declining aid to Bukhara. Before the year 1866 closed Bukharan forts had capitulated, and a formal treaty of submission soon followed. In 1868 Russian columns entered Samarkand. Khiva, long-coveted by the Russians and the object of a disastrous 900-mile march in 1839, was still unconquered. Preparations were made for its reduction. 'The dignity of the Empire, the material interests of Russia, and our political views, all necessitated the subjection of Khiva to our influence.'[2] Three separate expeditionary forces set out from Orenburg (Chkalov), Ak Masjid (Perovski), and Tashkent to converge on Khiva. In the summer of 1873 the Khivan oasis[3] was occupied, and the town soon captured. By the autumn of that year the ruler had signed a treaty by which he acknowledged himself to be a vassal of the Czar. This phase of Russian

[1] Belyavsky, *loc. cit.*   [2] *Ibid.*
[3] The oasis itself, which is surrounded by vast deserts, is about one hundred versts long by forty versts wide. One verst equals about two-thirds of an English mile.

expansion was rounded off in 1876 by an Imperial decree which incorporated the khanate of Khokand into the empire under the title of the Farghana province. The twelve years after 1863 had added thousands of square miles and nearly three million Muslims to the Russian empire. But the conquests were not cheap. The cost to the Imperial Exchequer for the annexation and administration of Turkestan had exceeded one hundred million roubles by January 1884.

From time to time the British discussed these transformations with the Russians. Always they were assured that the Imperial Government had no intention of increasing its responsibilities by territorial increments. Nevertheless, the generals pushed their forces forward, and where they went they always stayed. Occasionally some deference was shown to British protests. In 1866 General Tchernaieff was recalled for having exceeded orders, but he was presented with a diamond-hilted sword and then sent back as Governor-General to the province from which he had been removed as Commander-in-Chief. In 1865 part of the Czar's 'immutable policy' had been to respect the independence of Tashkent, but he formally annexed it as well as Khojand in the next year. In January 1873 Count Schuvaloff, then in London on a special mission regarding Central Asian affairs, assured Lord Granville that his Emperor had issued explicit orders against the occupation of Khiva. In the words of Count Schuvaloff, 'Not only was it far from the intention of the Emperor to take possession of Khiva, but positive orders had been prepared to prevent it.' He gave permission to the British Government to lay these 'positive assurances' before Parliament.[1] In spite of all this Khiva formed part of Russia before the year was out.

The annexation of Khiva brought Russia into contact with the outlying portions of Afghan Turkestan. Only the semi-independent Turkomans, over whom Persia had some historical

---

[1] Correspondence, from 1864 to 1881, respecting the movements of Russia in Central Asia and her relations with Afghanistan, secret, A.W.M., India Office, Political and Secret Department, 8 February 1882: F.O. 65/1150. Granville to Loftus, 8 January 1873. Correspondence with Russia respecting Central Asia, October 1872–January 1873. [C. 699]. pp. 706–7. *Accounts and Papers*, vol. lxxv (1873), pp. 693–711. See also Central Asia and Afghanistan. Chronological table of events from 1855 to 1885: F.O. 65/1246.

claim, remained. A new phase, and a different direction, in Russia's drive through Central Asia was represented in the campaigns which resulted in the reduction of the Akhal, Yomut, and Tekke Turkomans whose lands lay to the east of the Caspian Sea. These new movements, more alarming than the absorption of the khanates, were most carefully watched by the British in India. General Roberts believed that while the acquisition of the khanates was undoubtedly of importance to Russia, these gains were 'of little account to us, when compared with the conquests she soon afterwards made in the neighbourhood of the Caspian'.[1] In Russia, Prince Dondoukoff-Korsakoff noticed that the extensions made from Tashkent southwards had less effect in England than 'the movement from the shores of the Caspian in a south-easterly direction, a direction which threatened, in the highest degree, the interests of Great Britain in Afghanistan and North-western India'.[2]

There were, then, not one but two Russian movements in the general direction of India. The first, originating from the Orenburg base line, aimed perhaps at Kabul. This wave of expansion gathered momentum after the Crimean war, engulfed the trans-Oxus khanates, and then died away. The second movement, which occurred mainly after the Russo-Turkish war of 1877–8, was based on the Caspian and had for its objectives Merv and Herat. That there were two separate and distinct advances, and that they took place in remote and little-known regions, have led to numerous misconceptions. In the debates and writings of the period the two were often confused. It was commonly argued that the forbidding mountain ranges, if nothing else, would halt the Russians. This argument may be valid if applied to troops moving from Tashkent or Samarkand upon Kabul and Peshawar because the Hindu Kush bar the way, but it is less convincing when applied to the Caspian line because there are no such obstacles between

---

[1] Confidential memorandum by Roberts, Is an Invasion of India by Russia Possible?, 31 December 1883, enclosure in Ripon to Kimberley, private, 19 February 1884: bound volume, Letters from the Marquis of Ripon, January 1884 to December 1884, Pte Kimberley Papers.

[2] Memorandum on the Condition of the Trans-Caspian Province, secret, St. Petersburgh, 14/26 January 1887, enclosure in Dering to Salisbury, No. 294, secret, 23 August 1888, printed for the use of the Cabinet, 30 August 1888: F.O. 65/1352.

Krasnovodsk and Merv and Herat. In the half century preceding 1880, Russia advanced some 1,200 miles towards India.
In the four years ending in June 1884, she advanced about 600
miles along the line based on the Caspian.

Russo-Persian rivalry over the Caspian was long-standing.
Peter the Great himself led an expedition against one of the
Safavid monarchs. But not until treaties were concluded early
in the nineteenth century did Russia acquire the provinces
adjoining the western shore and obtain exclusive rights on the
sea itself.[1] Later, in 1836–8, the Russians first set foot on the
island of Ashurada off the Caspian's south-eastern littoral and
within a few years had transformed it into a naval base. The
Persian Government protested but lacked the power to do more,
and English remonstrances came too late to have any effect.
The process of erosion continued. Krasnovodsk on the east
shore of the Caspian was occupied in 1869. The following year
found the Russians on the other side of the bay at Mikhailovsk.
In 1872 a fort was built at Chikishliar, at the mouth of the
Atrek river, from which the reconnoitring of the Atrek valley
and the Kopet Dagh range took place. By 1874 enough territory had been seized to call for separate administration, and the
district known as trans-Caspia came into being, extending as far
south as the Atrek river. At first its affairs were supervised by
the Governor-General of the Caucasus, but in 1890 trans-
Caspia became an independent unit with the ambitious General
Kuropatkin as its Governor-General. He was responsible to the
Minister of War in St. Petersburg. His appointment reflected
the growing importance of the province for he was by many
considered the 'most prominent figure in the Russian army'.[2]

The Turkish war of 1877–8 slowed down activities in the
trans-Caspian region, but the Russians were quick to take
advantage of Great Britain's preoccupation with Afghan

[1] Aitchison, *op. cit.*, p. 8; Appendix No. V, translation of the treaty of Gulistan
between Russia and Persia, 1813, pp. xv–xviii: Appendix No. VII, translation of
the treaty of Turcmanchai between Russia and Persia, 1828, pp. xxiii–xxxiv. See
especially Article 8 relating to the Caspian.

[2] Enclosure in Morier to Salisbury, No. 98, 3 April 1890. This enclosure is a
memorandum on Major-General Alexis Nicholaevitch Kouropatkine, drawn up
by the British military attaché in St. Petersburg: Home Correspondence, Political
and Secret Department, vol. cxviii, India Office Records.

problems as they resumed their probing movements in 1879. A force sent out in that year under General Lomakin suffered a severe defeat. The Turkomans' triumph sealed their doom. The news of the reverse spread through Central Asia, shook Russian power in the entire area, and encouraged hitherto submissive peoples to enkindle afresh the sparks of resistance. If prestige were not regained at once, Russia's new empire would be in danger of crumbling. In this emergency, General Mikhail Skobeleff, the picturesque and brilliant 'White General' of the Turkish wars, took command. He carefully prepared for the siege of the main enemy stronghold—Geok Tepe (Blue Hill), where in January 1881 his forces crushed the Turkomans in their last bitter stand.

As a condition of his taking charge of this expedition General Skobeleff demanded that the first section of the trans-Caspian railway be constructed from Mikhailovsk, on an inlet of the Caspian Sea, across the desert to Kizil Arvat.[1] Constructed under the direction of General Annenkoff, the railway ran for nearly three hundred miles parallel with the Persian frontier, and very near to it. It was, according to Curzon, 'a sword of Damocles perpetually suspended above his [the Shah's] head'.[2] By the end of 1885 the railway had been completed to Ashkabad, and in the next year it was extended via Merv as far as Charjui on the Oxus. In 1888 it reached Samarkand with branches out to Tashkent and into Farghana. Various projects were put forward for lines into Persia itself, and Russian engineers even surveyed the land. The spur from Merv to Kushk, finished in 1898, was to point like a dagger at Herat—less than 100 miles away.[3] Materials for the extension to Herat were stacked at the terminus. The astuteness and foresight of Generals Annenkoff

---

[1] Mikhailovsk was selected as the Caspian terminus because it was twenty miles inland at the head of an inlet and thus shortened the distance over which the railway had to be laid. Only small tugs could navigate the channel. In 1886 Annenkoff decided to change the terminus to Uzunada, situated on the coast about sixteen miles southwest of Mikhailovsk. Its bay could accommodate any vessel then on the Caspian. It provided a suitable base for receiving large quantities of supplies from Russia for trans-Caspia. In 1888 the terminus was again changed to Krasnovodsk, about fifty miles away, because of its excellent harbour with deep water close inshore.   [2] Curzon, *Russia in Central Asia*, pp. 275-6.

[3] Hamilton to Curzon, private, 11 October 1900: Private Correspondence, India, part ii, vol. v, Pte Hamilton Papers, India Office Library.

and Skobeleff was fully admitted by the British, for in 1887 the
Intelligence Division of the War Office pronounced the railway
'in every way a strategic success'. By it troops in trans-Caspia
and Turkestan could be reinforced from the Caucasus, always
a great reservoir of Russian manpower.[1]

Thus in the twenty years from 1863 to 1883 the relative
positions of Great Britain and Russia in Asia changed fundamentally. In 1863 the Russians were separated by nearly 1,700
miles of mountains and deserts from the most advanced outposts of British India. In 1883 that distance was reduced by
almost half. The British had moved up some 200 miles from
Jacobabad to Quetta, and the Russians accounted for the rest.
General Roberts explained in 1883 that this proximity was by
no means the only consideration:

Previous to 1878, an invading Russian army would have had to
solve for itself the problem of the formidable Hindu Kush barrier,
or if it took the line by Herat, it would have had to face the terrors
of the deserts of Bokhara and Merv. Many months must have
elapsed before reinforcements could have reached it in case of
disaster, while hordes of Turkomans would have hovered on its
flanks, ready to swoop down at the first signs of weakness.

By 1883 that same army could proceed from its base at Ashkabad
through the recently conquered Turkoman country and it could
obtain supplies from the rich province of Khorassan in nearby
Persia. General Roberts reasoned, perhaps mistakenly, that the
trans-Caspian railway placed Persia completely at the mercy of
Russia, and compelled the Shah to do the bidding of his neighbour to the north whether he wanted to or not. The Russian
army, in 1883, would have, Roberts continued, 'no dread
mountain chain ranged directly across its path', and it would be
able to proceed secure in 'the knowledge that, should the
occasion arise, thousands of men, from the very heart of Russia
itself, could be forwarded rapidly to reinforce it'. The advantages gained by the new railway lines were striking.

So late as 1878, troops would have taken some six months to reach
Samarkand from Orenberg, the terminal point of the Russian railway; while now, reinforcements could be marched in six days to

[1] Military Report on the Trans-Caspian Railway, confidential, June 1887:
F.O. 65/1321.

Askabad from Kizil-Arvat, which is in direct rail and steam-boat communication with St. Petersburg, *viâ* Michaelovsk, Baku, and Batoum. We may shortly expect to hear of the extension of the trans-Caspian railway from Kizil-Arvat to Askabad, 146 miles, and Sarakhs, 186 miles, leaving a distance of 202 miles only to Herat.[1]

After General Skobeleff's victory at Geok Tepe the Merv oasis was left as one of the last of the independent Turkoman possessions. The nineteenth-century city bore few traces of its earlier glories—the ancient commercial emporium, the medieval seat of learning, and the site of a Nestorian diocese. Peace had rarely dwelt there. Most of the conquerors of Asia, from Alexander of Macedon to Nadir Shah, had subjugated Merv. Jenghis Khan had paused there in his descent to the Indus; and in 1212, Tuli, his son, in pillaging the city with true Mongol ferocity had demolished the great dam on the Murghab—thus transforming a flourishing oasis into a desert swamp. Yakut, the geographer, who was forced to flee at the onslaught of Tuli, wrote sadly that the abodes of the people and the public buildings which had housed among other things the great libraries he had so enjoyed were now but dwellings 'for the owl and the raven'.[2]

The dereliction of the city was within the next three centuries followed by a great Muslim renaissance which made it one of Asia's foremost centres and a metropolis of culture. Under Persian rule, Merv 'rose to a great and opulent country, and the waters of its river, which before had wasted themselves in the desert, were distributed by canals and a judicious use of dams throughout the territory.' Yet again, in 1794, it was sacked by the Amir of Bukhara.[3] In spite of these repeated misfortunes, the life of the city and its surrounding oasis again and again revived, as the power of the successive overlords waned

[1] Confidential memorandum by Roberts, Is an Invasion of India by Russia Possible?, 31 December 1883, enclosure in Ripon to Kimberley, private, 19 February 1884: bound volume, Letters from the Marquis of Ripon, January 1884 to December 1884, Pte Kimberley Papers.

[2] Quotation from Sykes, *History of Afghanistan*, i, 222–3. Le Strange, *op. cit.*, pp. 401–2.

[3] Quotation from A. Burnes, *Travels into Bokhara; containing the Narrative of a Voyage on the Indus from the Sea to Lahore; and an Account of a Journey from India to Cabool, Tartary, and Persia* (London, 1839), iii, 218–19. Curzon, *Russia in Central Asia*, pp. 108–16, 122, 135–8.

and civic independence was recovered. But in Lord Salisbury's time, Merv was once more in ruins. It was a 'Golgotha of cities'. In 1881, a correspondent from the *Daily News*, Edmond O'Donovan, visited it. 'I climbed', he wrote,

to the summit of a ruined building, half dwelling-house, half fort-alice, whence a commanding view was obtained over the crumbling expanse of cities. A feeling of oppressive loneliness comes over the spirit as the eye ranges across that voiceless wilderness, so deserted, so desolate, yet teeming with eloquent testimonies of what it had been of old. The heart of Zenghis Khan himself would feel exultant at the absolute, hopeless lifelessness of those sites, where great cities had stood and myriad populations swarmed. . . . It was strange to think that a few yards of dam upon the Murgab, some trenches dug by illiterate toilers, had once made these present deserts vernal, and had entitled this Golgotha of cities to the proud name of Queen of the World.[1]

Merv may have been a disheartening spectacle. Indeed, Lord Northbrook dismissed it as 'a few mud hovels in the desert'.[2] But for all that, it had in times past been of great strategic importance, and it was now again to occupy a prominent place in military calculations. In centuries gone by, the Asiatic conquerors who had poured down from the north, through the lofty mountain passes, and over some of the oldest roads known to man, had first captured Merv and Herat. They rested in these places, and then pushed on to the Indus.[3] No less a person than the Viceroy of India, Lord Lytton, endorsed this view of its possibilities in a dispatch dated 2 July 1877:

Russia may establish herself at Merv almost without Europe being aware of it. And yet Merv is undoubtedly the most important spot in Central Asia. Situated in a country of almost fabulous fertility, it commands equally Turkistan, Afghanistan, and Khorassan. All the lines of communication for military and commercial purposes between Meshed and Bokhara, Khiva and Herat, necessarily converge upon Merv. In every respect, and especially with respect to

---

[1] E. O'Donovan, *The Merv Oasis*, ii, 254.

[2] *P.D.*, Third Series, Lords, 10 March 1884, cclxxxv, 1005.

[3] Fraser-Tytler, *op. cit.*, pp. 9–10. Holdich, *Gates of India*, pp. 60–1, 239–47. 516–29. Sykes, *History of Afghanistan*, I, vii, 90, 110, 125, 160. For a Russian view of the significance of Merv see Dondoukoff-Korsakoff to Giers, 15 June 1884: Meyendorff, *op. cit.*, i, 117–22.

Russia, the position of Merv is infinitely superior to that of Herat; and the very fact that this celebrated capital of Khorassan is in ruins testifies to that superiority of position which, placing it in the pathway of all our conquerors, has marked it out as the blood-stained stage on which the barbarous hordes of Asia contend. To understand Merv, one must not judge by what it is now; one must consider what it has been, and especially what it may become. To judge of Merv by what it actually is, would be like judging of Sevastopol by what it was under Turkish dominion. . . . The capture of Merv, and the reduction of the surrounding Turkomans, present in themselves no serious difficulty. Only a small part of the sacrifices which enabled the Russians to reach Khiva would quite suffice to establish definitely their dominion from Astrabad to the gates of Herat. On the day when the Russian flag restores order and security in Merv, that destined capital will be re-established; and nature itself, aided by Russian administration, will inevitably render it the most active centre of new enterprises and certain successes . . .[1]

In 1882 even the poetic effusion of Sir Alfred Lyall could not but reflect the Russian advance which had been allowed to continue notwithstanding the warnings of the Viceroy.

> From Merv, last home of the free-lance, the clansmen are
>   scattering far,
> And the Turkmán horses are harnessed to the guns of the
>   Russian Czar.[2]

Sir Alfred Lyall was by no means unaware of the rumours of a Russian expedition to Merv which had been rife for three years before he published his poem. General Lazareff, who was intrepid and determined, had in 1879 led a column from Chikishliar across the Kara Kum sands towards the Merv oasis, but his campaign failed and he died.[3] In the next year, 1880, when General Skobeleff took over the trans-Caspian army, military manœuvres began which seemed more clearly directed

[1] Government of India, Foreign Department, to the Secretary of State for India, No. 21 of 1877, secret, 2 July 1877: F.O. 65/992.

[2] A. Lyall, *The Amir's Message*, 1882.

[3] Russian movements towards Merv began as early as 1873. The Lomakin and Lazareff expeditions carried out orders from the Grand Duke Mikhail. These expeditions usually, but not always, had the approval of the Emperor. See, for example, Memorandum by Hertslet on the Attrek, or Northern, Frontier of Persia, confidential/3325, printed for the use of the Foreign Office, September 1877: F.O. 65/991.

against India. By 1882 ominous tales concerning visits of Colonel Alikhanoff and General Dondoukoff-Korsakoff to Merv were filtering through the bazaars of Central Asia.[1] The British from being vaguely uneasy became positively anxious. Lord Cranbrook had observed earlier that 'Even Lord Derby spoke of Merv as a place the seizure of which might affect our relations materially with that power [Russia].'[2] The India Office told the Foreign Office that if the calamity of war 'is not rendered inevitable it is at least rendered more probable by the nearer approach of Russia to the frontier of Afghanistan'.[3] Once again the British ambassador discussed the problem with the Russian Minister for Foreign Affairs, and once again he reported to London the familiar chant that the Emperor had no intention of extending the frontiers of Russia. This assurance was frequently repeated between 1874 and 1884.[4]

The announcement by Giers, on 15 February 1884, that the Emperor of Russia had decided to accept the allegiance of the Merv Turkomans coincided with British troubles in the Sudan. Philip Currie believed that Egypt was 'an encouragement to the Russians as it is to every enemy of this country'.[5] There was indeed a close relationship between the affairs of Egypt and those of India, and the happenings in the Sudan could not but have repercussions upon the policy in India. Lord Kimberley once declared: 'Does any one really suppose that if we did not possess an Indian Empire we should have interfered in Egypt!'[6] He, like Lord Salisbury, often wished that the British had never

[1] Correspondence respecting the occupation of Merv by Russia and her proceedings on the Khorassan Frontier of Persia, secret, A.W.M., India Office, Political and Secret Department, 15 August 1884: F.O. 65/1209.

[2] Cranbrook to Lytton, private, 3 August 1878: Letters from the Secretary of State, iii, Pte Lytton Papers.

[3] India Office to Foreign Office, secret and immediate, 21 February 1882: F.O. 65/1150.

[4] Granville to Thornton, No. 42E, draft dispatch, 29 February 1884: F.O. 65/1203. Memorandum on Correspondence with the Russian Government in regard to Merv: 1874–1884, confidential, printed for the use of the Foreign Office, 26 February 1884: F.O. 65/1203. Burne's memorandum on English and Russian declarations in regard to Merv, 1 March 1884: loose papers, Pte Kimberley Papers.

[5] Currie to Kimberley, private, 12 January 1885: loose papers, Pte Kimberley Papers.

[6] Kimberley to Dufferin, private, 13 March 1885: bound volume, Letters to the Earl of Dufferin, November 1884 to July 1885, Pte Kimberley Papers.

gone there.[1] To Lord Kimberley it seemed plain that in annexing Merv the Russians had 'chosen the moment when we are in difficulties in Egypt'.[2]

Prolonged discussions ensued in which Lord Granville expressed to Baron Mohrenheim, the Russian ambassador in London, his 'real surprise' at the forward movement and recalled the previous assurances. Baron Mohrenheim said that his Emperor's surprise equalled Lord Granville's, apologized for the untimeliness of the incident, and alluded to the absurdity of quarrelling over the Turkomans—adding that had Mr. Gladstone not held office 'the Russian Cabinet would have formally declined to discuss the matter at all'.[3] Lord Kimberley considered the latter a 'novel doctrine'.[4]

Russia's incorporation of the oasis precipitated a mild flurry of activity in London—Cabinet meetings, debates in Parliament, consultations with the India Office, and a rapid exchange of telegrams with St. Petersburg and Simla. The Cabinet decided that, for reasons of self-respect alone, a remonstrance must be made, but they had no intention of straining relations with Russia. One tangible result ensued. The Government of India was ordered to resume work on the Quetta railway as a demonstration to all that the British guarantee to Afghanistan was seriously meant. The construction which had been suspended in October 1880 was thus recommenced in April 1884. Lord Kimberley, informing the Viceroy of the Cabinet's views on this 'difficult and important' subject, described the occupation of Merv as 'a very grave occurrence, bringing as it does Russia into immediate contact with the Herat territory'.[5]

The Government's decision to respond with calmness but

---

[1] Salisbury to Wolff, private, 23 February 1887; quoted in Cecil, op. cit., iv, 41–2.

[2] Kimberley to Ripon, private, 22 February 1884: bound volume, Letters to the Marquis of Ripon, January 1884 to November 1884, Pte Kimberley Papers.

[3] Foreign Office draft to Thornton, No. 42A, 28 February 1884, endorsed 'The Queen, Mr Gladstone, Circulate (immediate)': F.O. 65/1203. Granville to Thornton, No. 73A, draft dispatch, 1 April 1884, endorsed 'The Queen, Mr Gladstone, Cabinet': F.O. 65/1205. Same to same, No. 81B, confidential, 9 April 1884, endorsed 'The Queen, Mr Gladstone': F.O. 65/1205.

[4] Case 435, Minute by Kimberley of 25 May 1884: Home Correspondence, Political and Secret Department, vol. lxiii, India Office Records.

[5] Kimberley to Ripon, private, 22 February 1884: bound volume, Letters to the Marquis of Ripon, January 1884 to November 1884, Pte Kimberley Papers.

not with indifference was endorsed by Parliament, and supported generally in the Press. *The Times* tried to soothe its readers by pointing out that Russia had regarded her pledge as 'rather conditional than absolute'. The leading article, without being alarmist, reviewed Merv's strategic significance and prophesied that Persia would require more attention in the future.[1]

In Parliament, too, a moderate line predominated. The Duke of Argyll, having already diagnosed the late Conservative Government's ills as 'Mervousness',[2] spoke again in that vein, but at the same time he emphasized the increasing significance of Persia.[3] Lord Lytton, on the other hand, rebuked the Government for its apathy, and sarcastically observed that if the Liberals would create two new departments of the Foreign and War Offices 'devoted to the careful preparation of measures to be taken only when too late' they would be the busiest in Downing Street.[4] Edward Stanhope saw the history of the Merv question as one of 'prevarication . . . even more melancholy' than that of Khiva.[5]

Lord Salisbury, out of his greater experience, joined in the criticism of the Liberal Government's relative inactivity at this crisis. In his view the course of annexation which had recently taken Russia to Merv had been motivated, at least superficially, by the 'dens of robbers' on her frontier. Since 'dens of robbers' still inhabited the borderlands along Persian Khorassan and Afghan Turkestan the force which had drawn the territory from the Aral Sea to the Murghab river into Russia was probably not yet spent.[6]

None the less, Lord Salisbury's chief concern was not with these dens of robbers, but with a problem of more general importance, that 'impalpable power'—prestige. 'Your frontier

---

[1] Leading Article in *The Times*, 11 March 1884.

[2] The Duke of Argyll, *op. cit.*, ii, 370–1.

[3] *P.D.*, Third Series, Lords, 10 March 1884, cclxxxv, 980–1.

[4] *Ibid.*, pp. 959–75.

[5] *Ibid.*, Commons, 22 February 1884, cclxxxiv, 1762.

[6] His reasoning coincided with that of Rawlinson who wrote: 'The same law of advance which has taken Russia from Ashkabad to Merv, must necessarily take her from Merv to Herat, unless some counter law be applied.' Case 212, Merv: Conversation between Lord Granville and the Russian Ambassador: Home Correspondence, Political and Secret Department, vol. lxii, India Office Records.

may be as strong as you please; your fortress may be as impregnable as you please', he argued, 'but if the *prestige* of the
Power coming against you is greater than your own, it will
penetrate through that barrier; it will undermine your sway;
it will dissolve the loyalty and patriotism of those you rule.'
From this point of view the absorption of the Turkoman oasis
was clearly a grave event. As Secretary of State for India and
as Foreign Secretary, from 1874 to 1880, he had endeavoured
to keep Merv out of Russian hands and to uphold the chieftains
who wished either to remain independent or to give their
allegiance and their tribal lands to the Shah of Persia. He
explained why the capitulation of Merv was a danger to India.

. . . if it should so happen that any Viceroy should occupy the position which Lord Dalhousie was said to desire—of being the Viceroy
of India when the Russian invasion takes place—what he would have
to contend with would not be a direct attack of the Russian Army
coming through the Khyber and Bolan Passes. It would be the
undermining of his strength in India by the production of intrigues
and rebellions among the Natives of India, the gradual weakening of
the respect for the English arms, disaffection towards the English
Raj, and the gradual crumbling away of our resources before Russia
has struck a blow against our frontier. That is the real danger we
have to fear; that is why it is a matter of life and death to us that
Afghanistan should be kept clear not only of Russian soldiers, but of
Russian influence and intrigue. That is why the acquisition of Merv
must not be put aside by platitudes about the advantage of having a
humane instead of an inhuman Power upon the borders of Afghanistan, or with the consolation that Merv is not on the route to anywhere in particular. The event must be looked on in a graver light
than that. It is the gravest that has happened with respect to our
Empire in the East.[1]

Russia's incorporation of Merv had two immediate results.
It quickened Persia's sense of common interest with England,
and it led the British and Russian governments to try to agree
upon a joint delimitation of the frontier between Russia and
Afghanistan. The Shah, helpless and frightened, was likened by
Curzon to a fly in a spider's web.[2] His representative in London,
Malkom Khan, called frequently at the Foreign Office and

[1] *P.D.*, Third Series, Lords, 10 March 1884, cclxxxv, 1008–10.
[2] Curzon, *Russia in Central Asia*, p. 374.

pleaded for the re-establishment of closer ties with England. But
the Salisbury scheme of 1879 and 1880 had failed. The attempt
of the Liberal Government in 1882 to induce the Shah to re-
assert his authority over the Merv Turkomans had also failed.
In these circumstances the Foreign Office entered into new
discussions without enthusiasm. Lord Granville, nevertheless,
gave some encouragement to the flagging Persian Government;
he assured the Shah that the Anglo-Russian agreements
relating to the independence and integrity of Persia were still
in force.[1] He also declared that England would support Persia
diplomatically at St. Petersburg if Russian encroachments on
the Khorassan frontier continued.[2] Lord Kimberley, in a letter
to Lord Ripon, discussed the effect of these recent Russian
advances on Anglo-Persian relations, the plight of the Shah, and
the obstacles in the way of effective British support. Nevertheless, some assurance had to be given, for as Lord Kimberley
put it:

. . . we can hardly look on with indifference whilst Russia turns the
flank of Afghanistan and gets, as she cleverly intends to do, possession of the direct and easy road from Meshed to Herat. If she can
establish herself there, the question of the N[orth] W[estern]
Boundary will sink into comparative insignificance.[3]

Early in 1882 the Government of India had advocated
settling the Persian and Afghan frontiers as a deterrent to
Russia's movement south.[4] At that time the Foreign Office was
endeavouring to revitalize Persia's rule over the territory east
of the Caspian—unaware that the Shah had relinquished his

[1] See Appendix III.
[2] Granville to Thomson, No. 88, draft dispatch, confidential, 17 July 1884,
endorsed 'The Queen, Mr Gladstone': F.O. 65/1208. Foreign Office to India
Office, 18 July 1884: F.O. 65/1208. Granville to Thomson, No. 89, draft dispatch,
confidential, 19 July 1884: F.O. 65/1208. Draft memoranda by Granville and
Kimberley on conversations with Malcom Khan, 16 August 1884, endorsed 'Mr
Gladstone': F.O. 65/1209. Correspondence respecting the movements of Russia in
Central Asia, and her relations with Afghanistan, part iv, 22 January 1884, continuation of memorandum of 30 May 1882, secret: F.O. 65/1202.
[3] Kimberley to Ripon, private, 8 August 1884: bound volume, Letters to the
Marquis of Ripon, January 1884 to November 1884, Pte Kimberley Papers.
[4] Memorandum by Tenterden, 20 February 1882: F.O. 65/1150. Government
of India, Foreign Department, to Secretary of State for India, No. 115 of 1883,
secret, 13 July 1883: F.O. 65/1173.

claims by a secret agreement with Russia in the previous year. While the fruitless negotiations between Great Britain and Persia dragged on, the Russian generals crossed the sands and deserts that finally led to Merv. The cartographers in St. Petersburg also promoted the business of expansion. In 1884 an official map appeared which stretched Russia's southern boundary beyond the oasis for more than two hundred miles and terminated it less than twenty miles from Herat.[1]

The British had to act. The Government of India again in March 1884 pressed for a demarcation of frontiers—this time to a more receptive Lord Granville.[2] The British and Russian Governments agreed in May 1884 that a joint commission should survey Afghanistan's northern boundary, but the Russians persistently refused to recognize any British claims to representation in the Russo-Persian negotiations over Khorassan. The Foreign Office selected Major-General Sir Peter Lumsden to head their side of the commission,[3] and he reached the Afghan frontier with his party in the autumn of 1884.

[1] War Office to Foreign Office, No. 7603/4382, 16 April 1884, endorsed 'Cabinet': F.O. 65/1205. Memorandum by Hertslet on Russian maps in Central Asia, 19 April 1884, endorsed 'Cabinet': F.O. 65/1205.

[2] Government of India, Foreign Department, to Secretary of State for India, No. 16 of 1884, secret, 11 March 1884: F.O. 65/1205. Telegram from Viceroy, secret, 24 February 1884, endorsed 'Seen by Ld. Granville': F.O. 65/1203.

[3] For Lumsden's general instructions see India Office to Lumsden, August 1884, and Foreign Office to Lumsden, No. 1, 25 August 1884: F.O. 65/1209.

F

CHAPTER V

The Penjdeh Crisis, 1885

THE agreement between the British and Russian Governments to conduct the survey of Afghanistan's northern boundary still left a number of matters unsettled. There was much argument whether the survey should be made from west to east or from east to west, whether the decisions should be made in London and St. Petersburg or left to the men on the spot, and whether the work should commence in 1884 or await the arrival of the next warm season. The departure of the Russian commission under General Zelenoi was delayed month after month, and his alleged illness postponed the work until the spring of 1885. Tedious as these problems were, they were overshadowed in the autumn of 1884 by disquieting reports of continued Russian probing actions and encroachments.[1]

These negotiations between England and Russia, and between England and Afghanistan, did not proceed smoothly. Lord Granville complained of the difficulty of advising the Amir 'to yield indefinitely territory which has never been in the possession of Russia'.[2] On 19 February the British ambassador in St. Petersburg, Sir Edward Thornton, said that affairs on the

---

[1] Thornton to Granville, No. 297, 3 October 1884: F.O. 65/1211. Same to same, private, 20 November 1884: Pte Granville Papers, P.R.O. 30/29/186. Memorandum by Barrington on Negotiations with the Russian Government for the Demarcation of the Boundary of Afghanistan since the Annexation of Merv, confidential, 21 March 1885, endorsed 'The Queen, Mr Gladstone, Kimberley, Hartington, Northbrook, Dilke, India Office, Petersburgh, Tehran, Lumsden, Embassies.' Bears notation: 'I am much obliged for this excellent and useful Memorandum. G.': F.O. 65/1238. See also memorandum in reply to the memorandum enclosed in M. de Giers' dispatch of 16 January 1885, confidential, printed for the use of the Cabinet, 11 March 1885, endorsed 'Agreed to by the Cabinet': F.O. 65/1237.

[2] Granville to Thornton, No. 80, draft telegram, confidential, 3 March 1885: F.O. 65/1237.

frontier were growing 'very delicate'.[1] Less than a week later Lord Granville wrote: 'This question of the Affghan boundary is becoming very serious.'[2] General Lumsden reported that Russia's advance was continuing and her forces were approaching Penjdeh.[3] The Queen had already appealed personally to the Emperor of Russia to prevent the 'calamity' of an armed conflict.[4]

On 30 March, Russian and Afghan troops met and fought at the Penjdeh oasis. The Afghans acquitted themselves well, lost heavily, and finally retreated. Their loss was said to be 900 killed and 300 wounded. Two companies were killed to a man in entrenchments. The British boundary commissioners intervened as effectively as they could for peace; then dispatched protests to India and to London condemning the Russian offensive.[5] No one could fail to see in these events a crisis of acute difficulty. Mr. Gladstone, in an address to Parliament, described the clash as a 'grave occurrence', admitted that it looked like 'unprovoked aggression', and asked for £11,000,000 for war preparations—not a paltry sum in 1885.[6] Indeed, the Prime Minister observed that it was the largest vote of credit requested in the preceding seventy years with the possible exception of the Crimean War supply.[7] Gone was the mildness which had characterized the British Government in the Merv crisis twelve months before.

General Komaroff's occupation of Penjdeh seemed the more

[1] Thornton to Granville, private, 19 February 1885: Pte Granville Papers, P.R.O. 30/29/186.

[2] Note by Granville, 24 February 1885: B.M. Add. MSS., No. 44769, vol. dclxxxiv, Pte Gladstone Papers.

[3] E. Fitzmaurice, *The Life of Granville George Leveson Gower, Second Earl Granville, 1815–1891*, ii, 421–3. See for example Lumsden to Granville, No. 21, secret, 16 March 1885: F.O. 65/1237.

[4] The Queen to His Imperial Majesty the Emperor of Russia, telegram, 4 March 1885: Pte Granville Papers, P.R.O. 30/29/45.

[5] Lumsden to Granville, No. 29, confidential, 16 April 1885, enclosure by Yate, Memorandum on the recent Russian advance on Penjdeh, 15 April 1885, endorsed 'Circulated to Cabinet': F.O. 65/1240. Details of the Russian Advance on Penjdeh, 10 April 1885, confidential, Foreign Office memorandum, printed for the use of the Cabinet: loose papers, Pte Kimberley Papers. Telegram from Viceroy, secret, 11 April 1885: F.O. 65/1240. A. C. Yate, *England and Russia Face to Face in Asia: Travels with the Afghan Boundary Commission*, ch. ix, pp. 311–60.

[6] *P.D.*, Third Series, Commons, 9 April 1885, ccxcvi, 1159, 1162–3.

[7] *Ibid.*, Commons, 27 April 1885, ccxcvii, 859.

provocative since Giers, only two weeks previously (16 March), had in an interview with Thornton promised that there would be no advance of Russian troops into the debatable territory. Giers later told Thornton that the Emperor had approved the statements he had made. Gladstone proclaimed:

... it was a very solemn covenant. It was a covenant involving great issues. . . . What has happened? A bloody engagement on the 30th of March followed the covenant of the 16th. . . . The cause of that deplorable collision may be uncertain. What is certain is that the attack was a Russian attack. What was the provocation is a matter of the utmost consequence. We only know that the attack was a Russian attack. We know that the Afghans suffered in life, in spirit, and in repute. We know that a blow was struck at the credit and the authority of a Sovereign—our ally—our protected ally—who had committed no offence.

The pledge of the British Prime Minister to have 'right done in the matter' brought his nation to the verge of war with Russia.[1]

When the Foreign Office received the news of the Penjdeh encounter, the major embassies were warned by telegraph that a situation of 'utmost gravity' had arisen.[2] Documents announcing a state of war between England and Russia were printed. It was expected that most other nations would declare their neutrality, and the effects of such neutrality on the conduct of the war were investigated. Particular interest was shown in the state of the Japanese naval yards.[3] Lord Dufferin was informed that the Admiralty were watching all Russian ships.[4] Vice-

[1] *Ibid.*, pp. 863-5.

[2] Lumsden's telegram announcing the engagement between the Russians and Afghans, dated 1 April, was not received until 7 April. It had to be conveyed by pony express from his camp on the Afghan frontier through the mountains and deserts to the telegraph office at Meshed, Persia. See Foreign Office memorandum and telegram to Currie, 8 April 1885, instructing him to draw up a telegram to Thornton. Granville to Thornton, No. 129, draft extender telegram, 8 April 1885: F.O. 65/1239. Granville to Embassies, Paris No. 15, Rome No. 31, Vienna No. 13, Berlin No. 33, St. Petersburg No. 46, Constantinople No. 36, draft telegram, 9 April 1885: F.O. 65/1239.

[3] The extent of preparations can be gauged by an examination of the documents, most of which were never used, in the volume entitled 'Russia. Maritime and Commercial Questions which would be raised by outbreak of war, 1885': F.O. 65/1253.

[4] Kimberley to Dufferin, private telegram, 20 April 1885: bound volume, Telegrams to and from India, March 1885 to June 1885, Pte Kimberley Papers.

Admiral Sir William Dowell, then Commander-in-Chief of the China Station, was instructed by telegraph to 'occupy Port Hamilton, and report proceedings'.[1] On 26 April the governments of Japan, China, and Korea were notified that such action had been taken.[2] It was intended that Port Hamilton should be used as a base for operations against Vladivostock.[3] In India the Viceroy quietly prepared to move 25,000 men to Quetta, placed General Roberts in command, considered several possible plans of campaign, and received assurances that reinforcements from England would be forthcoming.[4] Throughout the anxious months of April, May, and June the letters from Lord Kimberley to Lord Dufferin were dominated by the idea that England was 'hovering . . . on the very brink of war'.[5] Thornton, in St. Petersburg, foresaw a 'very possible rupture'.[6] The French ambassador in London said that his German and Italian colleagues regarded war as inevitable.[7] The Queen wrote to Lord Granville:

She feels naturally all the responsibility wh[ich] a declaration of war with Russia entails upon herself & her Government—as well as the very serious consequences wh[ich] may result to the country therefrom, tho she has not a moment's anxiety as to the ultimate issue. But on the other hand, after having done what she can to avert such a painful Eventuality, she feels it to be our bounden duty to be very firm & not to agree to any *patching* up of this *question*

[1] Port Hamilton, Précis of telegrams, confidential, cypher telegram, No. 42, drafted and sent on 14 April 1885: Adm. 116/70, part i.

[2] Fitzmaurice, *op. cit.*, ii, 440. Decypher telegram from O'Conor, No. 48, secret, Peking, 9 June 1885: B.M. Add. MSS. 44769, vol. dclxxxiv, Pte Gladstone Papers.

[3] Memorandum by Northbrook on Port Hamilton, 28 July 1885: Pte Granville Papers, P.R.O. 30/29/22A.

[4] Kimberley to Dufferin, private, 10 April 1885; same to same, private, 17 April 1885; same to same, private, 24 April 1885: bound volume, Letters to the Earl of Dufferin, November 1884 to July 1885, Pte Kimberley Papers. Dufferin to Kimberley, private, 23 March 1885: bound volume, Letters from the Earl of Dufferin, December 1884 to June 1885, Pte Kimberley Papers.

[5] Kimberley to Dufferin, private, 10 April 1885: bound volume, Letters to the Earl of Dufferin, November 1884 to July 1885, Pte Kimberley Papers.

[6] Thornton to Granville, private, 9 April 1885: Pte Granville Papers, P.R.O. 30/29/186.

[7] *Documents diplomatiques français, 1871–1914* (First Series, 1871–1900, 11 vols., Paris, 1929–); hereafter cited as *D.D.F.* Waddington to Freycinet, telegram, 10 April 1885; vi, 5–6.

wh[ich] goes *much further* & is of *much* more serious import than appears on the surface.[1]

The British Government, in spite of its fiery pronouncements and military measures, hoped to surmount the crisis without going to war. Fortunately, neither the Viceroy and his military advisers nor even the Amir of Afghanistan thought that Penjdeh was worth a full-scale fight.[2] But a few more miles to the south lay Herat—the cause of two British wars with Persia, and long regarded as the 'gate' or 'key' to India.

Herat was an ancient city, and had in the days of Tamerlane and his son been a metropolis of Muslim culture and the glory of Asia. Now it was poor and ruinous, important only for its strategic situation on 'the main highway to India'.[3] Lumsden, when asked for a report on Herat by the Secretary of State for War, recounted the many sieges Herat had undergone, by Mongols, Uzbeks, Turkomans, and Persians. 'The Herat valley', he continued, 'has in past times subsisted very large bodies of men for considerable periods, and there can be no question but that under favourable circumstances the resources of the valley will again in the future be capable of producing all the food and forage required for a large army.' He pointed out that in almost every invasion of India from the north, 'Herat has afforded a resting place, base, and depôt of supply, whilst from its position it covers Turkestan, overawes Khorassan, and threatens Afghanistan and India.' Its value to an invader of India was great since 'in it concentrate the highways from Persia, the Caspian, Merve, Bokhara, and Afghan Turkestan; and from it, roads lead by Hazara to Kabul, and by Furrah to Kandahar and Seistan'. Herat, Lumsden concluded, 'has

[1] The Queen to Granville, private, Aix-les-Bains, 17 April 1885: Pte Granville Papers, P.R.O. 30/29/31.

[2] Dufferin to Kimberley, private telegrams, 4 and 5 April 1885: bound volume, Telegrams to and from India, March 1885 to June 1885, Pte Kimberley Papers. For published accounts of the Amir's visit to India and the Penjdeh crisis see A. Lyall, *The Life of the Marquis of Dufferin and Ava*, ii, 89–101; M. Durand, *Life of the Right Honourable Sir Alfred Comyn Lyall*, pp. 299–304; and F. Roberts, *Forty-One Years in India*, ii, 390–7.

[3] Quotation from Fraser-Tytler, *op. cit.*, p. 7. A. Conolly, *Journey to the North of India, overland from England, through Russia, Persia, and Affghanistan*, ii, 2–3, 301 ff. Benjamin to Frelinghuysen, diplomatic series, No. 72, 4 June 1884: Persia, i, American Department of State.

displayed a recuperative power in recovering from blows which would have entirely obliterated any place that did not possess great advantages in natural productiveness and commercial development'.[1]

Thus, in 1885 the fate of Herat was the subject of immediate and grave concern. Many statesmen feared that the Russian drive which had incorporated Penjdeh on 30 March aimed at Herat as its real objective. The Duke of Argyll, who accepted the label of Russophil without shame, stated plainly that the whole situation altered 'the moment that Russia . . . put one step forward towards Herat'.[2] His questions in Parliament caused Lord Granville to exclaim: 'I am almost inclined to say to him, "Et tu, Brute!"'[3]

The British Government had for several weeks before the incident at Penjdeh begun to consider the problem of Herat. As early as 29 January Thornton told Lord Granville privately that the military men were steadily gaining influence over the more moderate elements in the Russian Foreign Office,[4] and on 17 February the military attaché at St. Petersburg reported that the Russian military party talked of taking Herat. He suggested that it be put in readiness.[5]

Lord Kimberley commented:

This is a very important mem[orandum]:—The suggestion that our escort should in the event of the negotiations breaking off take up its quarters in Herat appears to me to be a very good one.

[1] Note by Lumsden on the Aspect of Affairs at Herat and in Central Asia, secret, India Office, 24 July 1885: F.O. 65/1248. General Lumsden was relieved of command by Lord Granville. Lord Kimberley, who did not believe that Lumsden had been 'ill treated' by the Foreign Office, wrote that 'his deeds have been much better than his words, and his views on the future policy to be pursued in Afghanistan appear to me to be marked by no extravagance'. Kimberley to Dufferin, private, 12 June 1885: bound volume, Letters to the Earl of Dufferin, November 1884 to July 1885, Pte Kimberley Papers. Lord Randolph Churchill told Lord Salisbury that Lumsden and Burne 'form my little private cabinet here on frontier matters, and both are undoubtedly most useful wise and influential'. Churchill to Salisbury, private, 30 July 1885: loose papers, Pte Salisbury Papers.

[2] P.D., Third Series, Lords, 27 March 1885, ccxcvi, 805.   [3] Ibid., p. 806.

[4] Thornton to Granville, private, 29 January 1885: Pte Granville Papers, P.R.O. 30/29/186.

[5] Memorandum by Colonel Trench on State of Opinion at St. Petersburg regarding the delimitation of Russo-Afghan Frontier, Intended Russian occupation of Herat, etc., 17 February 1885, endorsed 'Circulate among Members of the Committee. G.' F.O. 65/1236.

I will telegraph today privately to Dufferin to ask his opinion on it, and whether the Amir might not, as Dufferin suggested to me as a possible measure, receive some money to put Herat in a state of defence against a coup-de-main.[1]

An exchange of views took place among members of the Cabinet. Later, when Lord Dufferin asked if it was intended to keep Herat out of Russian hands at any price, he was told at once that 'An attack on Herat will mean war with Russia everywhere.'[2] Lord Kimberley amplified this declaration in a private letter two days later:

Both my 'secret' and 'private' telegrams of the 25th about Herat were seen and approved by the Cabinet, and expressed our 'innermost' mind on the subject. Our feeling is that it is now not a mere question about a few miles more or less of Afghan territory but of our whole relations with Russia in Asia.[3]

Simultaneously, Thornton carried out his instructions to inform Giers that any attempt by Russian troops to occupy Herat would be considered tantamount to a declaration of war.[4]

This determined opposition forced the Russians to halt in the Kushk valley. The British were anxious to avoid hostilities, and they struggled for a compromise settlement. The tension gradually relaxed, and negotiations continued in a less-charged atmosphere. Thornton reported, early in May, that the peace party was gaining strength in Russia. Moreover, it had been pointed out in a council summoned by the Emperor that the moment was not opportune for beginning a great war. The Russian army was in the midst of reorganization, the navy and the coast defences were unprepared, and the treasury was empty.[5] The turning-point in the crisis came when the Russian

[1] Minute by Kimberley of 19 February on Colonel Trench's Memorandum: F.O. 65/1236. Telegram to Viceroy, secret, 23 February 1885: F.O. 65/1236.

[2] Kimberley to Dufferin, private telegram, 25 March 1885: bound volume, Telegrams to and from India, March 1885 to June 1885, Pte Kimberley Papers. See Appendix I.

[3] Kimberley to Dufferin, private, 27 March 1885: bound volume, Letters to the Earl of Dufferin, November 1884 to July 1885, Pte Kimberley Papers.

[4] Thornton to Granville, No. 77, confidential, 29 March 1885, endorsed 'Cabinet': F.O. 65/1238.

[5] Thornton to Granville, private, 7 May 1885: Pte Granville Papers, P.R.O. 30/29/186.

Emperor agreed to the principle of arbitration.[1] The Germans believed that their pressure on Turkey for the closing of the Dardanelles to British warships had also contributed to the maintenance of peace.[2] Early in June, Lord Kimberley could tell the Viceroy that, although the Government was still, as he said, *aux prises* with the Russians, the fundamental differences had been narrowed to the single question of the disposition of Zulficar Pass—an issue about which the British Government remained adamant. This pass, which runs from east to west, and connects Khorassan with north and western Afghanistan, concerned Persia more immediately than Herat and India, since it constituted the old plundering road of the Turkomans and was the traditional 'way out to Persia'.[3]

The Liberal Government, however, did not survive to conclude its Afghan negotiations. Newspaper articles and narrow divisions in Parliament manifested the growing popular discontent. This dissatisfaction had been produced largely though not wholly by a combination of incidents in foreign policy—the Khartoum crisis and General Gordon's death, the Merv capitulation, and the Penjdeh encounter. The Government which had rashly declared its intentions to crush the Mahdi and to see right done in Afghanistan had ended by retreating from the Sudan and leaving Penjdeh to the Russians. British prestige suffered a series of blows, whose repercussions extended beyond the mountains of the Hindu Kush and the waters of the Nile to react upon the major Courts in Europe.

Early in May 1885 the Liberals failed to muster sufficient votes in a division over a relatively minor issue. A month later Lord Salisbury, as Prime Minister and Foreign Secretary, assumed leadership of a minority government which lasted for

[1] Granville to Staal, 1 May 1885, endorsed 'The Queen': F.O. 65/1242. Waddington to Freycinet, telegram, very confidential, 3 May 1885: *D.D.F.*, vi, 18–19.

[2] Bismarck to Prince Henry VII of Reuss, in Vienna, No. 60, secret telegram, 9 April 1885, iv, Nr. 765, 113–14. J. Lepsius, A. Mendelssohn Bartholdy, and F. Thimme (eds.), *Die Grosse Politik der europäischen Kabinette, 1871–1914* (Berlin 1922–1927); hereafter cited as *G.P.*

[3] Kimberley to Dufferin, private, 4 June 1885; same to same, private, 12 June 1885: bound volume, Letters to the Earl of Dufferin, November 1884 to July 1885, Pte Kimberley Papers. Memorandum by Kimberley of 16 April of conversations between Lord Granville and Lord Kimberley, and M. de Staal and M. Lessar on 14 April 1885: F.O. 65/1240.

seven months. Sir Michael Hicks Beach, later in his life, recalled that Lord Salisbury had boarded the train for Balmoral intending to decline office, but in deference to the Queen's wishes he had changed his plans and consented to form a government.[1] Irish issues were ablaze; Parliamentary reform was in progress once more; and England's relations with other Powers were, as the Queen told him, in a sorry plight. Upon returning from Balmoral, he remarked: 'They [the Liberal Government] have at least achieved their long desired "Concert of Europe". They have succeeded in uniting the continent of Europe—against England.'[2]

From a general diplomatic point of view the British position was indeed, as Lord Salisbury said in a letter to Sir William White, 'not enviable'.[3] At the outset, the Afghan frontier constituted the most acute danger zone, and the crisis with Russia intensified momentarily. The dispute over Zulficar Pass was not settled; one of Lord Granville's last acts was to accept General Lumsden's resignation as head of the boundary commission; the Government of India relayed reports of renewed Russian troop movements; and the Conservative Cabinet had also to consider war preparations.[4]

When Sir West Ridgeway took command of the frontier commission, he faced incessant Russian probing actions, tense and dissatisfied Afghans, and the threat of a collapse in the morale of his staff.[5] Salisbury, Dufferin and Ridgeway worked together smoothly. After long and tiresome negotiations, interspersed

[1] Lord St. Aldwyn to Lady Gwendolen Cecil, undated but filed between 16 December 1913 and 23 January 1914: Pte Hicks Beach Papers.

[2] Quoted in Cecil, *op. cit.*, iii, 136.

[3] Salisbury to White, private, 11 July 1885: Pte White Papers, F.O. 364/1.

[4] The work of the British boundary commission deserves fuller treatment than it has yet received. The commission itself, partly appointed by Lord Granville and partly by Lord Ripon, does not seem to have been happily constituted. General Lumsden's resignation was the climax to a series of differences existing within the commission itself and between it and higher authorities in London and Simla. Nevertheless, it acquitted itself well as far as its actual task was concerned. The F.O. 65 series for 1884 and 1885 contains an abundance of pertinent material, and so do the records in the Commonwealth Relations Office.

[5] Colonel Sir West Ridgeway replaced General Lumsden. The Afghan negotiations continued until 1887, and Ridgeway was on the frontier until they terminated. He wrote an interesting article on the frontier delimitation, 'The New Afghan Frontier', *Nineteenth Century*, xxii (1887), pp. 470–82.

with more than one anxious moment, a partial settlement of the boundary was achieved late in 1885.

This diplomatic triumph was not easily won. Controversy over Zulficar slowed the negotiations nearly to a halt, and so strained relations that the British investigated the possibility of a stand at Herat. The strategic position of Zulficar and its relations to Persia and to India had been all too clearly delineated by General Petrusevitch on his military maps several years before. His pamphlet and illustrative work in cartography reached the British Foreign Office on the last day of 1881. These documents were studied carefully and still had point in 1888 when copies were given to the new minister at Tehran, Sir Henry Drummond Wolff.[1] General Petrusevitch lucidly demonstrated that the Afghan barrier could be outflanked by penetrating Khorassan and that Zulficar unlocked the Persian door. Both Lord Kimberley and Lord Salisbury tenaciously refused to consider the pass as anything but a *sine qua non*. As Lord Kimberley put it to Lord Dufferin:

> There is one slight inaccuracy in the *Times* report of what I said about Zulficar. I did not say 'we thought the Amir should have the pass' but 'we informed the Amir he would have the pass'. Outwardly, at all events, there is a substantial concurrence of opinion between us and Salisbury as to the Afghan policy. I hope it will continue.[2]

The Queen urged Lord Salisbury to hold firm on Zulficar 'whatever results may be'.[3]

In April, when a state of war between England and Russia lacked little more than the official declaration, the Russians had accepted the formula—Penjdeh for Zulficar.[4] But before Lord Granville left the Foreign Office the question had been

---

[1] See Appendix III. (General Petrusevitch died at Geok Tepe.)

[2] Kimberley to Dufferin, private, 10 July 1885: bound volume, Letters to the Earl of Dufferin, November 1884 to July 1885, Pte Kimberley Papers.

[3] The Queen to Salisbury, private telegram, 11 July 1885: bound volume, From The Queen, 1885–1886, Pte Salisbury Papers.

[4] Kimberley to Dufferin, private, 4 June 1885: bound volume, Letters to the Earl of Dufferin, November 1884 to July 1885, Pte Kimberley Papers. Salisbury to Grosvenor, No. 352, draft dispatch, 17 September 1885: F.O. 65/1250. The sacrifice of Penjdeh was severely criticized in England. Even Ridgeway, whose views were moderate, referred to the 'humiliating Penjdeh story', *op. cit.*, p. 474. Morier in his letter to Salisbury of 17 February 1892 referred to 'the men who borrowed 11 million to cover their retreat'.

reopened, and discussions were taking place over whether Zulficar was a pass or a village.[1] The Amir's attitude added to the
delicacy of the question. 'Abd-ar-Rahman had accepted the
loss of Penjdeh without a remonstrance, but he told the Viceroy
plainly that he would not honour any settlement which relinquished his rights to certain other districts. One of these was
Zulficar.[2] On the frontier itself Colonel Ridgeway was appre-
hensive about the outbreak of war, and feared that 'Colonel
Alikhanoff's first endeavour may be to capture mission and
parade it through Turkistan'.[3] The Queen thought the Afghan
situation 'very ugly', and confided to Lord Salisbury her dread
of an 'explosion' before anything could be done.[4] In his report
to the Queen about his first reception of the diplomatic corps,
Lord Salisbury described the Russian ambassador's bearing as
'stiff and reserved'.[5] Such was the situation in the summer of
1885.

Under Lord Salisbury's supervision the preparations for war
went forward. His handling of the crisis was in harmony with
his principle that 'willingness on good cause to go to war is the
best possible security for peace'.[6] The boundary commissioners
received detailed instructions in case war broke out.[7] A collision
between Russian patrols and Afghan outposts seemed possible.
Sir West Ridgeway telegraphed for guidance about what he
should do in the event that 'Russians, few or many, advance into
the Herat valley'.[8] Lord Salisbury consulted the India Office
and the Government of India. The latter unanimously declared

[1] Giers to Staal, telegram, 4/16 April 1885: Meyendorff, *op. cit.*, i, 192. Thornton
to Granville, private, 17 June 1885: loose papers, Pte Salisbury Papers.

[2] Sykes, *Durand*, p. 154.

[3] Ridgeway to Foreign Department, Government of India, No. 35, telegram,
7 June 1885: Letters from India, Political and Secret Department, vol. xliv, India
Office Records.

[4] The Queen to Salisbury, private telegram, 17 July 1885: loose papers, Pte
Salisbury Papers.

[5] Salisbury to the Queen, private, 26 June 1885: bound volume, To The Queen,
1885–1886, Pte Salisbury Papers.

[6] Robert Cecil, Third Marquis of Salisbury, *Essays—Biographical*, p. 22.

[7] Case 1044, Afghan Boundary, Instructions in the event of hostilities, July
1885: Home Correspondence, Political and Secret Department, vol. lxxv, India
Office Records.

[8] Ridgeway to Salisbury, No. 132, decypher telegram, 16 August 1885: F.O.
65/1248.

that any such advance would be so 'unwarrantable' that it would 'justly constitute a *casus belli*'.[1] The Russian Foreign Minister received another warning about Herat.[2]

The drafts and minutes in his own hand, including telegrams to the Viceroy, reveal the extent to which Lord Salisbury personally conducted these negotiations, and also his amazing grasp of detail in Central Asian affairs.[3] To judge by his drafts and his private writings, he thought it unlikely that this present crisis would lead to war. In a letter to the Viceroy he set forth his analysis of the situation.

The military party would like war; Bismarck wishes war; the Emperor of Germany wishes peace; so does M. de Giers; and the Emperor of Russia, with whom the decision lies, is very vain of his diplomatic skill, and convinced that he has an inborn genius for managing men. Bismarck's inclination would be a more potent factor—only that his position just now is precarious. The Emperor may die. . . . His death will change things very much, for the next people are very anti-Russian.[4]

To his ambassador in St. Petersburg he wrote:

. . . The Russian negotiation seems as if it had arrived at an impasse. I don't think that at present they mean war—but I fear they have pledged themselves too strongly not to grant the whole pass, and that they cannot retract. Of course we cannot retract, for we are bound to the Ameer.[5]

A fortnight later, he continued:

I do not apprehend any change in Afghanistan so long as the heat continues, but I do not feel at all secure against an *incident facheux* as soon as October begins. However the defences of Herat are going

[1] India Office to Foreign Office and minutes by Currie and Salisbury, secret, 28 August 1885: F.O. 65/1249. Salisbury to Ridgeway, No. 65, draft telegram, confidential, 21 September 1885: F.O. 65/1250.

[2] Salisbury to Grosvenor, No. 336, draft dispatch, confidential, 11 September 1885: F.O. 65/1250.

[3] Both the F.O. 65 series and the F.O. 60 series (Russia in Central Asia and Persia) contain numerous drafts and minutes in his own hand. Some of his drafts to the Viceroy appear in the Home Correspondence, Political and Secret Department, India Office Records, for 1885.

[4] Salisbury to Dufferin, private, 7 August 1885. Pte Dufferin Papers.

[5] Salisbury to Thornton, private, 21 July 1885: bound volume, To Austria, Belgium, China, France, Egypt, Germany, Greece, Holland, Italy, Russia, Turkey, Sir H. D. Wolff, 1885–1886, Pte Salisbury Papers.

forward, and barring treachery I do not believe that they will be open to a *coup de main*.[1]

Sir Edward Thornton agreed. He did not think that the Russians intended to go to war in the immediate future, nor over the Afghan boundary. But their military preparations looked serious:

These preparations were begun when there really seemed to be a danger of a conflict with England, and they have not been discontinued: indeed the change of our Government seemed rather to have intensified them. . . . My impression is that their real objective is always Constantinople and that their threatening attitude towards India through Afghanistan is merely a detail and intended to induce us to send as many troops as possible to India and keep them there far away from the real object of their ambition.[2]

Throughout July and August, the constant Russian protractions and obstructions threatened to wreck the attempt to define the boundary. The Cabinet, at a meeting on 29 July, considered the withdrawal of the commission on the grounds that such large-scale military preparations could not be financed indefinitely and that the negotiations were involving 'no inconsiderable humiliation and discredit' for Her Majesty's Government.[3] The recall of the commission and the consequent breakdown of the deliberations seem to have been averted by the combined efforts of the Government of India and Colonel Ridgeway. They argued that the departure of British officers would probably be followed immediately by the loss of Herat.[4]

The month of August produced ominous reports of Russian troop movements, a crisis over Herat, and negligible progress with the Zulficar dispute. On the first day of September, Lord Salisbury wrote in a letter to Sir Henry Drummond Wolff: 'The

[1] Salisbury to Thornton, private, 5 August 1885: bound volume, To Austria, etc., 1885–1886, Pte Salisbury Papers.

[2] Thornton to Salisbury, private, 29 July 1885: bound volume, From Turkey, Russia, Bulgaria, Greece, Egypt, Sir H. D. Wolff, 1885–1886, Pte Salisbury Papers.

[3] Case 1112, Secretary of State for India to the Viceroy, secret telegram, 30 July 1885: Home Correspondence, Political and Secret Department, vol. cxxvi, India Office Records. This document is also in F.O. 65/1248.

[4] Case 1129, Viceroy to the Secretary of State for India, secret telegram, 3 August 1885: Home Correspondence, Political and Secret Department, vol. cxxvi, India Office Records.

Afghanistan negotiation hangs fire but I do not think the war will come out of that. Barring accidents I do not think it will come till the Russian railway to Sarakhs is finished.'[1] Sir Philip Currie thought that the reports from St. Petersburg confirmed 'Bismarck's view that the Russians mean business'. He suggested:

In view of the likelihood of the crisis some months hence, might it not be useful if a Committee of representatives of the India Office, F[oreign] O[ffice], War Office, and Admiralty were appointed to put together all the information we have got in the respective offices, bearing on hostilities with Russia, with the view of a complete plan of operations being prepared for the consideration of the Cabinet. . . .[2]

Within two weeks, however, the Russians had abandoned their claims to Zulficar, had accepted Lord Salisbury's terms, and had signed a preliminary protocol (10 September) which defined in general terms over three hundred miles of boundary from Zulficar on the Heri Rud to Khwaja Salar on the Oxus.[3] In one of his last private letters from St. Petersburg, Sir Edward Thornton remarked on the Russian Government's 'come down from their previous pretensions'.[4]

It is difficult to account for this *volte face*. Clearly, Baron de Staal believed that it was useless to treat for Zulficar. He reminded Vlangaly, Giers' deputy in the Russian Foreign Office, that the British Government possessed a formal written statement acknowledging Afghan rights to Zulficar Pass. Furthermore:

Si lord Granville n'a pas cru pouvoir rétracter cette promesse, lord Salisbury, qui a accepté l'héritage politique de son devancier sous bénéfice d'inventaire, le peut encore moins. . . .[5]

[1] Salisbury to Wolff, private, 1 September 1885: bound volume, To Austria, etc., 1885–1886, Pte Salisbury Papers.

[2] Currie to Salisbury, private, 22 August 1885: loose papers, Pte Salisbury Papers.

[3] Protocole, confidential, printed for the use of the Foreign Office, 10 September 1885: F.O. 65/1250.

[4] Thornton to Salisbury, private, 27 August 1885: bound volume, From Turkey, Russia, Bulgaria, Greece, Egypt, Sir H. D. Wolff, 1885–1886, Pte Salisbury Papers. A full summary of the Afghan negotiation is given in Ridgeway to Salisbury, No. 8, confidential, 15 August 1887: F.O. 65/1321.

[5] Staal to Vlangaly, No. 90, 26 July/7 August 1885: Meyendorff, *op. cit.*, i, 254.

But Lord Salisbury emphasized that the Russian Government paid little heed to Staal.

Meeting in central Europe, Giers and Sir Robert Morier took up the question of Zulficar. While *en route* to St. Petersburg as the newly appointed ambassador, Morier stopped at Franzensbad for the purpose of meeting with Giers. There began the frank and friendly discussions, which were continued at Marienbad, which characterized the relationship of the two men for many years. Morier said that the British lion was a peaceful beast, but it had 'a chorde sensible, like all respectable carnivora'. It had a bone to defend—India. Any British Government would fight for India and its outposts, including Herat. Philip Currie, too, discussed the Central Asian problem with Giers at Friedrichsruh.[1]

Yet these conversations may have had little bearing. A curious time relationship exists in the rising in Roumelia, which occurred eight days after the Afghan settlement. It seems highly probable that the eruption in the Balkans did not come as a complete surprise to the Russians.[2]

---

[1] Morier to Salisbury, private, Marienbad, 1 September 1885: loose papers, Pte Salisbury Papers. Currie to Salisbury, private, 29 September 1885: loose papers, Pte Salisbury Papers.

[2] Thornton to Salisbury, No. 314, confidential, 21 September 1885, endorsed 'The Queen, Cabinet'; same to same, No. 322, confidential, 23 September 1885, endorsed 'The Queen, Cabinet': F.O. 65/1218.

CHAPTER VI

The Approach to Germany

THE connection, if any, between the stirrings in the Balkans and the temporary calm that settled over Afghanistan remains obscure, but the effect of the Afghan frontier proceedings upon the neighbouring country of Persia was pronounced and clear-cut. The news from Penjdeh, even more than that from Merv, reverberated in Tehran.

In the years immediately preceding 1885 the Russians had whittled away at the Shah's loosely controlled north-eastern territories. The reports from Lieutenant-Colonel Charles Stewart, on duty on the Khorassan frontier, graphically depict the Russian incursions into the Atrek and Akhal country, the ever-slackening hold of the Shah on his outlying regions, the increasing number of Persian officials in the pay of Russia, and the gross misgovernment which sapped the people's will to resist encroachments. By 1885 Russian bases dotted Persia's border—at Chikishliar, Kizil Arvat, Geok Tepe, Ashkabad, Merv, and even Sarakhs—and the fighting at Penjdeh took place less than one hundred miles from the Shah's domain. Would Khorassan, the Parthia of the Romans and a bone of contention throughout the centuries between Turkoman and Persian, be next?[1]

---

[1] Case 148, Lieutenant-Colonel Stewart's report and minutes by India Office staff, report printed 3 March 1883: Home Correspondence, Political and Secret Department, vol. lv, India Office Records.

Case 177, Central Asia: M. de Giers declines to admit that the Atek territory is an integral part of Persia, 12 March 1883: Home Correspondence, Political and Secret Department, vol. lvi, India Office Records.

Case 432, Central Asia: Report by Mr Stephen, 11 May 1883: Home Correspondence, Political and Secret Department, vol. lvii, India Office Records.

Case 828, Perso-Afghan Frontier, Letter from Colonel Stewart, 5 December 1883: Home Correspondence, Political and Secret Department, vol. lx, India Office Records.

The excitement in northern Afghanistan roused Nasir ad-Din. Seized with a dread of impending danger, he turned to the British for help. In conversations with the British minister in Tehran, Sir Ronald Thomson, he asked for a formal territorial guarantee and for protection against possible Russian aggression. Little was said about Persia's own precarious position, but the Shah stressed the danger to India arising from Khorassan's unsettled frontier.[1] Lord Granville, beset with graver troubles, replied that the representations would be 'borne in mind', and gave the usual advice—that the Shah should strengthen his hold in Khorassan by appointing a reliable governor and by improving the quality of his administration. 'Prompt and energetic measures' should also be taken to establish better means of communication between the Gulf and Tehran.[2]

Several questions involving Persian policy were pending when the Conservatives came into power in mid-1885. Lord Salisbury attached real significance to the rôle of Persia in Indian defence, and Persian issues soon attracted his attention. On 17 July 1885 a relatively minor dispute brought forth a firm statement. The Russian Minister for Foreign Affairs had asserted that Great Britain had no interest in Persia's rights over the Atrek country. Sir Philip Currie suggested in one of his minutes that the reference should be allowed to pass unnoticed. Lord Salisbury disagreed, and directed that the Russians should be told that 'in our view the integrity of Persia is a matter of serious importance to this country'.[3] He had some

Kimberley to Ripon, private, 25 July 1884: bound volume, Letters to the Marquis of Ripon, January 1884 to November 1884, Pte Kimberley Papers.

[1] Thomson to Granville, No. 44, confidential, 7 April 1885: F.O. 65/1239. Same to same, No. 129, decypher telegram, 25 May 1885: F.O. 60/471. See also Foreign Office draft to Thomson, No. 28, confidential, 18 March 1885, endorsed 'The Queen, Mr Gladstone, Ld. Kimberley': F.O. 60/486.

[2] Minute by Currie on Thomson to Granville, No. 44, confidential, 7 April 1885: F.O. 65/1239. Granville to Thomson, No. 81, draft telegram, 27 May 1885: F.O. 60/471. Thomson to Granville and minutes by Currie and Granville, No. 4, confidential, 10 January 1885: F.O. 65/1235. Granville to Thomson, No. 25, 11 March 1885: Home Correspondence, Political and Secret Department, vol. lxxi, India Office Records.

[3] India Office to Foreign Office and minutes by Currie and Salisbury, 17 July 1885: F.O. 65/1246. Salisbury to Thornton, No. 276, draft dispatch, 22 July 1885: F.O. 65/1247. Memorandum by Sanderson on Rights of Persia over the Atak, 25 August 1885: F.O. 65/1249.

weeks earlier received a dispatch from Sir Ronald Thomson describing Nasir ad-Din's fright and his unsettled state of
mind. Thomson advocated a limited assurance for the Shah,
and suggested that attempts might be made to bring Germany
on to the Persian scene. This dispatch was, at Lord Salisbury's
instructions, printed for the Cabinet.[1]

Lord Salisbury gave several lengthy interviews to the Persian
minister in London. Malkom Khan, a man of considerable
literary and political ability, was genuinely distressed by the
deplorable state of affairs within his country and by its growing
subservience to Russia. He had long believed that the continued
existence of his country as an independent state depended upon
the identification of her interests with those of Great Britain
together with the inauguration of a serious reform programme.
Arthur Nicolson (later Sir), in charge of the Legation in 1886
and 1887, criticized Malkom Khan for devising schemes which
would bestow the 'paraphernalia of civilization' upon a people
whose experience had not included self-government, or good
government, or in some districts any government at all.[2] It is
true that an element of unreality crept into his plans. This indeed is not surprising since his long residence in England could
be measured not merely in years but in decades. His concern
and unremitting efforts for the improvement of his country
separated him from the vast majority of his countrymen who
had all but ceased to struggle against the gathering speed of the
downward trend.[3]

The evidence indicates that Malkom Khan's interviews with
Lord Salisbury in 1885 stemmed from his own initiative, and
not from Nasir ad-Din's instructions. He apparently hoped that
messages from London would draw the Shah's thoughts from
the pleasures of the hunt, and would stimulate some action
for the public good. In these conversations Malkom Khan asked
how Persia might meet both her external challenge and the
progressive deterioration of the state itself. Lord Salisbury

[1] Thomson to Granville and minutes by Currie and Salisbury, No. 65, secret,
9 June 1885: F.O. 65/1244.
[2] Nicolson to Iddesleigh, No. 142, confidential, 3 December 1886, endorsed
'Interesting. The Queen, Prince of Wales, Ld. Salisbury': F.O. 65/1293.
[3] E. G. Browne, *The Press and Poetry of Modern Persia*, pp. 18–23, 125; *The
Persian Revolution of 1905–1909*, p. 32.

replied by restating the principles which formed the pillars of his Persian policy—the improvement of communications between the Gulf and the northern regions, and a programme for arresting the decay of order and government. He spoke frankly to Malkom Khan:

... if England in the future was to be of any use in sustaining Persia against the probable encroachments of and gradual absorption by Russia, two things were necessary. In the first place, that such strategic precautions should be taken as should oppose the greatest difficulty to a Russian attack, and give the greatest facility for possible English succour; and, in the second place that the corruptions which were eating into the Kingdom and bringing it to decay should be attacked with a firm hand.

In the course of these conversations Lord Salisbury alluded to the desirability, both from Persia's and Britain's point of view, of moving the capital city 300 miles south to the old Safavi palace centre—Isfahan. Tehran was, as he put it, 'uncomfortably near to the Russian strongholds on the Caspian, and dangerously distant from the more friendly shore of the Indian Ocean'.[1]

A complete record of these conversations was transmitted to Tehran, and Sir Ronald Thomson was told to give similar advice to the Shah. Lord Salisbury's concluding words, written in his own hand, have an almost optimistic ring:

It is evident that the Persian Government is seriously impressed by the dangers which are gradually closing round it: & it is possible that even yet it may derive from them the resolution and energy which it seemed to have finally lost. Any such appearance of returning vigour should be watched for, & carefully encouraged. It may not, even now, be too late to undertake the arduous work of internal reform, & to make the necessary preparations for self-defence. The sympathy, & so far as it can be practically given, the assistance of H[er] M[ajesty's] G[overnment] may be counted on by the Government of Persia in any such endeavours. But the appearance of Russia on the Heri Rud sufficiently proclaims that there is no time to lose.[2]

[1] Salisbury to Thomson, No. 102, draft telegram, 12 August 1885: F.O. 60/471.
[2] Salisbury to Thomson, No. 75A, draft dispatch, 6 August 1885, endorsed 'The Queen, Lord Iddesleigh': F.O. 65/1248.

British statesmen indeed concerned themselves more with Persia's welfare than did its ruler. The Shah was progressive in the sense that he thought of visiting the United States whose Gatling guns intrigued him. His three trips to Europe illustrate his innate curiosity. They show also that he felt his rule secure enough in Persia for him to go abroad. Yet in his conduct of government he displayed a conspicuous lack of realism. He wanted, indeed he would plead for pathetically, British support, but he consistently denied his would-be protectors the means by which aid could be given. In this particular instance, Nasir ad-Din sulked after receiving the dispatches from London and ignored the advice they contained until after Lord Salisbury had made way for the brief Liberal administration of 1886.

Meanwhile, the India Office tackled the Persian dilemma. Sir Ronald Thomson's dispatch (No. 65 of 9 June 1885) inspired a thorough re-examination of possible courses of action. Sir Owen Burne recalled that in 1883 the question had arisen 'for the hundredth time, and was as usual shifted off to the shoulders of the futurity'. But each year the problems grew more acute, England's position more difficult, the Persian Government weaker, and the feasible alternatives fewer. By 1885 the India Office visualized only two real solutions: either a joint guarantee by Germany, Austria, and England, or a wholesale withdrawal from northern Persia and Afghanistan— Herat included—to be accompanied by the occupation of Kandahar, Girishk, and Bandar 'Abbas, and the recognition of the Zil es-Sultan as the lawful and British-protected ruler of southern Persia. But no middle course. As a prologue to 'active measures Persia-wards' they strongly urged the appointment of Sir Henry Drummond Wolff as minister to Tehran, since Sir Henry Rawlinson probably could not undertake the duties.[1]

On 25 July 1885 Lord Randolph Churchill sent a cogently argued letter to the Foreign Office advocating steps which would inject new life into England's Persian policy. He emphasized the incongruity of protecting Afghanistan and not

---

[1] Case 1049, Persia: Russian movements on Khorassan border. Shah's views, etc., 24 July 1885: Home Correspondence, Political and Secret Department, vol. lxxvi, India Office Records.

Persia, and counselled a corresponding extension of responsibility. The Persians could not stand against the Russians on good intentions and resolutions alone. Unless the Persians believed that England would support them in a struggle for independence they would drift along on their lethargic course which could only end in further, and perhaps complete, Russianization. Finally, he recommended that Prince Bismarck be invited to join with England in sponsoring enterprises designed to rescue Persia from final subordination to her powerful northern neighbour. Lord Salisbury agreed that a stronger line was needed, but he was impressed by the unpleasant facts of geography. He wrote:

Reply that the difficulty of supporting Persia against Russia lies in the fact that the regions in which Russian encroachments are likely to be made lie wholly beyond the reach of any material assistance wh[ich] H[er] M[ajesty's] G[overnment] could furnish to the Persian Gov[ernmen]t. Any promise, therefore, of assistance to Persia runs the danger of inducing the Persian Gov[ernmen]t to rely upon support which, if the occasion arose, it would probably be impracticable to give.[1]

Sir Owen Burne described the Foreign Office reply as 'disappointing',[2] but the India Office was unwilling to let the matter drop. In a few days they wrote again.[3] The minutes of the permanent officials in the India Office indicate that these letters represented more than Lord Randolph's personal views, which were denounced as swashbuckling in Liberal circles.[4]

Lord Salisbury rejected the proposal to extend to Persia the same protection accorded to Afghanistan, but he considered the possibility of German co-operation worth investigating. The suggestion for an Anglo-German guarantee for Persia coincided with and gave impetus to an already existing trend in policy. In his last private letter to the Viceroy in 1885, Lord Kimberley

[1] India Office to Foreign Office and minute by Salisbury, secret and immediate, 25 July 1885: F.O. 65/1247. Foreign Office to India Office, secret, 3 August 1885: F.O. 65/1248.

[2] Case 1132, Letter of 3 August 1885 from Foreign Office; Policy towards Persia: Home Correspondence, Political and Secret Department, vol. lxxvi, India Office Records.

[3] India Office to Foreign Office, secret, 11 August. 1885: F.O. 65/1248.

[4] Kimberley to Dufferin, private, 14 May 1885: bound volume, Letters to the Earl of Dufferin, November 1884 to July 1885, Pte Kimberley Papers.

had expressed regret over the continuous reports of Russian aggression on the frontier. But, he said: 'The present Gov[ernmen]t have one advantage over us that Bismarck is better disposed towards them.'[1]

Lord Salisbury founded his policy in 1885 on the assumption that this friendly disposition might exist, and might be exploited.[2] Although he expended some effort in fostering better relations with Italy, it was towards the Iron Chancellor that his most significant overtures by far were directed. The Queen, though displeased with Berlin on several scores, considered it necessary 'to cultivate the most friendly relations with Germany'.[3] Sir William White, who probably was Lord Salisbury's most trusted ambassador, wrote from Constantinople:

Austrian policy is obscure indeed. Calice is most unsatisfactory and I always considered Kalnoky more Russian than German. If I c[oul]d venture to suggest anything I should advise our getting as close to Germany as we properly can. . . .[4]

In his first interviews with Count Münster, the German ambassador in London, Lord Salisbury disclosed the direction of his policy. According to Count Münster's report, Lord Salisbury said that his basic premise was the restoration of close relations with Germany—'ein gutes Einverständnis mit Deutschland zu erhalten und zu pflegen'.[5] In another conversation, Lord Salisbury recalled Prince Bismarck's statement that the combination of Germany, England, and Austria could maintain the peace of Europe.[6]

These observations were followed by a more direct overture. On 2 July 1885 Lord Salisbury wrote privately to Prince Bismarck, spoke warmly of his recollections of Berlin in 1876

[1] Kimberley to Dufferin, private, 17 July 1885: bound volume, Letters to the Earl of Dufferin, November 1884 to July 1885, Pte Kimberley Papers.

[2] Cecil, op. cit., iii, 222–3. H. W. V. Temperley and Lillian M. Penson (eds.), *Foundations of British Foreign Policy from Pitt (1792) to Salisbury (1902)*, p. 429.

[3] The Queen to Salisbury, private, 6 October 1885: loose papers, Pte Salisbury Papers.

[4] White to Salisbury, private, 29 September 1885: bound volume, From Turkey, etc., 1885–1886, Pte Salisbury Papers.

[5] Münster to the German Foreign Office, No. 174, cypher telegram, 26 June 1885: *G.P.*, iv, Nr. 779, 131.

[6] Münster to the German Foreign Office, No. 176, cypher telegram, 29 June 1885: *G.P.*, iv, Nr. 781, 132.

and 1878, and stated more clearly his objective in foreign policy:

. . . to restore the good understanding between the two countries which we value as of supreme importance, but which in recent times has been slightly clouded. I think you may reasonably count on a continuity of policy in this matter.

I do not know what the real intentions of the Russian Cabinet are: but our wish is distinctly for peace. To speak candidly, our railroad towards Candahar will not be finished for two years; and I believe Russia is in precisely the same condition. We have both, therefore, the strongest interest to keep the peace for that time, if no longer: but I hope it may be for much longer.[1]

Bismarck's reply was polite but non-committal. He expressed friendship for England—but for Russia too—and he looked upon war between them as a calamity.[2]

Lord Salisbury's efforts for improved relations with Germany were not confined to conversations with the ambassador and letters to Prince Bismarck. In his own words he sought to 'gain some credit' with Bismarck by the attitude he took over the problems of Zanzibar and the Caroline Islands. Moreover, in August and September the negotiations between the Assistant Under-Secretary of State, Sir Philip Currie, the 'avowed though unofficial emissary of the Foreign Secretary',[3] and Prince Bismarck and Count Herbert Bismarck took place. The evidence is still incomplete since Lord Salisbury's original instructions and his letters to Currie are missing. Nevertheless, the frequent and full reports written by Currie to Lord Salisbury throw light on the reasons for the mission and recount the conversations in detail. Affairs on the Afghan frontier, and the Zulficar crisis particularly, seem to account for Currie's presence at Königstein, Homburg, and Friedrichsruh in the late summer of 1885.[4]

[1] Salisbury to Bismarck, private, 2 July 1885: *G.P.*, iv, Nr. 782, 132–3. A copy of this document is in the private Salisbury papers: bound volume, To Austria, etc., 1885–1886. An extract has been printed in Cecil, *op. cit.*, iii, 224.

[2] Bismarck to Salisbury, 8 July 1885: *G.P.*, iv, Nr. 783, 133–4. See also Cecil, *op. cit.*, iii, 226. Prince Bismarck's letter is in the private Salisbury Papers.

[3] Cecil, *op. cit.*, iii, 226–30. It seems possible that the idea of this approach to Germany originated with Lord Randolph Churchill. See Churchill to Dufferin, private, 2 and 24 July 1885: Pte Dufferin Papers.

[4] See Appendix II.

In his first conversation with Count Herbert Bismarck at
Königstein in the opening days of August, Currie summarized
the leading features of the Anglo-Russian crisis in Central Asia.
He gave a brief historical survey and discussed the current outlook. His words to Count Herbert Bismarck indicate that the
crisis was not yet passed:

The position is critical and, if a settlement is not arrived at within
the next few months, is very likely to lead to war. The Russian
Commanders are enterprising and are eager for a dash at Herat. The
Afghans are rash, and another Penjdeh affair may occur at any
moment. Either of these contingencies would inevitably produce a
rupture between England & Russia, which would lead to hostilities, not only in Central Asia, but in every part of the world where
England could deal a blow at her antagonist.

Currie also indicated that the British would attempt, if a full-
scale war with Russia broke out, to sever Russia's communication lines with her trans-Caspian provinces. This could be
accomplished only after acquiring access to the Black Sea, and
'this we should unquestionably do by some means or other,
whatever view Europe might hold as to the localisation of the
war'.[1] Currie's declaration seems to have been a considered one.
It coincided with a similar statement made by Lord Salisbury
in one of his letters to Sir Henry Drummond Wolff. Prior agreements on the subject would be worthless, Lord Salisbury wrote,
but if war between England and Russia did occur, 'we should
in one way or another force a passage [of the Dardanelles]'.[2]

Currie asked for Bismarck's mediation of the Zulficar dispute
in order to avert the catastrophe of a war between the two great
Asiatic Powers. He presented the British view of the claims over
Zulficar, and pledged his country's adherence to the Chancellor's decision, whatever it might be. His arbitration would
enhance Prince Bismarck's already great reputation as a peace-
maker. From England he could expect 'lasting gratitude':

. . . and he would be laying the foundations of a closer and more
intimate alliance between the two Countries.

[1] Copy of paper shown to Count Herbert Bismarck at Königstein, 3 August
1885: loose papers, Pte Salisbury Papers.
[2] Salisbury to Wolff, private, 1 September 1885: bound volume, To Austria,
etc., 1885–1886, Pte Salisbury Papers.

The present Prime Minister of England is known to be favorable to such an alliance in the fullest sense of the terms, and once established, the English people, who have the strongest leaning towards their old Protestant ally, would not allow their Government (from whatever party it might be taken) to swerve from it. A close union between the greatest military power and the greatest naval power would produce a combination that would not only secure the peace of the world, but would also be in the highest degree advantageous to the interests of the two Countries. It would put Germany at ease as regards the safety of her Colonial possessions in the event of European complications, and it would leave England free to defend her interests in the event of unprovoked aggression on the part of Russia against her Indian Empire, without fear of hostile neutrality on the part of the European Powers.[1]

These conversations continued for nearly two months. Count Herbert Bismarck seemed to be favourably disposed to the idea of an Anglo-German alliance, but two obstacles existed. Such a friendship might not be continued by Gladstone when he returned to power, and a Liberal victory in the not-too-distant future seemed probable. Moreover, closer association with England would irritate Russia, and Germany's eastern frontier was long, exposed, and vulnerable. 'The water', said Count Herbert Bismarck, 'is too hot for us to put our finger in.' He did, however, arrange for Currie to discuss these issues with his father.[2]

Prince Bismarck received Sir Philip Currie in September at Friedrichsruh. Prussia's traditional policy had been friendship with England, Prince Bismarck said, but it was impossible to deal with Gladstone, although there was the warmest personal regard for Lord Salisbury. As a step forward to better relations Count Münster would be recalled, and Count Hatzfeldt would take his place. The selection of Count Hatzfeldt as the new ambassador to London proved to be a wise move. Lord Salisbury considered him trustworthy, and spoke to him with a rare frankness.

In the course of the September discussions, Prince Bismarck observed that England's two potential enemies were France and Russia. He promised aid in the event of trouble with the

[1] Copy of paper shown to Count Herbert Bismarck at Königstein, 3 August 1885: loose papers, Pte Salisbury Papers.

[2] Currie to Salisbury, private, 4 August 1885: loose papers, Pte Salisbury Papers.

former, but if England and Russia went to war he could pledge neutrality only. Russia, though despicable in attack, was not easily accessible. Prince Bismarck and Sir Philip Currie also discussed Near-Eastern problems—Bulgaria, the Straits, and Egypt—at length.

The views and objectives of both England and Germany were clarified by the conversations, and Currie concluded:

When I took leave of the Prince, he spoke very kindly of the pleasure he had felt in seeing me at Friedrichsruh, desired me, to convey his best regards to you & said he hoped there would now be the best possible understanding between the 2 Countries. I said I hoped he would not forget to instruct his agents in Egypt to support our Rep[resentative]. He said that they would certainly do so.[1]

It is not clear whether other members of the Cabinet were informed of these conversations. They seem indeed to have been, to some extent at least, informal and unofficial. Several months later, however, Lord Randolph Churchill complained to Count Hatzfeldt about Germany's uncooperative attitude. 'A nous deux nous pourrions gouverner le monde. Mais vous n'avez pas voulu'.[2] Prince Bismarck, in reply to his ambassador's report, declared that he did not understand the reference to an alliance. No offer was made to him, he maintained, that he could refuse. Moreover, he believed, perhaps rightly, that for an alliance with England to have any prospect of long continuance, it would need to be fortified by the approval of Parliament. Without this, agreements were but as castles in the air.[3]

In still another sphere, Lord Salisbury attempted to harmonize the policies of England and Germany. The roots of these negotiations go back to the Shah's kingdom in the previous decade. In 1872 the Persian Grand Vizier, thinking that if England had a stake in the country she would protect it, had persuaded Nasir ad-Din to grant a startling concession.

Baron Julius de Reuter, a former Coburg subject who became British by naturalization, obtained a concession giving almost

[1] Notes by Currie of conversations with Prince Bismarck at Friedrichsruh, 28/29 September 1885: loose papers, Pte Salisbury Papers. A summary is given in Cecil, *op. cit.*, iii, 257–61.

[2] Hatzfeldt to Count Herbert Bismarck, 5 December 1885: *G.P.*, iv, Nr. 788, 138–40; quotation from p. 139.

[3] Prince Bismarck to Hatzfeldt, 9 December 1885: *G.P.*, iv, Nr. 789, 140–1.

complete control over Persia's resources for seventy years. He was empowered to construct a railway from the Gulf to the Caspian, and any branches he deemed feasible; to build tramways throughout the country; to work all mines except gold and silver; to undertake irrigation projects; to establish a national bank; to construct roads, bridges, and telegraphs; and to manage the customs for twenty-five years. For his part Baron Reuter agreed to pay a fixed sum for the privilege of operating the customs for the first five years and then sixty per cent of the net revenue for the period remaining. Twenty per cent of the profits from railways and fifteen per cent of the profits from all other sources were to be paid to the Shah. After seventy years all improvements reverted to Persia.[1]

The Shah travelled to Europe in the following year. His bargain with Baron Reuter was severely criticized, and the Russians were very angry. Upon returning to Persia he cancelled the concession. Shortly thereafter, the Persian minister in London held a confidential conversation with Lord Tenterden in which he explained why the concession had been granted originally and disclosed 'the real fact . . . that the Concession had been broken at the demand of the Russian Government'.[2]

Sir Henry Rawlinson quickly pointed out the significance of the proposed railway to Turkey, England, and Persia. If no interest was shown in upholding the legal rights of a British subject, he warned, an inevitable gravitation towards Russia would ensue. The execution of Reuter's proposals 'might conduce most essentially to the prosperity of Persia and to the improvement of our political position in the East'. With the construction of other railways in Persia the trans-Caspian would only be a competing line and Russia's hold proportionately reduced.[3] The Duke of Argyll, then Secretary of State for India, regretted the cancellation since the railway lines and irrigation

---

[1] Little has been written about this concession. Three case volumes, however—F.O. 60/405, 406, and 407—deal with the Reuter negotiations. The best printed summary is in Rawlinson, *England and Russia in the East*, pp. 123–30; an abstract of the concession is given in Appendix V. A useful article is that by L. E. Frechtling, 'The Reuter Concession in Persia', *The Asiatic Review* (1938), pp. 518–33.

[2] Memorandum by Tenterden on Baron Reuter and Persia, 9 November 1874: F.O. 60/406.

[3] Memorandum by Rawlinson on Baron Reuter's Railway proposals, 5 June 1873: F.O. 60/405.

works would benefit Persia, 'and would subserve the only interest which England can have—namely that of making the country stronger and more prosperous'.[1]

The British Government adopted a moderate official policy. On the one hand they approved of the Shah's decision to nullify the contract since the mammoth concession was considered unworkable and it left only a shadow of independence to the Persian Government. On the other hand, Nasir ad-Din's repudiation was difficult to justify on legal grounds since Baron Reuter had tried to uphold the terms of the agreement. Moreover, the projects for internal development would have been beneficial both to Persia and to British interests there. Consequently, Baron Reuter was given unofficial diplomatic support at Tehran. From this the principle evolved that no concession for railways should be granted to a foreign power or to its subjects until a settlement of the Baron's claims had been reached. For twelve years the negotiations produced a bulky correspondence, but nothing more.[2]

In 1885, when the Penjdeh crisis was at its height, Baron Reuter pressed his claims for compensation with renewed force. His threats to sell his rights to Russia or Germany had long been troublesome, and in May and June of 1885 his case went before the Cabinet. Lord Northbrook, at the Admiralty, wanted to dismiss the question summarily.[3] Lord Hartington, however, looking at the situation from the War Office point of view, held that 'means of making our influence felt in Persia might be useful just now'.[4] Ultimately, it was decided that Baron Reuter should discuss his proposals with Rawlinson.[5] He was engaged in doing so when the Liberal Government fell.[6]

[1] India Office to Foreign Office, 13 December 1873: F.O. 60/405.
[2] Much of the correspondence in F.O. 60/406 concerns the evolution of the official British attitude. See for example Derby to Tenterden, undated but filed between 19 and 28 May 1874. Salisbury to Nicolson, No. 21, 21 February 1887: F.O. 60/485.
[3] Cabinet Opinion of Northbrook, 25 April 1885: Pte Granville Papers, P.R.O. 30/29/145.
[4] Cabinet Opinion of Hartington, 26 April 1885: Pte Granville Papers, P.R.O. 30/29/145.
[5] Cabinet Opinions of Granville, Kimberley, and Hartington, 27/28 April 1885: Pte Granville Papers, P.R.O. 30/29/145.
[6] Memorandum by Rawlinson on conversations with Baron Reuter, 15 May 1885, endorsed 'Drawn up for the Cabinet': F.O. 60/476.

These discussions were continued by Lord Salisbury.[1] Baron Reuter saw Sir Julian Pauncefote, Permanent Under-Secretary at the Foreign Office. The Baron planned to organize an international company, backed by Prince Bismarck and Lord Rothschild, for the purpose of working his railway concession and establishing Persia as a strong bulwark against Russia. Lord Salisbury wrote on Pauncefote's report: 'I am very much disposed to recommend him to associate England & Germany in this matter: & England will go as far as Germany will.'[2]

Pauncefote interviewed Lord Rothschild privately. The financier seemed pleased to co-operate, but he doubted whether sufficient monetary backing would be forthcoming unless both the concession and the integrity of Persia were guaranteed by England and Germany. Pauncefote asked Lord Salisbury if he would still go as far as Germany. Lord Salisbury replied that he was 'disposed to agree: for I am sure Germany will not commit herself rashly. But it is a rather grave pledge.' Then he decided to ask for the opinions of the other members of his government.[3]

Memoranda were circulated. Lord Iddesleigh, though cautious and prone to see difficulties, approved. The Chancellor of the Exchequer, Sir Michael Hicks Beach, thought that action in concert with Germany would be 'very advantageous', but he doubted whether it could be obtained. W. H. Smith, the Secretary for War, favoured the inflow of British and German capital into Persia as a 'check to Russian ambition'. Lord Randolph Churchill rejoiced to find that the Foreign Office project coincided with that put forward earlier by the India Office. Protection of Persia as well as Afghanistan was axiomatic to Lord Randolph Churchill. He argued:

Generally, any arrangement under which the integrity of Persia might become an object of material solicitude to Germany so as to

---

[1] Abstract of Correspondence relating to the Concession granted to Baron Reuter by the Persian Government in 1872, confidential/5120, printed for the use of the Foreign Office, 11 June 1885, endorsed 'Copy to Queen, Lord Iddesleigh': F.O. 60/476.

[2] Memorandum by Pauncefote on conversation with Baron Reuter and minute by Salisbury, 11 August 1885: F.O. 60/476.

[3] Notes exchanged between Salisbury and Pauncefote, 14 August 1885: F.O. 60/476.

lead her to join with England in guaranteeing it could not fail to be of the utmost advantage to Indian interests to which the integrity of Persia, or at any rate the independence of Persia from Russian influence, is as essential as the integrity of Affghanistan & the independence of that country from Russian influence.[1]

Simultaneously, Lord Randolph Churchill discussed Anglo-Russian relations with Count William Bismarck. Churchill repeated his conviction that Persia was as important to England as Afghanistan. In fact, Russia's machinations in the former country were even more dangerous since material support was so difficult to give. 'Es würde ihm, Churchill, erwünscht sein, wenn die Integrität Persiens von Deutschland und England zusammen garantiert würde, und das ganze settlement in Persien, wie der Ausbau der Eisenbahnen pp. in deutsche Hände käme.' Count William Bismarck's reaction was discouraging; such co-operation, he said, could only be interpreted as a spearpoint against Russia.[2] Here, as so often happens, the extent to which the conversation was authorized is uncertain.

The negotiations which stemmed from the Reuter memoranda, however, were official and concrete. Lord Salisbury sent the memoranda relating to Baron Reuter's concession to Sir Edward Malet in Berlin. Malet was instructed to acquaint the Chancellor with British hopes for the development of Persia, and to inform him that in this task 'there is no one whose opinion and co-operation they would more value than Prince Bismarck's.'[3] The Foreign Office decided, after receiving recommendations from the India Office, that the association of Austria was also desirable. France and Russia would not be welcomed.[4]

Three days later the British ambassador reported that he had

[1] Minutes by Iddesleigh, Hicks Beach, Smith, and Churchill on memoranda presented by Salisbury on the Reuter Concession, 18/24 August 1885: bound volume, Miscellaneous, Government Departments, etc., 1885–1886, Pte Salisbury Papers.

[2] Count William Bismarck to Prince Bismarck, private, 19 August 1885: *G.P.*, iv, Nr. 784, 134–6.

[3] Salisbury to Malet, No. 371, draft dispatch, confidential, 2 September 1885, endorsed 'The Queen, Lord Iddesleigh, Copy to India Office for concurrence': F.O. 64/1074.

[4] India Office to Foreign Office, secret and immediate, 3 September 1885: F.O. 64/1100.

submitted the documents and made the explanations to Count
Herbert Bismarck who, without comment, promised to submit
the material for Prince Bismarck's consideration.[1] September
passed—October—November—and December neared its close.
On 22 December Lord Salisbury telegraphed to Malet saying
that he would be 'very glad to learn' if any hint had been given
regarding Germany's attitude.[2] Late in January 1886 the Chancellor announced his verdict. Perhaps the vision of the *Speer-
spitze* of Russian diplomacy turning west to probe the line of
Germany's eastern frontier seemed no more attractive to Prince
Bismarck than it had been in the preceding May.[3] For whatever
reason, he refused to involve Germany in Persian affairs, and
he was 'unwilling to side for or against England or Russia on
points where their interests were opposed'.[4]

Thus the attempts to develop an Anglo-German policy for
Persia failed. It would seem that Lord Salisbury's exertions in
cultivating the friendship of the Bismarcks paid very small
dividends. But perhaps not. Lord Kimberley's first letter to the
Viceroy, written after the return of the Liberals to power early
in 1886, commented on the work of his predecessor:

Salisbury has greatly advanced his own reputation by his successful management of foreign affairs, and I am hopeful that Rosebery,
whose appointment gives general satisfaction, will keep us in the
right path. It is no small gain that he is persona grata to the
Berlin Dictator.[5]

[1] Malet to Salisbury, No. 389, very confidential, 5 September 1885: F.O.
64/1079.
[2] Salisbury to Malet, No. 550, decypher telegram, very confidential, 22 December 1885: F.O. 64/1075.
[3] Prince Bismarck to the Emperor William I, 27 May 1885: *G.P.*, iv, Nr. 777,
124–6.
[4] Malet to Salisbury, No. 17, very confidential, 9 January 1886, endorsed 'The
Queen'; same to same, No. 51, 23 January 1886: F.O. 64/1113.
[5] Kimberley to Dufferin, private, 5 February 1886: bound volume, Letters to
the Earl of Dufferin, February 1886 to September 1886, Pte Kimberley Papers.

CHAPTER VII

The Persian Problem: 1885–8
Attempts at Anglo-Russian Agreement

I N the waning years of the last century the anxiety caused by
the Indian frontier outposts of Afghanistan and Persia was
often grave, sometimes needless, but seemingly endless. The
Amir's health, the Shah's vacillations, Herat's vulnerability,
Khorassan's effeteness, the ever-recurring war scares, the ever-
increasing defence burden combined to exasperate. Negotiations
invariably became entangled in a web of Oriental intrigue,
and they frequently closed abruptly with the disclosure of a
secret agreement signed much earlier which prohibited the
desired action. Rare was the conversation between the British
minister and Persian officials which did not reach, at least in a
distorted form, one of Russia's representatives. The reverse was
also true, and one British diplomat upon leaving Persia said
that he had felt 'like a jellyfish in a whirlpool'.[1] Tehran drove a
thriving trade in secret and official documents—with treaties
commanding a particularly high price.[2] The machinations
never ceased. Even when the general relations between England
and Russia seemed harmonious, the good feeling did not filter
down to far-away Tehran where their agents continued to wage
an undeclared war of their own.

The policy of ending the sordid rivalry and embarking upon
a new age of friendship and co-operation is popularly associated
with Sir Edward Grey, but the idea of settling controversial

[1] Quoted in Lord Newton, *Lord Lansdowne: A Biography*, p. 232. The diplomat
was Sir Mortimer Durand.

[2] See for example Benjamin to Frelinghuysen, diplomatic series No. 23, confidential, 19 July 1883: Persia, i, American Department of State. The American
minister wrote to his chief in Washington about a treaty between Persia and
Russia 'secretly placed at my disposal for the modest sum of $8,500. I might have
had a copy for $100, but the disavowal by England suddenly sent the price up.'

issues by an arrangement with the Russians had always been attractive, and the thoughts of many a nineteenth-century foreign secretary, ambassador, and viceroy turned longingly in that direction. Partition of Persia into spheres of influence, as eventually accomplished by Grey in 1907, was only one and perhaps the most extreme of the 'agreement with Russia' themes.

In 1834, when rivalry in Central Asia was passing through one of its more acute phases, Palmerston succeeded in obtaining Russia's adherence to the principle that both Governments were 'animated by a sincere desire to maintain, not only the internal tranquillity, but also the independence and integrity of Persia'.[1] The British extracted from St. Petersburg a reiteration of this pledge in 1838, 1865, 1873, 1874, and 1888.[2] But not until 1873 did the Shah learn of this territorial guarantee.[3] The Russian view of these pledges was expressed sixteen years later by one of the architects of her foreign policy, Count Vladimir Lamsdorff, in a dispatch to the newly appointed Russian minister to Tehran:

Two incidents in this struggle, namely the so-called 'agreements' of 1834 and 1888, serve as the object of constant reference from England which endeavours on that basis to make a settlement in our relations with Persia. These assurances . . . concerned circumstances of the immediate moment. . . . It must be borne in mind that they by no means served as final words.[4]

This interpretation had never been made public and throughout the Salisbury era the agreements constituted one of the cornerstones of Great Britain's Persian policy.

[1] *British and Foreign State Papers* (His Majesty's Stationery Office, 1841–); hereafter cited as *B.F.S.P.* Palmerston to Bligh and enclosure, 5 September 1834, xxiii, 863. Memorandum by Currie, 28 June 1877: F.O. 65/990.

[2] Buchanan to Russell, 12 September 1865: *B.F.S.P.*, lxiii, 1313–14. Loftus to Derby and enclosure, 23 December 1874: *B.F.S.P.*, lxv, 981–2. Foreign Office memorandum by Hertslet, Assurances on independence and integrity of Persia, 26 November 1874: F.O. 65/904.

[3] India Office to Foreign Office, secret and immediate, 21 February 1882: F.O. 65/1150. Correspondence respecting the occupation of Merv by Russia and her proceedings on the Khorassan Frontier of Persia, secret, A.W.M., India Office, Political and Secret Department, 15 August 1884: F.O. 65/1209. See also Appendix III.

[4] Lamsdorff to Speyer, secret, 30 September/13 October 1904: *Krasny Arkhiv*, liii, 15–16. I am indebted to Mr. Myrl Powell, formerly of the University of Kansas, for the translation of these and other Russian sources.

Lord Ripon, Viceroy of India from 1880 to 1884, proposed a more formal and far-reaching arrangement. In his private letters to Lord Kimberley and in an official Government of India dispatch, he advocated the opening of negotiations with Russia for a treaty which would adjust the differences between the two countries *sur toute la ligne*. The London authorities were united in their scepticism. The India Office drew up an exhaustive review, nearly 150 printed pages, contrasting Russian assurances and actions during the preceding two decades. From these marshalled facts they concluded that past experience did not justify any trust in pledges—even if sincerely undertaken by the Emperor and others in St. Petersburg.[1]

Considerable weight was attached to the opinion of Lord Dufferin, formerly ambassador to Russia and soon to be Lord Ripon's successor. Lord Dufferin asserted that such a treaty would have value as 'collateral security' only. As diplomat and Viceroy he consistently maintained that 'no promise, assurance, undertaking, convention, or treaty would have the slightest effect in permanently arresting the advance of Russia'. Her progress could be stopped only by the exhibition of and perhaps the resort to force.[2] This opinion is the more instructive when it is recalled that Dufferin was quite opposed to what was called the 'forward school'.

Lord Kimberley, too, lacked confidence in Russian promises. His private letters reveal that his experience as ambassador to St. Petersburg, though long ago, still strongly influenced him.

---

[1] Ripon to Kimberley, private, 3 February 1883: loose papers, Pte Kimberley Papers. Correspondence, from 1864 to 1881, respecting the movements of Russia in Central Asia and her relations with Afghanistan, secret, A.W.M., India Office, Political and Secret Department, 8 February 1882: F.O. 65/1150. Case 224, Memorandum by Sir Lepel Griffin, 5 March 1884: Home Correspondence, Political and Secret Department, lxii, India Office Records.

See also Lord Ripon's memorandum, strictly confidential, 2 September 1881, printed for the use of the Cabinet, endorsed 'It was circulated to the Cabinet 20/10/81': loose papers, Pte Kimberley Papers. Louis Mallet, then an official in the India Office, was also in favour of a treaty with Russia over Central Asia.

[2] Quoted in Correspondence, from 1864 to 1881, respecting the movements of Russia in Central Asia and her relations with Afghanistan, secret, A.W.M., India Office, Political and Secret Department, 8 February 1882: F.O. 65/1150. He used the same expressions in Dufferin to Kimberley, private, 30 March 1885: bound volume, Letters from the Earl of Dufferin, December 1884 to June 1885, Pte Kimberley Papers.

He argued that a treaty with Russia was not practicable, and even if practicable England would derive no benefit from it. Russian governors and military officers on the frontier would not consider such an instrument binding. Furthermore, the danger of a conflict would actually be increased since the violation of a fixed and recognized border could not be lightly ignored.[1] The Cabinet at a meeting on 20 April 1883 rejected the Viceroy's proposed overture on the grounds set forth by Lord Kimberley.[2]

The Merv and Penjdeh incidents precluded any further movements in the direction of an all-embracing treaty. The Liberal Government was, in fact, fully occupied in defending its Russian policy against the Conservative onslaught. The Afghan negotiations which Lord Granville had begun in 1884 presupposed some goodwill on the part of the Russians, but the subsequent battle on the banks of the River Kuskh disillusioned the Liberals and provided the opposition with deadly ammunition. Early in May 1885 Lord Randolph Churchill presented to the House of Commons a vivid description of previous breaches of engagements and scornfully derided the Government for having faith in the Russian word.[3] His indictment was closely followed by Lord Salisbury's forceful speech at Hackney. He told his audience:

My belief is that it was a fundamental error to attempt to engage in negotiations with Russia for the determination of a boundary in Afghanistan. I do not mean to say that if you could have got a trustworthy engagement it would not have been a good thing. That I am entirely ready to admit, but then experience surely should have taught us that trustworthy engagements with Russia are not things

[1] Kimberley to Ripon, private, 11 January 1883; same to same, private, 14 February 1883: bound volume, Letters to the Marquis of Ripon, December 1882 to December 1883, Pte Kimberley Papers. His reasons for opposing an agreement are succinctly outlined in Kimberley to Mallet, private, 4 November 1883: loose papers, Pte Kimberley Papers.

[2] Kimberley to Ripon, private, 20 April 1883: bound volume, Letters to the Marquis of Ripon, December 1882 to December 1883, Pte Kimberley Papers. See also memorandum by Burne, confidential, 30 November 1881: loose papers, Pte Kimberley Papers.

[3] *P.D.*, Third Series, Commons, 4 May 1885, ccxcvii, 1524-41. Waddington to Freycinet, No. 64, 20 May 1885: *D.D.F.*, vi, 30-2. Münster to Count Herbert Bismarck, 4 May 1885: *G.P.*, iv, Nr. 774, 120-1.

which we can count upon obtaining. . . . I do not attribute to the Russian Government an intention to deceive. It is not necessary for my purpose that I should make any such disagreeable suggestion. When they said that they would not go to Khiva, and immediately did go to Khiva; when they said they would not extend their boundaries to the east of the Caspian, and immediately did so; when they said they would not take Merv, and allowed Merv to be surrendered to them, it is very possible that they were not acting with any intention to mislead the English Government, but that circumstances were stronger than men. But it really does not matter. If a man does not keep his promise in commercial matters, if he does it intentionally you say that he is a swindler; if he fails to keep his promise because he cannot keep it you say he is a bankrupt. But whether swindler or bankrupt you are very careful about trusting him the next time, and therefore, making the fullest allowance for the difficulties of the vast Russian Empire, and the impossibility of controlling the military element, which is the only sure foundation for the Throne—making all these allowances I still say that where we are now, with the lessons of history behind us, it was not wise to seek as the main object of our policy to rest the defence of India upon the guarantee of Russia. If we wish to defend the frontier of India we must do it as Lord Beaconsfield proposed—we must do it ourselves.[1]

Thus the advent of the Conservatives in 1885 did not presage a bright new era of good feeling between England and Russia. Throughout that year the Afghan crisis overshadowed all other Central Asian considerations, and the boundary negotiations continued to absorb a great deal of diplomatic energy in 1886 and 1887. During these years the single British bid for co-operation with Russia over Persia concerned the delimitation of the Khorassan frontier. The authorities in St. Petersburg, however, emphatically denied that Great Britain had any right to a voice in the matter, and for obvious reasons preferred to deal with the Shah alone.

The British and the Persians occupied themselves with interminable discussions about railway building, but the monotony of these conversations was interrupted by the discovery of

[1] *The Times*, 6 May 1885. This speech caused considerable comment. Lord Granville denounced it in the House of Lords. *P.D.*, Third Series, Lords, 12 May 1885, ccxcviii, 293–9. See also Commons, 11 May 1885, p. 272. Karolyi to Kalnoky, No. 28, 20 May 1885: *Vienna State Archives*, England, 8/102.

several disquieting Russian documents. In April 1886 the chargé d'affaires, Arthur Nicolson, relayed copies of secret Russian plans which had been acquired surreptitiously from their Legation. The first was a memorandum written by Colonel Kaesmin Karavieff, nominally in charge of the Persian Cossack Brigade but actually still on the headquarters staff in St. Petersburg. This memorandum announced the cession of a sizeable slice of Khorassan. The second was penned by General Aleksyey Nikolaevich Kuropatkin, the successor and disciple of General Skobeleff, who followed the example of his former chief and mapped out his own plan for the invasion of India. His scheme provided for a simultaneous advance by the Russian army on three lines—upon Kabul via Balkh, upon Herat via Maimana, and upon Herat through Khorassan.[1] Sir Philip Currie called Gladstone's attention to these papers as of great urgency.[2] Here, he wrote, was something 'very serious, if true'. He thought that the documents probably represented the desiderata of the Russian officials rather than accomplished facts but he agreed that the strictest attention must be paid to events in Persia.[3]

The Karavieff and Kuropatkin revelations had scarcely been digested by the British Foreign Office when General Schepeleff appeared in Tehran. General Schepeleff, who held the post of Chief of Chancery, ranked second to Prince Dondoukoff-Korsakoff in the Caucasus Government.[4] Ostensibly his business concerned minor rectifications of the Khorassan frontier, but prevailing rumours attributed a more sinister motive to his journey. Nicolson soon verified the worst suspicions when he procured a copy of a draft secret convention drawn up by the Russian general. It was verbose and involved, but when the fundamentals were laid bare it was found to provide that

[1] Nicolson to Rosebery, separate and secret, 29 April 1886: F.O. 65/1285.

[2] It was Gladstone's practice to look at only the most important papers. See Rosebery to Gladstone, private and confidential, 15 January 1889: B.M. Add. MSS. 44289, vol. cciv, Pte Gladstone Papers. 'I remember when I took the Foreign Office you said to me that the important matter was to keep foreign affairs from disturbing us in England, where we had a great enterprise [Ireland] on hand which would fully occupy our energies.'

[3] Minutes on Nicolson to Rosebery, separate and secret, 29 April, 1886: F.O. 65/1285.

[4] Morier to Salisbury, No. 326, 26 September 1887: F.O. 65/1298.

Russia would assist the Shah in his disputes with Turkey if in the event of war with England Khorassan could be used as a base for operations against India. In effect, the Persians were required to divest themselves of all interest in events occurring on their eastern frontier, although Khorassan was guaranteed to the Persian Government and the sanctity of Meshed was not to be violated. Article eighteen provided that if Persia failed to fulfil her conditions 'Russia will forthwith annex Mazanderan and Ghilan'. The draft convention and Nicolson's secret dispatches were printed for the Cabinet.[1] In the India Office, Sir Owen Burne observed that even if the convention were only partially carried out Persia would become 'a feudatory of' Russia. Kimberley directed that 'the special attention of my successor should be called to this important paper'.[2]

In the summer of 1886, however, General Schepeleff left Tehran as suddenly and as mysteriously as he had come. The Shah consistently declared that Schepeleff had put no pressure upon him and that their discussions had been limited to inconsequential details. Nicolson, in private and official letters to Lord Salisbury, expounded his interpretation of the visit. He believed that the general, having found the moment unpropitious, gave the draft convention to a Persian deputy with instructions to tempt Nasir ad-Din with specious offers of assistance against Turkey when the circumstances seemed more favourable. Nicolson attached real significance to the Karavieff, Kuropatkin, and Schepeleff papers and on more than one occasion stressed their authenticity and implications. Nicolson did not intimate that Russia would violate Persian territory by a precipitate and outright invasion, but he warned the Foreign Office that the Russian Legation appeared to be preparing the ground for a diplomatic coup and that their ends could

[1] Nicolson to Rosebery and enclosure, separate and secret, 3 June 1886, endorsed 'The Queen, Mr Gladstone': F.O. 65/1287. Same to same, No. 85, very secret, 25 June 1886: F.O. 60/479. Memorandum by Thomson, secret and confidential, 8 June 1886: F.O. 60/479. See also F.O. 60/480.

Case 23, Correspondence on Nicolson's secret documents, printed for use of the Cabinet, 21 December 1886: Home Correspondence, Political and Secret Department, vol. xci, India Office Records.

[2] Minutes on letter from Persia, 25 June 1886, Russia and Persia, Draft of Secret Convention drawn up by General Schepeleff: Persian Correspondence, 1886, vol. cix, Political Department, India Office Records.

be achieved by the 'insidious terms of the Draft Convention'.[1]

Before the tumult caused by the generals had subsided, a new Russian minister arrived in Tehran. A picturesque and ambitious nobleman with powerful family connections in St. Petersburg, Prince Nicolas Dolgorouki came to Persia intent on winning his diplomatic spurs with all dispatch and moving on to the more coveted post of Constantinople. He was vain and arrogant, disdainful and demanding, and he scornfully refused to treat the Shah with the respect or the courtesy due to the head of a sovereign nation.[2] Dolgorouki's intimidation, more than the intrigues of the military men, annoyed and alarmed Nasir ad-Din who reiterated anew his appeals to Great Britain.[3]

In 1885, when he was terrified by the Penjdeh incident, Nasir ad-Din's entreaties had such a ring of desperation that Sir Ronald Thomson advised giving a limited guarantee.[4] Likewise, in 1888, the Shah's despair became acute enough to convince Nicolson that some definite statement of goodwill and sympathy had to be forthcoming in order to avert a wholesale capitulation to Russia. He thought that an offer of moral support would be enough to give him temporary confidence, though the Shah's ultimate goal was the promise of material aid.[5]

Early in 1888 the British tested a Persian policy which, in order to be understood, must be viewed not only in its Central Asian setting but also against the general background of Anglo-Russian relations. Sir Robert Morier often stressed the 'action and reaction on each other of political events at the European and Asiatic poles of the Russian cosmos'.[6] The impact of the Afghan settlement and the Bulgarian crisis upon British conduct at Tehran exemplifies this dictum.

[1] Nicolson to Currie, private, 1 July 1886: F.O. 65/1288. Nicolson to Salisbury, No. 12, very confidential, 24 January 1887: F.O. 60/486. Same to same, private, 1 February 1887: bound volume, Persia, Pte Salisbury Papers.

[2] Nicolson to Salisbury, No. 60, 4 May 1887: F.O. 60/486. Morier to Salisbury, No. 368, secret, 9 November 1887, endorsed 'Lord Cross': F.O. 65/1324.

[3] Nicolson to Salisbury, No. 19, very confidential, 20 February 1887: F.O. 60/486. Same to same, No. 4, records telegram, secret, 5 January 1888: F.O. 60/496.

[4] Thomson to Granville, No. 65, secret, 9 June 1885: F.O. 65/1244.

[5] Nicolson to Salisbury, No. 12, secret, 10 January 1888: F.O. 65/1347. Nicolson to Currie, private, 12 January 1888: F.O. 60/492.

[6] Morier to Salisbury, No. 144, 25 April 1887, endorsed 'The Queen': F.O. 65/1296.

In the winter and spring of 1887 the reports from Ridgeway on the Amir's northern frontier once more became alarming, and a complete breakdown seemed likely. During the summer, however, the atmosphere suddenly improved, and the final protocol was signed in St. Petersburg. Sir West Ridgeway's 'summing up' for Lord Salisbury is dated 15 August 1887.[1] This sharp change on the Central Asian front is probably accounted for by Russia's preoccupation with the transformations which were occurring in the western peripheral regions of her empire.

The tense moments in the Afghan delimitation negotiations during the winter of 1886–7 coincided with a darkening horizon elsewhere. Sir William White in his first letter to Lord Iddesleigh in 1887 used the word 'sombre' to describe the outlook for the new year and dwelt particularly upon the Austro-Russian rivalry in the Balkans which, it seemed, must inevitably lead to a collision.[2] In the opening days of 1887 European Chanceries were dominated by the question: Would Russia forcibly occupy Bulgaria? If she took such a forward step it seemed certain that Austria would resist.[3] And Lord Salisbury instructed the ambassador in St. Petersburg to impress upon Giers that Austria would not stand alone. This message was not intended to be provocative but was aimed at deterring the Czar from a course which would be catastrophic for Europe and for Russia alike.[4]

Morier had often asserted that leaders of nations rarely pursued a course of calculated suicide, and Russia's conduct in 1887 seems to bear out his maxim. She faced the combined opposition of England, Austria, and Italy—a grouping which the Mediterranean Agreements of February and December of 1887 turned into a more solid front.[5] Gradually Russian wartalk subsided, and her leaders set off on a new policy designed to gain their ends in south-eastern Europe. The result was concession and negotiation in Central Asia. While the winter and spring of 1887 saw the Afghan discussions deadlocked, the summer found them drawing swiftly to a successful end.

[1] Ridgeway to Salisbury, No. 8, 15 August 1887: F.O. 65/1347.
[2] White to Iddesleigh, private and confidential, 1 January 1887: Pte White Papers, F.O. 364/1.   [3] Cecil, op. cit., iv, 10, 14–16.
[4] Salisbury to Morier, private, 19 January 1887: bound volume, Russia, Pte Salisbury Papers.
[5] Temperley and Penson (eds.), Foundations, pp. 430–2, 445–8, 454–8.

Just before the Afghan settlement, the Sobranje in Bulgaria had voted in favour of Ferdinand of Coburg as their ruler. Prince Ferdinand reached Sofia in August. The Russians considered him totally unacceptable, proclaimed his election illegal, and worked for his expulsion. Since 1885, however, Great Britain had supported the ' "living barrier" formed by the "breast of freemen" ' in the embryonic Balkan states as a bar to Russia's drive towards Constantinople.[1] It was this check to Russian aspirations that Giers hoped to remove by concessions in Central Asia.

Immediately after the Afghan protocol was signed, Giers, both verbally and in writing, expressed his hope that the two countries would discuss the Bulgarian question 'in the same friendly tone'.[2] At Constantinople, Sir William White complained of Nelidov's taking every opportunity to make 'political capital' out of the Central Asian settlement by representing it as the beginning of a comprehensive rapprochement.[3] After some preliminary conversations Giers made a more direct overture in mid-August which, at his request, was telegraphed to London. The Russian Foreign Minister hoped that the 'restoration of good will' produced by the boundary agreement might be extended to Bulgaria.

He [Giers] said there were those who had very keenly hoped that the Afghan frontier negotiations would have led to a serious rupture and who bitterly lamented its favourable issue. This was the more reason to make it a stepping stone to a better understanding all round, and this was the light in which the Emperor as well as himself regarded our late accord.[4]

[1] Quotation from A. J. Grant and Harold Temperley (revised by Lillian M. Penson), *Europe in the Nineteenth and Twentieth Centuries, 1789 to 1950* (London, 1950), p. 306. See also Lillian M. Penson, 'The Principles and Methods of Lord Salisbury's Foreign Policy', *Cambridge Historical Journal*, v (1935), pp. 95–6. Cecil, *op. cit.*, iii, 237–56; iv, 64–5. An interesting account of British policy in the Balkans is the 'Memorandum on the Situation', confidential, September 1886: Pte White Papers, F.O. 364/1.
[2] Morier to Salisbury and enclosures, No. 260, confidential, 26 July 1887, endorsed 'The Queen; Prince of Wales': F.O. 65/1297. The Protocol regarding the Afghan delimitation was signed at St. Petersburg on 10/22 July 1887: see F.O. 65/1351.
[3] White to Salisbury, decypher telegram, private and confidential, 3 August 1887: Pte White Papers, F.O. 364/1.
[4] Morier to Salisbury, No. 61, decypher telegram, secret, 18 August 1887,

Sir Villiers Lister denounced the two-and-a-half-page
message as a 'monstrous waste of money', and another member
of the Foreign Office staff computed the exact cost of the telegram.[1] Lord Salisbury personally drafted the reply. He almost
curtly set forth the reasons why Her Majesty's Government
could not 'safely draw closer to Russia on the subject of Bulgaria'.[2]

Upon learning of England's cold reaction, Giers shifted the
emphasis from Bulgaria to the necessity for Anglo-Russian
co-operation in the event of a Franco-German war. Agreement in the Balkans constituted the door which opened the
way for the development of a 'frank understanding between
the two Governments'. The bait failed to tempt the British,
but tentative Russian approaches continued throughout
1887.[3]

Sir Philip Currie was the first to suggest that this new diplomatic atmosphere might be used in Persia. He declared, in a
long minute following one of Nicolson's appeals on behalf of the
Shah, that the 'only chance' of helping Persia 'would be to take
advantage of the friendly disposition of the Russian Gov[ern-
men]t and try to have some kind of exchange of ideas with them'.
Currie had faith in the essential prudence of the Czar, though
he believed Prince Dolgorouki and the trans-Caspian officials
were 'eager for the fray'. He urged Lord Salisbury to use the
frenzied outburst in the Russian press, caused by Sir Henry
Drummond Wolff's appointment as minister to Tehran, as a
basis for broaching the subject of Persia with Staal.[4] According
to this journalistic hysteria, which Morier thought was inspired,
Wolff intended not only to re-establish British paramountcy in

endorsed 'Seen by Lord Salisbury': F.O. 65/1300. See also same to same, No. 287,
secret, 17 August 1887, endorsed 'The Queen; Embassies': F.O. 65/1298.

[1] Minutes following Morier to Salisbury, No. 61, decypher telegram, secret,
18 August 1887: F.O. 65/1300.

[2] Salisbury to Morier, No. 112, draft telegram, 19 August 1887; same to same,
No. 113, draft telegram, 22 August 1887: F.O. 65/1300. See also the extenders of
these telegrams, Salisbury to Morier, No. 237, 19 August 1887; same to same, No.
239, 22 August 1887, endorsed 'Seen by Lord Salisbury': F.O. 65/1294.

[3] Morier to Salisbury, No. 294, 24 August 1887, endorsed 'The Queen: Embassies'; same to same, No. 325, 21 September 1887, endorsed 'The Queen,
Prince of Wales, Paris, Berlin': F.O. 65/1298.

[4] Minute by Currie of 17 February following Nicolson to Salisbury, No. 12,
secret, 10 January 1888: F.O. 65/1347.

Persia but also to launch an anti-Russian pan-Islamic crusade throughout the East.[1]

Currie then laid down the essentials of the British side of the proposed Salisbury-Staal conversation. He recommended that the importance attached to the Wolff mission be admitted. But hostility to Russia did not follow as a logical deduction. England coveted no exclusive rights in Persia, and she would welcome co-operation in upholding the integrity of the country and in promoting its development. Commercial enterprise, particularly, should be encouraged. In that connection the British Government took special interest in the improvement of communications from the Gulf inland. Currie argued, finally, that even if nothing tangible emerged, the Shah would have proof of England's solicitude. Lord Salisbury's sole comment was that the attempt should be made through Morier since 'they pay no attention to Staal at all'.[2]

Action soon followed. In Tehran, information reached Nicolson by telegraph of the Foreign Office decision to assuage the Shah's fears through representations in St. Petersburg. Nicolson was assured that his secret messages would not be mentioned; the communications would be based entirely on Wolff's impending departure and on the already existing agreements over Persia.[3] Simultaneously, Currie drafted a long dispatch to Morier, and Salisbury revised it extensively.

This joint composition elaborated Currie's minute. It explained the purpose of the Wolff mission, stressed the futility of Anglo-Russian rivalry in Persia, and emphasized the need for co-operation in the development of the country. The British dexterously returned the Afghan ball by putting forward their hope of supplementing that agreement by an accord in Persia. They argued that the commercial field was extensive enough to provide an outlet for the enterprise of both nations, and they restated their primary aims of opening the Karun to navigation and building railways in order to tap fertile but torpid districts. Britain promised not to oppose Russia commercially in northern

[1] Morier to Salisbury and enclosures, No. 398, 5 December 1887: F.O. 65/1299.
[2] Minutes by Currie and Salisbury of 17 February following Nicolson to Salisbury, No. 12, secret, 10 January 1888: F.O. 65/1347.
[3] Salisbury to Nicolson, No. 9, draft telegram, secret, 21 February 1888: F.O. 60/494.

Persia. Lord Salisbury, however, put on record the interest his government had in northern Persia since any frontier changes in Khorassan affected the independence and integrity of the country, which both England and Russia were pledged to uphold. Thus Russian commercial supremacy did not imply political subservience.[1]

Herein, Lord Salisbury's Persian policy illustrates one of his more elusive concepts—what he called a 'partition of preponderance'. In this he seems mainly to have thought of economic development. Here arise the questions: What were the motives behind this policy, and what did this policy imply? Lord Salisbury seems not to have envisaged economic preponderance as a preliminary to partition into spheres of influence with ultimate absorption by England and Russia of their particular areas. Partition into spheres of economic preponderance would serve a dual function. It would mitigate the friction between England and Russia by reducing their points of contact. It would at the same time strengthen Persia herself by the opening of the country by railways, by the ever-increasing trade and industrial development, and by the flow of capital into the respective spheres. Once the process began, other nations, such as Germany and the United States, would trade and invest in Persia—not only in the British-dominated south but also in the north. After Great Britain and other powers had established their stakes in the country, Russian designs would be thwarted. The improved condition of Persia itself would constitute an obstacle as would the combined opposition of the interested parties. One of Lord Salisbury's aims in Persia was to bring other Powers into the field and to transform the question from an Anglo-Russian into an international one.

The Foreign Office sent their Persian dispatch to Sir Robert Morier, and told him that he might read it to Giers and leave a copy with him.[2] Not even this communication escaped Sir Robert's revisionist pen, although here his changes were minor.[3]

---

[1] Salisbury to Morier, No. 51, draft dispatch, 21 February 1888, endorsed 'The Queen': F.O. 65/1347. Salisbury to Morier, No. 52, secret, 21 February 1888, endorsed 'The Queen': F.O. 65/1347.

[2] Salisbury to Morier, No. 51, 21 February 1888, endorsed 'The Queen': F.O. 65/1347.

[3] Morier to Currie, private and confidential, 2 March 1888: F.O. 65/1330.

Exactly a week later Morier reported that Giers wished to see the Emperor before giving a definite reply. He had, however, apologized for the behaviour of Prince Dolgorouki, and seemed generally well disposed to the English overture. Morier concluded with the happy prophecy that the Russians would 'fully enter into the view of Her Majesty's Government as recorded in Your Lordship's above-mentioned dispatch [No. 51]'.[1]

Once again the affairs of Bulgaria and Persia interacted. The Russians, in the meantime, had renewed their agitation for the removal of Prince Ferdinand. Their new plan was to unseat him by pressure of the powers acting through the Porte.[2] This programme was essentially negative since it provided for the downfall of a régime without putting anything in its place. Lord Salisbury unhesitatingly refused to participate in the scheme since Prince Ferdinand's overthrow would deprive Bulgaria of its main element of stability.[3]

This refusal annoyed St. Petersburg. Morier reported that Giers was discouraged and that the Emperor was disappointed by the 'summary dismissal' of their Bulgarian programme.[4] When Morier and Giers again turned to Persia the tone of their discussion was set by the impasse in Bulgaria. Giers made no effort to conceal his pique. He agreed, but without enthusiasm, to send instructions to Staal authorizing him to discuss the Persian problem in London. Morier still felt optimistic and seemed hopeful that the Russians would co-operate to lessen the tension in Persia, but his conviction was less sure as the appendage marked 'secret' to his telegram reveals.

I found M. de Giers much less warm on the subject [Persia] than he had been on Monday. I attribute this to his great discouragement at our attitude in regard to Bulgaria & to the belief which I strongly suspect he holds that the opposition to the scheme has been mainly organized by us.

[1] Morier to Salisbury, No. 77, 28 February 1888: F.O. 65/1347.
[2] Morier to Salisbury, No. 60, 15 February 1888, endorsed 'The Queen': F.O. 65/1329.
[3] Salisbury to Morier, No. 62, draft dispatch, 26 February 1888, endorsed 'The Queen': F.O. 65/1328.
[4] Morier to Salisbury, No. 65, very confidential, 22 February 1888, endorsed 'The Queen'; same to same, No. 72, 24 February 1888, endorsed 'The Queen': F.O. 65/1329.

Emperor has returned the copy of your despatch without comment.

The Foreign Office staff did not view the situation as tragic. Sir Thomas Sanderson commented: 'This is as much as we could expect while they are out of temper.'[1]

The scene of negotiations shifted to London. Giers sent the instructions, but they are not included in the published Giers–Staal correspondence. Both Lord Salisbury and Sir Henry Drummond Wolff exchanged views with Staal. Memoranda by them are extant, as are Staal's reports to St. Petersburg. The London conversations concerned three issues. The British pressed for a renewal of the 1834 and 1838 assurances, and secured Russia's consent. Then they sounded the Russians on a programme for the joint development of Persia and advocated an understanding as to the railways each country would build. The Russians were frigid on the subject of railways. In their opinion, it was an individual matter which each should take up separately with the Shah. Finally, the British referred to the desirability of concluding the Khorassan frontier negotiations, but the Russians consistently maintained that the delimitation concerned Russia and Persia alone. Staal, however, assured Lord Salisbury that Russia intended to treat Persia 'equitably', and that Prince Dolgorouki would do all he could in Tehran 'to make relations harmonise'.[2]

Negotiations along similar lines were to be carried forward by Wolff and Dolgorouki in Tehran. The Shah was informed of the representations which had already resulted in the Russian promise 'to attach the greatest value to the integrity of Persia'.[3] Nasir ad-Din received the news with lively satisfaction and said that the tone of the Russian Legation was less severe.[4]

---

[1] Morier to Salisbury, No. 16, decypher telegram, 1 March 1888; appendage marked 'secret'; minute by Sanderson of 1 March: F.O. 65/1348. This telegram is sometimes dated 29 February 1888. It was sent at midnight.

[2] Wolff to Salisbury, 3 March 1888, endorsed 'The Queen': F.O. 65/1348, Memorandum by Salisbury, 8 March 1888, out as Salisbury to Morier, No. 73, 8 March 1888, endorsed 'The Queen'. See also Salisbury to Morier, draft No. 73a, 12 March 1888, endorsed 'The Queen': F.O. 65/1348. Sir H. D. Wolff, *Rambling Recollections*, ii, 338–9. Staal to Giers, No. 23, 28 February/11 March 1888: Meyendorff, *op. cit.*, i, 402–3.

[3] Salisbury to Nicolson, No. 14, draft dispatch, 9 March 1888: F.O. 60/494.

[4] Nicolson to Salisbury and enclosure, No. 31, secret, 13 March 1888, endorsed 'The Queen': F.O. 65/1348.

Sir Henry Drummond Wolff, meanwhile, crossed Europe and the Caucasus on the way to his new post. Before reaching his destination he began to collect interesting information. At Tiflis he was entertained by the Governor-General of the Caucasus and the trans-Caspian provinces—Prince Dondou-koff-Korsakoff. The Governor-General was ambitious and able, powerful and popular. Most British authorities credited him with the Penjdeh coup. By 1888, however, Penjdeh was three years past, and no further Russian advances had strained relations in Central Asia. Prince Dondoukoff received Wolff with an impressive display of hospitality and *désinvolture*. While banqueting, the Prince and the British diplomat recalled old times in Bulgaria where each did unpleasant things to the other in pursuance of his duty. Then, in the midst of this entertainment, Prince Dondoukoff and his adjunct, General Cherametieff, turned their talents to general prognostications. Cherametieff confessed that even Russian extremists saw the difficulties involved in holding India if taken. But it could, he mused, serve as a useful bargaining lever. The Prince, in one of his gloomier moments, predicted the partition of Persia and suggested that the surgeon's knife be sharpened for an impending operation. Then he brightened the conversation by extolling the blessings of Russian rule in Central Asia. Dondoukoff-Korsakoff even foresaw his responsibilities increased by an Herati petition asking for incorporation into the Czar's trans-Caspian provinces.[1]

Wolff's account of his visit to Tiflis produced a reaction in the Foreign Office. The proposed Persian bisection was disquieting. Far more serious, however, was the probing of that ever-sensitive area—Herat. Sir Thomas Sanderson drew up a memorandum on Herat.[2] Sir Philip Currie suggested that if Wolff's Russian colleagues talked further of incorporating Herat they should be informed that war would automatically follow such a territorial transformation.[3] Lord Salisbury directed that

[1] Wolff to Salisbury, separate, secret, and confidential, 9 April 1888, endorsed 'The Queen, Prince of Wales': F.O. 65/1348. Nicolson to Salisbury, No. 39, records telegram, 6 April 1888: F.O. 60/496.

[2] Memorandum by Sanderson, Warnings that advance to Herat would be a *casus belli*, undated but endorsed by Salisbury on 6 April 1888: F.O. 65/1348.

[3] Minute by Currie following Wolff to Salisbury, separate, secret, and con-

simultaneous instructions be drafted for Sir Robert Morier. He should open a conversation with Giers by expressing thanks for the hospitality accorded Wolff during his journey through the trans-Caspian province. In alluding to Prince Dondoukoff's conversation, however, Morier was to 'remind Giers that he has been several times instructed to say that Herat means war', and to recall the previous warnings which had been given.[1]

Sir Robert Morier was *persona grata* in St. Petersburg. On more than one occasion he had irritated his own superiors by toning down communications which, in his opinion, might be wounding. He strove towards a resolution of differences between the two empires as the crowning of his diplomatic career. As an effective instrument for remonstrance, he could hardly be surpassed since his pro-Russian proclivities were so well known. A grave or bellicose tone from Sir Robert had the most salutary effect on Russian officials. Threatening the Russians with war whenever a Cossack pony turned its head towards Herat did not suit Morier's taste. Nevertheless, he resolutely held his 'Herat interview' with Giers and apparently carried out his instructions without independent interpretation. His report to the Foreign Office is a masterpiece of English prose.

Having cordially thanked Giers for the hospitable entertainment provided for Sir Henry Wolff, he mentioned that the new minister to Persia had been charmed by the 'sprightliness' of Prince Dondoukoff's witticisms. The Russian Minister for Foreign Affairs, immediately suspecting the Prince of indiscretions, pressed for an elaboration. Giers showed genuine apprehension over Lord Salisbury's reaction. Morier assured him that Lord Salisbury had 'seized the humorous side of Prince Dondukow Korsakow's observations'. The real importance attached to them, he went on to say, was that of the straw which indicates a current—and that there was a current sweeping towards Herat in Russian military circles was undeniable. Giers did not contradict this statement, but he insisted that nothing was more remote from his own mind and from that of the

---

fidential, 9 April 1888: F.O. 65/1348. Salisbury to Wolff, No. 17, draft telegram, 9 April 1888, endorsed 'Lord Cross': F.O. 60/494.
[1] Minute by Salisbury on Wolff to Salisbury, separate, secret, and confidential, 9 April 1888: F.O. 65/1348.

I

Emperor than the annexation of Herat. Morier expressed gratification, but he also explained that British statesmen of all
political shades were united in their conviction that a move on
that fortress would be a *casus belli*. He continued:

. . . if, for the sake of argument, we took Prince Dondukow's diag-
nosis *au sérieux* and the Heratis signed a monster petition for annexation to Russia and the signature of this petition synchronized with
the appearance on the frontier of Colonel Alikhanow with a body of
Cossacks and Turkoman cavalry His Excellency might be quite sure
that this would mean war.

Morier then turned to Prince Dondoukoff's pessimistic reflections on Persia. Giers hastened to repudiate any thought of partition, and passed off the Governor-General's remarks as the
idle speculation of one who knew nothing of foreign policy. The
renewal of the 1834 agreement represented a working basis
for Anglo-Russian co-operation, and Prince Dolgorouki had
already received his instructions to continue the conversations
so auspiciously begun in London. Giers concluded with the hope
that Wolff would not be misled by what he clearly regarded as
the useless wanderings of a remote Russian frontier officer.

Thus the admonition seems to have been conspicuously
successful. The Russians had categorically repudiated any
designs on Herat. Moreover, Giers had spoken reassuringly on
Persia. In the course of this conversation Morier also gained
additional information about the Penjdeh incident. During that
prolonged crisis, both Liberal and Conservative Governments
had informed the Russians that an advance on Herat would
plunge the two countries over the precipice. A Cabinet which
met in March 1885 decided that Great Britain would have to
declare war if Herat were threatened. The question arises: Did
the Russians plan an advance on that city? In his résumé
Morier referred to the

. . . great council to which many of the military notabilities had
been summoned, and which, I gathered, must have met about the
period of the Penjdeh incident and when the issues of peace and
war trembled in the balance. There was a strong expression of
opinion, His Excellency said, in favour of a march upon Herat, and
of the annexation of that city. He himself opposed the project with

all his might and main and the one General who had rallied to his opinion had been the Prince Dondukow who now rhapsodised about annexation by petition.[1]

[1] Morier to Salisbury, No. 146, confidential, 18 April 1888, endorsed 'The Queen': F.O. 65/1348.

CHAPTER VIII

The Wolff Mission, 1888–91
Its Contribution
to Anglo-Russian Agreement

THE appointment of Sir Henry Drummond Wolff as minister to Tehran in 1888 was a manifestation of the stronger British line in Persia. Consultations between the India Office and the Foreign Office had been taking place since 1885 on the subject of Sir Ronald Thomson's successor. The chargé d'affaires, Arthur Nicolson, had performed his duties assiduously in the long three-year interval between ministers. He was inexperienced, however, and in certain critical negotiations failed to fathom the intricacies of the never-ending plots which characterized the Persian Court. This junior diplomat, who developed into one of the architects of the Anglo-Russian Convention of 1907, received a decoration at the close of his Tehran service. According to his biographer this portion of his early career 'ended in triumphant success'.[1]

Nicolson worked, however, under one unavoidable handicap. He lacked prestige. He was himself aware of this defect, and in a private letter to Sir Henry Rawlinson he explained why the new minister should be a man of standing as well as one of innate capacity. The appointment of an ambassador extraordinary to Persia was, for a time, under consideration. Nicolson advised against this innovation on two grounds. First, such a challenge would antagonize the Russians and stimulate them to even greater activity. Secondly, the Shah would develop an exaggerated notion of his own importance and would become

---

[1] Harold Nicolson, *Sir Arthur Nicolson, First Lord Carnock, A Study in the Old Diplomacy*, pp. 60–77; quotation from p. 60.

still more refractory.[1] The idea of sending an ambassador to Persia was ultimately abandoned.

Those who selected the new minister, however, took into account the fact that worship of the golden calf prevailed at Tehran. Lord Dufferin, then Viceroy of India, put forward Sir Donald Mackenzie Wallace as his candidate for the post. Currie suggested Sir Donald Stewart, formerly Commander-in-Chief in India, who would be not only firm but also dexterous and conciliatory. The India Office recommended either Rawlinson, then in the twilight of his eminent career, or Sir Henry Drummond Wolff. The choice finally devolved upon Wolff whom Lord Salisbury described as 'a great master of Oriental diplomacy'.[2] He was the son of Joseph Wolff, the missionary who made a dangerous journey to Bukhara in 1843.

Wolff's diplomatic experience had already been long and his work praiseworthy. He was fresh from two special tours of duty in Constantinople. These missions did not accomplish their immediate objectives, but the failure was caused by the outside forces of French and Russian interference.[3] In the judgment of Sir William White, the Wolff negotiations of 1885 and 1887 served a useful purpose.[4]

Wolff was a many-sided and ambitious man, gifted with boundless energy, keen insight, and an inquiring mind. He probed and investigated every imaginable line of procedure. That he left a stone unturned was not a criticism to be applied to Sir Henry Drummond Wolff. But he inspired little affection. He was respected—at a distance. Subordinates and colleagues found their work difficult and at times vexing,[5] but on the other

[1] Nicolson to Rawlinson, private, 26 April 1887: Case 630, Home Correspondence, Political and Secret Department, vol. xcv, India Office Records. See also Nicolson to Sanderson, private, 28 May 1887: F.O. 60/486. Nicolson, *op. cit.*, p. 68.

[2] Salisbury to Morier, private, 22 October 1890: bound volume, Russia, Pte Salisbury Papers.

[3] Cecil, *op. cit.*, iii, 234-7; iv, 28-47. Lillian M. Penson, 'The Principles and Methods of Lord Salisbury's Foreign Policy', *Cambridge Historical Journal*, v (1935), pp. 99-100. Rosebery to Gladstone, private, 22 May 1893: B.M. Add. MSS. 44290, vol. ccv, Pte Gladstone Papers. C. L. Smith, *The Embassy of Sir William White at Constantinople*, pp. 77-82.

[4] White to Salisbury, private and confidential, 31 May 1887; same to same, private and confidential, 16 July 1887: Pte White Papers, F.O. 364/1.

[5] Cartwright to White, private, 4 September 1888: Pte White Papers, F.O.

hand his temperament frequently provided an outlet for humorous asides. Sir Thomas Sanderson wrote:

The Wolff from the mountains will be down upon us very soon. He is coming home to look after [the] Shah.

I hope you will get the Persian O[rder] in C[ouncil] out of the office somewhere before he arrives—or he will rend us in pieces.[1]

Wolff's restiveness and his determination to explore all possibilities exposed him to the criticism of having 'fads' in his conduct of affairs. In Persia he embarked on innumerable projects. But he successfully carried through, after long and tedious negotiations, more schemes for the mutual benefit of Persia and Great Britain than had any British minister for many a year.

Wolff fostered a dual Persian policy. He sought to conclude an agreement with Russia whereby the two countries would cease their rivalry, co-operate in the promotion of commerce, encourage better government, and recognize their respective superior positions. Though a preponderance of influence was admitted, he did not envisage a division of the country. The goal of his proposed Anglo-Russian activity was the improvement of Persia and its transformation into a stable buffer state.

His other line of approach consisted of the immediate bolstering of Persia by various devices. Measures were sponsored designed to promote trade, to improve internal security, and to develop the country's rich natural resources. He attached particular importance to the introduction of western capital, not only from Great Britain but from Continental and American Powers as well. Untiringly, Wolff pressed the Shah to favour legitimate foreign enterprise. He reasoned that when other nations invested in Persia they too would take an interest in its preservation as an independent state.[2]

From Wolff's point of view the two aims of his Persian policy were not contradictory. Both were pursued with equal intensity, but not with equal success. In the final analysis not only

364/1. Kennedy to White, private and confidential, 27 November 1889: Pte White Papers, F.O. 364/1.

[1] Sanderson to Davidson, private, 4 May 1889: F.O. 60/518.

[2] Wolff to Salisbury, private and confidential, 21 April 1888, printed for the use of the Cabinet, 23 May 1888, endorsed by Salisbury 'Print. Send to Queen & Cabinet. S.19.5': F.O. 60/492. Same to same, private, 24 May 1888: bound volume, Persia, Pte Salisbury Papers. Wolff, op. cit., ii, 332–3.

his but all efforts to bring about a reconciliation with Russia in the latter part of the nineteenth century failed. No statesman put forth more sincere and pertinacious efforts in that direction than the British minister to Persia. One of his subordinates, intending no compliment, described his zeal as 'Randolphian'.[1] Wolff expended an immense amount of time and energy in these negotiations, and he mentions in his recollections that a substantial part of his time at Tehran was 'occupied in devising some arrangement with Russia'.[2] This project, however, seems to have been doomed at the outset. Count Lamsdorff maintained:

All efforts of this statesman [Wolff] to involve Russia in a definite agreement with England concerning Persian affairs were not and could not be successful on account of the primordial aim of Russian politics.[3]

Wolff's policies had a single objective—the improvement of Persia. For such resuscitation drastic reforms were needed. These changes could be inaugurated by the Persian central government itself, or they could be imposed from without by the two great neighbouring powers. After a preliminary study Wolff concluded that sweeping innovations would not mark the close of Nasir ad-Din's reign. The old Shah thought primarily of his own peace of mind, and was entrapped in a succession of dilemmas and vicious circles which would have discouraged far greater men. The character of the Shah and the acuteness of the Persian crisis account, at least in part, for Wolff's stubborn insistence upon an agreement with the Russians.[4]

The London interviews of March, held between Salisbury and Wolff on one side and Staal on the other, were to be continued in Tehran. The original topics, however, encompassed

[1] Kennedy to White, private and confidential, 27 November 1889: Pte White Papers, F.O. 364/1.   [2] Wolff, *op. cit.*, ii, 372.

[3] Lamsdorff to Speyer, secret, 30 September/13 October 1904: *Krasny Arkhiv*, liii, 16.

[4] Wolff to Salisbury, private and confidential, 21 April 1888. F.O. 60/492. Same to same, private, 20 May 1888: bound volume, Persia, Pte Salisbury Papers. His letters of 15 June 1888 and 9 September 1888, private and confidential, are also pertinent. Memorandum by Wolff, confidential, 21 April 1891, printed for the use of the Foreign Office, 3 May 1891; draft memorandum endorsed by Salisbury 'To be printed for Queen & Cabinet—but not to go abroad. S. April 27, 91': F.O. 65/1413.

three specific issues only—the renewal of the previous agreements, the Khorassan boundary, and the construction of railways. Wolff widened the scope of the discussions and drew up
a comprehensive programme for the rejuvenation of Persia.
Soon after reaching his post he launched 'completely unofficial
and personal' conversations with Dolgorouki.[1]

To implement his elaborate plans Wolff advocated the formation of mixed commissions with British, Persian, and
Russian members. These bodies were to perform diverse func-
tions. The first task was to define Persia's elusive boundaries.
Thus the perennial problem of the Khorassan frontier might be
laid to rest. Moreover, the Perso-Turkish boundary was one of
the few in the world which throughout the nineteenth century
remained 'unmaterialized and unknown'.[2] Indefiniteness gave
rise to chronic disturbances which threatened to involve both
Great Britain and Russia. Since 1843 efforts had been made to
adjudicate the line, but Wolff's attempt was abortive and the
last pillar was not erected until the autumn of 1914.[3]

The second commission, composed of officers with special
qualifications, was to perform tasks of a scientific and technical
nature. Its members were to survey the country, and then draw
up a report on resources with recommendations for improving
means of transportation. Persia's commercial interests, not
strategic considerations, were to be the criterion for the projected roads, canals, and railroads. After assembling the preliminary data and agreeing upon the objectives England and
Russia should jointly undertake to facilitate the realization of
the internal development programme. Wolff told Dolgorouki:

It seems to me that by establishing the prosperity of this country,
and by assisting in the development of her resources, her two neighbours will interpose between their frontiers a neutral territory,
which, while profiting by their support and legitimate influence,
would remove the friction which is the inevitable result of a state of
uncertainty.[4]

[1] Wolff to Salisbury, No. 43, most confidential, 2 May 1888, endorsed 'The
Queen, Prince of Wales': F.O. 65/1349. Wolff, op. cit., ii, 345–6.
[2] Curzon, Frontiers, The Romanes Lecture for 1907, p. 49.
[3] Aitchison, op. cit., xiii, The Treaties, etc., Relating to Persia and Afghanistan,
pp. 11, 19.
[4] Wolff to Salisbury and enclosure, private and confidential, 21 April 1888:

Prince Dolgorouki professed himself converted to the idea of an Anglo-Russian rapprochement, and he conversed pleasantly during the summer of 1888. His interest centred less on co-operation in Persia, however, than on reaching a general understanding with England. Indeed, it was a gloomy Dolgorouki who spoke of Persia and its fate. He usually returned to one of two themes: the opposition of England to Russia's policy in Bulgaria, or the opposition of the military party in Russia to a pacific policy in Persia.[1]

Nor was the Russian alone in his doubts. Both Sir Henry Rawlinson and Sir Alfred Lyall, though for different reasons from those of Prince Dolgorouki, viewed Wolff's draft convention with the 'gravest suspicion' and opposed it vigorously. The Indian authorities conceded that Persia's neighbours, without *arrière pensée*, had it within their power to cleanse the Augean stable. But Rawlinson was unable even to imagine Russian endeavours to transform Persia into a flourishing state. Both Lyall and Rawlinson detected a hidden motive in Russia's willingness to participate—assuming that willingness existed. Since the scope of the proposed mixed commissions included the whole of the country, the two Indian experts reasoned that the Russians saw in these commissions a stratagem for establishing a foothold in southern Persia and penetrating to the Gulf. Sir Alfred Lyall reminded his colleagues that the reform of a third country by two outsiders was at best a delicate operation, and historically England and Russia had differed fundamentally *inter se* in their ideas of good government, their political and commercial interests, and their missions in Asia. In conclusion Lyall suggested that one limited and specific reform—such as Persian finance—should be attempted as a test before Wolff's complicated machinery was set up, misunderstandings occurred, and the mutual distrust intensified.[2] These opinions

F.O. 60/492. Same to same, No. 71, decypher telegram, urgent and secret, 13 June 1888: F.O. 60/495. Wolff to Dolgorouki, very confidential, 13 June 1888: reproduced in full in Wolff, *op. cit.*, ii, 347–50; quotation from p. 347.

[1] Wolff to Salisbury, No. 43, most confidential, 2 May 1888, endorsed 'The Queen, Prince of Wales': F.O. 65/1349. Same to same, No. 105, decypher telegram, secret and confidential, 15 July 1888: F.O. 60/496. Same to same, private, 30 July 1888: bound volume, Persia, Pte Salisbury Papers.

[2] Case 574, memorandum on the State of Affairs in Persia by Major-General Sir H. Rawlinson, 26 June 1888; note by Sir A. Lyall on Affairs in Persia, 27 June

went to Lord Salisbury, who confided privately to Wolff:

Some of the Indian Council are very much distressed at the policy you are pursuing in coming to an agreement with Russia. I have begged them to write down their views in full & send them out by this mail for your consideration. I do not attach very much value to them—as Indian opinions so soon become obsolete. And as far as I understand their views (I have not seen their papers) they do not take into consideration the almost hopeless dilemma in which we find ourselves. Until some road or railway is made we can not help Persia: & at present it is only with Russia's leave that we can get these made. If we get that leave from her, it will be a real success. But if we do not, at least our negotiations may amuse her & keep her from mischief until either Germany or Russia [sic: Austria] take off our hands the task of keeping her employed. The gist of the information I get is that Russia will be ready for the swoop on Constantinople, possibly next summer, certainly the summer after: & all appearances—so far as preparations go—are in favour of her making it. But I do not believe in a merely naval attack: & a land attack must bring the Central Powers into the field. I hope our frontier defences in India will be ready by the time I have named . . .[1]

Earlier he had said officially: 'I am not in love with the proposal to appoint Commissions. On a joint Commission the Russians will generally have the best of us.'[2]

Since Dolgorouki had not responded with alacrity to his joint commissions scheme, Wolff changed his objective to the making of a tripartite treaty. Having decided to induce the Shah to initiate the proceedings, he requested Lord Salisbury's permission to plant such a thought with the Persian ruler. Lord Salisbury consented but not without reservations. 'Take care Russia does not use the Shah to ask impossible conditions from us, & put us in the wrong if we refuse', he telegraphed in reply.[3]

1888: Home Correspondence, Political and Secret Department, vol. cii, India Records Office. The papers are also in the Foreign Office records and in Lord Salisbury's private papers. See also Case 450, Home Correspondence, Political and Secret Department, vol. cii, India Office Records.

[1] Salisbury to Wolff, private, 27 June 1888: bound volume, Persia, Pte Salisbury Papers. Memorandum by Wolff, 26 July 1888: F.O. 60/492.

[2] Salisbury to Wolff, No. 28, draft telegram, 12 June 1888, endorsed 'Lord Cross': F.O. 60/494.

[3] Wolff to Salisbury and draft telegram by Salisbury, private, 30 May 1888: bound volume, Persia, Pte Salisbury Papers. Same to same, decypher telegram, urgent, private, and confidential, 10 June 1888; F.O. 60/495.

The permanent Foreign Office staff shared Lord Salisbury's doubts. Sir Julian Pauncefote, for example, commented: 'He seems to be stirring up muddy waters rather vigorously.'[1]

Three-sided conversations seem to breed complications spontaneously, and the tripartite treaty discussions fulfilled the worst expectations. Wolff was treading on dangerous ground when he attempted to carry on concurrent negotiations with the Shah and the Russian minister. Versions of the Dolgorouki-Nasir ad-Din talks varied with the nationality of the speaker. Wolff was distressed still more by the distortions which reached him of his own proposals to the Russian and the Persian. Reluctantly he resigned himself to the interpretation that the Shah was holding a 'Dutch auction' and that 'Dolgorouky is somewhat of a *liar*'. Sanderson remarked: 'A national quality of Russians.'[2]

The negotiations nevertheless bore some fruit. When Wolff first requested approval of his project, Lord Salisbury inquired about a precedent for such a treaty. Sir Edward Hertslet's research led to the compilation and publication of an excellent reference volume on nineteenth-century Anglo-Persian relations.[3]

Despite the early demise of the joint commissions and the tripartite treaty the Wolff–Dolgorouki exchanges continued throughout the summer. Dolgorouki assumed the initiative. But he interjected the affairs of south-eastern Europe into Persian discussions. He suggested that if Lord Salisbury would settle the Bulgarian dispute with Staal, he then would conclude a Persian agreement with Wolff. He argued that an Anglo-Russian understanding should not be restricted to Persia but should extend

[1] Wolff to Salisbury and minutes by Sanderson and Pauncefote, No. 71, secret and confidential, 1 June 1888, endorsed 'The Queen, Prince of Wales': F.O. 65/1350.

[2] Wolff to Salisbury, private and confidential, 4 October 1888; same to same, private, 20 June 1888: underlining in pencil and comment by Sanderson: bound volume, Persia, Pte Salisbury Papers. Wolff to Salisbury and minute, No. 94, secret and confidential, 22 June 1888: F.O. 65/1350.

[3] Wolff to Salisbury and minutes by Salisbury and Currie, decypher telegram, urgent, private, and confidential, 10 June 1888: F.O. 60/495. Memorandum by Hertslet, 13 June 1888: F.O. 60/498. Hertslet to Foreign Office, 23 September 1889: F.O. 60/501. E. Hertslet, *Treaties, etc., Concluded between Great Britain and Persia, and between Persia and other Foreign Powers, Wholly or Partially in Force on the 1 April 1891* (London, 1891).

'*sur toute la ligne*'.[1] Wolff's competence did not include Bulgaria, and Lord Salisbury was not convinced that 'overtures from us to Russia on the Eastern Question are desirable at present'.[2] The insistence upon Bulgaria stultified the negotiations.

The British reasoned that a *détente* in Persia, similar to that in Afghanistan, would be as beneficial to Russia as to England. Concessions in Bulgaria were therefore superfluous. Moreover, the Persian question concerned the British and Russians alone, but the Bulgarian imbroglio involved the interests of the Powers signatory to the Berlin Treaty. Finally, Lord Salisbury thought the Dolgorouki overture lacked substance and reality. He wrote privately to Wolff:

Your Eastern Question negotiations with Dolgorouky have puzzled me a good deal: for they do not correspond to any simultaneous action of Russia in other parts of the world. No overtures have been made at St. Petersburgh, or at Vienna, or at Const[antino]ple. Staal has been here this afternoon: he talked very agreeably about everything: professed great confidence in the maintenance of peace: but he did not utter a single word—suggestive of special & separate negotiations between England & Russia. Nor do we get any such suggestions from the Germans, who have hitherto been generally employed by Russia when she wants to approach us for any particular question. I conclude, therefore, either that Dolgorouky's language was a mere belated edition of the conversation held with Randolph in the beginning of the year: or that he was acting entirely on his own hook without any instructions at all.[3]

The ministers carried on subsequent discussions, but in a desultory fashion, until Wolff left Persia in 1889 to accompany the Shah on his trip to England. He took advantage of his

[1] Wolff to Salisbury, private, 30 July 1888: bound volume, Persia, Pte Salisbury Papers. Same to same, No. 104, 6 July 1888, endorsed 'The Queen': F.O. 65/1351. Same to same and minutes by Sanderson and Salisbury, No. 97, decypher telegram, secret and confidential, 6 July 1888; same to same, No. 111, decypher telegram, most secret and confidential, 20 July 1888: F.O. 60/495.

[2] Salisbury to Wolff, draft telegram, 1 August 1888: F.O. 60/494.

[3] Salisbury to Wolff, private, 25 July 1888: bound volume, Persia, Pte Salisbury Papers. Wolff to Salisbury and minute by Salisbury, decypher telegram, private and confidential, 28 July 1888; same to same and minute by Currie, private telegram, 30 July 1888: F.O. 60/495. Salisbury to Wolff, No. 47, draft telegram, 6 August 1888; same to same, No. 50, draft telegram, 15 August 1888: F.O. 60/494. Same to same, No. 94, draft dispatch, 15 August 1888: F.O. 65/1352.

journey home to clarify the lines of Central Asian policy. Many possibilities were considered, but Wolff's belief in the necessity for an agreement with Russia remained unshaken.

While he was still in England, Wolff learned that Czar Alexander III's visit to Berlin would coincide with his own journey across the Continent *en route* to Tehran. He had suspected for several months that Giers was not providing the Emperor with full reports of his approaches for co-operation in Persia, and he longed to take his '*grand dessein*' to the 'fountainhead'. On 22 September 1889 Wolff sent to Lord Salisbury a memorandum on Anglo-Russian relations in Persia, and he suggested in his covering letter that the Emperor be informed of its contents.[1]

Three days later Wolff dined with the Prince of Wales. Lord Randolph Churchill had introduced them several years earlier, and a cordial friendship had developed. 'The cynical frankness of Wolff's conversation and his lively epistolary style made him welcome to the Prince as a companion and a correspondent.'[2] At the luncheon Wolff discussed his Persian problems, and the Prince of Wales 'undertook to speak to the Emperor whom he will see next week'. Lord Salisbury was informed at once.[3]

Lord Salisbury did not forbid the meeting, but he refused to promote it. He wrote:

The message must be entirely from you in no sense from me. I could not be party to it without exposing myself to the imputation of intriguing against Giers. Under these circumstances the precise language had better be left to you.[4]

Wolff and the Prince of Wales went on with the arrangements. Eight days after their first conversation the Prince of

[1] Memorandum by Wolff on the Relations of England and Russia in Persia, 22 September 1889 and covering letter to Salisbury: loose papers, Pte Salisbury Papers. Staal to Giers, 23 October/4 November 1889: Meyendorff, *op. cit.*, ii, 56–8.

[2] Sidney Lee, *King Edward VII. A Biography*, i, 685.

[3] Wolff to Salisbury, private, 25 September 1889: loose papers, 'Drafts, Copies, Minutes, Memoranda, etc., 1889', Pte Salisbury Papers. Wolff, *op. cit.*, ii, 367–8. According to Sir Sidney Lee the idea of the meeting with the Czar originated with the Prince of Wales. The documents indicate that the plan was suggested by Wolff, and the Prince of Wales made the arrangements. Lee, *op. cit.*, i, 686.

[4] Draft telegram to Wolff, private, Chalet Cecil, Puys, Dieppe, 25 September 1889: loose papers, 'Drafts, Copies, Minutes, Memoranda, etc., 1889', Pte Salisbury Papers. Cp. Lee, *op. cit.*, i, 687.

Wales telegraphed from Fredensborg Castle the news that the Russian Emperor had consented to discuss Persian affairs with Wolff.[1]

In Berlin, Wolff supplemented his audience with the Czar by two short talks with Count Herbert Bismarck. Earlier in the year, attempts had been made on the German side to draw closer to England.[2] Views concerning Persia, however, had not altered since 1885. Interference there, Count Bismarck said, would only irritate Russia and might lead to reprisals on Germany's eastern frontier.[3]

The interview with Czar Alexander III, however, appeared to be a real triumph. Wolff described his conference of nearly an hour as 'long and most satisfactory'.[4] He presented his case for an Anglo-Russian understanding and emphasized that its objective was the joint development of Persia. The Czar responded with a three-point message for Lord Salisbury: he too wanted an agreement over Persia, such an agreement must be completely reciprocal in so far as it applied to railways, waterways, and industrial undertakings; if the British ambassador in St. Petersburg would state formally to the Imperial Government that Wolff was authorized to negotiate in the above sense the new Russian minister would be given like instructions. At the close of the session Alexander III said:

I am most desirous to come to an understanding with England in Persia. We have no interests in common in Europe. Our common interests lie in Asia. There I desire to live in friendship with her, and to establish an understanding which will enable us to be friends.[5]

The Queen, who disapproved generally of negotiations and treaties with Russia, did not at all like the Berlin talks. She saw

[1] The Prince of Wales to Wolff, private and confidential, 3 October 1889: loose papers, Pte Salisbury Papers.

[2] Memorandum by Currie of a conversation with Count Herbert Bismarck, 26 March 1889: loose papers, Pte Salisbury Papers.

[3] Wolff to Salisbury, confidential, Berlin, 12 October 1889, endorsed 'The Queen': F.O. 60/502.

[4] Wolff to Salisbury, decypher telegram, very secret, Berlin, 13 October 1889: F.O. 60/503. Cp. Lee, op. cit., i, 686–8; he overlooks, as do many other writers, the joint development aspect of Wolff's Anglo-Russian programme.

[5] Wolff to Salisbury, secret and confidential, Vienna, 14 October 1889, endorsed 'The Queen': F.O. 65/1379; reproduced in full in Wolff, op. cit., ii, 368–70.

Russian traps.[1] Sir Philip Currie, on the other hand, commended Wolff's skilful handling of the Emperor. Optimistically he wrote to Lord Salisbury: 'I think, after what we have obtained, the Russians, whether they like it or not, must go in for developing Persia.'[2]

Sanderson and Currie composed a dispatch for Petersburg, and Lord Salisbury praised it as a 'well-drawn draft'. This and the dispatch of 21 February 1888 are two of the fundamental official explanations of Persian policy and of its Anglo-Russian refinements. The principles put forward in the previous instructions were re-stated. The British continued to hope that Persia's material and political progress might be accompanied by increased friendship instead of jealousy and discord between the two major powers. The preliminary efforts of Wolff and Dolgorouki were noted, and a more definite invitation to open negotiations for an understanding was extended.[3] Still, Lord Salisbury shared the Queen's doubts at least to some extent. In a telegram which intercepted Wolff at Constantinople, he set forth the salient features of the dispatch to Morier and authorized Wolff to continue conversations at Tehran. But, he warned, 'The discussions will require careful conduct. Material development may mean [to Russia] only an easier way to Herat.'[4]

Queen Victoria and Sir Robert Morier rarely agreed, least of all about Russia. She made little attempt to conceal her dissatisfaction with Morier's management of the St. Petersburg Embassy.[5] Not only the Queen, but Liberal and Conservative Foreign Secretaries alike collided with their ambassador's recalcitrant nature. 'Sir R. Morier's despatches are expositions of Russian not British policy', complained Lord Rosebery,[6] and

---

[1] The Queen to Salisbury, private, 2 June 1888, 19 October 1889, and 5 November 1889: loose papers, Pte Salisbury Papers.

[2] Currie to Salisbury, private, undated but filed between 3 and 14 October 1889: loose papers, Pte Salisbury Papers.

[3] Salisbury to Morier, No. 307, draft dispatch, 28 October 1889: F.O. 65/1379.

[4] Salisbury to Wolff, unnumbered, draft telegram, secret, 21 October 1889: F.O. 60/503.

[5] The Queen to Rosebery, 3 March 1886, in G. E. Buckle, *Letters of Queen Victoria*, Third Series, i, 70. The Queen to Salisbury, private, 6 August 1886; same to same, 17 November 1886; same to same, 17 February 1887; same to same, 14 November 1889; same to same, 18 February 1890: loose papers, Pte Salisbury Papers.

[6] Rosebery to The Queen, 4 March 1886: *Letters of Queen Victoria*, Third Series, i, 72.

Lord Iddesleigh alleged: 'he [Morier] . . . writes as if he enjoyed a controversy with his own chief much more than with M. de Giers'.[1] The Queen and Sir Robert, unusually agreeing together, took the same unfavourable view of Wolff's negotiations with the Emperor.

Morier preached settlement with Russia with the persistency of monomania, but he preached settlement in Bulgaria. In his correspondence with Lord Salisbury about Persia he repeatedly used the phrase 'let sleeping dogs lie'. After Wolff's appointment he was uncooperative if not obstructive. 'I fear I shall have no means at my disposal to prevent the Shah when here from signing IOU's. It will be Wolff's business to prevent his meeting them', Morier told Lord Salisbury in 1889.[2] Originally, Wolff had planned his itinerary back to Persia to include St. Petersburg, but Morier effectively discouraged this visit. Giers, who had not relished locking horns with Wolff over Persia—indeed the very suggestion 'seemed to produce a kind of shiver'[3]—received the news of Morier's victory with a 'satisfied chuckle'.[4]

The Foreign Office dispatch concerning Persia coupled with orders to transmit to Giers the summary of Wolff's audience with Alexander III had a dampening effect. Morier's displeasure at Wolff's 'Pauline appeal to Caesar', though hidden in brilliant prose, occasionally betrays itself. According to him, Giers listened uncomfortably to the recital of Wolff's interview, and observed that it was 'exceedingly rare that the Emperor entered into political conversation with anyone'. Indeed, Giers told Morier that in his own interview with the Czar he 'had playfully alluded to the fact that he himself (the Czar) had fallen into the trap which he (Giers) had with HM approval avoided!'[5]

[1] Iddesleigh to Salisbury, confidential, 16 September 1886: loose papers, Pte Salisbury Papers.

[2] Morier to Salisbury, private, 17 April 1889: bound volume, Russia, Pte Salisbury Papers. Cp. Smith, *White*, p. 171.

[3] Morier to Salisbury, private, 3 September 1889: bound volume, Russia, Pte Salisbury Papers. Salisbury to Morier, private telegram, 29 August 1889: bound volume, Russia, Pte Salisbury Papers.

[4] Morier to Salisbury, No. 330, very confidential, 25 October 1889, endorsed 'The Queen': F.O. 65/1379.

[5] Morier to Salisbury, No. 342, secret, 6 November 1889, endorsed 'The Queen:

Giers received the proposals regarding Persia pessimistically. He recounted the difficulties involved in raising Persia to a higher level of civilization. Furthermore, Russian finances were in no condition to permit expenditure abroad since M. Wyshnegradsky had more projects to provide for within Russia than funds. Giers spoke glumly of Great Britain's experience, capital, and resources, and argued that this superior equipment for launching enterprises in Persia was inconsistent with the Russians' prospering there.[1] He would have agreed with what Dolgorouki said to Wolff: 'the principal difficulty in the way of an arrangement was the fact that where British commerce flourished, Russian trade failed.'[2]

Morier, taking his cue from Giers, discouraged the whole concept of developing Persia. He referred to a memorandum from General Brackenbury, the Director of Military Intelligence, denouncing the promotion of railway building in northern Persia as 'little short of treason'. Morier explained that 'co-operation in Persia' to Giers and the Emperor meant railway construction—in the north by the Russians and in the south by the British.[3]

A week later Giers returned to the subject of Wolff's Berlin stroke. He maintained that the British diplomat had misunderstood his Emperor on two vital issues:

The first had reference to the parties between whom the negotiations contemplated should take place. The Emperor's wish had been to convey that they should be carried on between the two Governments (de gouvernement à gouvernement) and not at Tehran between the representatives of the two governments.

The second touched the concluding words attributed by Sir Henry Wolff to His Majesty, when the Czar used '*almost*' the words "we have no interests in common in Europe. Our common interests lie in Asia. There I desire to live in friendship with her (England) and to establish an understanding which will enable us to be friends,"

Prince of Wales': F.O. 65/1379. Same to same, private, 8 November 1889: bound volume, Russia, Pte Salisbury Papers.

[1] Morier to Salisbury, No. 341, secret and confidential, 6 November 1889, endorsed 'The Queen': F.O. 65/1379.

[2] Wolff, *op. cit.*, ii, 346.

[3] Morier to Salisbury, No. 353, most secret, 13 November 1889, endorsed 'The Queen, Intelligence Department, Lord Cross'; Salisbury added 'Prince of Wales': F.O. 65/1379.

K

His Majesty did not intend to contrast Europe and Asia, as they appear drawn upon a map but Europe and the East. His meaning distinctly was that, whilst England and Russia had few common interests in European Europe (if I may so call it), their common interests lay in the East, that is in Asia, and if I may so say, in Asiatic Europe. It was here and especially in the so called Eastern question that we both had great interests on which we were at present divided and on which, as is well known, the Emperor desires to arrive at an understanding with us.[1]

Great was the discrepancy. Morier suggested that the mis-understanding had conceivably arisen because the Emperor was shy and his French was not fluent.[2] Wolff countered by saying that the Czar spoke excellent French.[3] The Wolff–Morier controversy raged around these issues for the remainder of their professional lives, and the lack of co-operation between Tehran and St. Petersburg inevitably brought all schemes for Anglo-Russian co-operation in Persia to the ground. Lord Salisbury expressed his opinions in a private letter to Wolff:

I hope that the great Wolff-Morier conflict on the question of Persian railways is approaching its truce. I always thought your interview with the Czar a mistake. Giers was certain to look upon it as poaching, & to do what in him lay to prevent it having any effect: & that is what has happened. But I do not applaud Morier's treat-ment of the difficulty—which he did little to remedy or diminish. As for the railways—I have never believed in an agreement with Russia —not because I doubted the value of such an agreement if honestly carried out—but because I thought the light of the past sufficient to show that co-operation of the most formal kind was the utmost that was to be expected. The Emperor is probably honest—but he is probably unique among Russians in that respect. An agreement would have been at best a truce from which neither side could hope anything except the opportunity of gaining time. I do not say that it is not wise to *ask* for an Agreement: but it would not be at all wise to trust it, if obtained. The Russians are deceptive in the same way that

[1] Morier to Salisbury, No. 361, most secret, 20 November 1889, endorsed 'The Queen, Prince of Wales': F.O. 65/1379. Salisbury to Wolff, private, 10 December 1889: bound volume, Persia, Pte Salisbury Papers.

[2] Morier to Salisbury, secret and separate, 27 November 1889, endorsed 'The Queen, Prince of Wales': F.O. 65/1379. Same to same, private, 20 November 1889: bound volume, Russia, Pte Salisbury Papers.

[3] Wolff to Salisbury, No. 37, 5 February 1890, endorsed 'The Queen, Prince of Wales': F.O. 60/509.

they are aggressive. The Czar would deny, probably with perfect honesty, that he is either one or another. He does not tell his officers to lie: or to invade territory that does not belong to him. But when they lie, or encroach, he has to approve what they have done and to accept all the responsibility of their acts.[1]

Wolff left Persia in the spring of 1891 after a breakdown in health. His departure was a great loss, but his experience was of value after his return to England. In 1891 the Persia question, both *per se* and in its Anglo-Russian setting, was passing through one of its critical phases. Lord Salisbury requested Wolff to draw up a memorandum setting forth the condition of the country and possible alternative policies. This memorandum was considered by the Cabinet. Again, one of the features of Wolff's Persian policy was an understanding with Russia.[2]

The possibility of coming to an agreement over Persia was put forward by Wolff's successor, Sir Frank Lascelles. Lord Rosebery studied the question thoroughly and asked for the Wolff papers.[3] But the crisis over the Pamirs so strained relations between the two countries that negotiations for an understanding were not feasible. Tentative approaches to Russia were made by Lord Salisbury in 1896 and 1898 and by Lord Lansdowne in 1900–1. Not until 1907, under Sir Edward Grey, was a convention between England and Russia concluded.[4] One of the few Eastern authorities who approved of the 1907 agreement was Sir Henry Drummond Wolff.[5] Yet the Grey Convention bore little resemblance to Wolff's plan since it failed to provide for the development of Persia and constituted essentially a division of the country into spheres of influence. That such an arrangement offered any real solution is certainly open to doubt.

[1] Salisbury to Wolff, private, 27 May 1890: bound volume, Persia, Pte Salisbury Papers.

[2] Memorandum by Wolff, secret and confidential, 21 April 1891, printed for the use of the Foreign Office, 5 May 1891; Draft memorandum, endorsed by Salisbury 'To be printed for Queen & Cabinet—but not to go abroad. S. April 27, 91': F.O. 65/1413. He never abandoned the idea of an understanding with Russia; for example, Wolff to Salisbury, private, 8 October 1899: loose papers, Pte Salisbury Papers.

[3] Currie to Rosebery and minute by Rosebery, 28 October 1892: F.O. 60/533.

[4] For the full text of the convention together with a map of Persia showing the areas of the respective spheres of influence, see *B.D.*, iv, 618–20.

[5] Wolff, *op. cit.*, ii, 372, 378.

Persian issues grew even more acute during the years from 1907 to 1914, Russian aggressiveness intensified, and Sir Edward Grey reflected: 'Persia tried my patience more than any other subject.'[1]

[1] Grey of Fallodon, *Twenty-five Years, 1892–1916*, i, 169.

CHAPTER IX

The Persian Problem, 1885–8
The Buffer Principle as a Practical Policy

THROUGHOUT the whole of the nineteenth century there were two main threads running through Great Britain's Persian policy. The weaker one was 'agreement with Russia'. This line of policy periodically faded away, but in spite of all its defects it persistently re-emerged with ever-increasing tendencies towards predominance. The buffer principle, by contrast, was the strong and unbroken cord. Statesmen pursued the buffer state policy with varying points of emphasis and with violent fluctuations in the degree of success achieved. It, nevertheless, supplied British policy in Persia with such elements of consistency and reality as it possessed.

The preservation of a zone of outlying independent states on the fringe of her Indian Empire was England's answer to the challenge of Russia's Asiatic drive. By the 1880's Russia's southward movement had assumed menacing proportions and had begun to look as if it would never stop. Nicolson's experience in Persia convinced him that the approach of his country's rival 'towards the Indian Frontier was no mere Cossack adventurism but some slow tidal movement'.[1]

Judged by European standards, Russian governments were primitive and crude indeed. Yet the political practices of the Czars were at any rate less barbaric than those of the bordering khanates and countries. One by one the little states gravitated towards the neighbouring colossus. Local Russian officials hastened this natural trend by military pressure and internal intrigue. The Turkomans and Uzbeks, and even many Persians and Afghans, gradually came to envisage the giant to the north

[1] Nicolson, *op. cit.*, p. 59.

as the cynosure of the Asiatic peoples. Russian border officers actively promoted deterioration in the successive frontier regions as a premeditated technique in softening a country or group of people staked out for annexation. The Czar and Giers, at least nominally, disavowed the 'rotting process'. But the powerful military party in St. Petersburg, backed by such men as Zinovieff, Kapnist, and Chichkine, believed in Russia's ruling destiny, and worked for it with crusading faith and dogged determination. They competed with the more moderate Foreign Office officials for control of policy, and acted as defence counsel for overzealous officers whose incursions into adjacent states or massacres of Turkomans had become too outrageous to pass unnoticed. Sir Robert Morier, in a typical analysis of Russia's Persian policy, wrote:

The worse the condition of these neighbours therefore, the more hopeless their squalour and decadence, the nearer she [Russia] is to the attainment of her goal and the less she can look with equanimity on any attempts made to endow them with the blessings of civilisation otherwise than as annexes of the Russian Empire; therefore, that Persians and other Asiatics similarly situated should go on stewing in their own gravy is the simple *credo* which she opposes to your earnest prayers for joint energetic action.[1]

While statesmen from the banks of the Neva watched Persia's stagnation with contentment and satisfaction, the British struggled to avert her transformation into a Russian province or puppet state. Several motives account for this interest. Russian control over the north-eastern province of Khorassan would bring the Russians within striking distance of Seistan, and have the effect of turning the flank of the British land defences in Afghanistan. The backbone of Sir Edward Grey's case for the Anglo-Russian Convention was the 'real' strategic gain achieved by the safeguarding of Seistan.[2] It was also known that the Russians contemplated, in their long-range plans, the construction of railways connecting their trans-Caspian system with a port on the Gulf. Besides breaking the British monopoly in the Persian Gulf, this would have much the same effect as

[1] Morier to Salisbury, No. 330, very confidential, 25 October 1889, endorsed 'The Queen': F.O. 65/1379.
[2] Grey to Nicolson, private, 24 February 1908: *B.D.*, iv, 616-17.

the occupation of Herat and Seistan. Finally, when Russia wielded an iron grip over Central Asia and entrenched herself firmly in Persia, she could apply pressure from those positions to influence Britain's policy in Europe.

In hammering out Persian and Central Asian policy, Lord Salisbury laid down the main lines, made many decisions on immediate questions, and wrote frequently to his minister in Persia and to the Viceroy of India. The Foreign Secretary's second-in-command was Sir Philip Currie. His minutes on Persian policy outnumber those of any other individual, but Lord Salisbury personally drafted and revised a surprising amount of the outgoing correspondence. Both the Foreign Secretary and his subordinate realized that the Czar's empire waxed strong on the weakness of its neighbours. Zinovieff, one of Russia's most astute policy makers, prophesied that Persia would soon fall like an overripe pear, and 'we will walk in when the time comes without striking a blow'. Currie's answer was that 'Our policy should be, as far as we can, to *make* Persia *something*.'[1]

In the task of strengthening Persia the British encountered resistance not only from the Russians but from the Persians as well. The Shah's inertia was partly justifiable. At the close of the nineteenth century two trends prevailed in his realm—the ever-tightening shackles of foreign domination, and the rapid internal disintegration. Russia ruled the trans-Caucasian and trans-Caspian regions, held the Caspian as a national lake, and negotiated for control over the rich frontier provinces of Azerbaijan, Gilan, Mazandaran, and Khorassan. Confronted with overwhelming strength along a 1,200-mile frontier and with his only efficient military unit officered by Cossacks, the Shah lived with a pistol at his head. Nasir ad-Din's sympathies seem unmistakably pro-British, but he was thoroughly cowed by Russian might. In this conflict of emotions, fear emerged predominant.[2]

[1] Memorandum by Currie on Persian Railways, 16 March 1889: F.O. 65/1378. Thornton to Granville, No. 65, confidential, 12 March 1883: F.O. 65/1151. Kennedy to Currie, private, 13 March 1884: F.O. 65/1204. Same to same, private, 8 October 1884: F.O. 65/1211.

[2] Thomson to Granville, No. 44, confidential, 7 April 1885: F.O. 65/1239. Nicolson to Salisbury, No. 12, secret, 10 January 1888: F.O. 65/1347. Nicolson to

The Russians did not constitute the only obstacle to Persian regeneration. In the last decade of his life, the Shah thought more of his personal indulgence than of his country's welfare and preferred tent life to the affairs of state. With few exceptions Nasir ad-Din surrounded himself with uninspiring and parasitic men who undermined reforms, discouraged innovations, and nurtured suspicions of western enterprise.

A notable exception was Mirza Ali Asghar Khan, the Amin as-Sultan (Trusted of the Sovereign). Although he lacked the advantages of noble birth, he had by 1888 gathered for himself the offices of Minister of the Palace, the Interior, of Finance, and Customs. In practice he was Foreign Minister. He supervised other departments, and the headquarters of several ministries were in his house. At the age of thirty he had reached a position which 'few functionaries in Persia have hitherto enjoyed'.[1] After the Shah, over whom he exerted considerable influence, the Amin as-Sultan was the most important individual in Persia. He was alive to the dangers which threatened his country. Although his first consideration was probably to further his own ambitions, nevertheless he seems to have tried in these years to support whatever course would push Persia into the path of progress and did not hesitate to use British assistance for this end. He had many enemies. He was thoroughly unacceptable to the Russians, and he was the constant target of court intrigue. His position was substantially weakened in 1892 as a result of the events connected with the tobacco concession. His attitude towards the British also changed. Near the end of his reign Nasir ad-Din bestowed upon him the title of Sadr A'zam (Grand Vizier). He was dismissed in disgrace upon the accession of the new Shah in 1896, but was later recalled and raised to Atabeg A'zam—a title which he held until 1903.[2]

Currie, private, 12 January 1888: F.O. 60/492. Wolff to Salisbury, private, 20 May 1888: bound volume, Persia, Pte Salisbury Papers. Same to same, No. 172, most secret and confidential, 5 September 1888, endorsed 'The Queen': F.O. 65/1353.

Case 555, Memorandum by Durand on the Present Position in Central Asia, 21 May 1887: Home Correspondence, Political and Secret Department, vol. xciv, India Office Records.

[1] Nicolson to Salisbury, No. 33, 20 March 1888, endorsed 'The Queen': F.O. 65/1348.

[2] Wolff to Salisbury, No. 188, most secret and confidential, 10 April 1890, endorsed 'For the Queen, Prince of Wales': F.O. 60/517. Miscellaneous Papers,

In his latter years the Shah's idiosyncrasies became more pronounced. He doted on cats; he bestowed the rank of Field Marshal in the Persian army upon a child of twelve[1]—a child moreover who before he was fifteen had made more than one attempt on the life of his patron and king. A British Legation secretary described the lad as a 'snake seedling'.[2] The moods and unpredictability of the Persian ruler affected his conduct of state business. Today's project was shelved tomorrow. Little that was constructive emanated from Tehran. Curzon, upon returning from his travels in Persia, maintained: 'The Shah is about as likely to undertake a genuinely great public work as he is to turn Protestant.'[3]

In the final analysis, the main reason for Nasir ad-Din's inaction was his determination to avoid crises and to have the remainder of his days in peace. The embers of internal discontent smouldered in the eighties and were clearly discernible.[4] The Shah proclaimed few measures designed to alleviate the misery of his people; however, he hoped that the flames of revolution would not burst forth until after his death. But this hope was not fulfilled. In 1896, as he entered the Mosque of Shah Abdul Azim to hear the Friday prayers, an assassin's bullet killed him.

Nasir ad-Din also strove to postpone the day of reckoning with Russia. If he remained inactive, he reasoned, the Russians would have no excuse for intensifying their harassing tactics on the frontier. The Shah was haunted by the nightmare of a Russian ultimatum which would deprive him of territory and infringe his sovereign rights. The resolution to retain his power unimpaired was the corollary to his 'live in peace' principle. The British understood all this. Lord Salisbury wrote privately to Sir Frank Lascelles:

. . . if circ[umstanc]es move you, as well they may, to try & diminish in any respect or instance the misgovernment under which the Persians labour, you should be very careful not to inspire the Shah

Rough Notes, etc., by Colonel Ardagh, confidential: case entitled 'Persia. Reigning Family and Official Hierarchy', P.R.O. 30/40/12.

[1] Curzon, *Persia and the Persian Question*, i, 399–400.
[2] Lascelles to Salisbury and enclosures, No. 116, secret, 15 July 1892, endorsed 'The Queen': F.O. 60/532.   [3] Curzon, *Persia and the Persian Question*, ii, 317.
[4] See for example Nicolson to Salisbury, No. 35, 25 March 1887: F.O. 60/486.

with suspicion that you have any settled plan for diminishing his power. He has a mortal dread of reform, & of all that may lead to it, & the fear lest measures for the development of his country should issue in the curtailment of his own power, stands for very much in the passive resistance which he has offered to most of our attempts to benefit his people. If he once suspects you mean to clip his wings, he will start away from you, & never let you get near him again.[1]

In order to implement their buffer policy the British repeatedly attempted to induce the Shah to build roads, construct railways, and open the Karun river to navigation. The years over which these negotiations spread slipped into decades. Still, by 1885, no roads other than pack-saddle trails existed, no railroads connected Persia's cities, and no steamer traffic plied along the Karun. When the Shah was frightened by Russia's annexation of Merv and frantically appealed to Gladstone's government for assistance, Lord Granville urged him to facilitate ingress by providing good roads and by opening the Karun.[2] No tangible results ensued.

Lord Salisbury's conception of Persia's position in British foreign policy germinated in the decade of the seventies—when he was Secretary of State for India and later Foreign Secretary.[3] He attached greater significance to the Persian question than did his Liberal countrymen, and he encouraged internal development schemes more earnestly and hopefully. In his 1885 conversations with Malkom Khan, Lord Salisbury stressed both the importance of grappling with the evils of a corrupt administrative system and of constructing roads and railways from the Gulf inland.[4] This advice was relayed to the Shah. Nasir

[1] Salisbury to Lascelles, private, 6 October 1891: bound volume, Persia, Pte Salisbury Papers. Sir Frank Lascelles succeeded Sir Henry Drummond Wolff as minister to Persia.

[2] Granville to Thomson, draft dispatch, 16 August 1884: F.O. 65/1209. The rough outline of this communication is in Granville's hand, but Kimberley revised the dispatch extensively.

[3] For his Persian negotiations of 1879-80, see above, pp. 50-1. His interest in Persia also reveals itself in many small ways. For example: dispatches in the commercial series rarely bore endorsements by the Foreign Secretary; Commercial No. 3 from Tehran, 30 July 1879, however, analysed the importance of improving transportation in southern Persia. It was endorsed by Lord Salisbury 'Print. Circulate to Anatolian Consuls—Bagdad—Damascus—Bayrout': F.O. 60/424.

[4] Salisbury to Thomson, No. 75A, draft dispatch, 6 August 1885, endorsed 'The Queen, Lord Iddesleigh': F.O. 60/468. See also another draft of this same document in F.O. 65/1248.

ad-Din did not respond to the communication warmly, but instead adopted a resentful tone. Again, action did not follow.

In one of his last official dispatches Sir Ronald Thomson recapitulated the story of his own negotiations for Persian reform and improved transport. He maintained that the Legation had strained every nerve in sponsoring such measures. Nor could the absence of roads be explained by lack of foreign capital. Persia's retrograde condition, the British minister asserted, must be 'attributed to the strong disinclination of the Shah himself to grant the Karun concession or to seriously enter even into a discussion of projects of internal development and improvement.'[1]

Sir Ronald Thomson returned to England on leave from Persia late in 1885. Subsequently, he resigned his post because of ill-health. For several years thereafter, however, he acted as an adviser on Persian affairs, and attended official meetings in London. Upon the minister's departure in 1885, when Arthur Nicolson took over the management of the Legation, he immediately interested himself enthusiastically in the problem of Persia's internal communications, in this continuing the efforts made by his predecessor.[2]

In May 1886 the Shah suddenly announced his conversion to progress, and stated his belief in the 'absolute necessity' of facilitating ingress from the Persian Gulf. He preferred the construction of a railway by a European or a Perso-European company. Nasir ad-Din also declared that the opening of the Karun would follow the railroad as a natural consequence. If the railway project proved impracticable, he would revert to road-building. Nicolson's representations undoubtedly account, at least partially, for this *volte face*, but other factors may have had bearing on it.

The Shah had recently elevated Yahya Khan, the Mushir ad-Dowleh, to the post of Minister for Foreign Affairs. Yahya Khan's pro-Russian proclivities were notorious, and he had for many years induced the Shah to make territorial concessions to

[1] Thomson to Salisbury, No. 111, 28 September 1885, endorsed 'Lord Iddesleigh': F.O. 60/470.

[2] Harold Nicolson in his life of Lord Carnock, however, leaves the reader with the impression that Arthur Nicolson initiated the idea of improving transportation and opening the Karun river. Nicolson, *op. cit.*, p. 63.

Russia. His return boded ill for British influence.[1] Sir Philip Currie called Lord Rosebery's attention to the appointment.

Sir Ronald Thomson, our Minister at Tehran, spoke to me yesterday about the recent app[ointmen]t as Foreign Minister of Yahya Khan, who is known to be a creature of the Russians, and of the probability that he will connive at further cessions to Russia of territory in Khorassan. The result of this would be very injurious to our own interests, as it would enable Russia to push southwards along the left bank of the Herirud towards Seistan, and thus to turn the flank of the N[orth] W[estern] boundary of Afghanistan.[2]

While deferring to Russia by favouring Yahya Khan, the Shah also angled for a territorial guarantee from England. Expediency dictated, therefore, at least an outward display of interest in traditional British projects.

The Foreign Office responded with alacrity to the Shah's sudden preoccupation with railway-building. Sir Philip Currie, after calling attention to Baron Reuter's prior claims, urged a speedy decision: 'The matter should be considered *at once* with Sir R[onald] Thomson & the India Office, as we ought to clench it before the Shah changes his mind.'[3] A telegram was soon on its way to Nicolson instructing him to express 'gratification' over the decision and to inform the Persian Government that the project was receiving 'immediate consideration'.[4]

The Foreign Office became the headquarters for Persian railway conferences. Sir Philip Currie apparently assumed the administrative burden and conducted the discussions when more pressing business precluded the attendance of the Foreign Secretary. The India Office sent Sir Owen Tudor Burne as its

---

[1] Thomson to Currie, private, 19 March 1886: F.O. 65/1284. Appointed Minister for Foreign Affairs early in 1886, Yahya Khan, the Mushir ad-Dowleh, resigned that post in July 1887. He was reputed to have been the key figure in the intrigue which led to the escape of Eyoub Khan from Tehran. His behaviour at this time made him still more *persona ingrata* to the British. Yahya Khan held other offices afterwards, but he continued to work, without success, for reinstatement as Foreign Minister. He died of pneumonia in January 1892. An interesting summary of his life is given in Lascelles to Salisbury, No. 38, 18 February 1892, endorsed 'The Queen': F.O. 60/532.

[2] Memorandum by Currie for Lord Rosebery, 19 March 1886: F.O. 65/1284.

[3] Minute on Nicolson to Rosebery, No. 88, decypher telegram, 17 May 1886: F.O. 60/481.

[4] Rosebery to Nicolson, No. 25, draft telegram, 18 May 1886: F.O. 60/481.

representative. Lord Kimberley and Lord Cross, however, kept abreast of the consultations.[1] Sir Ronald Thomson regularly attended the sessions, and supplied information from the local point of view. Two business men, Sir William Mackinnon and Sir George Mackenzie, completed the group. They immediately computed Persian railway costs and estimated future returns on the investment.[2]

On the British side the consideration appears to have been sincere and realistic. Experts scrutinized the possible routes. Draft concessions were formulated, subjected to searching criticism, and then revised.[3] In Tehran, meanwhile, firmness and conviction gave way to haggling and delay as the Shah renounced his former stand. Less than two weeks had elapsed since Nasir ad-Din had approached Nicolson. Already, however, the Persian spoke timorously of Russian reprisals.

The Shah's initial modification of policy was comparatively minor. He asked that the railway be constructed by the nationals of a remote and neutral Power—preferably America. The official attitude towards the hypothetical American company indicates that the British genuinely thought in terms of Persian advancement, not merely of their own developments in that country. The Foreign Office welcomed the newcomers since 'the great thing is to get the Railway made'.[4] Two ministers in particular from the United States, Mr. S. G. W. Benjamin and Mr. E. Spencer Pratt, endeavoured vainly to interest their Government in sponsoring enterprises in Persia, and emphasized the benefits which would accrue from railway construction. In 1886 a private American scheme was submitted to the Shah, who did nothing about it. The British denounced

[1] Case 1245, 'Persia, Railway projects', 12 August 1886: Home Correspondence, Political and Secret Department, vol. xc, India Office Records.
[2] India Office to Foreign Office and minute by Currie, secret and immediate, 27 May 1886: F.O. 65/1286. India Office to Foreign Office, secret, 15 June 1886, with enclosure, Note on a Railway for Southern Persia by Colonel E. C. S. Williams, India Office, secret, 12 June 1886: F.O. 65/1287.
[3] See for example: Draft Concession for the Formation of a Railway from Ahwaz to Tehran, viâ Dizful, Khoramabad, Buroojird, Sultanabad, and Küm, confidential, printed for the use of the Foreign Office, 11 January 1887: F.O. 60/485.
[4] Nicolson to Rosebery and minute by Currie, No. 98, decypher telegram, 28 May 1886: F.O. 60/481.

the plan as 'visionary', and then redoubled their own efforts.[1]

Nasir ad-Din's preference for a neutral Power was natural, but his subsequent waverings throw doubt upon the sincerity of his request for the railway. Mackenzie, after consulting with Mackinnon and Baron Reuter, prepared a draft concession.[2] It was therefore possible for Nicolson to present the Shah with a tentative outline less than a month after having received the initial appeal. The British envisaged the formation of an international company, domiciled in London, which would undertake to construct a narrow-gauge line from Ahwaz to Burujird, with an extension to Tehran and branch lines to follow later. For his part the Shah should furnish the land and timber. Since the railway could not be sufficiently remunerative in its first few years of operation the Company should be allowed to take over the management of the customs of Bushire, Moham-merah, and Shushtar as a temporary expedient. Nasir ad-Din was guaranteed a yearly sum equivalent to his annual return under Persian management, and he would receive in addition the amount that remained after the company had paid a seven per cent dividend. The company thus considered opening the Karun a *sine qua non*.[3]

The Shah objected to the customs provisions; then shifted ground completely. His enthusiasm for railways waned, and road-building absorbed attention for the moment. Nicolson told Nasir ad-Din frankly that such vacillation made the work of negotiation 'weary and disheartening', but he recommended nevertheless to his own superiors that the new project be received in a co-operative spirit.[4] Currie investigated the cost of roads, and estimated the expenditure required to be only

[1] Nicolson to Rosebery, No. 100, decypher telegram, 31 May 1886: F.O. 60/481. Rosebery to Nicolson, No. 28, draft dispatch, 31 May 1886: F.O. 60/481. Translation of Memorandum given to Mr. Nicolson by the Shah, 28 May 1886: F.O. 65/1286. Memorandum written by Mr. Nicolson and sent to the Shah, 28 May 1886, in reply to His Majesty's Memorandum: F.O. 65/1286.

[2] Foreign Office to India Office, secret, 4 June 1886: F.O. 65/1287. Nicolson to Rosebery and minute by Currie, No. 102, decypher telegram, 2 June 1886: F.O. 60/481.

[3] Rosebery to Nicolson, No. 31, draft telegram, 4 June 1886: F.O. 60/481.

[4] Nicolson to Rosebery, No. 115, text telegram, 10 June 1886: F.O. 65/1287. Same to same, No. 77, 11 June 1886; same to same, No. 81, 21 June 1886: F.O. 65/1287.

slightly below the amount calculated for the railway.[1] Nicolson expatiated incessantly to Nasir ad-Din 'on the necessity of doing something', and felt reasonably certain of obtaining a road if not a railway. Early in July, however, the Shah departed abruptly for the hills, and the negotiations fell into temporary abeyance.[2]

In England, the month of July brought a Conservative victory at the polls. Lord Salisbury again became Prime Minister. His first choice for the office of Foreign Secretary was Lord Iddesleigh, but in January 1887 he took over that position himself. Lord Cross was Secretary of State for India.

Persian railway talks were resumed. The British prepared draft concession after draft concession, but the shadow of fear hung over Tehran. Trepidation over possible Russian retaliation and anxiety over his authority being curbed by Western innovations combined to lessen the Shah's desire for internal improvements. He became progressively more dubious as the negotiations became more concrete, and his attitude did not augur favourably for the ultimate success of the scheme. As the British revised drafts, the Persians raised fresh objections.[3]

The Shah ingeniously invented excuses for maintaining the *status quo*. He spoke intermittently about his preference for a neutral power, and he sounded warnings over too rapid changes, but his most consistent objection to the British proposals concerned the hypothecation of his customs. The negotiations eventually broke down on the financial issue.[4] The British finally realized that the Shah was adamant about the customs, and they attempted to solve the money question by other means. Neither Mackinnon nor Mackenzie felt able to help to build Persian railroads without a guarantee, reminded the Foreign

[1] Foreign Office to India Office, secret and immediate, 22 June 1886: F.O. 65/1287. Minute by Currie on Nicolson to Foreign Office, No. 124, 21 June 1886: F.O. 60/481.

[2] Nicolson to Currie, private, 1 July 1886: F.O. 65/1288.

[3] Nicolson to Iddesleigh, No. 133, 26 October 1886: F.O. 65/1292. Nicolson to Currie, private, 29 October 1886: F.O. 60/480. Salisbury to Nicolson and enclosures, No. 2, 11 January 1887: F.O. 60/485.

[4] Nicolson to Salisbury, No. 33, 21 March 1887: F.O. 60/486, Nicolson to Currie, private, 30 March 1887: F.O. 60/486. Nicolson to Salisbury, No. 43, 30 March 1887; same to same, No. 62, confidential, 4 May 1887: F.O. 60/486. Salisbury to Nicolson, No. 57, 24 June 1887: F.O. 60/485.

Office that the project had its origin in that office, but promised to assist with the enterprise as a public service if proper financial arrangements could be made.[1]

Lord Cross, in a letter of 5 March 1887 of his own drafting,[2] set forth the salient features of his stronger policy. He believed that England should demonstrate more tangibly her active interest in the welfare of Persia. With regard to the railway, he said:

... even if the Shah's acquiescence be obtained ... it may be found difficult to obtain the necessary funds from the English public for the carrying out of the scheme without some guarantee from the Imperial and Indian Governments; but he proposes to communicate on this matter with the Government of India, and to address the Secretary of State for Foreign Affairs separately in regard to it when the occasion shall arise.[3]

On this occasion the Government of India were unable to co-operate. The Viceroy and his Council acknowledged the significance of Persia, and the need for taking steps which would recover Britain's once superior position. But they had railroads to build within India itself. They not only refused to carry the entire burden of the guarantee, but even hesitated to share the expense with the Home Government. This decision, however, was reached by a vote of four to three, with the Viceroy, the Commander-in-Chief, and Mr. Scoble dissenting.[4]

Lord Salisbury did not believe that a subscription of English capital would be forthcoming without a guarantee.[5] Searching for a solution to the financial problem, he asked whether the mineral resources in the mountains of southern Persia would be

[1] Memorandum by Mackinnon for Foreign Office on proposed Persian Railway and Navigation Concession, 4 April 1887: F.O. 60/490.

[2] Case 262, Persia—Future Policy towards, 5 March 1887: Home Correspondence, Political and Secret Department, vol. xcii, India Office Records. Minute by Cross of 28 April on Letters from Persia: Persian Correspondence, 1887, vol. cx, India Office Records.

[3] India Office to Foreign Office, secret and immediate, 5 March 1887: F.O. 60/490. India Office to Government of India, No. 13, secret, 22 April 1887: Dispatches to India, Political and Secret, vol. xiii, India Office Records.

[4] Government of India, Foreign Department, to Secretary of State for India, No. 100A, secret/external, 24 June 1887: F.O. 60/490. India Office to Foreign Office and enclosed telegram from Viceroy, 27 June 1887: F.O. 60/490.

[5] Minute by Lord Salisbury of 29 June on India Office to Foreign Office, 27 June 1887: F.O. 60/490.

sufficient to attract capital investment. This inquiry seems to be the first evidence of official interest in natural resources. The report returned was so uninspiring, however, that the matter dropped.[1] The railway discussions proceeded capriciously and with little hope of positive results. The Persians, still anxious for a British assurance, submitted several counter-proposals. The Foreign Office considered them unrealistic and unacceptable. As Lord Salisbury observed, 'We shall never raise a farthing on these terms.'[2] Nevertheless, policy in Persia could not be effective without means of ingress, and as Lord Salisbury laconically put it: 'Unless he [the Shah] will make a railway to the Sea Coast—all advice is bunckum.'[3]

By 1888 the British position had already been compromised. The question was also of importance for Russia, and her agents had not been idle. The Russians planned eventually to connect Persian lines with their own system, but since they could not as yet afford it, they therefore determined to persuade the Shah to postpone construction until the moment was more propitious.[4] By a secret agreement of September 1887 Nasir ad-Din had pledged himself 'not to give orders or permission to construct railways or waterways to Companies of foreign nations *before consulting with His Majesty the Emperor*'.[5] Sir Harold Nicolson was apparently unaware of this Russo-Persian agreement when he wrote:

[1] Minute by Salisbury on Wolff to Salisbury, No. 186, decypher telegram, 30 September 1888: F.O. 60/495. Lord Salisbury's enquiry as to any trustworthy account of the mineral resources of southern Persia, 15 October 1888: F.O. 60/495.
[2] Minute by Salisbury on Nicolson to Salisbury and enclosure, No. 7, 4 January 1888: F.O. 65/1347. See also Observations by Mackenzie on the draft concession communicated by the Persian Government to Mr. Nicolson [17 February 1888]: F.O. 65/1347.
[3] Minute of 4 May by Lord Salisbury on Currie's memorandum concerning his conversation with Malcom Khan, 3 May 1888: F.O. 60/497.
[4] Lamsdorff to Speyer, secret, 30 September/13 October 1904: *Krasny Arkhiv*, liii, 16–17, 34. 'Die zaristische Diplomatie über Russlands Aufgaben im Orient im Jahre 1900', *Die Kriegsschuldfrage*, vi (1928), 649–50; a translation into German of Count Muravieff's Memorandum of 1900 from the Russian in *Krasny Arkhiv*, xviii.
[5] Enclosure No. 2 in Wolff to Salisbury, No. 201, secret and confidential, 1 October 1888: F.O. 60/495. The enclosure is a translation of a secret and confidential Memorandum concluded between the Shah and Prince Dolgorouki in the Month of Zi Hejjeh, 1384 [sic 1304] (21 August to 18 September 1887). This agreement was kept secret for a year. See also Wolff to Salisbury, No. 199, most secret and confidential, 30 September 1888: F.O. 60/495. See below, pp. 166, 180.

L

. . . twelve months after Nicolson's arrival the Shah pledged his word of honour that he would not enter into any secret agreement with Russia without first 'consulting' Her Majesty's Government. This interview took place in a garden: the Shah, grunting enormous under his diamond aigrette, twirling his huge moustaches, sat on one side of a little stream under a bower of jasmine. Nicolson, on the other side of the stream, was shaded by a pine tree. It was in such idyllic circumstances that the pact was made. Nasr-ed-Din Shah, who was a man of honour, maintained his promise in the spirit and the letter.[1]

In striving for their Persian railway the British did not negotiate with the Shah alone. His eldest son, Sultan Mas'ud Mirza, the Zil es-Sultan (Shadow of the King), ruled over much of southern Persia from his palace at Isfahan. Being the son of the Shah by a morganatic marriage, he was disqualified from succeeding his father, but he was a man of conspicuous talents and progressive tendencies. Many of his contemporaries considered him to be the ablest man in Persia.

He had been pensioned off with the governorship of Isfahan, and it was up to him to make what he could of it. The control exerted by Tehran over outlying areas was ineffective, and the Zil enjoyed a free hand in his vaguely defined theatre of ascendancy. Territory after territory was incorporated until, in 1887, he ruled nearly half of Persia—including the provinces of Isfahan, Arabistan, Burujird, Kurdistan, Kermanshah, Kamareh, Luristan, Yazd, Fars, Mahallat, Gulpaigan, Khunsar, Irak and Dargazin. The population of these regions contained good military material. The Zil subdued the warlike and usually uncontrollable tribesmen, and out of these rugged individuals forged a well-drilled and disciplined army.[2] With at least two-fifths of Persia under his sway and with 20,000 admirably trained men as an instrument of persuasion, the Zil seemed a strong candidate for the Peacock Throne despite the legal claims of his half-brother, the Valiahd, in Azerbaijan.

The British therefore cultivated the Zil. Three-fourths of their

---

[1] Nicolson, op. cit., pp. 64–5.

[2] Wolff to Salisbury, separate—secret and confidential, 13 April 1890, endorsed 'For the Queen. Not to be printed': F.O. 60/511. Report on the Persian Army, Compiled in the Intelligence Branch of the Quarter Master General's Department in India, confidential, 1 August 1892: F.O. 60/536.

telegraph lines passed through his territories; while the Zil ruled, trouble in keeping the lines intact was reduced to a minimum. His realm was orderly, and trade flourished. Moreover, he made no secret of his pro-British leanings, and he showed acute awareness of the evils which stemmed from the rapacity abounding in the central government.

Lieutenant-Colonel R. Murdoch Smith, who had supervised the British telegraph system in Persia for twenty years, was sent to Tehran on a special mission in 1887. His primary objective was to renew one of the telegraph conventions, but he was also instructed to promote the railway project if the opportunity arose.[1] He held a most encouraging conversation with his old friend the Zil at Isfahan, who professed friendship for England, said that he would help with the railway, but asked for a 'sign' that his assistance would be welcomed. The Zil said:

But with every desire to do a service to England, and win her friendship, I must think of many things. We Princes, especially those of us who are Asiatic, occupy very precarious positions. Since I first began to be occupied in affairs of Government, and I am hardly 40 years old, what have I myself seen? Abdul Aziz, Sultan of Turkey, kicked off his throne and killed. Khedive Ismail sent off to wander about the different capitals of Europe. Napoleon first a prisoner and then an exile. The Emperor Alexander blown up in the streets. Amir Shir Ali dying while a fugitive, and his sons prisoners, one in India and another in Tehran. Cetewayo, poor devil, carried off to England and sent back to his country, only to have his throat cut. Alexander, of Bulgaria, snapped up in the night. The King of Burmah dethroned, exiled, and imprisoned. All this makes a Prince think.

He did not follow the recital of these ominous precedents with an outright request for support. He asked for a 'sign' that his services were wanted. The 'sign' he wanted was the G.C.S.I.[2]

[1] India Office to Foreign Office, secret and immediate, 5 March 1887: F.O. 60/490. Memorandum by Sanderson on conversation with Smith, 12 March 1887: F.O. 60/490. Foreign Office draft instructions to Smith, 22 March 1887: F.O. 60/490.

[2] Nicolson to Salisbury and enclosures, No. 98, 26 July 1887: F.O. 60/487. The enclosures consist of Colonel Smith's reports of his interviews with the Zil es-Sultan. Smith also had long conversations with the Amin ad-Dowleh, the Amin as-Sultan, the Mushir ad-Dowleh, and the Mukhber ad-Dowleh. See enclosures in Nicolson to Salisbury, No. 96, 22 July 1887, endorsed by Salisbury 'Not hopeful': F.O. 60/488.

The idea of a decoration for the Zil had much to recommend it. The French, a short time previously, had conferred upon him the Grand Cross of the Legion of Honour.[1] Nicolson pointed out that if the 'sign' were refused, the Zil would despair of British friendship and would become more susceptible to Russian cajoleries.[2] There were two conceivable drawbacks— the attitude of the Shah and the jealousy of the Valiahd. But as Nicolson put it in a private letter to Rawlinson:

Although he [the Zil] has many faults he is the only real man in Persia. If it were skilfully done, I do not think the Shah would resent any attention we paid to the Zil. The Valiahd and the other brother might possibly do so, but they are both lost to us & the latter is a wretched creature. But I do think that the Zil is beginning to despair of our being of any support to him: & it is always possible he may make terms with the other side.[3]

A decoration, moreover, committed Great Britain to no definite line of policy, but could be interpreted merely as a recognition of the Zil's distinction.

Both the Foreign Office and the India Office considered the Zil's request within the framework of the larger issues of their policy in southern Persia. Lord Salisbury asked for the opinion of the Council, and expressed his own tendency to concur with Nicolson's recommendations. 'What we want is a hold over the South of Persia', he declared.[4] Sir Henry Rawlinson also inclined to that view. He, like many others, envisaged the breakup of Persia after Nasir ad-Din's death with the Zil ruling the southern regions from Isfahan and the Valiahd holding the north from Tabriz.[5] The India Office had decided in favour of the investiture, and maintained that a 'commanding influence

[1] Nicolson to Salisbury, No. 51, 16 April 1887: F.O. 60/486.
[2] Nicolson to Salisbury, No. 92, decypher telegram, 30 August 1887: F.O. 60/488.
[3] Case 630, Nicolson to Rawlinson, private, 26 April 1887: Home Correspondence, Political and Secret Department, vol. xcv, India Office Records.
[4] Case 630, Minute by Lord Salisbury on Cross to Salisbury, 23 May 1887: Home Correspondence, Political and Secret Department, vol. xcv, India Office Records. See also Case 649, Persia: British Interests in Persia, Bestowal of G.C.S.I. on Zil, Memorandum by Lord Cross: Home Correspondence, Political and Secret Department, vol. xcv, India Office Records.
[5] Case 630, Rawlinson to Neil, 26 May 1887: Home Correspondence, Political and Secret Department, vol. xcv, India Office Records.

in Southern and Central Persia should be secured for the English Government'.[1] Colonel Smith also favoured the more active course since 'to do nothing is to let Russia go on unchecked'.[2] The one dissenting voice was that of Sir Ronald Thomson, who appreciated the wisdom of encouraging the Zil, but he gave a warning against antagonizing other members of the Royal Family.[3]

The India Office decided to confer the decoration, and so advised the Foreign Office.[4] Lord Salisbury authorized Nicolson to proceed with the formalities. He was delighted.[5] The Zil responded warmly to the honour and talked cordially with Nicolson during his visit to Tehran early in 1888.[6] Then, suddenly, the wheel of fortune turned. The Zil, isolated while he was in Tehran, and far from his supporting forces, was compelled to resign all his governorships except Isfahan and was stripped of all but a fragment of his fine army. Currie commented: 'It is unfortunate & shews that we did not bestow the G.C.S.I. wisely.'[7] The Foreign Office instructed Nicolson to proceed carefully since their information indicated that the Shah was in a 'suspicious state' and 'incaution might cost the Zil his life'.[8] Subsequently, however, Nicolson was authorized to explain to the Shah the implications of his unfortunate action upon Anglo-Persian relations. The Shah professed the most

[1] Resolution of the Political Committee, 8 June 1887: Home Correspondence, Political and Secret Department, vol. xcv, India Office Records, H. C. Rawlinson, R. Montgomery, and A. Eden were members of the Political Committee.

[2] Case 905, Zil's Decoration, Smith to Neil, 13 September 1887: Home Correspondence, Political and Secret Department, vol. xcv, India Office Records.

[3] Thomson to Sanderson, private, 31 August 1887: F.O. 60/487.

[4] Case 934, Zil's Decoration, India Office to Foreign Office, 24 September 1887: Home Correspondence, Political and Secret Department, vol. xcvii, India Office Records.

[5] Nicolson to Currie, private, 29 September 1887: F.O. 65/1323. See also Salisbury to Nicolson, No. 43, telegram, 29 August 1887: same to same, No. 52, telegram, 20 September 1887, endorsed 'The Queen': F.O. 60/488. Salisbury to Nicolson, No. 104, extender telegram, 7 November 1887: F.O. 60/485.

[6] Nicolson to Salisbury, No. 16, secret, 30 January 1888, endorsed 'Very interesting. The Queen': F.O. 60/492. Nicolson to Currie, private, 2 February 1888: F.O. 60/492.

[7] Nicolson to Salisbury and minutes, No. 25, decypher telegram, 24 February 1888: F.O. 60/495.

[8] Salisbury to Nicolson, No. 12, secret telegram, 27 February 1888: F.O. 60/494.

friendly feeling for England, but firmly refused to reinstate the Zil.[1]

The reasons for the Zil's fall are still obscure. His rivalry with the Amin as-Sultan and the latter's intrigues with the Shah undoubtedly had some effect. The Shah's own susceptibilities were also probably aroused. Nasir ad-Din might have regarded his son as a potential threat not only because of his widespread and ever-growing domain, but also because of the enterprises he advocated. Nicolson reported that the Zil was going to discuss the railway question with the Shah, impressing upon him the 'absolute necessity of taking some serious step in the direction we desired'. Beside this statement Lord Salisbury wrote: 'This accounts for the whole explosion.'[2] But some saw the hand of Russia. That the incident occurred shortly after a visit of three days by the Russian minister to the Shah's shooting camp seems more than a remarkable coincidence.[3] Ominous too was the robe of honour given to Yahya Khan who had recently become a constant visitor at the palace. He boasted to his friends that he would again be Minister for Foreign Affairs before the New Year, a forecast which did not come true probably because of Nicolson's energetic representations.[4]

Ultimately the Zil received his decoration, but never again did he regain a fraction of the authority he had at his zenith in 1887. The event was untimely since it coincided with a period when the British Government was alive to the importance of Persia and were disposed to depart somewhat from their traditional refusal to pledge themselves to support the Shah in an emergency. While Nasir ad-Din was stripping the Zil of his possessions the British were working out a new attack on the Persian problem. Shortly after the Zil's downfall Nicolson

[1] Nicolson to Salisbury, No. 30, secret, 5 March 1888, endorsed 'The Queen'; same to same, No. 32, confidential, 13 March 1888, endorsed 'The Queen': F.O. 65/1348.

[2] Nicolson to Salisbury and minute, No. 16, secret, 30 January 1888, endorsed 'Very interesting. The Queen': F.O. 60/492.

[3] Nicolson to Salisbury, No. 30, records telegram, 28 February 1888: F.O. 60/496. Same to same, No. 26, confidential, 28 February 1888, endorsed 'The Queen'; same to same, No. 27, secret, 28 February 1888, endorsed 'The Queen': F.O. 65/1347.

[4] Nicolson to Salisbury, No. 29, confidential, 1 March 1888, endorsed 'The Queen': F.O. 65/1348.

delivered to the Shah a formal assurance of Britain's intention—
to uphold the integrity of Persia. In other circumstances, this
message might well have been a step on the way to a closer
relationship between the two countries.[1]

For the British the blow to their prestige was great. Few
decorations were given in later years. The Foreign Office
promptly took up the attitude, when any foreign candidate was
recommended, that 'the result may be as fatal to him as to the
Zil'.[2] Lord Salisbury summarized the effect of the episode in a
letter to Lascelles:

... in the past we have made a mistake, as we have done elsewhere,
by running a special candidate for power. We backed the Zil, the
second son of the Shah, a man of English proclivities & considerable
ability. But we backed him so clumsily that the Shah took fright, &
stripped him of all his dignities & power, & now he is of very little
value. All that we have got from the support we gave him is the ill
will of the eldest son, the Veliahd, who is his competitor in his
father's good graces, & who, by a more reserved line of conduct, has
contrived to maintain his position.[3]

[1] Message communicated to the Shah, 12 March 1888, enclosure in Nicolson
to Salisbury, No. 31, secret, 13 March 1888, endorsed 'The Queen': F.O. 65/1348.
[2] Minute by Currie on Wolff to Salisbury, No. 211, decypher telegram, very
secret, 29 October 1888: F.O. 60/495.
[3] Salisbury to Lascelles, private, 6 October 1891: bound volume, Persia, Pte
Salisbury Papers.

CHAPTER X

The Wolff Mission
Its Contribution to the Buffer Policy, 1888

ALTHOUGH the British were more vitally interested in the south, the cardinal principle of their policy in Persia was to maintain the country intact and to encourage its regeneration and reform.[1] The success of any undertaking, whether it concerned the north or the south, depended upon the influence of the minister in Tehran. That influence was almost always proportionate to his standing in his home country. This applied not only to Britain but to Russia. Thus, in spite of all his faults, Dolgorouki served Russia well. He was a Prince and one of the Emperor's favourites. Moreover, the first secretary in the Russian Legation was the son of the Russian Minister for Foreign Affairs. Nasir ad-Din, therefore, felt that the hand of the government in St. Petersburg was never far away, and in the end he usually capitulated to the demands made by the Russian Legation.[2]

The India Office staff had, for many years, contended that the surest way of regaining lost ground was to strengthen the British Legation staff. Two of the most competent advisers, Sir Owen Burne and Sir Henry Rawlinson, attached more importance to the appointment of an able and dynamic minister to Tehran than to any of the other projects under consideration.[3] When Lord Salisbury sought to win the Shah by the

[1] Lansdowne to Hardinge, No. 2, 6 January 1902: *B.D.*, iv, 369–70. Grey, *op. cit.*, i, 154.

[2] Case 630, Nicolson to Rawlinson, private, 26 April 1887: Home Correspondence, Political and Secret Department, vol. xcv, India Office Records. Nicolson to Sanderson, private, 28 May 1887: F.O. 60/486.

[3] Rawlinson to Lytton, private, 3 January 1879: Letters from England, vii, Pte Lytton Papers. Burne to Lytton, private, 20 June 1879: Letters from England, vii, Pte Lytton Papers.

cession of Seistan in 1879, Burne had advised him: 'Don't cede
the Shah territory *before* you settle our position in Teheran.
What you *really* want is to make Rawlinson (for instance) a
Baronet & send him out as Minister.'[1] But nearly a decade
elapsed before a person of distinction proceeded to that
post.

The strong recommendations from Lord Cross at the India
Office, coupled with Lord Salisbury's natural inclinations to
take the Persian question seriously, culminated in the appointment of Sir Henry Drummond Wolff. Before his departure, the
Foreign Office acquainted their new minister with the salient
features of Persian policy by presenting him with seven printed
pages of detailed instructions and eighteen enclosures.[2] The
basic premise, and it is significant that here Lord Salisbury
himself was responsible for the final wording, was:

It is to the interest of this country that the *integrity of Persia* should
be maintained, that its resources should be developed, and that its
Government should be strong, independent, and friendly. It is to
the promotion of these objects that your attention should be directed,
and so long, at least, as there is any reasonable hope of their being
realized, the efforts of H[er] M[ajesty's] G[overnment] w[oul]d be
directed to frustrate any policy incompatible with them.[3]

Thus the objective of the Wolff mission, as the Foreign Office
envisaged it, was the revitalization of the buffer policy.

On his journey *en route* to Tehran, Wolff took a keen interest
in the regions through which he passed. He saw in the Persians
an 'aptitude for civilization', but their innate capacities were
choked by extortion and maladministration.[4] The observations
of other travellers and officials verify his conclusions. Nicolson,
though often critical of the Persians, wrote privately to Currie:
'I think we should all be surprised how rapidly this country

---

[1] Quoted in Burne to Lytton, private, 30 January 1879: Letters from England,
vii, Pte Lytton Papers.

[2] See Appendix IV.

[3] Salisbury to Wolff, No. 14, very confidential, 29 February 1888, printed for
the use of the Foreign Office, 17 February 1888: F.O. 60/491.

[4] Wolff to Salisbury, private and confidential, 21 April 1888, printed for the use
of the Cabinet, 23 May 1888, endorsed by Salisbury: 'Print. Send to Queen &
Cabinet. S. 19.5': F.O. 60/492. There is a copy of this document in the Pte
Salisbury Papers.

would civilize.'[1] General Smith, after long residence in Persia, described the people as 'one of the finest races in the world, physically and intellectually'. In spite of the 'monstrous abuses', he declared that the 'condition of the country is, in my opinion, far from hopeless'.[2] Rawlinson rated the capabilities of the Persians far above the Turks, Indians, Uzbeks, and Afghans. He consistently maintained that training and encouragement would pay handsome dividends.[3]

Decay and inertia, not advancement and enterprise, were the distinguishing characteristics of the country, however. Since their governors could extract from the people, through *pishkesh*, any profits or valuable possessions, a very large part of the population lived at a subsistence level and nothing more. In 1887 a British officer traversed the country on a special mission to purchase horses for the Indian Army. He, too, deplored the deterioration everywhere about him and the suppression of a potentially creative people. Even horse-breeding, an occupation in which the Persians had long taken pride, had so far declined that Colonel Williams had trouble in filling his quota with satisfactory animals. Any good foal was requisitioned by the local authorities. The Colonel attributed Persia's ills to the 'utterly unscrupulous' governing classes.[4]

Wolff discussed his impressions with Nicolson, and then concluded that improvements would not be forthcoming until individual initiative was restored. Further investigation soon convinced him that laws for order and stability were as urgently needed as roads and railways.[5] He therefore pressed the Shah for the promulgation of a decree declaring that all Persian subjects were secure in their lives, liberties, and possessions

---

[1] Nicolson to Currie, private, 29 September 1887: F.O. 65/1323. Nicolson, *op. cit.*, p. 75.

[2] W. K. Dickson, *The Life of Major-General Sir Robert Murdoch Smith*, pp. 275-6. Observations by Smith on Herbert's Report on the Internal State of Persia, 14 March 1887: F.O. 60/490.

[3] Rawlinson, *England and Russia in the East*, pp. 137-8. Report on the Persian Army, 1 August 1892, F.O. 60/536.

[4] Colonel B. Williams, on special duty in Persia, to Lieutenant-Colonel E. H. H. Collen, Government of India, Military Department, Calcutta, No. 70, 1 February 1887: F.O. 248/450.

[5] Wolff to Salisbury, No. 43, most confidential, 2 May 1888, endorsed 'The Queen, Prince of Wales': F.O. 65/1349.

until publicly condemned by a competent tribunal. The aim of this projected reform was twofold. It would encourage the Persians to work, save, and invest. It would also favourably impress public opinion in other nations—nations to whom Persia might look for help in the not-too-distant future.[1]

At this time Nasir ad-Din was negotiating for a territorial guarantee. At the beginning of the year he had appealed plaintively for support. He accused England of giving 'honeyed words—but nothing else', and he asked for a definite pledge to resist Russia if she seized Persian territory.[2] The substance of England's reply is contained in Sir Philip Currie's minute.

. . . that we cannot pledge ourselves to go to war in unknown eventualities: but that the maintenance of the integrity of Persia is a part of the policy of England & that the Shah may rest assured that she will use her best efforts to secure it.

Lord Salisbury added: 'but that without a railway our assistance must be in any case less efficacious'. In the official reply to Nicolson he stressed the 'great advantage' of railways in 'enabling the Persian Gov[ernmen]t in having recourse to external support in resisting attacks or pressure from the north'.[3]

In their initial conversations with Wolff, the Shah and his powerful minister, the Amin as-Sultan, recalled the days of Fath 'Ali Shah when the relations between England and Persia were closer. Indeed, a defensive alliance bound the two countries. When Wolff talked of reform measures and proclamations, the Shah and the Amin as-Sultan turned to assurances and guarantees.

Wolff argued that if Persia wanted protection she should clearly demonstrate to her potential friends that she was worth sustaining. He pressed for the life and property decree 'as a preliminary which should at once be carried out'.[4] The Amin

[1] Wolff to Salisbury, No. 56, most secret and confidential, 14 May 1888, endorsed 'The Queen, ?Cabinet': F.O. 65/1349.

[2] Nicolson to Salisbury, No. 9, secret, 5 January 1888, endorsed 'The Queen': F.O. 65/1347.

[3] Minutes by Currie and Salisbury of 5 February on Nicolson to Salisbury, No. 9, secret, 5 January 1888: F.O. 65/1347. These points were amplified in Salisbury to Nicolson, No. 6, secret, 8 February 1888, endorsed 'The Queen': F.O. 65/1347.

[4] Wolff to Salisbury, No. 56, most secret and confidential, 14 May 1888, endorsed 'The Queen, ?Cabinet': F.O. 65/1349.

as-Sultan soon reported that the Shah had decided in favour of such a proclamation, and he would promulgate it in the most public manner. He went on to allude to the Shah's desire to build railroads and to foster more cordial relations with England. But, he asked, 'What support would be given to him if his so doing should entail upon him the execution of the threats of Russia.'[1] Wolff said that he would have to obtain more specific instructions, but he urged that no time should be lost in publishing the decree.

The Amin as-Sultan, with Wolff's assistance, drafted the proclamation, and the Shah announced it at a levée on 22 May 1888.[2] Later, it was read in the mosques and the public meeting-places, and subordinate officials were required to give bonds to ensure the execution of its provisions.[3] Wolff was delighted with the outcome of his first efforts in Persia, and asked Lord Salisbury to convey an encouraging message to the Shah. He suggested:

Continuance in the course thus inaugurated will double the claims of His Majesty on the support of H[er] M[ajesty's] Gov[ernmen]t & the Shah will find in the moment of difficulty that the friendship of England will not be wanting.[4]

Lord Salisbury, though pleased with these hopeful signs, was more guarded. He replied:

You may add that continuance in the course thus inaugurated cannot fail to enhance the claims of His Majesty to the friendship of the English nation.[5]

[1] Wolff to Salisbury, No. 57, most secret and confidential, 18 May 1888, endorsed 'The Queen, Cabinet': F.O. 65/1349.

[2] Wolff to Salisbury, No. 57, decypher telegram, most secret and confidential, 17 May 1888: F.O. 60/496.
Aitchison, *op. cit.*, XIII, *The Treaties, etc., Relating to Persia and Afghanistan*, appendix no. xx, translation of a Proclamation of the Shah of Persia respecting the protection of lives and properties of Persian subjects, dated 26 May 1888, pp. lxxvi–lxxvii.

[3] Wolff, *op. cit.*, ii, 340–2. Wolff to Salisbury, 23 May 1888: *B.F.S.P.*, lxxix, 704. Same to same, 25 May 1888: *B.F.S.P.*, lxxix, 705–6.

[4] Wolff to Salisbury, decypher telegram, private and confidential, 23 May 1888: F.O. 60/495.

[5] Salisbury to Wolff, 23 May 1888; see also same to same, 22 June 1888: *B.F.S.P.*, lxxix, 704–7; quotation from p. 705.

Stimulated by his swift initial success, Wolff turned his attention to a project which is traditionally associated with British policy in Persia—the opening of the Karun river to navigation. Sir Henry Layard, as early as 1841 and 1842, had described the potentialities of that river as a means of entry into the Shah's central provinces.[1] The possibilities were investigated, but active negotiations did not begin until Mackenzie revived the idea in 1874. According to the provisions of Lord Salisbury's abortive treaty of 1879, part of the price Nasir ad-Din would have had to pay for Herat and Seistan was the opening of the Karun. Lord Granville, too, had pushed this project. In 1884 he had drafted a dispatch to be communicated to the Shah in which he recalled previous efforts in this direction, and advised the Persian ruler to take 'immediate & effective' steps if he wished to see British interest in his country 'greatly & speedily developed'.[2] No action had followed.

The British promotion of the Karun scheme was consistent and serious. The Shah demurred—partly because of Russian hostility, and partly because of internal complications. The Arab and Bakhtiari tribes in their remote mountain strongholds of the south-west maintained little connection with the central authorities and did not conceal their hostility to the Qajars. Since ties of neither race nor loyalty bound them to the Tehran government, the Shah suspected that they would become pliant tools in the hands of a foreign power. Nor did those who governed Persia seem anxious to have the task of developing the southern part of the country undertaken 'by those from whom they could expect to make no *mudakhil* and to receive no bribes'.[3]

Nasir ad-Din doubted and procrastinated, but some Persians favoured the enterprise. The Zil es-Sultan, whose territories would be directly affected, was an enthusiastic convert. The Nasr al-Mulk wrote a memorandum in which he depicted the former prosperity of the region and argued that with irrigation and proper care the rich alluvial soil could again support a thriving population. Rawlinson wrote on his paper: 'This is a

[1] G. N. Curzon, *Persia and the Persian Question*, ii, 332–3. W. F. Ainsworth, *The River Karun: An Opening to British Commerce* (London, 1890).

[2] Granville to Thomson, draft dispatch, 16 August 1884: F.O. 65/1209. This dispatch is extensively revised by Kimberley.

[3] Curzon, *Persia and the Persian Question*, ii, 383.

very excellent report and does credit to its Persian author.'[1]
The ideas of the Nasr al-Mulk cannot be dismissed as chimeri-
cal. Those who explored the Persian south-west thought the
Karun plains were potentially productive.[2]

Rawlinson nevertheless believed that the Karun project was
'a delusion and a snare'. He preferred the construction of a
metalled road to Isfahan. He stood alone, however, in his opposition. Other authorities considered it advantageous both commercially and politically.[3] Commercially, it would place
England on a more equal footing. The Russians had persuaded
the Shah to build roads from the Caspian to Tehran and
Meshed, and they constantly developed transportation facilities
in the north. Their goods were penetrating into the heart of the
country and were providing keen competition as far south as
Isfahan. In the south the British had to transport their products
over picturesque but expensive caravan trails. The Indian Intelligence Department summarized the effects from the political
point of view.

... it would give England, as the country which would most largely
employ the new route, paramount influence in Southern Persia,
while the possibility of bringing troops within a few hundred miles
of the most important Persian towns naturally would contribute
largely to the re-establishment of British influence at Tehran.[4]

Wolff believed that the hardy and warlike tribes of the south-
west could be made into an effective counterpoise to Russia's
Cossack Brigade in Tehran.[5]

[1] Enclosure in Thomson to Granville and minute by Rawlinson, No. 18, Commercial, 26 December 1882, printed for the use of the Foreign Office, 17 February
1883: Home Correspondence, Political and Secret Department, vol. lx, India
Office Records.

[2] G. N. Curzon, 'The Karun River', *Proceedings of the Royal Geographical Society*,
xii (1890), pp. 514, 526–7. H. F. B. Lynch, 'Notes on the Present State of the
Karun River', *Proceedings of the Royal Geographical Society*, xiii (1891), p. 593.

[3] Memoranda on the Karun River by Sir H. Rawlinson, Sir O. St. John, Mr.
W. Baring, Capt. H. Wells, and Mr. Ronald Thomson; Intelligence Department,
India, secret, 1882: F.O. 248/472. Rawlinson held that 'Persia can never become a
rich or a producing, or a manufacturing country, but it will doubtless be turned to
great account some day or other as a nursery for soldiers'. Quoted in Curzon, i,
612, who dissociated himself from the first part of this statement.

[4] Karun River Précis, 1879–1883, Intelligence Department, India, secret, 16
August 1883: F.O. 248/472.

[5] Wolff to Currie, private, 9 October 1888: F.O. 65/1354.

In 1885, following his return from Persia after many years there, Colonel Smith acquainted the Foreign Office with his views on Persian affairs. His plans provided for the improvement of communications in southern Persia and in Mesopotamia by putting steamers on the Tigris and the Karun rivers and by building a carriageable road from Shushtar to Qum. The results would be mutually beneficial. Persia's trade and revenue would increase, and England would establish supremacy along a line from Mosul, through Kermanshah, Isfahan, and Yazd, to Herat. Sir Philip Currie considered the question 'very important', and added that 'we have been urging the Persian Gov[ernmen]t continually to make a road to the Karun'. Not until the energetic days of Sir Henry Drummond Wolff was the Shah's opposition overcome.[1]

When the Shah and the Amin es-Sultan spoke of their need for support, Wolff pointed to the practical obstacles which precluded effective help. Troops could not advance over mule tracks. Furthermore, English public opinion was not sufficiently alive to Persia's difficulties, and did not understand the nature of her struggle for continued existence as an independent state. He also remarked that Russia justified her annexations to the world by alleging that conditions improved in the countries and districts she incorporated.[2]

Wolff suggested to Lord Salisbury that Britain might, under the most-favoured-nation clause of her treaty with Persia in 1857, demand the right of putting steamers on the Karun, since Turkish vessels used the river.[3] The Law Officers decided, however, that the presence of these small Turkish grain and cargo boats did not justify a claim for steamers. Ultimately, Wolff and the Shah worked out the formula—an assurance in exchange for the opening of the Karun.

The Foreign Office consulted George Mackenzie about

---

[1] Smith to Stokes and minute by Currie, private, 24 July 1885: F.O. 65/1247. Case 1255, Letter from Lieutenant-Colonel Murdoch Smith as to improvement of communications in Southern Persia and Turkish Arabia: Home Correspondence, Political and Secret Department, vol. lxxvii, India Office Records.

[2] Wolff to Salisbury, No. 56, most secret and confidential, 14 May 1888, endorsed 'The Queen, ? Cabinet': F.O. 65/1349. Same to same, No. 71, secret and confidential, 1 June 1888, endorsed 'The Queen, Prince of Wales': F.O. 65/1350.

[3] Wolff to Salisbury, No. 106, 7 July 1888, Asia/confidential/883: F.O. 60/492.

business details. He had pressed this scheme for many years, and his connection with the firm of Gray, Dawes and Company, of Bushire, enabled him to make recommendations based upon local knowledge. Mackenzie believed that the Karun region offered exceptionally promising opportunities for development. He had wanted to sponsor Persian enterprise from the outset. A mixed company with Persian and European shareholders should undertake to establish steamer trade on the Karun between Mohammerah and Shushtar, and, in return for the right, the company should construct a wagon road from Shushtar to Burujird. The road when finished would belong to the Persian Government, and subsequently other branches connecting the central cities could be built. Mackenzie suggested getting into contact with the Tigris and Euphrates Steam Navigation Company, which would, he thought, assist in the inauguration of the enterprise for a proportionate increase in their subsidy.[1] The Foreign Office took up the financial question with the India Office. Lord Cross responded favourably, and pledged the Government of India to contribute a 'material share'.[2]

Wolff carried on these negotiations throughout the summer of 1888. He did not ask for a concession, but for a Royal Proclamation opening the river for trade to all nations. Wolff and the Amin as-Sultan worked out the terms, and in mid-October the Shah decided in favour of the measure.[3] His circular of 30 October 1888 permitted commercial vessels of all nations to use the Karun.[4] The broad and swift river was navigable for 81 miles from Mohammerah to the little village of Ahwaz. There rapids intervened, and the great dams of the Sassanian monarchs were useless—though still imposing in

[1] Smith to Stokes, private, 24 July 1885: F.O. 65/1247. Salisbury to Wolff, No. 23, telegram, 31 May 1888: F.O. 60/494. Mackenzie to Sanderson and minutes by Ferguson, Lister, Sanderson, Hertslet, Currie, and Salisbury, private, 27 June 1888: F.O. 97/590.

[2] Foreign Office to India Office, secret, 5 July 1888: F.O. 97/590. India Office to Foreign Office, 26 July 1888: F.O. 97/590.

[3] Wolff to Salisbury, No. 199, 30 September 1888; same to same, No. 202a, 2 October 1888: F.O. 97/590. Same to same, No. 219, secret and confidential, 10 October 1888: F.O. 65/1354.

[4] Aitchison, op. cit., appendix no. xii, translation of a Persian circular announcing the opening of the Karun river from Mohammerah to Ahwaz, 30 October 1888, p. lxxviii. Wolff to Salisbury, No. 204, decypher telegram, 25 October 1888: F.O. 97/590.

decay. Consequently their cargoes had been unloaded, and loaded again on to smaller ships. In its upper course the river was navigable up to the plains which surrounded Shushtar—an ancient royal centre. By opening the Karun, approximately 177 miles of water carriage could be substituted for many miles of fatiguing travel over hazardous mountain trails.[1] General Smith in an address to a London audience explained:

To realise what this means, let us imagine for a moment the whole traffic between London and Scotland carried on by means of beasts of burden, and then a line of steamers to be suddenly started between London and Berwick.[2]

The American minister in Tehran described it as a 'step in the direction of true progress'.[3] The British Resident at Bushire, in his annual report, predicted that it would be a boon not only to British trade but also to south-western Persia itself.[4] Lord Salisbury, in his Guildhall address, said:

In Persia, the Shah has recently by a wise and statesmanlike measure, opened the only navigable river of his dominions to all nations for their commerce. It is not a favour for England, it is a favour to all the world, but it is the beginning of a policy by which new life can be breathed into Persia, and new prosperity brought to its commerce and industry.[5]

Much was accomplished despite Persian obstruction. Messrs. Lynch, of the Tigris and Euphrates Steam Navigation Company, transferred steamers to the Karun and operated a regular

[1] Curzon, *Persia and the Persian Question*, ii, 330–1, 346–8, 363–5. Lynch, *ibid.*, pp. 592–3. Smith, 'The Karun as a Trade Route', *Journal of the Society of Arts*, xxxvii (10 May 1889), pp. 561–79.

[2] Quoted in Wolff, *op. cit.*, ii, 343. This speech is quoted in Ainsworth, *op. cit.*, pp. 217–18. Smith's calculations are based on a comparison with the Bushire route. He shows that 'the end of the Karun navigation at Shuster is nearer to the central part of Persia than Bushire, not only by the 170 miles of river and estuary, but also by the 180 miles of sea between Bushire and the mouth of the Shat-al-Arab'.

[3] Pratt to Bayard, diplomatic series, No. 311, 2 November 1888: Persia, iv, American Department of State.

[4] *Selections from the Records of the Government of India* (Calcutta), cclix. *Administration Report on the Persian Gulf Political Residency and Muscat Political Agency for 1888–89*, p. 29.

[5] Speech at the Guildhall on 9 November 1888, reported in *The Times*, 10 November 1888. See also *P.D.*, Third Series, Lords, 18 December 1888, cccxxxi, 1738–39.

M

service on both the lower and upper river.[1] A British vice-consulate was established at Mohammerah, and the agent's first report was published in 1891. British trade in the Karun region in that year was valued at £16,000, but by 1902 it had risen to £271,732. The tonnage of shipping which passed through the port of Mohammerah increased steadily, and the city's population trebled within a decade.[2] By the turn of the century, the superior merits of the Karun route had been proved. From Bushire to Isfahan, a distance of about five hundred miles, the journey took approximately a month. Travelling via the Karun reduced the time by half. The freight rates were considerably cheaper. When the telegraph company brought in 157 tons of material they saved $2,682 by choosing the waterway.[3] In later years, the developments which accompanied the Karun river enterprise became the keystone for British predominance in the south.[4]

Throughout the Karun river negotiations the Shah bargained for an assurance from England. His secret agreement with Russia of September 1887, however, had to be revealed. It prohibited waterway and railway concessions to foreign powers, but its restrictive provisions were circumvented by the opening of the Karun river to all nations.[5] The fact that Nasir ad-Din had entered into another secret agreement with Russia made the British still more doubtful of his reliability. Nevertheless, they assumed a limited obligation. The Shah hoped for a promise of direct material assistance, but Lord Salisbury specifically forbade any such pledge 'as we are really powerless till there is

[1] Lynch, ibid., pp. 592–3.

[2] Selections from the Records of the Government of India, cclxxxv. Administration Report of the Persian Gulf Political Residency and Muscat Political Agency for 1890–91, pp. 47–50. Chirol, The Middle Eastern Question, pp. 167–8. Special articles by Chirol in The Times, 15 December and 23 December 1902.

[3] An impartial account of British developments on the Karun river is given in a long and detailed trade report from the American minister in Tehran, Griscom to Hay, No. 25, 25 November 1902, endorsed by Adey 'valuable report': Persia, xi, American Department of State.

[4] Hamilton to Elgin, private, 6 December 1895; same to same, private, 7 and 14 February 1896: Private Correspondence, India, part i, vol. i, Pte Hamilton Papers, India Office Library.

[5] Wolff to Salisbury, No. 199, most secret and confidential, 30 September 1888; same to same and enclosures, No. 201, secret and confidential, 1 October 1888; same to same and minute, No. 215, decypher telegram, 1 November 1888: F.O. 60/495.

railway communication with the Coast'.[1] But a written promise to make 'earnest representations' at St. Petersburg in case Russia infringed Persia's sovereign rights was given.[2]

The Russians made persistent inquiries during the course of the negotiations, and protested 'in a very blustering manner'[3] against the opening of the river, M. de Poggio, the chargé d'affaires, said that the Emperor would be very angry. Prince Dolgorouki, feeling secure with his 1887 secret engagement, had left Tehran temporarily in order to accompany the Emperor in his progress through his Caucasus dominions. At the Imperial Court he was *persona gratissima*. The *Herold* printed glowing accounts of his triumphant service at Tehran; the Emperor received him cordially. Victory over Sir Henry Drummond Wolff had been easy for Prince Nicolas Dolgorouki. Into this serene and complacent atmosphere dropped the bomb of the Shah's circular of 30 October 1888—opening the Karun river.[4]

Dolgorouki fumed; the Emperor chafed; the press ranted; and Giers brought this 'serious matter' before Morier. The 'greatest irritation' had been caused by the opening of the Karun, and the equilibrium had been upset in Persia. Russia would have her *revanche*, Giers said, and corresponding measures would be taken. Morier reported that the Shah was regarded as a 'sort of traitor to the interests of the White Czar'.[5] In Tehran, too, Poggio reproached the Shah in strong and insulting terms.[6]

[1] Salisbury to Wolff, No. 21, draft telegram, 23 May 1888; same to same, private, 25 May 1888: F.O. 60/494.

[2] See Appendix V. Wolff to Salisbury, decypher telegram, very secret, 11 October 1888: F.O. 97/590. Salisbury to Wolff and minute, No. 78, draft telegram, 13 October 1888: F.O. 97/590. Assurances given by British Minister to Shah respecting maintenance of Integrity of Persia, Tehran, 24 October 1888: Treaty series 14B, Persia, F.O. 93/75/14B.

[3] Wolff to Salisbury, No. 212, decypher telegram, very secret, 29 October 1888: F.O. 97/590.

[4] Morier to Salisbury, No. 382, most secret, 14 November 1888: F.O. 65/1355.

[5] Morier to Salisbury and minute by Currie, No. 396, extender of telegram No. 66, most secret, 21 November 1888, endorsed 'The Queen': F.O. 97/590. Same to same and enclosure, No. 383, most secret, 14 November 1888, endorsed 'The Queen, Lord Cross, Sir E. Bradford'; same to same and enclosure, No. 402, 23 November 1888: F.O. 65/1355. Same to same, No. 423, 12 December 1888: F.O. 65/1356.

[6] Wolff to Salisbury, No. 228, decypher telegram, most confidential, 21 November 1888: F.O. 97/590. Same to same, No. 257, most confidential, 21 November 1888, endorsed 'The Queen': F.O. 65/1355.

Currie thought that Nasir ad-Din should be supported, and with Sanderson's assistance he drafted a telegram to Morier.

The Foreign Office registered 'pain and surprise' at the attitude of the Russian Government. Their dispatch of 21 February 1888 had clearly set forth the British views, and the opening of the Karun river had formed an essential part of their stated programme. The Russian Government had not expressed opposition in February. Moreover, England had obtained no concession, and certainly the Shah retained the right to do as he pleased with his own rivers. Lord Salisbury drafted the conclusion, with his own hand, and hoped that Russia would not quarrel with England over 'a policy on our part which has only been inspired by the common interests of civilization, & to which she herself [Russia] has in principle emphatically assented'.[1]

The Russians did not frame their retaliatory demands immediately. They accused Wolff of blocking their efforts to obtain a consul at Meshed and of obstructing their negotiations for a road from Ashkabad to Meshed.[2] Soon they would fix their own demands for compensation. 'La réalité est', wrote Giers to Staal, 'que nous ne sommes nullement à bout de moyens d'obtenir quelques équivalents des avantages que s'est assurés le Gouvernement anglais . . .'[3]

When Morier held his 'Karun river' interview with Giers—a conversation which was delayed for several days because of Morier's indisposition—he laid much emphasis upon the February dispatch. Giers was obviously embarrassed, and he gave no articulate reply. He pointed to the violence of the Russian press and explained that public opinion had to be soothed by compensation of some type. That compensation, however, had not yet been determined. Morier concluded, in his report to Lord Salisbury, that the Emperor had taken a personal interest in the issue since it touched one of his favourites—Nicolas Dolgorouki. The concern of the Emperor, who was impulsive and stubborn, turned the minor dispute into one not 'free from

[1] Salisbury to Morier, No. 64, draft telegram, 23 November 1888, endorsed 'The Queen': F.O. 65/1355.

[2] Morier to Salisbury, No. 69, decypher telegram, secret, 5 December 1888: F.O. 65/1334.

[3] Giers to Staal, 16 November/14 December 1888: Meyendorff, *op. cit.*, i, 448.

danger'. As the year 1888 drew to a close, Morier foresaw breakers ahead for England and Russia in Central Asia. He warned Salisbury:

. . . in the present temper of the Czar, of his military advisers, and of public opinion, were Baron Reuter by means of Sir H[enry] D[rummond] Wolff's indefatigable energy to secure his concessions behind the back of Russia, I believe there would be no small risk of some violent and ill-considered step, which might force on earlier than would perhaps be convenient to us, the moment when we should be bound in honour to afford material support to the Shah of Persia.[1]

---

[1] Morier to Salisbury, No. 421, secret, 11 December 1888, endorsed 'The Queen, Lord Cross, Sir E. Bradford. Print Asia (very secret section)': F.O. 65/1356. Later he thought 'that the very strong language employed by Monsieur de Giers in his first conversation with me about the Karun concession . . . was to a great extent a *scène de circonstance*, which he was bound to act in order to satisfy . . . the irritation prevailing at the time in the highest circles here'. Morier to Salisbury, No. 439, confidential, 26 December 1888, endorsed 'The Queen, Lord Cross, Sir E. Bradford': F.O. 65/1356.

CHAPTER XI

The Wolff Mission
Its Contribution to the Buffer Policy, 1889–91

RUSSIA's tone continued to be strident long after the initial shock of the opening of the Karun had been absorbed. Some newspapers advocated military action,[1] and Morier referred to the 'super-excited state of feeling which still prevails here in regard to Persia'.[2] Attention was focused on three issues—the new Reuter concession then in process of negotiation, the Meshed consulate, and the construction of railways. Intemperate language was not uncommon. The Russian chargé d'affaires, Poggio, stormed to the Persian Minister for Foreign Affairs about Baron George de Reuter, then in Tehran on business for his father. The Persian Government should, he said, 'either send him away or strike him in the mouth if he again ventured to open it concerning his concession'.[3] Zinovieff talked of reconsidering the territorial guarantee if further privileges were granted to England.[4] The French minister in Tehran 'insinuated very clearly that how-

[1] Morier to Salisbury, No. 423, 12 December 1888: F.O. 65/1356. Wolff to Salisbury, No. 286, secret and confidential, 15 December 1888, endorsed 'The Queen, Lord Cross': F.O. 97/590. Same to same, No. 288, secret and confidential, 20 December 1888, endorsed 'The Queen, Prince of Wales, Lord Cross, Sir E. Bradford': F.O. 65/1356.
[2] Morier to Salisbury, No. 439, confidential, 26 December 1888, endorsed 'The Queen, Lord Cross, Sir E. Bradford': F.O. 65/1356.
[3] Wolff to Salisbury, No. 235, secret and confidential, 30 October 1888: F.O. 65/1354.
[4] Morier to Salisbury, No. 441, secret, 28 December 1888, endorsed 'Lord Cross, Sir E. Bradford': F.O. 65/1356.

ever unreasonable the anger of Russia energy on our part in the extension of trade might lead Russia to war'.[1]

The first demand was for a consulate at Meshed. That city of 60,000 occupied a position in the north-east comparable to Tabriz in the north-west. It was important to the Russians as an approach to Herat, to the British as a base for observations in Central Asia, and to the Persians as a religious centre. Because it was a sacred city, where there was the tomb of the Imam 'Ali al-Rida, all requests by foreign powers to establish any type of official headquarters there had been refused. Russian imperiousness in 1888 and 1889, however, induced the Shah to reverse this decision.[2] After his capitulation to the Russians, Nasir ad-Din asked the British to send a representative to Meshed in order that the Russian flag would not fly alone. General Maclean, already on duty along the Khorassan frontier, was ordered to proceed to that city as its first British consul general.[3]

Severe pressure was applied over railways. In the initial stages of the long discussions which continued through 1889 and 1890, the Russians seemed to be angling for a concession—in spite of the fact that Morier had always maintained: 'So long as Wyshnegradsky remains Minister of Finance, not one copeck will be found for a Persian railway.'[4] The British did not object to a commercial line for, when Staal had complained about the Karun, Lord Salisbury had suggested that a railway might suffice for compensation.[5] But strategical construction was a different matter. A line to the capital, either from Astrabad or from Resht and Kazvin, was an obvious Russian move. The British, however, decided not to oppose these projects since their

[1] Wolff to Salisbury, No. 27, confidential, 29 January 1889, endorsed 'The Queen': F.O. 60/500.

[2] Morier to Salisbury, No. 69, decypher telegram, secret, 5 December 1888: F.O. 65/1334. Wolff to Salisbury, No. 255, decypher telegram, most confidential, 14 December 1888: F.O. 60/496.

[3] Minute by Salisbury on Wolff to Salisbury, No. 247, decypher telegram, confidential, 7 December 1888: F.O. 60/495. Same to same, No. 13, decypher telegram, 14 January 1889: F.O. 60/503. Same to same, No. 25, records telegram, very secret, 29 January, 1889: F.O. 60/504. Maclean to Wolff, private, Mashad, 30 March 1889, endorsed 'For the Queen': F.O. 60/500.

[4] Morier to Salisbury, private, 10 June 1891: bound volume, Russia, Pte Salisbury Papers.

[5] Salisbury to Wolff, No. 18, draft telegram, very secret, 4 February 1889: F.O. 65/1377.

military advisers had long ago decided that Tehran was an easy
prey for invasion and already lay at the mercy of her neighbour
to the north—with or without railroads.[1] Construction in
Khorassan would be far more dangerous. Its eastern districts
constituted 'the highway for Russian flank attack on Afghanistan',[2] and Wolff should resist lines in that province 'to the
utmost' of his power.[3]

In the summer of 1889 the Shah journeyed to Europe for the
third and last time. Thus railway negotiations were temporarily
suspended, although conversations were held on that subject
both in St. Petersburg and in London. The Emperor spoke in a
friendly vein, but 'insisted very strongly on the maintenance of
the Shah's promise not to grant Railway Concessions for five
years'.[4] In London, on the other hand, the benefits which
would be derived from such construction were emphasized.
Wolff accompanied the Shah during the month he spent in
England. Nasir ad-Din came with a suite of forty, was entertained at England's expense, and was shown every honour. He
had expressed the desire to arrive in London via the Thames,
and Wolff thought that he should be conveyed in an impressive
vessel. The royal yacht, the *Victoria and Albert*, brought him from
Antwerp to England, and while there he stayed at Buckingham
Palace.[5] The Prince of Wales was 'assiduous in personal
attendance', and Wolff arranged for the Shah to meet many
leading financiers and to visit industrial centres.[6]

The Shah's sojourn in England was, on the whole, most successful, but there was one unfortunate repercussion. Malkom
Khan obtained a concession for state lotteries, and then sold

[1] Minutes by Salisbury and Sanderson on Wolff to Salisbury, No. 26, most
confidential, 29 January 1889: F.O. 65/1377. Memorandum by Law on Persian
proposed concessions to Russia, confidential, 7 March 1889: F.O. 60/505.

[2] Salisbury to Wolff, Nos. 17 and 19, draft telegrams, most confidential, 4 and
9 February 1889: F.O. 65/1377.

[3] Salisbury to Wolff, unnumbered, draft telegram, secret and confidential, 19
May 1890: F.O. 60/513; see Appendix VI.

[4] Wolff to Salisbury, No. 211, most confidential, 21 November 1889, endorsed
'The Queen': F.O. 60/502.

[5] Wolff to Salisbury, No. 81, 5 April 1889: F.O. 60/500. Same to same, No. 103,
records telegram, very secret, 4 April 1889; same to same, No. 107, records telegram, very secret, 10 April 1889: F.O. 60/504. Ponsonby to Currie and minute by
Salisbury, 16 April 1889: F.O. 60/506.

[6] Lee, *op. cit.*, i, 686; Wolff, *op. cit.*, ii, 350-1.

his rights to the Anglo-Asiatic Syndicate. Upon returning to Persia the Shah found his people in an angry mood because of his indulgence in an expensive European tour at a time when the country was on the brink of bankruptcy. There was general irritation at the lottery concession. The Russian chargé d'affaires remonstrated against it. The British law officers believed the enterprise to be illegal. Nasir ad-Din tried to secure its repeal. The personal rivalry between the Amin as-Sultan and Malkom Khan aggravated the controversy, and finally Malkom Khan was recalled. In December the concession was cancelled without compensation.[1] This episode together with the memory of Reuter made capitalists all the more sceptical of Persia as a sound field for investment.

Not all financial enterprise was discouraged, however. In mid-1888 the New Oriental Bank Corporation which operated throughout the East—in Aden, Bombay, Colombo, Hongkong, Singapore, and Yokohama—extended its business to Persia. When Mr. Charles Duffield arrived in Tehran to begin his work as permanent head of the branch in that city, he was welcomed enthusiastically by Wolff who thought that the plans for a bank were of a 'most promising character'.[2] The undertaking flourished, and soon agencies had spread to Tabriz, Resht, Meshed, Isfahan, Shiraz, and Bushire.[3] No concession was required for the bank to carry on its work, and it performed such services as the transmission of taxes from the provinces to the capital, the issue of paper currency, and the loaning of money at moderate interest rates. The Foreign Office tried to promote its growth by transferring to it the Legation account,[4] but the Treasury were unwilling to agree to the change.[5]

While the New Oriental Bank was laying its groundwork, the son of Baron Julius de Reuter arrived in Tehran. Nasir ad-Din had told Wolff that he would give Reuter the right to found a

---

[1] Wolff to Salisbury, No. 167, records telegram, secret and confidential, 30 November 1889; same to same, No. 176, records telegram, 8 December 1889: F.O. 60/504, *The Times*, 11 January 1892. Memorandum on Persian Lottery Loan Concession, 20 August 1902: F.O. 60/657.

[2] Wolff to Salisbury, No. 145, confidential, 14 August 1888: F.O. 60/493.

[3] Curzon, *Persia and the Persian Question*, i, 474.

[4] Foreign Office to Treasury, immediate, 14 August 1888: F.O. 60/498.

[5] Treasury to Foreign Office, immediate, 22 August 1888: F.O. 60/498.

national bank as compensation for the 1873 abrogation, and he asked the British minister to prepare a draft concession.[1] But Reuter pressed for the Karun railway in addition.[2] The negotiations were rendered more delicate by the irritation which Wolff's Karun coup produced. In Tehran the Russian chargé d'affaires spoke 'very loudly' against Reuter,[3] and Morier sent a warning from St. Petersburg that further concessions to England would be regarded as a 'hostile act'.[4]

Poggio argued that the Shah's secret agreement, which he regarded as a treaty, prohibited the granting of concessions without Russia's consent. The Amin as-Sultan, however, upheld Baron Reuter since his claims long preceded the secret undertaking with Russia. Moreover, he saw in the Reuter concession a 'means of liberating Persia from the dictation of Russia'.[5] Early in 1889 permission to establish a national bank was given in lieu of the original grant. Wolff's part in the negotiations was limited to extending to 'Baron George de Reuter such advice as he asked from time to time and to counsel the Shah and his Government to terminate as speedily as possible this long standing claim'.[6] The Foreign Office expressed 'gratification' at the settlement since, although the original concession contained 'obvious objections', the construction had been begun and the expenditures made deserved some compensation. In the future, Lord Salisbury said, it should be easier for Persia to obtain foreign capital for the development of public works.[7]

The year 1889 closed with the promulgation of two British Orders in Council. The need for such enactments had been recognized for many years, but not until Wolff took up the question with typical energy and enthusiasm were they brought into force. The first Order in Council invoked the Foreign

[1] Wolff to Salisbury, No. 263, confidential, 28 November 1888, endorsed 'The Queen': F.O. 65/1355.
[2] Wolff to Salisbury, No. 241, decypher telegram, very secret, 3 December 1888; same to same, No. 251, decypher telegram, very secret, 12 December 1888: F.O. 60/496.
[3] Wolff to Salisbury, No. 213, decypher telegram, urgent and very secret, 29 October 1888: F.O. 60/496.
[4] Morier to Salisbury, No. 20, 23 January 1889: F.O. 65/1377.
[5] Wolff to Salisbury, No. 235, secret and confidential, 30 October 1888: F.O. 65/1354.   [6] Wolff to Salisbury, No. 28, 2 February 1889: F.O. 60/500.
[7] Salisbury to Wolff, No. 15, draft telegram, 1 February 1889: F.O. 60/503.

Jurisdiction Acts of 1843 and 1878, and established consular control over British subjects in Persia. The second extended the same privileges to the Gulf littoral and included the semi-independent shaikhdoms along the Arabian shore.[1] These acts were the natural outgrowth of the increased numbers of British subjects who resided in Persia as a result of the banking activities, the opening of the Karun, the operation of telegraph lines, and the mining explorations.[2] *The Times* pointed out that some stability had to be established before merchants and investors would risk their lives and fortunes in the development of Persia.

The day of doing nothing, and of letting the over-ripe Persian pear fall into Russia's mouth, of discouraging still further by our apathy the already disheartened Persians, seems to have passed away, and in its place has arrived one marked by energetic but not provocative action, by the resolve to uphold our legitimate rights against all comers . . .[3]

In 1890 the Imperial Bank of Persia acquired the assets of the Persian branch of the New Oriental Bank. The Imperial Bank was originally chartered for sixty years, was empowered to undertake 'all matters financial, industrial, or commercial', and had the exclusive right of issuing bank notes. In addition to its banking privileges it obtained a monopoly over all mines, except gold, silver, and precious stones, which were not already ceded. The caution money, £40,000, which was deposited in the Bank of England in 1872 by Baron Reuter was to be handed over to the Persian Government as a guarantee that the bank would be formed. Upon its establishment, however, the sum reverted to Reuter.[4]

The Bank was incorporated under a Royal Charter in London,

[1] The two Orders in Council of 13 December 1889 relating to consular jurisdiction in Persia and along the Persian Gulf have been reprinted in *British and Foreign State Papers*, lxxxi, 805–935.
[2] Foreign Office to Law Officers of the Crown, 7 May 1889: F.O. 60/518. Wolff to Salisbury, No. 3, consular, 30 March 1889: F.O. 60/518.
The Gulf ports, coasts, and adjacent islands were in close relationship to British India so that the laws and procedures of British India were applied in the Persian Gulf. No such special relationship existed between inland Persia and British India. Therefore a system similar to that in force in the Levant under the Ottoman Orders in Council was adopted.   [3] Leading article in *The Times*, 26 December 1889.
[4] Wolff to Salisbury, No. 28, 2 February 1889: F.O. 60/500. Copy of Concession for the Imperial Bank of Persia, 30 January 1889: F.O. 60/506.

in spite of the fact that the Treasury refused such applications as a general policy. In this case they apparently acceded to Lord Salisbury's request. He urged that every possible encouragement should be given to the institution since its failure would be detrimental politically. To the Lords Commissioners of the Treasury he wrote:

... Persia stands at this moment at a very critical point in her history. If no development of her resources can be accomplished, decay, which for several generations past has set in, can only be expected to continue, & her absorption by a powerful military neighbour can only be a question of years. On the other hand, if her wealth & prosperity can be increased, if advantage can be taken of her great natural capabilities, & above all, if communications with the sea & with India by railway can be established, the difficulties in the way of a Russian subjugation will be largely increased, & if sufficient interval for the accomplishment of that growth can be obtained, the danger will probably be dispelled altogether. If the railways are made, Persia will be able to fight for herself, & may obtain friends to fight for her: if the railways are not made, she must be the defenceless prey of an invader.

On this account it becomes a matter of capital importance to encourage the creation of the commercial machinery by which undertakings of this kind can be carried out. The accumulation of money in Persia is only possible through the medium of a successful banking system, & in face of the diplomatic conditions which exist, it is not probable that the necessary communications will ever be established with the sea, & with other countries, except by the action of native enterprise, nominally at least supported by native resources.[1]

The Lords of the Treasury honoured Lord Salisbury's 'urgent representations' and gave their consent for a Royal Charter. But they insisted upon certain modifications and pointed out that a twenty-five-year-old precedent was being broken.[2] By the time the prospectus of the Imperial Bank of Persia was published the venture seemed so secure that 'within a few hours of the date of issue, the capital, amounting to 1,000,000l, was subscribed fifteen times over'.[3] The capital of the bank was

[1] Foreign Office to Treasury, 2 July 1889: F.O. 60/507.
[2] Treasury to Foreign Office, 13 July 1889: F.O. 60/507.
[3] Curzon, *Persia and the Persian Question*, i, 475. According to the concession the bank was considered to be formed when the first series of shares, amounting to £1,000,000, had been subscribed.

fixed at four million sterling, and the Persian Government was guaranteed six per cent of the net profits annually, but not less than £4,000. Mr. Joseph Rabino was its first manager, and under his indefatigable and astute management the bank became an accepted national institution. Several years after its formation the American minister in Tehran said that the 'only banking business in Persia conducted in a regular and systematic manner is that of the Imperial Bank of Persia'.[1] Other concessions were acquired and lost, other enterprises were attempted and failed, but the bank continued its operations into the present decade.

A supplement to the concession provided that the mining rights should not be worked by the bank itself.[2] Hence, in 1890, the Persian Bank Mining Rights Corporation was formed in London with a capitalization of £1,000,000. Persia's latent mineral wealth was thought to be great. Sir Charles MacGregor Sir R. Murdoch Smith, Colonel Mark Bell, and General A. Houtum-Schindler had all returned encouraging reports.[3] The American minister in Tehran stated that Persia was 'abundantly supplied' with minerals, and he described the quantities of coal, iron, and copper as 'almost inexhaustible'.[4]

The petroleum deposits seemed especially promising, and those around the Karun were reported to be 'perfectly colourless and exceptionally pure'.[5] The company took drilling equipment to Daliki, near Bushire, but their drilling was not successful. Then they moved to the island of Kishm where some experimental shafts were sunk. The coal deposits around Bushire were investigated, and so were the manganese mines of Kerman. It had been thought that mining activity would more

[1] McDonald to Sherman, diplomatic series, No. 297, 24 May 1897: Persia, ix, American Department of State.

[2] Imperial Bank of Persia, Additions to Concession, Appendix No. 4: F.O. 60/501. Treasury to Foreign Office, 13 July 1889: F.O. 60/507.

[3] Special report on 'The Mines of Persia' in *The Times*, 10 April 1890.

[4] Pratt to Bayard, diplomatic series No. 153, 19 December 1887: same to same and enclosure, diplomatic series No. 163, 31 December 1887: Persia, iii, American Department of State.

[5] *The Times, loc. cit.* See also Great Britain, Foreign Office, *Diplomatic and Consular Reports, Miscellaneous Series No. 207* (London, 1891), 'Report on a Journey from Tehran to the Karun and Mohamrah, viâ Kum, Sultanabad, Burujird, Khoremabad, Dizful, and Ahwaz', p. 8. See also F.O. 60/528.

than amply reward anyone who undertook the task, but the obstructionism of the Persians and the cost of transportation had not been sufficiently taken into account. In 1893 the Company decided to disband its activities and soon after went into voluntary liquidation, although this was not completed until 1901.[1]

The Imperial Bank also acquired a concession, formerly held by Yahya Khan, for a wheel road from Tehran to Ahwaz. Wolff was enthusiastic over the advantages which would be obtained if its construction proved feasible.[2] The road was to pass through Qum, Sultanabad, and Burujird. Various branch roads were also planned. In 1890 the building began—proceeding from Tehran southward. Two years later the section to Qum, approximately one hundred miles, was completed, but the expenses had so far exceeded expectations that work was suspended. Not until Messrs. Lynch took over the concession at the close of the century did a road connect Ahwaz and central Persia.[3]

In 1890, when the railway dispute loomed up anew, neither the British nor the Russians presented a united front. Morier consistently opposed all activity which touched upon the construction of railways in Persia. Let sleeping dogs lie was his philosophy. Both Giers and Wyshnegradsky, too, thought the moment unpropitious for raising the issue of Persian railways, but they were constantly assailed by the military party which pressed for lines through Khorassan to Herat, Seistan, and the Gulf.[4] On the British side, Morier's contentions were reinforced by the Director of Military Intelligence, General Brackenbury. He argued that the British position in Baluchistan was not con-

[1] Reports of mining activity are given in the *Selections from the Records of the Government of India, Administration Report of the Persian Gulf Political Residency and Muscat Political Agency for 1890-91, 1891-92 and 1892-93*, vols. cclxxv, ccxciii, and ccciv. Report of the Persian Bank Mining Rights Corporation in *The Times*, 14 December 1893. For the claims of the company see the case volume entitled Persian Bank Mining Rights Corporation: F.O. 60/576.

[2] Wolff to Salisbury, No. 13, confidential, 14 January 1890: F.O. 60/509.

[3] Chirol, *The Middle Eastern Question*, pp. 133, 146-50, 161. Special articles in *The Times*, 27 October, 15 December 1902. For a short summary of the three interests of the Imperial Bank—banking, mining, and road building—see Rabino to Lascelles, 16 February 1892: F.O. 60/532.

[4] Morier to Salisbury, private, 8 November 1889: bound volume, Russia, Pte Salisbury Papers. Same to same, No. 353, most secret, 13 November 1889: F.O. 65/1379. Same to same, No. 41, secret, 8 February 1890: F.O. 65/1392.

solidated, and only when it had been developed would it be time to move on to Persia. Moreover, nothing should be done which might stimulate the Russians to build lines in the north:

. . . The construction of this railway [to Seistan] would be a direct incentive to Russia to push forward railways into Khorassan. It would strengthen the hands of the Russian military party, which is anxious to make such railways for purposes of aggrandizement, against the Finance Minister, who, from motives of economy . . . desires to prevent their being made, and any possible advantages that our Indian trade might derive from it would, in my opinion, be far more than counterbalanced by the advance of Russian railways, which would hasten on that evil day when, with an advanced and improved base of operations, Russia will be in a position to threaten our Indian frontier.[1]

Wolff, on the other hand, tried desperately to convince his government of the benefits which would be derived, and he believed that a railway to Seistan was the answer to Russian strides in Central Asia. This line, moreover, could be financially remunerative since it would facilitate the entry of Indian goods into Khorassan and it might lead to the revitalization of Seistan.[2] Herein, Wolff was supported by Lord Salisbury, who wrote in a minute to General Brackenbury's memorandum:

As Sir H. Wolff is unhappily not in a condition to defend his own thesis, with which in some respects I have much sympathy, I desire to add a few words to indicate a line of thought which General Brackenbury has not touched.

If Russia makes her railway through Khorassan the North of Persia is hopelessly lost. Will the South of Persia,—the region which stretches South of the desert & includes Shuster, Ispahan, & Seistan —be lost also? The answer to that question largely depends on some such line as under consideration. If it is not made, Southern Persia must fall too—Affghanistan so embraced must be indefensible—the

---

[1] Memorandum by Brackenbury on the subject of proposed Seistan Railway, secret, 2 October 1890: F.O. 60/517. Later, when he was the Military Member of the Supreme Council in India, Brackenbury modified these views. He said (27 April 1891) that he had objected to the Seistan Railway only so long as Russia made no extensions south of the trans-Caspian line.

[2] Wolff to Salisbury, No. 42, most confidential, 19 February 1889: F.O. 65/1377. Same to same, No. 230, most confidential, 22 December 1889: F.O. 65/1379. Same to same, Nos. 245 and 246, secret, 25 July 1890: F.O. 65/1394.

advanced Russian posts will be on the Helmund. I should, however, myself prefer a railway to Seistan from the sea.[1]

From time to time the Russians had attempted to obtain exclusive rights over railway construction in Persia. In the final analysis their counter-demands took the form of a prohibition on construction. In March 1889 the Shah agreed to a delay of five years.[2] Earlier, on 16 September 1888, he had given Wolff an oral promise of priority for Great Britain as to construction in the south; and of a concession for the line to Shushtar whenever any other power should be given railway privileges in Persia. This was later confirmed in writing.[3]

The new Russian minister, M. de Butzow, tried to persuade Nasir ad-Din to extend the prohibitory period to the end of his lifetime. Later he changed the demands, and asked for a ten-year restriction. At the end of that time the Shah, in consultation with the Russians, would decide whether to prolong further the period of inactivity, or, if not, what railways should be constructed. The British encouraged the Shah to oppose the monopoly provisions and to retain his freedom of action.[4] They believed that ten years was too long an interval but a temporary postponement was not distressing in view of their own difficulties in raising money for Persian railway construction. That the Shah should retain his authority was the main concern.

When it became obvious that the Russians were in earnest, the British interceded for Nasir ad-Din in St. Petersburg. Lord Salisbury informed Morier:

We cannot accept as valid so barbarous a measure as consent by the Shah that his subjects shall be permanently deprived of the bene-

[1] Minute by Salisbury on Brackenbury's memorandum on the subject of proposed Seistan Railway, secret, 2 October 1890: F.O. 60/517. See also Salisbury to Wolff, draft telegram, secret and confidential, 19 May 1890: F.O. 60/513.
[2] Wolff to Salisbury and enclosure, No. 68, 27 March 1889, Asia/confidential/1095: F.O. 60/513.
[3] Wolff to Salisbury, No. 62, most secret and confidential, 20 March 1889, Asia/confidential/1095: F.O. 60/513. See also F.O. 65/1378.
[4] Salisbury to Wolff, No. 87, draft telegram, very secret, 12 September 1890, endorsed 'Print—for Cabinet only': F.O. 60/513. Same to same, No. 101, draft telegram, 10 October 1890: F.O. 65/1395. Salisbury to Kennedy, No. 107, 27 October 1890: F.O. 65/1395. Same to same, No. 259, secret telegram, 29 October 1890: F.O. 60/513.

fit of railways: nor can we admit that their enjoyment of it is to depend on the will of Russia.[1]

He suggested that a *modus vivendi* might be reached according to which England, Russia, and Persia would agree to postpone railway construction in Persia for a fixed period. The British thought that ten years was excessive, but they would agree to it if the Shah were admitted to a tripartite treaty. Lord Salisbury objected strongly to 'the forced abdication by the Shah of his sovereign rights, *especially in regard to the South of Persia*'.[2] When Morier broached the subject of this joint delay, Giers 'gave an exclamation of pleased surprise'. Rarely had the Russian Foreign Minister displayed such 'unalloyed pleasure'. Giers looked forward to a period of 'rest and quiet'.[3]

These representations came too late. The Shah was determined to bury the railway question for the rest of his lifetime. He seemed, moreover, to be in a 'state of almost incredible dread of Russia's subsequent vengeance'.[4] Butzow talked of withdrawing the Russian Legation and said that he would leave Tehran before he would 'humiliate himself' by joining the British in a railway agreement.[5] Nasir ad-Din agreed to the ten-year restriction in negotiations with Russia alone. Morier found, in his next conversations over Persia, that the tone of Giers' remarks had changed abruptly as he recounted a long, inaccurate, and bitter survey of British misdeeds in Persia.[6]

One of the effects of these railway negotiations was to cause Lord Salisbury to look mainly to the south of Persia, and to concentrate more on upholding British interests there. In November 1890 his alterations in a dispatch pointed 'to a

[1] Salisbury to Morier, No. 34, draft telegram, 10 November 1890, endorsed 'Print for Cabinet': F.O. 65/1395.

[2] Salisbury to Morier, No. 29, draft telegram, 1 November 1890, endorsed 'Print for Cabinet': F.O. 65/1395. Salisbury to Kennedy, draft telegram, No. 109, 30 October 1890: F.O. 60/513.

[3] Morier to Salisbury, No. 283, confidential, 12 November 1890, endorsed 'The Queen, Prince of Wales': F.O. 65/1395.

[4] Kennedy to Salisbury, No. 266, decypher telegram, secret, 9 November 1890: F.O. 60/513.

[5] Kennedy to Salisbury, No. 309, secret, 5 November 1890, endorsed 'The Queen': F.O. 65/1395. Same to same, No. 312, 12 November 1890, endorsed 'The Queen, Prince of Wales': F.O. 65/1395.

[6] Morier to Salisbury and minutes, No. 284a, secret, 15 November 1890, endorsed 'The Queen, Lord Cross': F.O. 65/1395. Aitchison, *op. cit.*, p. lxxxi.

N

possible division of spheres of influence. Russia will never acknowledge a right in this country to interfere with what happens in the *north* of Persia.'[1] Several months later he expanded this in a private letter to Morier:

I feel that all the schemes which are devised by many British authorities for stiffening Persia will come to nothing. They are difficult in themselves; and the peculiarities of our system of administration make them really impossible. Things will go on much as they are—till the Slavonic storm bursts. To which side will it move, will it discharge itself on the Vistula or the Attrek? If the latter, nothing will save Persia, though we may possibly pick up some of the fragments that are left upon the south. But there may be many years before that happens.[2]

In another sphere, too, the British were unfortunate. Major Gerald Talbot obtained complete control over the production, sale, and export of all Persian tobacco, including *tutun* widely used in the water-pipe. Nasir ad-Din was to receive £15,000 annually in addition to a quarter of the profits. The company's prospectus appeared late in 1890, but it aroused little attention and the initial work of organization proceeded normally.[3]

The tobacco concession was in itself innocuous enough. Those who mentioned it at all in its early days predicted that it would be generally beneficial. It made no less good a pretext for a popular rising, because almost everyone in Persia smoked, and there were few whom the tobacco monopoly did not touch in some way. Some of Persia's people may have thought that 'De concession en concession, la Perse sera bientôt tout entière entre les mains des étrangers'.[4] But the movement which developed against the company was in the main an expression of discontent by a people—largely illiterate, impoverished, and denied legitimate means for expressing their protests—who had been subjected for many years to the most shocking misgovernment.

The situation which developed was indeed complex. Lascelles saw as the 'chief danger' the character of the Shah 'who is

---

[1] Minute on draft telegram to Morier, No. 29, 1 November 1890: F.O. 65/1395.
[2] Salisbury to Morier, private, 10 May 1891: bound volume, Russia, Pte Salisbury Papers.
[3] Wolff to Salisbury and enclosure, No. 104, 3 April 1890: F.O. 60/533.
[4] J. B. Feuvrier, *Trois ans à la cour de Perse*, p. 182.

always prepared to give anything for a quiet life and shows no inclination to resist the growing power of the Mollahs, or the intrigues in which his own sons are engaged'. Both the Zil and the Na'ib used the tobacco monopoly in an attempt to bring about the downfall of the Amin es-Sultan. Lascelles continued: 'It is evident that if the Mollahs succeed in asserting their power and introduce a fanatical and anti-European regime, we should have to give up all hope of seeing the regeneration of Persia by means of commercial enterprise'.[1] The religious teachers, in a campaign against the monarchy, led the agitations against the tobacco concession. For a time they demanded the abolition of all concessions to foreigners. This decree was to have been signed not only by the Shah, but also by two foreign representatives one of whom must be the Russian minister.[2] 'The Shah', commented Lord Salisbury, 'should maintain his own authority. If he allows the Mollahs to take the government out of his hand, he will suffer much worse things than have happened yet. The suppression of the Imperial Bank would be a most serious breach of faith'.[3]

The original connection between the British Legation and the concessionaire was vague. Wolff wrote:

Some time ago the Imperial Bank, on depositing the stipulated sum on behalf of Major Talbot, received a concession for him and registered it. At the same time I heard Major Talbot was forming an international company. Since then I know nothing. . . .[4]

The Russians protested against the tobacco monopoly— vigorously, officially, and immediately.[5] The Shah and the Amin as-Sultan seemed frightened at the outset, and Wolff's illness which later necessitated his permanent departure from Tehran handicapped the British in meeting the crisis.[6] Not until

[1] Lascelles to Salisbury, private, 24 December 1891: bound volume, Persia, Pte Salisbury Papers.
[2] Lascelles to Salisbury, No. 5, 4/5 January 1892, F.O. 60/533.
[3] Salisbury to Lascelles, draft telegram, 5 January 1892. F.O. 60/533.
[4] Wolff to Salisbury, No. 154, decypher telegram, 13 June 1890: F.O. 60/553.
[5] Wolff to Salisbury, No. 217, decypher telegram, very secret, 6 September 1890: Kennedy to Salisbury and enclosures, No. 286, decypher telegram, very secret, 23 September 1890; same to same, No. 272, decypher telegram, 12 November 1890: F.O. 60/553.
[6] Wolff to Salisbury and minutes by Sanderson and Salisbury, No. 240, decypher telegram, secret, 25 September 1890: F.O. 60/553.

the summer of 1891 did the Persian people become aroused, but at that time the tobacco monopoly become the all-engrossing topic of conversation in the bazaars. The first complaints centred around the excessive profits the company was expected to make. Nor was an influx of foreigners welcomed. Mr. Julius Ornstein, the company manager, worked assiduously to soothe the populace, but he would barely quieten one locality when risings would break out in another. By July the agitation was becoming violent, and in Tabriz an anonymous placard warned 'We will kill the Europeans first and then plunder their property.'[1]

The tone became progressively more menacing, and a full-scale fanatical outbreak was feared. Russian agents promoted the discontent, the mullas preached with ever-increasing vehemence, Malkom Khan supported the agitators, and the people obediently followed this leadership.[2] The Shah and the Amin as-Sultan wanted desperately to rescind the concession, but such a capitulation could only be interpreted as weakness. When they appealed to Lord Salisbury for advice, he said that severe measures should be taken only if necessary in the interest of the country and for the preservation of the Shah's authority. 'We do not wish to assume the invidious position of urging vigorous measures, in order that foreigners may make money', he asserted.[3]

The operations of the régie were temporarily suspended in Azerbaijan and in other localities where the excitement was intense.[4] In the autumn a temporary lull ensued, and a peaceful arrangement seemed in sight. Then, however, one of the chief mujtahids placed an interdict on smoking and branded all tobacco 'unclean' until the concession was repealed. The use of tobacco was declared to be a more heinous offence than indulgence in articles forbidden by the Koran itself. Sir Frank Lascelles, who had replaced Wolff, reported that those in high-

[1] Kennedy to Salisbury, No. 180, confidential, 27 July 1891: F.O. 60/553.
[2] Kennedy to Salisbury, No. 106, decypher telegram, 20 May 1891: F.O. 60/525. Lascelles to Salisbury, No. 242, decypher telegram, 19 December 1891: F.O. 60/553.
[3] Salisbury to Kennedy, private telegram, 6 September 1891: F.O. 60/553.
[4] Kennedy to Salisbury, No. 184, decypher telegram, 9 September 1891: F.O. 60/553.

est authority saw only two alternatives if the concession were maintained—civil war or the retirement of the Amin as-Sultan.[1] The American minister in Tehran described the uneasy Christmas spent by the European colony in Tehran amid incendiary placards reading: 'Death to the Infidel!'[2]

Ultimately, the company negotiated for compensation. Lord Salisbury instructed Lascelles to give advice and whatever unofficial support he could since the company had not been at fault. Such support was not unqualified. When demands seemed excessive Lord Salisbury telegraphed: 'Remember that the first thing we have to care for is the maintenance of the Persian State.'[3] The negotiations for compensation were protracted, but ultimately the Shah agreed to pay £500,000. The Persian Government had no reserve funds; indeed lack of revenue accounted for the original concession. Money was available from one source, for the Russians offered the sum on very liberal terms. Eventually, the Imperial Bank made the loan, and competed successfully with the Russian proposal.[4]

The loan inaugurated Persia's national debt. The long discussions had tried the patience of the British, the Shah, and the Amin as-Sultan. The crisis had arisen at an untimely moment for its early stages coincided with Wolff's illness. In 1891 he left Persia for ever. His departure was a severe blow for the British. Lord Curzon wrote to Lord Salisbury: 'The whole machinery of British prestige & success, political or commercial, at Teheran depended on Wolff.' He feared that the Amin might 'make friends with the mammon of unrighteousness and temporise a little'.[5]

The troubles over the tobacco concession lowered Persia's reputation in European financial circles and it halted the flow of capital into the country, but it produced no change in

[1] Lascelles to Salisbury, No. 238, decypher telegram, 12 December 1891, endorsed 'The Queen, Prince of Wales': F.O. 60/553. Lascelles to Salisbury, No. 261, 22 December 1891, endorsed 'The Queen, Prince of Wales': F.O. 60/553.

[2] Beale to Blaine, diplomatic series No. 29, 28 December 1891: Persia, v, American Department of State.

[3] Salisbury to Lascelles, Nos. 61 and 62, telegrams, 15 December 1891: F.O. 60/553.

[4] Sanderson to Lascelles, private, 20 April 1892: F.O. 60/555.

[5] Curzon to Salisbury, private, 6 October 1890: loose papers, Special Letters, Pte Salisbury Papers.

England's official policy. When Sir Frank Lascelles left England late in 1891 to begin his work as minister to Tehran, he carried with him private instructions from Lord Salisbury. His task was to build on the foundation laid by Wolff, for as Lord Salisbury put it:

Wolff has done very much to aid in the development of Persia. The Oriental Bank, the opening of the Karun, & the tobacco monopoly are all measures which, as they work, will strengthen Persia very much. We have to go on in the same lines, favouring every enterprise which will increase the well being of the Persian people & the strength of the Persian Gov[ernmen]t.

He added that it was vital to avoid the suspicion that the aim of British policy was the exploitation of Persia, for, as he put it, 'where we have very few but moral weapons to use, character is of great importance to us'.[1]

Lascelles found a disheartening situation. The reports of Kennedy, the chargé d'affaires in Tehran, frequently contained the details of riots and seditious plots in Persia.[2] Malkom Khan, now a minister in disgrace, assailed the Shah's government through his newspaper, *Qanun* (Law), which was published in London and distributed secretly throughout Persia. He did not preach violence and revolution, but favoured a gradual development and improvement through constitutional government, codified law, and fair tribunals. Still, such ideas presupposed the disappearance of the present rulers. From the very nature of *Qanun* it is impossible to know how widely it was circulated, or how far it affected the people. The mention of Malkom Khan's name was enough to throw the Shah into one of 'those paroxysms of irritation and alarm'.[3]

Persia's internal crisis was, by 1891, acute. In Khorassan, where the authority of the central government was almost non-existent, the most alarming events were taking place. Some of

[1] Salisbury to Lascelles, private, 6 October 1891: bound volume, Persia, Pte Salisbury Papers.
[2] Kennedy to Salisbury, No. 117, confidential, 2 May 1891, endorsed 'The Queen. Prince of Wales'; same to same, No. 120, 7 May 1891, endorsed 'The Queen': F.O. 60/523.
[3] Kennedy to Salisbury, No. 66, 10 March 1891, endorsed 'The Queen, Prince of Wales': F.O. 60/522. Same to same and minutes, No. 36, decypher telegram, 6 March 1891: F.O. 65/525. Browne, *Persian Revolution*, pp. 35-42.

the tribes of the Yomut Turkomans, equipped with Russian breech-loaders, were in revolt. This nomadic tribe passed part of its time in Persia and part in Russia—where it came under the influence of General Kuropatkin. He had been trained by General Skobeleff, and there were those who attributed Skobeleff's laurels to Kuropatkin's work. Personal scandal had relegated him to the position of Governor-General of the trans-Caspia. But, wherever he was assigned, Kuropatkin seemed determined to leave his mark. He intrigued with the Turkomans, bribed Persia's frontier officials, collected large quantities of military supplies in the Sarakhs-Zulficar vicinity, communicated with the Governor of Herat, and visited nearby Persian villages 'for a change of air' with two hundred 'invalid' soldiers.[1] Morier wrote that the reports of Kuropatkin's doings 'were not pleasant reading for nerves unstrung'. The danger was, in his view, that

the collision [in Central Asia] is impossible if the Emperor is warned, but if he remains with his eyes closed, there is no knowing to what extent a man like Kuropatkine, who, from all I hear is of the type of the Scopeleffs and Kaufmanns, may compromise his Government and force their hand.[2]

Since Khorassan had all but slipped from his grip, the Shah turned to England for aid and advice. Lord Salisbury urged him to send thoroughly reliable officials to the disturbed areas. He recommended that a chain of forts be built along the border

---

[1] Kennedy to Salisbury, No. 187, 1 August 1891: F.O. 60/524. Same to same, No. 10, decypher telegram, 29 January 1891: F.O. 65/1412. Same to same, No. 70, decypher telegram, 10 April 1891: F.O. 65/1413. India Office to Foreign Office, 13 May 1891: F.O. 65/1414. Morier to Salisbury, No. 130, 20 May 1891: F.O. 65/1414.

Memorandum on information regarding the course of affairs beyond the North-Western Frontier, received during the month of July 1891: Simla, Foreign Department, secret/frontier: F.O. 65/1415.

Persia, Traduction d'une Lettre Confidentielle, datée du Mois de Redjeb 1308 (Février 1891), écrite par Son Altesse Émînu-'s-Sultân (Grand Vézir) sous la dictée de Sa Majesté Impériale le Schâh de Perse, et adressée à Son Excellence Mîrzâ Muhammed-Ali Khân, Alâ 'u-s Sultâna, Ministre de Perse en Angleterre, pour être par lui remise confidentiellement à Lord Salisbury, confidential, printed for the use of the Foreign Office, 5 May 1891, endorsed 'The Queen, Cabinet': F.O. 65/1413.

[2] Morier to Salisbury, private, 12 May 1891: bound volume, Russia, Pte Salisbury Papers; same to same, No. 178, confidential, 4 July 1891, endorsed 'The Queen, Prince of Wales': F.O. 65/1415.

so that the Yomuts would feel under strict supervision, and he suggested the possibility of using the Yomuts themselves as soldiers.[1] The British had already transferred Colonel Charles Stewart from Tabriz to the critical region around Astrabad.[2] The Shah concluded that the advice given by Lord Salisbury and that relayed to him periodically by Colonel Stewart was wise. He took, however, no apparent action.[3]

But the anxiety over Khorassan was soon overshadowed by graver troubles. Count Hatzfeldt passed on to Lord Salisbury information that the Chancellor General Caprivi had acquired. A Russian expedition of three hundred cavalry and three hundred infantry had been ordered to the Pamirs to take the territory which controlled the passes through the mountains into India. Lord Salisbury thanked Hatzfeldt for the communication, but he very seriously doubted its correctness. Still, after consultations with the India Office and the Director of Military Intelligence, he decided to put the rumour before Giers with a few words added to convey the impression that the report had reached British authorities through an Eastern source.[4]

Mr. Howard, who was in charge of the Embassy in Morier's absence, brought the question to the attention of Chichkine, the Russian Assistant Minister for Foreign Affairs. Chichkine said, 'positively', that the rumour was 'absolutely' without foundation.[5] When Giers returned from Finland, however, the assurances were less categorical. A small force was proceeding to that

---

[1] Salisbury to Kennedy, No. 4, draft telegram, 28 January 1891: F.O. 65/1412. Draft memorandum to Mirza Mahomed Ali Khan, Foreign Office, 16 May 1891: F.O. 65/1414.

[2] Kennedy to Salisbury and minutes by Currie and Salisbury, No. 9, decypher telegram, 29 January 1891: F.O. 65/1412. Report by Stewart on the Yamoot Turcomans, No. 4, Political, 14 March 1891; No. 5, Political, 18 April 1891, British Consulate, Astrabad, Persia: F.O. 65/1413.

[3] Kennedy to Salisbury and minutes, No. 155, 25 June 1891, endorsed 'The Queen': F.O. 65/1414. Same to same and minutes, No. 181, 27 July 1891: F.O. 65/1415.

[4] Draft memorandum by Salisbury, secret, 15 July 1891, endorsed 'The Queen. Not to be printed': F.O. 65/1415. Foreign Office to India Office, secret, 16 July 1891: F.O. 65/1415. Director of Military Intelligence to Foreign Office and minute by Salisbury, secret, 27 July 1891: F.O. 65/1415. See also Memorandum by Salisbury, 15 July 1891: loose papers, Pte Salisbury Papers.

[5] Howard to Salisbury, No. 34, decypher telegram, 30 July 1891: F.O. 65/1415.

region, but only eighty men were involved and they were going to shoot big game.[1]

Within a few days the Viceroy telegraphed that Captain Francis Younghusband, who had been investigating the extent of Chinese authority in the Pamirs, had met the Russian party. In the beginning he was received cordially, but shortly thereafter he was informed by the Colonel in command that the Governor-General of Turkestan had decided to annex the region.[2] Captain Younghusband's expulsion from the 'newly acquired Russian territory' rapidly ensued, and his colleague, Lieutenant Davison, was seized and held temporarily.[3]

Indignation swept through the British Foreign Office. Howard was instructed to recapitulate the various phases through which the episode had passed—from 'no foundation', to game shooting, to the acquisition of territory—and explanations were requested.[4] Giers listened to the recital sympathetically, and insisted that there must be some 'great misunderstanding'. He did not, however, divulge any information which would clarify it.[5] The continued reports of Russian probing actions and excursions into territory considered under British protection threatened to produce a serious crisis. Lord Salisbury, anxious that Morier should fully understand the views of the Government before he returned to St. Petersburg, consulted with the India Office and the War Office before he drew up precise instructions.[6]

Morier and Giers, no longer working together, could find no immediate solution to the difficulty. Giers, ill and the victim of rivalry within his own department, was no longer a pleasant

[1] Howard to Salisbury, No. 35, decypher telegram, 5 August 1891: F.O. 65/1415.
[2] Telegram from the Viceroy, 28 August 1891: F.O. 65/1415.
[3] Telegram from the Viceroy, foreign/secret, 7 September 1891, endorsed 'Print for Cabinet. Immediate': F.O. 65/1415. Telegram from the Viceroy, foreign/secret, 12 September 1891, endorsed 'Cabinet': F.O. 65/1415. Howard to Salisbury and enclosure, No. 239, confidential, 14 October 1891: F.O. 65/1416. 'An Indian Officer', op. cit., ii, 259–60.
[4] Salisbury to Howard, No. 154, draft dispatch, 11 September 1891, endorsed 'The Queen, Copies to the Cabinet, India Office for concurrence': F.O. 65/1415.
[5] Howard to Salisbury, No. 220, confidential, 16 September 1891, endorsed 'The Queen, Cabinet, Immediate: 16 extra copies on separate sheets': F.O. 65/1415.
[6] Foreign Office to India Office, secret, 3 November 1891: F.O. 65/1417. Draft instructions to Morier, 15 December 1891, endorsed 'The Queen': F.O. 65/1417.

person with whom to deal,[1] and Morier's reports of these negotiations are strikingly different from those in former days. When he asked for an explanation of the proceedings in Central Asia, he was forced to describe the reply as 'so crude, so unfriendly, and so inconceivably fatuous'. The Russian note, he said, possessed the qualities of 'arrogance, superficiality, contempt for facts, and offensive self-assertion which we might expect to meet in a missive of the Czar to the Amir of Bokhara, but strangely out of place in a note to the representative of the Queen of the United Kingdom and the Empress of India'.[2] When his efforts with Giers proved unsuccessful, Morier discussed the crisis with Wyshnegradsky, the Russian Minister of Finance. Morier rarely resorted to a threatening tone, but in the Pamirs dispute he spared no one. If an apology were not forthcoming, he would leave St. Petersburg. Even a partial break in relations would necessitate the publication of a Blue Book, into which, Morier warned, certain damaging revelations about the precarious state of Russian finance would almost certainly find their way.[3] He explained the situation privately to Lord Salisbury.

The entire collapse of Giers was a contingency I could not have foreseen nor the hopeless incompetency of the new men who have been called upon to act as his right hand & his left. Zinoview was a dangerous man, but a thoroughly clever one who understood an argument & would never have let in his chief for such a hopelessly inextricable position as that in which the Russian Government stand in the presence of the notes of the 23d. The result is that I am really fighting the battle with the Emperor in person & a more unenviable task than fighting a stupid autocrat cannot be imagined. . . . It is the case, if ever, for my formula that diplomacy is the art of using the

[1] Morier to Salisbury, No. 97, 10 May 1891, endorsed 'The Queen': F.O. 65/1437. Same to same, private, 28 January 1892: bound volume, Russia, Pte Salisbury Papers.

[2] Morier to Salisbury, No. 27, very confidential, 27 January 1892, endorsed 'The Queen. Print separate section not to go abroad. Cabinet': F.O. 65/1434.

[3] Morier to Salisbury, No. 28, secret, 28 January 1892, endorsed 'Cabinet': F.O. 65/1434. One of Morier's greatest assets was his skill in diagnosing the forces at work within Russia. His dispatches on the internal situation and his analyses of the people with whom he dealt were often endorsed 'candid' or 'interesting'. See, for example, minutes on Morier to Salisbury, No. 24, confidential, 26 January 1887: F.O. 65/1295. Same to same, No. 92, 21 March 1887: F.O. 65/1296. Same to same, No. 389, 28 November 1887: F.O. 65/1299.

force of war *in posse* to prevent the calamity of war *in esse*. We have everything in our favour. They not only dare not risk a war, but they dare not risk the faintest rumour of war because it would bring about an immediate collapse in their finances when the back of the country is broken with this terrible famine.[1]

The almost militant representations were effective, and Staal delivered a vague apology to Lord Salisbury.[2] This was later reinforced by a more specific repudiation from Giers to Morier, and by the Emperor's admission that the proceedings had been 'illegal and regrettable'.[3]

In the summer of 1892, Lord Salisbury's long ministry came to an end. The flames of the Pamirs dispute were dying down, but Lord Rosebery still found it one of the three 'most pressing' issues with which he had to deal.[4] For several months preceding the Conservative defeat the questions connected with Persia had demanded less attention than the more acute controversies about the high plateau further east in Central Asia. The main direction of Russian pressure had now for the time being shifted away from Persia: but it still accentuated the problem of Indian defence.

[1] Morier to Salisbury, private, 21 January 1892: bound volume, Russia, Pte Salisbury Papers.

[2] Salisbury to Morier, No. 42, draft telegram, secret, 12 February 1892, endorsed 'The Queen': F.O. 65/1435.

[3] Morier to Salisbury, No. 98, secret, 10 May 1892, endorsed 'Seen at Berlin. The Queen': F.O. 65/1438.

[4] Rosebery to Gladstone, private and confidential, 27 August 1892: B.M. Add. MSS. 44289, vol. cciv, Pte Gladstone Papers.

CHAPTER XII

Conclusion

INDIA was frequently of the very first importance in the framing of British diplomatic policy; a fact which seems surprisingly often to have been overlooked. The special place of India was made clear in 1901 in a War Office document.

Speaking broadly, so long as the Navy fulfils its mission, the British Empire is impervious to the great land forces of continental nations except in one point—India.

Here alone can a fatal blow be dealt us. The loss of India by conquest would be a death-blow to our prosperity, prestige, and power. The damaging effects of even a near approach by hostile forces would be incalculable.

We cannot doubt, therefore, that whatever may be done or left undone, the greatest and most determined effort will be made by Russia against India.

Next in importance then, and second only to the security of the United Kingdom itself, comes the question of the defence of India.[1]

The defence of India involved chiefly the prospect of a Russian invasion. Knowledgeable persons could never agree amongst themselves whether an invasion, either by direct attack or by intrigue leading to treachery within India, was or was not practicable or likely. Lord Salisbury himself wrote to the Viceroy, Lord Lansdowne, in October 1891 that 'Of late years I think the balance has inclined to the positive or more gloomy side of that discussion.' In his view, recent developments pointed to 'an early effort on the part of Russia to make herself mistress of the Straits': an enterprise which he thought would certainly involve 'an expedition against India to put pressure upon England in order to paralyse her resistance in the

[1] Military Needs of the Empire in a War with France and Russia, secret, 1901: W.O. 106/48, E3/2.

Bosphorus'.[1] As late as 1896 the Viceroy, Lord Elgin, wrote: 'I found to my surprise that the Commander-in-Chief[2] was not prepared to say that a Russian invasion of India was beyond practical politics.'[3] This is the more remarkable when it is remembered that Russian expansion in the decade of the nineties was primarily eastward. Her centre of attention had shifted to China; her energies and available finance were largely taken up in building the trans-Siberian and Eastern Chinese railways; and her dream of a warm-water port in the East was realized by the acquisition of Port Arthur. As Lord George Hamilton put it: 'The danger of a direct attack by Russia upon India yearly lessens, as Russia has other and larger fish to fry.'[4]

The formulation and execution of a clear-cut and consistent policy for British India was made difficult by sharp cleavages which had developed during the nineteenth century. These differences substantially weakened Great Britain in her dealings with Russia in Asia. Of the several divisions the most basic was the conflict between Britain's Indian and Britain's European interests. They became so divergent that John Morley at the India Office once declared: 'The plain truth is . . . that this country cannot have two foreign policies.'[5] The triumph of European considerations was hastened by the telegraph but was not completed until the conclusion of the Anglo-Russian Convention of 1907—an agreement severely criticized in India. The American consul-general at Calcutta told his Government that the convention was regarded as 'all that it ought not to be'. He concluded with the observation: 'It would seem that a convention that was unacceptable to India, Persia, and Afghanistan was hardly one to be adopted by England.'[6]

[1] Salisbury to Lansdowne, private, 21 October 1891: loose papers, Pte Salisbury Papers.

[2] Sir George Stewart White, Commander-in-Chief 1893–8.

[3] Elgin to Hamilton, private, 30 September 1896: Private Correspondence, India, part i, vol. ii, Pte Hamilton Papers, India Office Library. It is also interesting to notice that Lord Elgin described the Commander-in-Chief as a 'levelheaded man' in his letter of 4 November 1896: Private Correspondence, India, part i, vol. iii, Pte Hamilton Papers, India Office Library.

[4] Hamilton to Elgin, private and confidential, 23 September 1897: Private Correspondence, India, part ii, vol. ii, Pte Hamilton Papers, India Office Library.

[5] J. Morley, *Recollections*, ii, 179.

[6] William H. Michael to the Assistant Secretary of State, Calcutta, 20 February

In India itself, two diametrically opposed schools battled fiercely for control of foreign and frontier policy. They disagreed fundamentally about the defence of India and relations with the border tribes. The problem was complex. It involved three distinct but related questions—first, how to deal with raids from the tribal belt; second, how to avoid both the annexation of more territory and increases of responsibility by treaties of guarantee; and third, how to deal with the new situation created by the approach of Russia.

These two schools came to be known as of 'masterly inactivity' and of 'mischievous activity'. The promoters of 'masterly inactivity' inevitably endeavoured to associate their principles with those expounded by Sir John Lawrence. They counselled a stationary or defensive policy, which implied little contact with the neighbouring tribes, no entanglements in the politics of Persia and Afghanistan, and a 'wait and see' policy towards Russia generally.[1]

The depredations and atrocities committed by the unruly tribesmen were for this school to be answered by punitive expeditions which entailed marching into tribal territory, burning villages and crops, and then withdrawing—a policy which was denounced by their opponents as 'alternate violence and inaction' or as 'butchery and scuttle'. They viewed the Russian threat less seriously. Indeed, Lawrence once ventured the opinion that Russia might 'prove a safer ally: a better neighbour than the Mahomedan races of Central Asia and Cabul'.[2] Should the tragedy of a war with Russia occur, it would be fought 'all over the world', in which event a tight defensive strategy for India was to be recommended. Lord Elgin, in 1896,

1908: Case 8570/17, American Department of State Numerical File. See also *The Times*, 26 August 1907 and 2 September 1907. Minto to Morley, 29 May 1907, quoted in Mary, Countess of Minto, *India, Minto and Morley, 1905–1910*, p. 175.

[1] J. W. S. Wyllie, 'The Foreign Policy of Sir John Lawrence', *Edinburgh Review*, ccxxv (1867), pp. 44–7; 'Masterly Inactivity', *Fortnightly Review*, new series, vi (1869), pp. 591–3, 613–15; 'Mischievous Activity', *Fortnightly Review*, new series, vi (1870), pp. 293–5, 303–8. See also Davies, *Problem of the North-West Frontier*, chs. i and ii.

[2] Minute by His Excellency the Governor General, Simla, 3 October 1867. Central Asia and Quetta. Dispatches from the Governor General of India in Council to the Secretary of State in 1867, with minutes enclosed; and Reply. H.C. 73, p. 41 (1879). lxxvii, 151.

wanted a policy of 'trust and co-operation' with Russia,[1] but if that were not possible his military principles were:

a defensive attitude . . . we lock up the smallest number of troops, our communications are absolutely secure, and our enemy can only reach us by a long and difficult march, directly away from his base, and open to attack by fighting clans . . .[2]

The advocates of 'mischievous activity' included such men as Rawlinson, Roberts, and Sandeman. They wanted to promote friendly relations with the border tribes, and to provide for the defence of India outside India—that is, to utilize Persia, Afghanistan, and Baluchistan as outworks in Indian defence. They regarded Russia's push southward with concern if not alarm. Rawlinson, for example, warned that:

Anyone who traces the movements of Russia towards India on the map of Asia cannot fail to be struck with the resemblance which these movements bear to the operations of an army opening parallels against a beleaguered fortress.[3]

Opinion on these subjects usually divided along party lines. The Liberals, led by Gladstone, tried to curtail expansion, and lacked an energetic colonial policy. They supported 'masterly inactivity' in India. Nevertheless, Liberal administrations, hardly less than Conservative ones, annexed territories, fought frontier wars, and built strategic railways. But the theory was different. Liberal sympathy for those under colonial rule reached such heights that Gladstone described the savages who murdered General Gordon as 'a people rightly struggling to be free'.[4]

Conservatives, as a rule, believed that England should make an effort to maintain her position as a great—even an expand-ing—Asiatic Power. During their intervals in office they launched a forward policy in many areas, including Central Asia. Disraeli declared: 'I have always been opposed to, and

[1] Elgin to Hamilton, private, 4 November 1896: Private Correspondence, part i, vol. iii, Pte Hamilton Papers, India Office Library.
[2] Elgin to Hamilton, private, 30 September 1896: Private Correspondence, India, part i, vol. ii, Pte Hamilton Papers, India Office Library.
[3] Rawlinson, *op. cit.*, pp. 293-4.
[4] J. Morley, *The Life of William Ewart Gladstone*, iii, 144.

deplored, "masterly inactivity".'[1] Lord Salisbury wrote that he 'could hardly speak charitably to Lord Lawrence, whom it was my fate to sit next [sic] for two hours, when I thought of all the mischief his masterly inactivity had caused'.[2] Many years later he said that he believed a forward policy to be 'inevitable'— and he went on to say that 'we must gradually convert to our way of thinking in matters of civilisation these splendid tribes'.[3]

Two underlying assumptions consistently run through Lord Salisbury's Indian policy: that the position of the British there was 'singularly unsuited for purely defensive strategy';[4] and that war with Russia 'all over the world' was a meaningless and misleading phrase. 'Russia knows perfectly well that she is unassailable by us', he wrote to Lord Lytton. 'The experience of 1854', he continued, 'proved to her that Cronstadt was too strong to be attacked with success. She has no longer a vulnerable point at Sebastopol. And without a military ally a land invasion would be ridiculous.' She was, therefore, deaf to British protests over her conquests in Asia. These diplomatic remonstrances 'have become a trite, and not very edifying Foreign Office form'. None the less, the story was not simply that of the bear and the whale, for there was one place where England and Russia could come to grips. As Lord Salisbury pointed out: 'If any check is to be applied, it can be applied in Asia only, and that is the part of the question to which alone it is worth while to devote our thoughts.'[5]

Here Lord Salisbury's principles were thoroughly in accord with those of Lord Roberts, the Commander-in-Chief in India from 1885 to 1892. Lord Roberts judged India's frontier to be indefensible; considered a defensive policy to be suicidal; and

---

[1] W. F. Monypenny and G. E. Buckle, *The Life of Benjamin Disraeli: Earl of Beaconsfield*, vi, 381; see also p. 377.

[2] Salisbury to Lytton, private, 2 June 1876: bound volume, Letters from the Secretary of State, i, Pte Lytton Papers.

[3] *P.D.*, Fourth Series, Lords, 8 February 1898, liii, 42.

[4] Salisbury to Lytton, private, 4 August 1876: bound volume, Letters from the Secretary of State, i, Pte Lytton Papers.

[5] Salisbury to Lytton, private and confidential, 22 June 1877: B.M. Add. MSS., No. 39164, vol. ccxxxiv, Pte Layard Papers. These views are borne out by a War Office paper of 1885, England's means of Offence against Russia, secret, 10 April 1885: loose papers, Pte Kimberley Papers.

believed Russia to be assailable, effectively, only through India. In one of his rare speeches in Parliament he said in 1898:

When the responsibility for the defence of the North-West Frontier devolved upon me, as Commander-in-Chief in India, I never contemplated any defence being possible along the Frontier, as marked on our maps by a thin red line—the haphazard Frontier inherited by us from the Sikhs—which did well enough so long as we had only to guard against tribal depredations. A Frontier more than 1,000 miles in length, with a belt of huge mountains in its front, inhabited by thousands of warlike men, over whom neither we nor any other Power had control, and with a wide, impassable river in its rear, seemed to me then, as it does now, an impossible Frontier, and one upon which no scheme for the defence of India could be safely based.[1]

In his official papers he tried many times to explain the unique position of the British in India—the artificiality of an alien rule —and the dangers which must ensue therefrom. In 1883 he wrote:

It must, moreover, be remembered that, whereas the invasion of any country is usually met by the determined opposition of all classes of the inhabitants . . . with the British in India, the conditions would be vastly different. At the best, we could only expect the natives to remain passive, while the first disaster would raise throughout Hindustan a storm, compared with which the troubles of 1857 would be insignificant.

This is a discouraging result of more than a century's rule; but I think that the truth of the statement will be admitted by most people who have been long associated with the natives of this country. It seems to me tolerably certain that, in the event of any serious disturbance, even if numbers were on our side, the strength of the country would be against us.[2]

Again in 1888 he declared officially that a defensive attitude in any conflict with Russia would give rise to grave internal troubles in India and would destroy the confidence of the native army and civilian population. It would thus undermine

---

[1] *P.D.*, Fourth Series, Lords, 7 March 1898, liv, 752–3.

[2] Enclosure in Ripon to Kimberley, private, 4/5 April 1884: Memorandum by Roberts on Is an Invasion of India by Russia Possible?, confidential, 31 December 1883: bound volume, Letters from the Marquess of Ripon, January 1884 to December 1884, Pte Kimberley Papers.

O

British prestige and supremacy throughout the East. 'Prompt offensive operations' were his answer.[1] Lord Roberts outlined his point of view concisely in a letter to Sir James Hills-Johnes, former Military Governor of Kabul. He said:

An idea prevails in some quarters at home, that in the event of war with Russia, India should act strictly on the defensive, while the offensive should be taken from England in the direction of the Black Sea, Asia Minor, or as circumstances at the time may direct. Such an opinion could only be held by men who are ignorant of India. We could not remain on the defensive out here; to do so would lose us India. We must act vigorously and without delay, and, as far as I can judge, we should have a much better chance of dealing Russia a deadly blow from India than from any other route.[2]

Lord Salisbury's stand in this matter is perfectly clear. In 1888 he assured Lord Roberts:

In my humble civilian way I have been preaching the same doctrine for the last twenty years. When first I was connected with Indian affairs in 1866, Sir John Lawrence and all under him were never tired of maintaining the doctrine that India was to stay at home in case of war; and England was to fight Russia 'in every part of the world'. No one seemed to take the trouble to ask themselves at what point 'in every part of the world' Russia was accessible to England. . . .[3]

But in the years that Lord Salisbury was Prime Minister and Foreign Secretary, he might well have remembered what he had said years before to Lord Lytton, for his words about Turkey then might equally well be applied to the north-west frontier.

The commonest error in politics [he wrote] is sticking to the carcasses of dead policies. . . . We cling to the shred of an old policy after it has been torn to pieces; and to the shadow of the shred after the rag itself has been torn away.[4]

[1] Memorandum by Roberts on What part should India take in the event of a war between England and Russia?, strictly confidential, 22 August 1888: loose papers, Pte Salisbury Papers.

[2] Roberts to Hills-Johnes, 14 May 1888; quoted in D. James, *Lord Roberts*, p. 204.

[3] Salisbury to Roberts, private, 19 October 1888: *ibid.*; see also Salisbury to Dufferin, private, 14 September 1887. Pte Dufferin Papers.

[4] Salisbury to Lytton, private, 25 May 1877: bound volume, Letters from the Secretary of State, ii, Pte Lytton Papers. The salient part of this letter is printed in Cecil, *op. cit.*, ii, 145.

Napier of Magdala had, to be sure, adjusted his views to fit new conditions. Once a distinguished exponent of 'masterly inactivity', he left no doubt as to the changes he thought the persistent advances of Russia had made necessary. In an official paper he argued that the nearer Russia came to India the more difficult and expensive the governing of that region would become. Of 'masterly inactivity' he said:

Our policy of masterly inactivity, or rather of receding from every difficulty until what were matters easy of suppression have grown into serious dangers, has continued too long, and, if it is maintained will lead us to disaster.

It has been frequently asserted, by people with pretensions to speak with authority, that we shall be secure if we remain within our mountain boundary.

But this is at variance with all history. A mountain chain that can be pierced in many places is no security if you hide behind it. India has been often entered through her mountain barrier, which was never defended. India waited to fight the battle in her own plains, and invariably lost it.[1]

Lord Kimberley, too, stated publicly on several occasions that 'as to the Lawrence policy . . . the time has passed when we can revert to it'.[2] But, as late as 1898, the Leader of the Opposition, Sir William Harcourt, still spoke in Parliament of 'the spirit and the policy of Lord Lawrence to which I, and I believe most Gentlemen on this side of the House, still constantly adhere'.[3]

The controversy persisted. Debates on the Indian frontier question were emotionally charged. Current issues were constantly being lost sight of in long reviews of past events and in mutual recriminations. There were ancient tales recited of the

---

[1] Memorandum by Napier of Magdala, 30 May 1878. Afghanistan, Correspondence respecting the relations between the British Government and that of Afghanistan since the Accession of the Ameer Shere Ali Khan: [C-2190], p. 226 (1878). lvi, 600.

[2] *P.D.*, Fourth Series, Lords, 7 March 1898, liv, 816. On 8 February 1898 he said: 'but the time has passed when we could take our stand on the Lawrence policy': liii, 28.

[3] *P.D.*, Fourth Series, Commons, 15 February 1898, liii, 729. See also Hamilton to Elgin, private and confidential, 21 January 1898; same to same, private, 11 February 1898; same to same, private, 25 February 1898: Private Correspondence, India, part i, vol. iii, Pte Hamilton Papers, India Office Library. Hamilton to Curzon, private, 13 February 1902: Private Correspondence, India, part ii, vol. vii, Pte Hamilton Papers, India Office Library.

application, misapplication, or non-application of various principles. Yet, the career of one frontier administrator won the
admiration of all, even though his policies did not win unqualified approval. This was Sir Robert Sandeman, the Scots officer
whose courage, tenacity, and character brought Baluchistan
into the British orbit. He devoted his life to the establishment of
personal relations with the tribes for the purpose of promoting
peace, order, and British supremacy. In 1885 Sir Charles
Aitchison, one of Lord Lawrence's most devoted and indefatigable assistants, wrote to the Viceroy, Lord Dufferin:

> Sandeman is doing noble work at Quetta; he knows personally all
> the heads of the tribes and all the leading men, and has great
> influence over them. The people are rapidly settling down and
> learning respect for law and order. I believe the change between
> Quetta now and Quetta five years ago is greater than between the
> India of to-day and the India as I knew it before the Mutiny, and
> that is saying a good deal. For this we have mainly to thank Sande-
> man, whose personal influence is something marvellous. Cultivation
> is rapidly spreading on the Quetta plateau, and villages with
> refreshing foliage are springing up all round the cantonment. I can-
> not speak too highly of the work he is doing. It is noble pioneer
> work.[1]

Sandeman, in 1891, brought the Persian question before Lord
Salisbury and once more into the foreground.

There was a remote but long-standing connection between
Sir Robert Sandeman and Lord Salisbury. That relationship
went back to the mid-seventies when Lord Salisbury was Secretary of State for India and Captain Sandeman was an obscure
frontier officer. The question of security on the north-western
frontier was pressing, and the private letters of Lord Salisbury
and Lord Lytton are filled with references to Baluchistan and
Khelat. On 5 May 1876 Lord Salisbury wrote that 'the doctrine
of non-intervention in Beloochistan has been carried a great
deal too far.'[2] Two months later he reiterated: 'Of course we
must bring Khelat into a more orderly state—& with the help
of that admirable treaty of 1854 we must try to outflank the

---

[1] Quoted by Roberts in *P.D.*, Fourth Series, Lords, 7 March 1898, liv, 755.
See also Thornton, *op. cit.*, p. 292.

[2] Salisbury to Lytton, private, 5 May 1876: bound volume, Letters from the
Secretary of State, i, Pte Lytton Papers.

Amir.'[1] Early in the following year he could congratulate the Viceroy with 'Khelat you have done admirably.'[2]

Sir Owen Burne once told Lord Salisbury: 'I always look upon Khelat as Your Lordship's own policy. You were the first to grasp the importance of that country to us.'[3] If the policy towards Khelat was conceived by Lord Salisbury and supported by Lord Lytton, it was executed by Sir Robert Sandeman. Fifteen years later he reminded Lord Salisbury of that history. The civil war between the Khan of Khelat's government and the confederacy of Baluch and Brahin chiefs had caused such widespread devastation that, in 1875, the Secretary of State for India had pointed out to the Government of India the necessity of 'settling once for all the distracted state of affairs in Baluchistan'. Thus Lord Lytton's government had, in 1876, renewed and re-established the treaty with Khelat, and in consequence of his activities Sandeman could write in 1891 that 'the whole of Baluchistan now enjoys profound peace from the frontier of Persia to the Gumal Pass'. Sandeman concluded his letter as follows:

As the officer directly responsible for the continued maintenance of the treaty reestablished by order of Her Majesty's Government in 1876, I feel that the extension of the Karachi line to Lus Beyla and ultimately to Panjgour [the border state adjoining the Persian Kohak], is daily becoming a question that, considering the grave issues at stake, ought not to be any longer delayed, in the interests of the Indian Empire, and in those of the States of Kalat, Lus Beyla, and Kharan, and of the Province of Kej-Mekran and Panjgour.[4]

It was concern for the north-west frontier that led Sir Robert Sandeman to revive interest in the affairs of Persia. In his recent frontier expeditions he had extended British influence up to the borders of Seistan. Impressed with the strategic importance and economic possibilities of that district, and with

[1] Salisbury to Lytton, private, 19 July 1876: bound volume, Letters from the Secretary of State, i, Pte Lytton Papers.

[2] Salisbury to Lytton, private, 9 February 1877: bound volume, Letters from the Secretary of State, ii, Pte Lytton Papers.

[3] Burne to Salisbury, private, 28 August 1878: loose papers, Pte Salisbury Papers.

[4] Sandeman to Salisbury, private, 2 September 1891: loose papers, Pte Salisbury Papers.

Russian activity there, he took positive steps to institute a more vigorous British line.[1] His actions are remarkable both in themselves and for the results they achieved.

Negotiating with high authorities in India and in England was not one of his characteristic activities. He hated red tape, rather disliked officialdom, resented reports, and once remarked: 'I might have been a great man, but for the telegraph.'[2] Yet it was in person that he placed his views on Persian affairs and his projected railway scheme before the Viceroy and his Council, and while in London on leave during the summer and early autumn of 1891 he interviewed Lord Salisbury more than once. At Lord Salisbury's suggestion he also had conversations with Lord Cross, General Chapman, and Sir Henry Drummond Wolff.

Lord Salisbury was kept informed of the substance of the discussions with Chapman and Wolff. Sandeman placed before General Chapman orally his views on the situation in Persia, and also gave to him a copy of the report he had submitted to the Government of India before leaving Quetta. General Chapman was sympathetic in that he desired to see the development of the resources of the border provinces proceed steadily, but he advocated a somewhat slower process of consolidation of British influence over the tribal territories in the direction of southern Persia and Seistan. Although General Chapman did not seem to be alive to the immediate necessity of the Seistan railway, Sandeman was encouraged in so far as he

fully recognises as I do the necessity for flank defence to Karachi and Baluchistan; the consolidation of British authority in Baluchistan and its development financially with the idea of securing our flank against a Russian advance; not however by the construction of fortifications but by the consistent organisation of the tribes and their gradual incorporation under our authority.

[1] From printed sources an idea of Sandeman's recommendations can be obtained from Sandeman to Curzon, Quetta, 22 November 1891: same to same, Camp, Sibi, 12 January 1892: quoted in Thornton, *op. cit.*, pp. 256–8.

An interesting postscript can be found in Curzon's book. 'I grieve to say that this excellent frontier officer has, just when starting upon a second tour in South Beluchistan, died at Lus Bela (Jan. 1892). An hour before hearing by telegram of his death, I received a long and enthusiastic letter from him about his frontier policy, of which I was a cordial advocate.' *Persia and the Persian Question*, ii, 265 n. 1.

[2] A. L. P. Tucker, *Sir Robert Sandeman*, p. 6.

These projects received Wolff's wholehearted support. Indeed, he had been preaching the Seistan railway for years. At this time, while in London on account of his illness, he was still minister to Persia and it seemed to be remotely hoped that he might return to his post. Sandeman's idea was to correlate his activities on the eastern frontier of Persia with general policy in Tehran. Wolff had no objection to the proposal for doing all that was possible to improve British relations from the Baluch side. He was, on the contrary, 'very anxious to see British influence extended into Southern Persia from Baluchistan and believed a railway ought to be constructed without delay from Karachi or some port on the Persian Gulf with the object of securing our flank and preventing a Russian advance via Southern Persia and Seistan in the direction of Baluchistan and Karachi'.[1]

The most outstanding result of the Sandeman representations was Lord Salisbury's decision to write to Lord Lansdowne himself. This was an unusual departure from the ordinary routine, for it was not customary for prime ministers or foreign secretaries to address the viceroy about a matter of Indian policy. It is noticeable that Lord Cross took care to allude to this in his reply to Lord Salisbury.

I had myself a long conversation with Sir R. Sandeman upon the subject of this railway some little time ago. I should like to see it very much. I am glad that you have written from a foreign office point of view, direct to the Viceroy, and I shall be curious to see his answer. I send you a copy of a paragraph in one of his letters to me on the subject written more than a year ago.

May he not possibly suggest that, as you ground your letter to him *direct* on the understanding that the foreign office is specially interested, the matter is an Imperial one and certainly not simply an Indian one, and that therefore Imperial funds must largely contribute? May he not also add that if it were otherwise India would be expected not only to make the railway but also to furnish the requisite troops when necessary?[2]

Lord Salisbury's letter was long and carefully drafted. It dealt mainly with Persia. That country, he thought, had not

[1] Sandeman to Salisbury, private, 11 June 1891: loose papers, Pte Salisbury Papers.
[2] Cross to Salisbury, private, 27 October 1891: loose papers, Pte Salisbury Papers.

received sufficient consideration by those who drew up the plans
for the defence of India. He wrote:

I have had two or three interviews & some correspondence with
Sir Robert Sandeman in reference to the policy which your Gov[ern-
men]t is pursuing in Beloochistan. . . . I write to you direct, rather
than writing through Lord Cross, because the chief grounds of my
own immediate interest in the matter are considerations arising out
of my own department at the Foreign Office. Though I was once
familiar with all the Indian conditions of the North-West problem,
my knowledge is a little dim, & much of it is antiquated. On the
questions therefore which exclusively belong to the I[ndia] O[ffice]
I do not venture to address you.

In recent years I have been deeply impressed with the conviction
that there is a defect or gap in the plans which your Gov[ernmen]t
has been forming & carrying out for some years for the defence of the
North West Frontier against a Russian attack. I will not discuss the
probabilities of that attack. . . .

The point about which I am anxious is *Persia*: which is strictly a
Foreign Office matter. The Russian forces, provided by sea & railroad passage, lie along the whole North of it. Its powers of resistance
are matter of speculation, but they are probably very small. The
only effective resistance it could offer would be of the irregular
kind—a predatory & partizan warfare which would make the
nourishment of troops & the supply of ammunition difficult. But is
there any chance under existing circumstances that Persia would
offer any such resistance, when once Russia begins to move? I see
nothing to make me think so. Persia will not resist without encouragement. The only encouragement that is of value is a certain support in troops, & a more considerable support in officers, money, &
munitions of war. Any such support is out of the question now, on
account of the distances which any Indian assistance would have to
cover. It is only by a railway from the sea, whether it starts from
Quetta, Kurrachi, or Gwadir, that that distance could be covered,
& the possibility of assistance to Persia on the part of the Indian
Gov[ernmen]t could become one of the elements in the calculation.

You will tell me that the distances are large, the chance of profit
infinitesimal, the burden too heavy for your already embarrassed
exchequer. I fully admit the force of all these considerations; but on
the other hand I ask you to consider what the effect on India of a full
Russian occupation of Persia would be. If Persia is not encouraged
to resist, I do not see why Russia should not become mistress of
Ispahan, Shuster, Teheran & Meshed, & of the country lying

between them. The material basis which such an occupation would give her for operations against India would not be trivial. Much of the country in proper hands is very fertile & full of resource, & the population had a great military reputation at no very distant date. But the moral value of such an occupation would be much greater. What chance would you have of securing the docility of Afghanistan except by mere force, if Meshed was occupied by Russia? And what would be the effect on your Indian populations, who know some-thing of their own history, & who would draw perilous auguries from the achievements of a Power which had been able to conquer Persia? It seems to me that this is the most serious danger on the North West that you have to confront, & from the policy that has been pursued I fear that it has been left altogether out of calculation. . . .[1]

Lord Salisbury in letters of 6 October 1891 to Sir Frank Lascelles and of 21 October 1891 to Lord Lansdowne most fully explained his views concerning Persia. His conclusions had been reached after years of experience and consideration. As early as 1867, in a memorandum written about the policy of the Bombay Government, he had turned his attention to the problems of the north-west frontier. The weakness of the Porte and of Persia he deplored, and he foresaw the coming of rivals in the Red Sea and the Persian Gulf. 'To any such enterprises England must always have the strongest objection', he main-tained, '& statesmen must be prepared for the necessity of forestalling it. It is not a matter for action: but for the careful collection of information.' Even then he felt that 'more vigilance is needed in this quarter than the Calcutta authorities are inclined to admit'.[2]

His interest in Persia continued. That more activity might be expected there is indicated in a short but cordial letter, chiefly about Cyprus, to Colonel Home in 1878.

[1] Compare his minutes on India Office to Foreign Office, secret and immediate, 25 July 1885, F.O. 65/1247, above, p. 90; and on Brackenbury's memorandum on the subject of proposed Seistan Railway, secret, 21 October 1890, F.O. 60/517, above, pp. 179–80 , with the views expressed in more detail in this letter.

Salisbury to Lansdowne, private, 21 October 1891: packet entitled 'Drafts, Copies, Minutes, Memo[randa] etc 1890–1892', Pte Salisbury Papers.

For Lansdowne's reply setting forth reasons for not building the railway see Lansdowne to Salisbury, private, 16 December 1891. Pte Lansdowne Papers.

[2] L[or]d Cranborne's Memo[randum] on policy of Bombay Government. Jan[uary] [18]67: loose papers, Pte Salisbury Papers.

I am glad to think [he wrote] that—at all events during my remaining term of office—our official intercourse is likely to continue—for 'intelligence' is a commodity we are long likely to require in the affairs of the East. If I do not err the next act will open in Persia—are your pigeon holes full of Persian facts?[1]

In the next year, though he was no longer Secretary of State for India, Lord Salisbury wrote to the Viceroy. After expressing his satisfaction over the current outlook in Afghan affairs, he proceeded to urge Lord Lytton to give his mind to Persia. He did not complain of the Government of India's decision to prefer an Afghan policy to a Persian one ('probably it was the wisest course'), but that decision increased the difficulty of dealing with Persia. With Afghanistan under British protection, and Afghanistan was never anything more than a motley collection of tribes in the mind of the Shah, Persia was drawing off towards Russia. Lord Salisbury urged the necessity of defining British aims in Persia.

The question that interests me—what is our objective point to be in Persian policy? Is the Russianization immaterial—& wholly to be disregarded? If not—are there any materials left for establishing counter influence, now that we have pledged ourselves to defend the integrity of Affghanistan & therefore have no territory to promise? If not—should we look forward to some species of partition—annexation of the sea coast as our security against this danger? The nature of the danger—be it distant or near—small or great—I take to be, lest Russia should so far make herself supreme in Persia as to make it a base of action either against the Euphrates Valley or the valley of the Helmund: & I am referring to diplomatic or agitating, as well as military action when I speak of a base.

Lord Salisbury did not think that the problem was immediately pressing, but he clearly saw that decisions taken then would very likely affect Foreign Office policy towards Persia for many years. Russia's future development was another consideration—'in the course of years Russia's pecuniary difficulties will be possibly overcome, if she lasts at all, & new enterprises may be imagined by her eager military spirits'. He had indeed proposed

---

[1] Salisbury to Home, private, 5 August 1878: loose papers, 'Drafts & Copies 1871–80', Pte Salisbury Papers.

to Lord Cranbrook handing Persia back to the India Office, but the advantages to be gained by such a step in bringing greater unity of action on the north-west frontier, and of giving Persia 'an adequate share of the political horizon as seen from Simla', were offset by the alarm which such action would cause to the Shah.[1]

Thus for more than a decade Lord Salisbury had tried to get facts assembled and ideas exchanged which would lead in the end to a rational and well-defined policy in Persia. He had asked the questions which needed answers. He had tried to jog the Government of India into taking as lively an interest in Persia as it did in Afghanistan. In this he was not successful. Lord Curzon, in 1899, wrote the Government of India's 'Persian Despatch' himself because there was no one in the Foreign Department at Simla who could do it.[2] Nor did there seem to be in the voluminous records, in London or in India, any document which went beyond stop-gap measures in laying down a policy for Persia. As Lord Curzon put it to Lord George Hamilton:

I cannot find anywhere in the records of our administration here, and there certainly was not in the Foreign Office records at home, any attempt to lay down, as the basis of common action, what our interests in Persia are, or what they demand; nor have I ever come across any one who could tell me either what our policy towards Persia is, or what it should be. I have endeavoured to supply both deficiencies, utilising a knowledge which is perhaps singular, in so far as it rests upon some acquaintance with Persia itself, as well as upon experience both of the India Office, the Foreign Office, and now of the Government of India.[3]

[1] Salisbury to Lytton, private, 23 May 1879: bound volume, Letters from England, vii, Pte Lytton Papers.

[2] Curzon to Hamilton, private, 10 May 1899: Private Correspondence, India, part ii, vol. xiii, Pte Hamilton Papers, India Office Library.

[3] Curzon to Hamilton, private, 19 September 1899: Private Correspondence, India, part ii, vol. xv, Pte Hamilton Papers, India Office Library.

That this surprising omission seems to have existed is borne out by War Office documents of 1902 in which it is stated that, while Russian activities and aims in Persia and their conflict with British interests had often been discussed, no practical policy for Persia had been set forth nor had means for implementing the several possible alternatives been considered: 'strange to say . . . as far as the records of the Intelligence Division shows, no authoritative opinion or discussion regarding them has ever been given'. War Office Memoranda on Sir A. Hardinge's Letter of 27 August 1902 and Papers Annexed to it, Persia, most secret, 1902: F.O. 60/657.

Any hope that a stronger and clearer policy for Persia would emerge from the 1891 consultations was cut short by a peculiarly unhappy coincidence of events. Sir Robert Sandeman, who had returned to Baluchistan and had already set out on another expedition in the direction of the Persian frontier, died of influenza at Las Bela in January 1892. Sir Henry Drummond Wolff was never able to go back to Persia, although he recovered from his breakdown sufficiently to serve in Spain later. Of even greater significance was the defeat of the Conservative Government in July. The Salisbury–Sandeman–Wolff combination might have had the insight and drive to overcome all obstacles and objections and to put their programme into operation. The occurrences of 1892 permanently shattered any such prospects.

Nearly a year elapsed from the time Wolff left Tehran until his successor, Sir Frank Lascelles, arrived there. In the interval, although the chargé d'affaires, Robert Kennedy, did his best, the domestic situation deteriorated. Riots became commonplace. The Shah's authority, especially along his northern frontier and with the mountain tribes of the south, steadily declined. The mullas became increasingly more radical and more formidable. Russian influence throve. Lascelles was a competent, but not a strong minister. The situation he encountered was depressing enough, and he worked under a severe handicap in that neither the London nor the Indian authorities would back any positive action on his part. The Liberal Government treated the Persian situation as regrettable but hopeless, and tolerable only in that the disagreeable consequences which must ensue from the country's decline and increasing subservience to Russia need not be faced for a few more years. Everyone agreed that the condition of Persia was critical, but the Government of India told the Foreign Office that the Persian question was an Imperial rather than an Indian matter so the responsibility rested on the Foreign Office, and the Foreign Office replied that as Persia was predominantly an Indian interest any action must come either from the Government of India or the India Office. Lord Lansdowne answered one of Lascelles' gloomy letters from Tehran by saying that he could provide no very satisfactory answer:

In the first place, our action must, it seems to me, depend upon the foreign policy of Her Majesty's Government, which again must be affected by the European situation for the time being. I have had a good deal of correspondence with the Secretary of State as to the action which might be taken here in the event of a serious Russian encroachment upon Afghanistan, and I have been given clearly to understand that even in this case, which concerns us more immediately than that of Persia, we shall not be allowed to commit ourselves beyond what might be termed the earliest phase of any operations which might become inevitable. Of one thing you may, I am afraid, be assured, which is that the military forces of which we in India can dispose are barely sufficient for our own requirements, and that anything like a military demonstration in force at a distant point would be out of the question, except in connection with larger operations, authorised, controlled, and directed from home.[1]

Lord Rosebery despaired over the 'Persian edifice . . . so frail and crazy'.[2] Lord Kimberley described the country as 'completely moribund', and took refuge in the thought that 'moribund Eastern States are wonderfully long in dying, and the final catastrophe may yet be distant'.[3]

Sandeman's successor, Sir James Browne, endeavoured to carry on the work along the Persian border. He went to Calcutta with hopes of reviving interest and of persuading the Council to continue the scheme more or less as Sandeman had projected it. He was received unenthusiastically by the Viceroy, Lord Elgin, who informed Lord Kimberley:

I find from the papers that somewhat similar schemes have frequently been brought up, not only by Sir James Browne, but also by his predecessor, Sir Robert Sandeman. The last occasion was in August last, and the proposals then made were declined. . . . My own view is that the proposal is objectionable politically, and in a direction on which I recollect your speaking somewhat emphatically, i.e., an increase of our responsibilities among the wild tribes

[1] Lansdowne to Lascelles, 7 January 1893, enclosure in Lansdowne to Kimberley, private, 11 January 1893: bound volume, Letters from Lord Lansdowne and Lord Elgin, August 1892 to February 1893, Pte Kimberley Papers.

[2] Minute by Rosebery on memorandum by Sanderson on the case of Seyd Mahomed, 10 January 1893: F.O. 60/547.

[3] Kimberley to Lansdowne, private, 3 February 1893: bound volume, Letters to Lord Lansdowne and Lord Elgin, August 1892 to May 1893, Pte Kimberley Papers.

outside our actual frontier: but I have decided to let Browne state his case before the Council to-morrow.[1]

Although he adhered to the principles of 'masterly inactivity', Lord Elgin found that to make plans for decreasing military expenditure and for abstaining from interference in frontier affairs was easier than to carry them into effect. The Amir was demanding an increase in his subsidy, the Waziris were restless, murders were being committed along several portions of the border, and the Lieutenant-Governor of the North-West Frontier Province was asking for reinforcements for Gumal. Thus Lord Elgin had to act in several directions, but his treatment of Sir James Browne shows that 'masterly inactivity' sometimes prevailed. He told Lord Kimberley:

On the other hand, I have taken a somewhat stronger line with regard to affairs in Khelat than I might otherwise have done, very much in order to establish at once my position as one of opposition to any advance beyond our frontier which is not absolutely forced upon us. I have laid it down that there must be no interference with the internal affairs of Khelat, and no occupation of Mekran. The only difficulty as to the latter is that we are under some obligations to Persia . . .

Browne was a man of considerable experience, and an accomplished linguist who had great personal influence with the tribes, so that his removal would be inexpedient. His obedience to the orders issued, orders which he would certainly find disagreeable, was insured by making the extension of his appointment contingent upon his ability 'to satisfy me that he will adhere strictly to the policy we prescribe'.[2]

In London the members of the Political Department of the India Office wrote the final epitaph on the Sandeman project. They went over the whole Persian situation and outlook. For them, Persia was the sick man, but they offered no suggestions for curing him. They simply prophesied collapse and the dominance of Russia, unless the agreements between England

[1] Elgin to Kimberley, private, 14 February 1894: bound volume, Letters from Lord Lansdowne and Lord Elgin, September 1893 to March 1894, Pte Kimberley Papers.
[2] Elgin to Kimberley, private, 28 February 1894: bound volume, Letters from Lord Lansdowne and Lord Elgin, September 1893 to March 1894, Pte Kimberley Papers.

and Russia might be used as a basis for an approach for an understanding over Persia. They alluded in passing to the Seistan railway scheme, but hastily dismissed it as impracticable and too expensive. Their report said:

Sir Robert Sandeman when he was in England, shortly before his death, made an endeavour to get the matter reconsidered, but it was not taken up here, and the Government of India declined to encourage any schemes in this direction, on the ground of want of men. It is not likely that in the existing state of their finances the Government of India will be willing to expend a couple of millions on a wholly unremunerative railway which would always have to be guarded, and which could only be of use for military operations if they were in command of much larger forces than are now at their disposal.[1]

This is to some extent a misleading account. There is evidence that some members of the Viceroy's Council had given support to Sandeman's policies. In 1890, while Sandeman was still at the height of his influence, Wolff planned a trip to India for the purpose of promoting the Seistan railway.[2] Lord Salisbury even extracted money from the Treasury for his excursion.[3] When Wolff was unable by reason of his physical collapse to go to India, General Gordon put the case before the Council. In one of his letters, which at Lord Salisbury's direction was printed for the Cabinet, General Gordon reported to the Foreign Office his conversation of 24 January 1891 with the Viceroy, the Commander-in-Chief (Sir Frederick Roberts), and the Military Member of the Council (Sir George Chesney). He described the outlook from India in hopeful tones.

It is possible that the Royal Engineer and other officers now engaged on the survey of the proposed railway, known as the Zhob Valley line (to make a direct connection between the Punjab frontier system and Quetta) may, next autumn, be made available for a survey of the suggested line west, towards and beyond Nushki.

[1] Persia, The Present Situation, The Policy of Her Majesty's Government, Minute Submitted by the Political Department, 9 January 1893: F.O. 251/58.
[2] Wolff to Salisbury, private and confidential, 15 April 1890: bound volume, Persia, Pte Salisbury Papers. Wolff also stated that he hoped to 'harmonize the views both of India & home with regard to Persia'.
[3] Minutes by Salisbury on Wolff's private telegrams of 2 August 1890 and 12 August 1890: bound volume, Persia, Pte Salisbury Papers.

Sir R. Sandeman is now strongly in favour of a railway from Pasni, on the Mekran coast, about 300 miles from Karachi (where there is said to be a splendid large harbour), to Quetta, through Panjgur and Khelat. This line would for some part of the way, near Panjgur, pass within 60 miles of the Persian frontier, and may be regarded as well calculated to support and strengthen British influence in Persia. It would also be of great strategical value as a direct alternative route from the sea to Quetta, and in flanking the main line from the Indus Valley. . . .[1]

Roberts had long advocated the construction of the Seistan railway. As early as 1889 he told Lord Salisbury:

We should be in a very different position if we had a railway to Kandahar, or what would be still better, to Seistan, with material ready to extend the line towards Meshed in one direction, and the Persian Gulf in the other.[2]

Sir George Chesney also promoted the project. He assured Sir Robert Sandeman: 'I am entirely in accord with you as to the importance of pushing on railway communication in that direction, and I have already placed my recommendations on record in this respect.'[3] Two months after writing this letter Sir George Chesney retired from his position of Military Member of the Supreme Council, and Lord Roberts' term as Commander-in-Chief in India expired in 1893.

With Chesney and Roberts gone the Seistan project drifted but did not die. A trade route was eventually opened between Persia and India. Separate figures were returned for the Nushki route for the first time in 1897. Commercially, the enterprise proved a profitable one. In 1897–8 the total trade amounted to Rs. 5,89,929, and by 1900–1 it had increased to Rs. 15,34,452.[4] Lord George Hamilton, by 1901, could describe the Nushki–Seistan venture as 'a great success'.[5] In

[1] Gordon to Foreign Office, 13 March 1891, printed for the use of the Cabinet, 30 May 1891: F.O. 60/528.
[2] Roberts to Salisbury, private, 5 September 1889: loose papers, Pte Salisbury Papers.
[3] Chesney to Sandeman, private and confidential, 25 February 1891, enclosure in Sandeman to McDonnell, private, 28 October 1891: loose papers, Pte Salisbury Papers.   [4] P.D., Fourth Series, Commons, 13 February 1902, cii, 1244–5.
[5] Hamilton to Curzon, private, 21 June 1901: same to same, private, 27 June 1901: Private Correspondence, India, part ii, vol. vi, Pte Hamilton Papers, India Office Library.

CONCLUSION

213

converting the track into a railway it was Lord Roberts who brought about belated but still beneficial action. When the question was being considered by interdepartmental conferences and by the Cabinet, Lord Roberts declared in an official minute in 1902: 'I am strongly of opinion that we must not let Seistan fall into the hands of Russia, and I hope that the railway to Nushki will be pushed on to Seistan.'[1] St. John Brodrick added that 'the crux of the position is Seistan and no doubt the Commander-in-Chief's opinion as to the Nushki Railway will weigh much with the departmental Conference'.[2] Lord Curzon, in India, was a vigorous champion of the scheme, and by 1905 the Quetta–Nushki branch of the railway was completed.[3]

At the close of Lord Salisbury's administration there were two other questions actively canvassed—one was the defence of India, and the other was Constantinople. Lord Cross in a letter to Lord Salisbury referred to a recent memorandum submitted by Lord Roberts. Its contents had 'much alarmed' the Secretary for War, Edward Stanhope, but Lord Cross had considered it 'very reasonable'.[4] The Government of India's dispatch did in fact contain two minutes by Lord Roberts.[5] Their arguments set into motion high-level discussions and a series of Cabinet meetings about the defence of India. The

[1] Minute by Roberts, 24 October 1902, on War Office memoranda on Sir A. Hardinge's Letter of August 27, 1902, and Papers annexed to it, Persia, most secret, 1902: F.O. 60/657.

[2] Minute by St. J.B., 4 November 1902, on War Office memoranda on Sir A. Hardinge's Letter of August 27, 1902, and Papers annexed to it, Persia, most secret, 1902: F.O. 60/657.

[3] Curzon to Hamilton, private, 29 May 1901: Private Correspondence, India, part ii, vol. xx, Pte Hamilton Papers, India Office Library. The Earl of Ronaldshay, *The Life of Lord Curzon*, iii, 154–5.

[4] Cross to Salisbury, private, 27 October 1891: loose papers, Pte Salisbury Papers.

The India Office correspondence on this subject is bulky. See for example Case 34, Minutes and memoranda on secret dispatch from India of 15 September 1891, October–November 1891: Home Correspondence, Political and Secret Department, vol. cxxvii, India Office Records. Lord Cross has written on this case: 'This is a most interesting and very valuable paper. As soon as the expected papers arrive I should like a very careful memorandum for the use of the Cabinet. 14/10/91. C.'

[5] Government of India, Military Department, to Secretary of State for India and enclosures, No. 180 of 1891, secret, separate, 15 September 1891: W.O. 32/264.

P

resolutions arrived at by a joint committee of representatives
from the India Office and the War Office were submitted to the
Prime Minister and were revised by him.[1] Lord Salisbury
studied the proposals carefully, and the following minute
illustrates his interest:

> Please look in my room A. [he directed] in the container near the
> window—& in the pigeonhole cave close by it—& see if you can
> find (& send here) any papers by Roberts—or Lansdowne—or
> Chesney—on the defence of the N.W. frontier of India.[2]

The changes which came out of these consultations did not
remove all the fundamental differences between London and
Indian authorities, but they tended to promote harmony.
Before the end of 1892 the Director of Military Intelligence,
General Chapman, could tell his colleagues that the government was prepared for 'eventualities in India', and possessed a
plan of mobilization actually *'based on the idea of war'*.[3] Not until
1901 and 1902, when the defence of India was again reviewed,
did the War Office accept the principle that 'in fighting for
India, England will be fighting for her Imperial existence'.
At that time it was also conceded that although war with
Russia would undoubtedly involve military action in many
parts of the world, the focal point would be Central Asia.

> England would be compelled by the necessity for maintaining her
> prestige to apply her main strength across the Indian frontier; and
> as Russia can nowhere put effective pressure on England except in
> Afghanistan, it is there that the contest must be decided.[4]

The military and naval authorities, during the years 1891
and 1892, pressed for a reorientation of British policy in another

---

[1] See for example War Office draft to India Office, secret, 15 March 1892:
W.O. 32/264.

[2] Minute by Salisbury of 23 September 1891 attached to memoranda by
Roberts: loose papers, Pte Salisbury Papers.

[3] Chapman to Badcock, private, 12 October 1892; Chapman to Buller, private,
3 November 1892; Chapman to Brackenbury, private, 21 November 1892: Letterbook of General E. F. Chapman, D.M.I., 1891–3, W.O. 106/16.

[4] The Military Resources of Russia, and Probable Method of their employment
in a war between England and Russia, secret, 1902: W.O. 106/48. E3/1. See also
Military Needs of the Empire in a War with France and Russia, secret, 1901:
W.O. 106/48, E3/2. This document is very important since it summarizes the
more significant letters and memoranda relating to the Indian defence negotiations.

region long considered vital because of its special relation to Russia and to India—that is, in Turkey, or more specifically in Constantinople. To acquire Constantinople was the traditional aim of Russia. To arrest her progress towards that goal was the equally consistent objective of Great Britain. Lord Salisbury put it thus: 'The protection of Constantinople from Russian conquest has been the turning point of the policy of this country for at least forty years, and to a certain extent for forty years before that.'[1]

In 1885 Sir Philip Currie told Prince Bismarck that 'ever since he had been at the Foreign Office, Belgium and Constantinople had been looked upon as questions about which England would fight'.[2] In 1891 this principle, so far as it related to Constantinople, was challenged. General E. Chapman and Admiral C. Bridge, Directors of Military and Naval Intelligence respectively, submitted a joint report approved by the Lords of the Admiralty in which they discussed the feasibility of a Russian attack upon Constantinople and how such a move might be thwarted by Great Britain.[3] Their report disclosed that 'the Foreign Office on the one side, and the defensive Departments on the other, have been proceeding on lines as far divergent as it is possible for lines of policy to diverge'. The military authorities maintained that the defence of Constantinople by Great Britain was no longer practicable.

The peril would arise [said the Foreign Office summary] not from any danger we might incur in meeting the Russian forces, not from the strength of any fortifications the fleet would have to pass, but from the fact that this is the extreme end of the Mediterranean; and that so long as the French fleet exists at Toulon, the function of the English fleet must be to remain in such a position as to prevent

[1] Foreign Office memorandum of 4 January 1892, most confidential, printed for the use of the Cabinet, 8 June 1892: Foreign Correspondence in hands of secretaries, 1892, Pte Salisbury Papers.

[2] Summary of the Memorandum, by Sir Philip Currie, of his Conversations with Prince Bismarck, September 28–30, 1885: quoted in Cecil, op. cit., iii, 259. See also Appendix II, p. 250.

[3] War Office to Admiralty and enclosure, secret, 11 May 1892: Adm. 1/7122. Hamilton, who noted that he agreed with the reasoning and conclusions of the joint report, recommended that 'a copy of this paper should go to Prime Minister, First Lord of Treasury & Chancellor of Exchequer, G.H. 17 May 1892'. A. J. Marder, *British Naval Policy 1880–1905*, ch. ix.

the French fleet at Toulon from escaping into the Atlantic and the English Channel, where it would be a grave peril to this country. They conclude . . . that unless we had the concurrence of France, which is of course an absurd hypothesis, or unless we had first destroyed the French fleet at Toulon, . . . it is not legitimate for us to employ our fleet at the eastern end of the Mediterranean. The presence of the French fleet therefore in the harbour of Toulon, without any declaration of hostile intention or any hostile act, has the power of entirely immobilizing, and therefore neutralizing, any force that we possess or could bring under existing circumstances into the Mediterranean.[1]

As early as 1889 Lord George Hamilton, then First Lord of the Admiralty, had called Lord Salisbury's attention to the shifting balance in the Straits, but then reference to the French fleet as a decisive factor was noticeably lacking. In a private letter to Lord Salisbury he enclosed a report from naval intelligence on the coast defences of Turkey. It was clear to Hamilton that 'when the Russians have three or four ironclads in the Black Sea Constantinople or at any rate the Sultan's palace is at their mercy. A determined rush at night down the Bosphorus could not be stopped.' The British could, however, stop the Russians from passing the Dardenelles, but there the forts were stronger and navigation was difficult. In fact, as the Admiralty well knew, the Turks had fortified the Dardanelles against British entry, but left the Bosphorus clear for the Russians. 'I thought', said Hamilton, 'that you should have placed plainly before you the position which a Russian ironclad fleet in the Black Sea & Turkish apathy & ineptitude outside have combined to make.'[2]

Within a year the emphasis had changed. When Hamilton returned to the subject of forcing the Dardanelles in 1890, he laid most stress on the difficulty of maintaining 'a line of communication from Gibraltar to Constantinople', and the risk of

[1] Foreign Office memorandum of 4 January 1892, most confidential, printed for the use of the Cabinet, 8 June 1892: Foreign Correspondence in hands of secretaries, 1892, Pte Salisbury Papers. The report itself of 18 March 1892 concludes that 'unless we are acting in concert with France, the road to Constantinople, for a British force bent on a belligerent operation, lies across the ruins of the French fleet': Adm. 1/7122.

[2] Hamilton to Salisbury, private and confidential, 5 June 1889: loose papers, Pte Salisbury Papers.

'the great French fleet at Toulon becoming master of the situation'.[1] Lord Salisbury pertinaciously insisted that the dangers
were being overrated, but Hamilton answered him in an almost
lecturing tone, declaring that if anything his account had not
been gloomy enough.

The incidents of 1878 are not a reliable precedent, on the contrary the Russians will take good care that if they do attempt a coup
de main it will be free from the mistakes they made in 1878. A fleet
cannot protect Constantinople from a land attack such as you con-
template except by being masters of the Black Sea. The forts of the
Dardanelles & Bosphorus would both have to be overcome before we
met the Russian fleet, & all supplies would have to pass through this
perilous water way.

Unless the Turks cooperated we should require the whole Mediterranean fleet for the job, & if anything went wrong we should be
in a terrible trap.[2]

In one of his private letters General Chapman alluded to
Lord Salisbury's continuing belief that, although the difficulties
may have increased, British power was still equal to the task of
applying effective pressure at Constantinople.[3] It was a question
of first-class importance. For nearly a century, in Europe and in
Asia, the defence of Constantinople had been looked upon as a
cardinal feature, an axiom and a tradition, of British foreign
policy. Any change would cause comment. Failure to act in the
event of a Russian *coup*, without having publicly announced a
revision of policy, would be attributed to impuissance. Great

[1] Hamilton to Salisbury, private and confidential, 29 April 1890: loose papers,
Pte Salisbury Papers.

[2] Hamilton to Salisbury, private and confidential, undated but endorsed 1890
and filed with the September correspondence: loose papers, Pte Salisbury Papers.

[3] Chapman to Brackenbury, secret, 8 September 1892: Letterbook of General
E. F. Chapman, D.M.I., 1891–93, W.O. 106/16.

General Chapman believed that Great Britain alone could not save Constantinople, but that did not necessarily imply the loss of Constantinople to Russia. He
explained it thus: 'My own view is, that if we wish to make our influence at the
Porte of real use to the country, we must work in harmony, & in close alliance,
with Germany.

'I think the Emperor is so bent upon thwarting Russia at Constantinople, that
he will also go with us in Persia to keep Russia from the Persian Gulf: if we have
Germany with us in both these ideas, we shall win!' Chapman to Chermside,
private, 14 February 1893: Letterbook of General E. F. Chapman, D.M.I., 1891–
1893, W.O. 106/16.

Britain might also be accused of bad faith, or at best of pursuing a policy of 'false pretences'.

The capitulation of Constantinople to Russia would be a serious blow to England because of the tradition alone. It would also react unfavourably upon the 'Oriental mind and our position in India, which is so largely dependent on prestige'. The route to India would be made more hazardous. But the greatest impact would be upon Great Britain's interests in the Mediterranean.

It is our principal, if not our only, interest in the Mediterranean Sea; for if Russia were mistress of Constantinople, and of the influence which Constantinople possesses in the Levant, the route to India through the Suez Canal would be so much exposed as not to be available except in times of the profoundest peace . . . the matter of present importance is its effect upon the Mediterranean: and I cannot see, if Constantinople were no longer defensible, that any other interest in the Mediterranean is left to defend.[1]

The Constantinople dilemma was no nearer a solution when Lord Salisbury went out of office in 1892, but the question of forcing the Dardanelles did not become acute until the autumn of 1895—shortly after his return to power.[2] At that time Lord Salisbury asked the Cabinet to sanction instructions to the fleet at Lemnos to pass the forts and appear before Constantinople (whether the Sultan approved or not)—indeed, he wanted to place the fleet under the ambassador's orders. But the evidence which the experts had compiled weighed heavily with the Cabinet. In the end the admonitions of caution, from the Admiralty especially, forestalled British action. Sir Michael Hicks Beach, Chancellor of the Exchequer in that Cabinet, recalled many years later in his life that the 1895 Constanti-

[1] Foreign Office memorandum of 4 January 1892, most confidential, printed for the use of the Cabinet, 8 June 1892: Foreign Correspondence in hands of secretaries, 1892, Pte Salisbury Papers.

[2] The Constantinople problem was considered by the Liberal Government. In 1894 General Chapman sent to Lord Kimberley, then at the Foreign Office, a report by Sir John Ardagh who had travelled through the Crimea and Constantinople for the purpose of considering the problem of a Russian *coup de main*. His conclusions coincided with those of the joint War and Admiralty report of 18 March 1892. Secret enclosure in Chapman to Sanderson, private, 5 December 1894: bound volume, From and to War Office, Admiralty, Home Office, 1894–5, Pte Kimberley Papers.

nople crisis was the one occasion when Lord Salisbury was more bellicose than his colleagues.[1] Although he yielded graciously and without reserve, Lord Salisbury almost bitterly told Goschen, the First Lord of the Admiralty, that 'In Armenia I have been told by the Cabinet practically to sit still.' Goschen answered that 'It was one particular movement, namely to pass our fleet alone through the Dardanelles to which some of us were strongly opposed.'[2]

Lord Salisbury's distrust of 'experts' was already proverbial, but it was intensified after his experience in 1895—a failure deeply and lastingly felt. A year later Goschen referred to 'the feeling which is clearly strong on your side, that the Admiralty action thwarts your policy', and he went on to say:

as Prime Minister and Foreign Secretary it is, I quite understand galling to you not to be able to secure a readier acquiescence in your views as to the disposition of the fleet than I have, unfortunately been able to give. To use your own expressive phrase 'it cuts me to the heart' just as our Admiralty action seems to have done to you.[3]

The Cabinet decision, in Lord Salisbury's opinion, wrote finis to an energetic British policy in Turkey.

Thus in the early nineties Persia, the Straits, and the defence of India were matters of serious and immediate concern. They all three hinged upon Great Britain's relations with Russia, and two of these, Persia and Turkey, bore more particularly on the defence of India. The Conservative defeat in 1892 occurred when deliberations on all the three were in mid-stream.

In Salisbury's last administration the task of providing for the defence of India was more definitely met. Two Cabinet

[1] Lord St. Aldwyn to Lady Gwendolen Cecil, private, undated but filed between 16 December 1913 and 23 January 1914: Pte Hicks Beach Papers.

[2] Goschen to Salisbury, private, 22 December 1895: loose papers, Pte Salisbury Papers.

[3] Goschen to Salisbury, private, 12 December 1896: loose papers, Pte Salisbury Papers.

The appraisal of the situation as given by Admiral Seymour to Sir Philip Currie, 29 June 1895, is interesting. 'If it came to forcing the Dardanelles, there is no doubt we could get through with more or less damage, but the forts are very different from what they were in Hornby's time—& it would be rash particularly if there was any doubt about the French to leave them in our rear, & really there ought to be a land force to take them in the rear. . . .' Bound volume, Turkey, Pte Salisbury Papers.

decisions—to enter into an alliance with Japan and to proceed with the Quetta–Nushki railway—were directly connected with the Russian menace. The hostility of Russia and France, the dread of having to fight those two powers together, was still the major determinant of British foreign policy.

The Russian threat in Asia and the growing might of the Dual Alliance therefore induced many British statesmen and public officials to look hopefully towards Germany. Sir Thomas Sanderson confided to Lord Salisbury in 1898 that 'I have not liked to say—what I feel—that France is pushing us more and more towards a German alliance.'[1] Sir Philip Currie wrote in 1900 that he had recently 'been reading over the rough notes of my conversations with Prince Bismarck in 1885, and I confess that they have to a certain extent revived my belief in the advantages of a close understanding with Germany'.[2] Lord George Hamilton, who had once been confident that Great Britain's burdens could be lightened by an agreement with Russia, had reluctantly but gradually altered his views. We must, he told Lord Curzon, 'throw in our lot, for good or bad, with some other Power. On the whole, I think the best alliance we could form would be to join the Triple Alliance. Such a combination would guarantee the peace of Europe, and, would, I believe, enable us to reduce our expenditure, both naval and military.'[3] When Lord Curzon demurred, Hamilton pointed out that if an alliance with Germany could be arranged, 'it would very greatly strengthen your position in India'.[4]

As late as the autumn and winter of 1902 the precarious and potentially dangerous situation in Persia caused the British to think of Germany. Lieutenant-Colonel Altham of the Intelligence Division wrote:

The occupation by Russia of Eastern Persia not only will lay India open to direct attack, but will also give Russia a new and inde-

[1] Sanderson to Salisbury, private, 3 April 1898: loose papers, Pte Salisbury Papers.

[2] Currie to Salisbury, private, Rome, 27 September 1900: loose papers, Pte Salisbury Papers.

[3] Hamilton to Curzon, private, 25 April 1901: Private Correspondence, India, part ii, vol. vi, Pte Hamilton Papers, India Office Library.

[4] Hamilton to Curzon, private, 17 October 1901: Private Correspondence, India, part ii, vol. vi, Pte Hamilton Papers, India Office Library.

pendent line of advance, and will thus enable her to largely increase the number of men she can launch against the Indian frontier.

This is a matter of serious moment to the Empire. Under existing conditions, it has been held that India will, in the contingency of war with Russia, require reinforcements of 70,000 men; but it will be seen from paragraph 13 of Lieutenant-Colonel Robertson's paper that in three years' time the completion of the Tashkent-Orenburg Railway will enable Russia practically to double the number of men she can throw into Afghanistan. This change in strategical conditions will leave India dangerously insecure, unless the permanent garrison is increased, and a provision of still larger reinforcements arranged. But if to this be added the necessity of providing a separate force to oppose the Russian advance through Seistan, an addition to our army of 100,000 men will barely suffice to place the defence of India on a satisfactory footing.

It is therefore highly desirable that, if possible, some counter-move should be devised to frustrate any attempt to make Eastern Persia, or at least, Seistan, a Russian province.

Before the British decided what they *would* do in Persia they had to ascertain what they *could* do. The plain issue was: Could England without the help of allies bring a war with the Dual Alliance to a successful conclusion? The facts were not encouraging. Her military status was pronounced 'distinctly inferior' to that before the South African war, and it was predicted that a single-handed conflict with France and Russia would 'entail on the Empire a period of humiliating disasters, from which recovery will be most difficult'.[1] On the other hand, 'the vital necessity is that our prestige must remain unimpaired both in India itself and among the border tribes. Each step Russia takes forward endangers this prestige.'[2] Lieutenant-Colonel Altham summarized the quandary and suggested a remedy.

These conclusions are extremely unpleasant to face, the more so in that they land us in an *impasse*. If we take steps to counteract a Russian advance into Persia, we risk a war, in which our chances of success are very doubtful; if we do nothing and let Russia gradually

[1] War Office memoranda on Sir A. Hardinge's Letter of August 27, 1902, and Papers annexed to it, Persia, most secret, 1902. Memorandum by Lieutenant-Colonel E. A. Altham, A.Q.M.G., dated 14 October 1902: F.O. 60/657.

[2] *Ibid.*, Memorandum by Lieutenant-Colonel W. R. Robertson, A.Q.M.G., dated 4 October 1902: F.O. 60/657.

absorb Persia, the evil day is but put off to a time when we shall be forced to fight for India under still more unfavourable conditions.

There is in fact no sound solution of the Persian question if we adhere to our present lines of military organization and to our present policy of isolation from all European alliances.

But if it be permitted to reconsider those two essential factors it will be found that a change in either, or still better in both, would place the defences of the Empire, from a military point of view, on a secure footing.

. . .

Germany is concerned equally with ourselves in thwarting a Russian advance which might end in Russia dominating not only all Persia, but Asia Minor, Mesopotamia, and the Persian Gulf. A mutual understanding between Germany and Great Britain as to Asia Minor and Persia, resulting in an agreement drawn up on lines similar to those of the Anglo-Japanese Alliance would enable Russia to be checkmated without her daring to risk a war, or, if war ensued, it would be a war the results of which we need not fear.

The report concluded with the recommendation that Germany be approached.[1] The Director-General of Mobilization and Intelligence, Sir William Gustavus Nicholson, passed these memoranda up to the Commander-in-Chief, Lord Roberts. General Nicholson agreed with the views expressed by Lieutenant-Colonels Altham and Robertson. He added some observations of his own, one of which was:

It seems almost impossible to maintain British interests in Persia unless we come to an understanding with either Germany or Russia. But while in the former case the interests of the two nations would not be dissimilar and the understanding would have some chance of being of a permanent nature, in the latter case the interests of England and Russia are so obviously antagonistic that any agreement as to spheres of influence in Persia would probably be infringed by Russia whenever it suited her purpose to do so.[2]

Thus it seems clear that anxiety for British interests in the Middle East bulked large among the motives which inspired the abortive alliance negotiations with Germany. As in 1885, the British were now again drawn to Germany because of

---

[1] *Ibid.*, Memorandum by Lieutenant-Colonel E. A. Altham, A.Q.M.G., dated 14 October 1902: F.O. 60/657.

[2] *Ibid.*, Memorandum by General W. G. Nicholson, D.G.M.I., dated 16 October 1902: F.O. 60/657. Roberts opposed alignment with Germany.

Russia's threat to India from Central Asia. This threat was an added reason for making an effort to counterbalance the Dual Alliance, which was the more alarming in general because the naval strength of Great Britain compared with that of France and Russia had in recent years distinctly deteriorated.

The tradition against an outright alliance with a European power was still very strong. Lord Salisbury, near the end of his career, had passed the time when he would initiate or even support fundamental changes. His experience with Germany in 1885 may well have contributed to his growing scepticism. He may have been hindered also by the hostility of the Liberal party to the Mediterranean Agreements, by the poisonous recrimination of British and German newspapers, and by Parliamentary considerations. The problem of Indian defence was not in the end to be met by that German alliance to which he had once been prone to look as a means of insuring the British position in the East. This was to be done, several years after his death, not by consorting with Russia's enemies, but by agreement with her, in the Anglo-Russian Convention negotiated by the Liberal government in 1907. In the words of B. H. Sumner:

The gain to Great Britain was very great; for her the removal of the threat to India was the major object of the convention and a necessary preliminary for any real entente with Russia. . . . For Persia, however, and for the British position in Teheran the Anglo-Russian agreement spelt nothing but loss . . . it was anathema to most Persians, and it became more and more of a stumbling block for liberal opinion in Great Britain as it became apparent that Russia was bent on the destruction of the Persian nationalist and constitutionalist movement. . . . By 1914 Anglo-Russian relations in Persia were if possible worse than ever . . .[1]

Lord Salisbury's legacy does not include a set of rigid and easily defined principles. He founded no school. His policy cannot be summarized in phrases like the 'sealed border' or the 'closed frontier'. Perhaps this is as well. Catch-phrases like 'masterly inactivity', and its opposite 'mischievous activity', commonly survive for years and are too often applied long after circumstances have changed and when their use has become positively dangerous.

[1] *Tsardom and Imperialism*, pp. 62–4.

Lord Salisbury's policy in Asia shows a consistent development, and it forms a coherent pattern. It was based upon certain underlying assumptions. He regarded India as a magnificent possession which deserved to be defended. He believed that Russia's territorial gains in Central Asia, consolidated as they were by a system of strategic railways, placed her in a position from which she might threaten India. It was an incontrovertible fact that Russia had once had an ideal boundary in the Kirghiz steppe; that she had conquered it only after more than a century of strenuous effort; and that she seemed determined to leave all deserts behind in her drive to the mountainous and relatively populous borders of Persia and Afghanistan. If she had sincerely wished to avoid clashes with the slave-trading tribes of the khanates and interference in the affairs of the Amir and the Shah, the obvious course would have been to keep a wide desert border in her front. Her advance had been continuous, and it was impossible to know when it would stop. Indeed, there seemed to be no reason to assume that it would ever stop. The engagements of the Russian Government were not kept. 'The promises given are not worth the breath with which they are spoken'—so said even the Duke of Argyll.[1] Nor were Russian expositions of policy comforting. Gortchakoff told Morier that 'in case of European complications England was to be paralysed in Europe by fear of complications in India'.[2] An official memorandum declared that 'if our establishment in the Trans-Caspian region demanded great sacrifices from the Empire, still they would be amply repaid by the advantages which, thanks to our position in Turkomania, Russia could extract from the yielding nature of England on disputed questions of general policy'.[3]

To counteract this, Lord Salisbury worked for the maintenance of a tier of buffer states along the outskirts of India. Persia was a vital link in this chain which stretched from Siam to Turkey. 'What we have to do in Persia', he explained to Sir

[1] P.D., Third Series, Lords, 10 March 1884, cclxxxv, 985.

[2] Morier to Salisbury, private, 1 September 1885: loose papers, Pte Salisbury Papers.

[3] Memorandum on the Condition of the Trans-Caspian Province, secret, St. Petersburgh, 14/26 January 1887, enclosure in Dering to Salisbury, No. 294, secret, 23 August 1888, printed for the use of the Cabinet, 30 August 1888: F.O. 65/1352.

Frank Lascelles, 'may be summed up in two sentences: we have to make Persia as strong as we can by internal development to resist the supposed aggression; & we have to obtain for ourselves the amount and the kind of influence which will enable us when the crisis comes to turn the efforts of Persia into the right direction.'[1] Unlike Sir Edward Grey he did not believe that the expression 'the independence and integrity of Persia' was a fiction and an illusion. Speaking in St. Andrew's Hall, Glasgow, on 21 May 1891, Lord Salisbury said:

A curious part of the duty of the Foreign Office in its great dominant mission of preserving peace and extinguishing all danger of war, wherever it may arise, is the relation in which it places us with the Mahomedan communities of Europe and Asia. One of the great provocations and dangers of war has arisen from the position of these great Mahomedan communities . . .

The danger was receding 'in the progressive improvement of the majority of these states under the contagious influence of more enlightened ideas'. He referred specifically to the 'hopeful revival' in Persia.[2] But in the reform of Persia, success did not come during his own lifetime. Conditions worsened steadily throughout the nineties, and the popular discontent was once more shown in the assassination of Nasir ad-Din in 1896. Improvement did not follow his removal, for the last of the Qajars were a wretched lot indeed. They took no steps to relieve the poverty and misery of the people they ruled. They virtually completed the thraldom to Russia by two disastrous loans. Nevertheless, the events of 1905 and 1906 proved that reform in Persia amounted to something more than a high-sounding and impracticable ideal.

Finally, Lord Salisbury believed that the maintenance of prestige was a basic necessity for the continuation of peaceful British government in India. Sir Robert Sandeman wholeheartedly endorsed his views. 'What Lord Salisbury said . . . regarding prestige is,' Sandeman declared, 'I most truly believe, soundly true and shows that His Lordship has a deep insight into the motives which influence the minds of such Orientals as

[1] Salisbury to Lascelles, private, 6 October 1891: bound volume, Persia, Pte Salisbury Papers.
[2] Cecil, op. cit., iv, 384–5. The Times, 21 May 1891.

Afghans and Persians.'[1] To Lord Salisbury maintaining prestige meant keeping his word and fulfilling the obligations he had undertaken. It did not mean making a quarrel of every dispute, which could be just as fatal as giving way to every pressure. He was forceful without being bellicose. His objective in Persia, as it was elsewhere, was to find and to follow what he called 'the difficult, the narrow line that separates an undue concession from that rashness which has, in more than one case in history, been the ruin of nations as great and powerful as ourselves'.[2]

---

[1] Sandeman to Burne, private, 19 April 1884: loose papers, Pte Kimberley Papers.

[2] *P.D.*, Fourth Series, Lords, 8 February 1898, liii, 43–4.

APPENDICES

I

Correspondence and Memoranda relating to Herat, 1885

Private telegram from Viceroy, 21 March 1885:

Before seeing the Amir, would it not be well that I should know the innermost mind of the Government up to date. The first question is—Are we determined to keep Herat out of the hands of Russia at any price?

The following is the situation as viewed from here—We calculate from information received that the Russians could place 30,000 men before Herat about the 21 May, & 70,000 men, if they mean business, by the 7 July. Herat itself seems almost destitute of proper ordnance. By reducing the British garrison left behind to 30,000 Infantry and 2000 Cavalry (and we are all agreed that this is a minimum) we should have 17,000 British, 38,000 natives, 178 guns at our disposal. But the several arms comprising the force are not in regulated ratio—front line at present available 32,000 men and 108 guns. Could get 12,000 men into Herat before 21 May—so small force ought not to go unless able to support by 5 divisions before end of June. If meet Russians at Herat shall require at once from England 22,000 Infantry, 1100 Cavalry, 2 batteries Horse Artillery, 18 batteries of Field Artillery. Total 25,800. Would give 40,000 British. Native Army should be increased. Once we know the reinforcements were on their way, we could afford to send to the front at once a considerable proportion of the 30,000 men already noted as the British Garrison to be left behind in India. To fight Russians at so great distance from base great strain. On the other hand, if we allow Herat to fall Amir would consider himself betrayed, and the effect in India would be very bad. Commander-in-Chief inclines to let Herat go. Other military authorities have no doubt of the issue if we receive proper and timely reinforcements, and admit great expense. Foreign Department believes that, as the struggle must come sooner or later, it would be better to fight now for Herat, with the Afghans on our side and the Turcomans unsettled, than after Russia has consolidated herself in Central Asia and we have alienated Amir. The second question is—Do we intend to declare war if the Russians cross Afghan frontier, even though defence of Herat not a necessary part of our military programme? Could you make the dog drop his bone by squeezing his throat (that is, blockade his ports, etc.), instead of taking it out of his mouth? In that case our army would take up position in front of Candahar. Either alternative requires troops. Important I should know intention of Government on these two points before seeing Amir, as it would not do for me to allow him to expect support which we were not determined to give. I trust you may be able to come to reasonable settlement, but ought negotiations to delay troops? They may be merely intended to mask Russian concentration. We have too much at stake to leave anything to chance. I have seen many Natives; all deprecate abandonment of Herat, and some spontaneously suggest income tax. Native Princes volunteering assistance.

Dufferin

This telegram raises in the most direct form the question whether we are to defend Herat with our whole strength and to take immediate steps for that purpose.

As far as I can form a judgment on a question which is in many aspects entirely military, I am not in favour of sending a great army to fight the Russians at Herat.

1. Herat is at a great distance from our frontier. It is 512 miles from Quetta our nearest military post, and it must be remembered that the railway to Quetta is unfinished, and that the railway only extends as far as Dadur at the mouth of the Bolan Pass. There is however a good military road through the pass.

2. I do not believe that by any exertions we could place a British force in Herat in time to prevent the Russians from taking it. Sir P[eter] Lumsden's reports show that it is miserably prepared for defence. If we send out such a force as is required according to Lord Dufferin to meet the Russians at Herat (and I do not question the numbers required), Russia will certainly believe we are determined on war, and I cannot think she would allow us to anticipate her at Herat.

3. Could we get so great a force as 25800 men to India before the

great heats? I suppose that by calling out all our reserves and militia immediately it might be possible.

Would not so great a demonstration render the continuance of negotiation almost hopeless?

4. I have always felt the greatest doubt as to the possibility of our defending Herat from any real attack of Russia, now that the Russians are so much nearer to it than we are, except through the Afghans. If the Afghans are not strong enough to hold it with such aid as we can afford them in arms and money, and officers to advise them, I believe we must give up the hope of doing so, and must look to a line of defence nearer India.

The difficulty is how to keep the Amir with us in present circumstances and to discharge our obligations to him.

This brings me to Dufferin's second question 'do we intend to declare war if the Russians cross Afghan frontier' etc.

I should answer, that, if they advance in force with a view of taking Herat, war is unavoidable, whether we make 'the defence of Herat a part of our military programme' or not.

We should discharge our obligations to the Amir by the fact of our resisting the act of Russia by war. We must be the sole judges how that war can be best carried on, and our engagement to him cannot bind us to any particular military operation. If therefore we do not consider it a wise military measure to send an army to Herat, we are not obliged by any consideration of good faith to do so.

Ought we not however to make immediate preparations at home to reinforce, if necessary, the army in India? As Dufferin justly says 'we have too much at stake to leave anything to chance.' I have drawn up two telegrams, one 'secret' (that is official), the other 'private'.

K[imberley]
21 March 1885

I am not well off for military advice at present, but I will obtain such as is available tomorrow on the question whether it is possible for us to send out such a force as would in Dufferin's opinion enable us to keep the Russians out of Herat.

If we can do this, and can therefore give the Amir the assurance that we will do it; and if we also send out at once or prepare to send out the first instalment of the troops required, I think that it would probably be the best chance of avoiding war, and of carrying it on successfully if this must be so.

Q

I do not believe Russia will deliberately encounter such a force as Dufferin speaks of backed up by the Affghans. The danger is that she will creep on gradually, seize Herat by a coup de main and force war on us in more unfavourable conditions.

H[artington]
22 March 1885

I agree with Kimberley——

Both alternatives are most serious.

Kimberley's view seems to be confirmed by the Commander in Chief in India, and by the Intelligence Dep[artmen]t here. But on this Hartington will be able to speak.

What confidence is it possible to place in the Ameer. If in earnest, and he is able to raise the Turcomans the diversion might save Herat.

G[ranville]
[undated]

I agree with the substance of the telegrams which Kimberley proposes to send—In fact Dufferin will be instructed to enter into an offensive & defensive treaty with the Ameer—Russia is only in my opinion to be stopped by a general war with her not by a war at Herat.

N[orthbrook]
22 March 1885

The only way of avoiding war is to lead the Russians to believe that we are in earnest. I doubt if they will think so as long as we go on with our preparations for going to Khartoum. The possibility of making the Suakin railway now seems more remote than ever. I should use grave language with regard to Russia;—send the Suakin force to India only holding the town as a post against the slave trade,—order Wolseley to India, & bring the Korti force down to the best Egyptian frontier.

I agree with Hartington subject to the Khartoum operations being at once abandoned.

Ch[arles] D[ilke]
23 March 1885

If this question had to be decided without a Cabinet, I should incline to Kimberley's views: not to have a race for Herat, or to urge military authorities in India, if against their judgment, to fight at 500 miles from our base.

But I think that, without any delay, the 7 or 8000 reserve men required to fill up the English battalions in India should be sent out. This ought, even for reasons of the season, not to be delayed. Dufferin should assure the Amir that any genuine invasion of undoubted Affghan territory should be a casus belli, and the fact that he had done so ought to be known. And the 25000 men should be advanced to Quetta. I do not think there should be any delay whatever in filling up our army in India, either for the safety of the country, or for the effect, serious but not menacing, which so reasonable a precaution would produce. To withdraw from the Soudan prematurely for the purpose of making a demonstration against Russia might bring on a Russian war, which would be much worse than a Soudanese war: but I am entirely in favour of winding up military operations in the Soudan as soon as the immediate affair with Osman Digna is over; sending a portion of the army to India, and withdrawing Wolseley's force northward in such a way as to show that, now that the real point of danger to India is ascertained, we do not mean to spend our strength elsewhere.

G. O. T[revelyan]
[undated]

I think that we should at once inform Russia that any further advance towards Herat will be a casus belli, and in proper diplomatic language insist on her repudiating any such intention, and on her arresting all movements of troops from the Caucasus & other provinces towards the frontier.

We should also insist on an immediate answer.

When we receive it, or when she shuffles, we should at once determine on the military movements necessary. But I should deprecate a retrograde movement at Souakin until Osman Digna has been chastised. Otherwise the moral effect of the two last skirmishes will be very mischievous, both in Europe & in the Army.

H. C. E. C[hilders]
23 March 1885

This is a very difficult & most anxious question: but of one thing I feel sure, that, unless actually at war with Russia, any sudden withdrawal, or decision to withdraw, from the positions we have taken up in the Soudan, would be discreditable and disastrous.

Lord Kimberley is of course right, when he says that, if we *are* forced into a Russian war, we must reserve to ourselves full discretion as to the measures to be taken, and the points of attack or defence to be chosen in any part of the world.

But, fully agreeing in this, it still seems to me, that we should not hesitate to send such a force, (at all events), as can be spared from India, to be in a position to assist the Ameer in the defence of Herat, if attacked, or in its recovery, if occupied and taken. I cannot help thinking, that the moral effect of its abandonment would be most dangerous in Affghanistan, and in India also. Of the military considerations proper, I do not presume to judge.

Selborne

23 March 1885

I concur generally with Kimberley as to the policy to be pursued in India and our attitude to the Ameer—

We should also I think free our hands as soon as possible by withdrawing from the Soudan affair. The further we are involved in this the greater will be our difficulties & the greater the inducement to Russia to follow a forward policy.

It may not be possible to withdraw the Suakin force until Osman Digna is dealt with: but would it not be well to instruct Lord Wolseley to withdraw his force to the frontier of Egypt as much as he can before the hot weather sets in?

G. [J.] S[haw] L[efevre]

23 March 1885

I incline to Lord Kimberley's view but reserve a final opinion till the matter has been discussed in Cabinet.

J. C[hamberlain]

23 March 1885

I believe that the answer to Dufferin's two questions should be affirmative. The fall of Herat, into Russian hands, means not merely the loss of what has always been called the Key of India and a spot which can of its own resources support a large army, but a deadly blow struck at our supremacy in India.

I believe further that the only peaceful way out of this crisis is by the most warlike firmness: and indeed I suspect that Russia is less ready than we are.

I think that Dufferin should be informed that we wish to make every preparation to prevent the Russian occupation of Herat; and that the Ameer should be told so, and asked what he would wish us to do, whether to send troops there or to supply him with arms to defend it himself.

And both the Russians and Dufferin should be told that any further advance by the former will be considered a casus belli: though it may not be necessary to tell the Russians so at once, nor indeed until Dufferin shall have seen the Ameer.

But of course this is so vital a matter that it can only be properly considered by the Cabinet itself——

R[osebery]
23 March 1885

I think we have no choice as to defending Afghanistan and Herat is undoubtedly a part of Afghanistan. We ought to tell Russia that an attack upon it will be a *casus belli*, and make such preparations as will show that we are in earnest.

To abandon Herat is to turn the Ameer into an enemy and it will not long put off the fight for India.

I think there is a fair chance, even a probability, of the Russians giving way if they see we mean business. It would be premature now to say that we shall let the Egyptian business stand over: but probably that will be the result, if Russia does not give way.

All details are best discussed in Cabinet.

D[erby]
23 March 1885

This is a desperate decision to have to take. The most disadvantageous position we could occupy would be to have to fight at the extremity of the frontier of Afghanistan. But then if we do not fight then Herat will fall without a blow & there is no likelihood of the Russians advancing beyond that point so as to come to meet us. Can we keep the Ameer if Herat is allowed to fall?

The best chance would be to inform the Russian Gov[ernmen]t at once that the capture of Herat will be a *casus belli*. But there ought to be a Cabinet before such a message is sent.

I agree with Dilke it is impossible to come to such a decision unless we have made up our mind to abandon the Khartoum expedition.

The news of yesterday shows that Souakin Berber expedition is an impossibility.

We have undertaken this Egyptian business in a great part for the interest of India & it is plain that our engagements there are the greatest peril to which our Indian Empire is exposed.

W. V. H[arcourt]
23 March 1885

I concur generally in the views you have so well expressed in your memorandum.

Besides the distance of Herat another consideration weighs with me namely that it is not precisely and properly Afghan though undoubted Afghan territory.

Please see my memo on the official (Secret) telegram—especially A and B.

As to A, I do not see how we can negotiate except with a reserved power to decide. Of course it would be right, and you might I think in the telegram properly engage, to communicate with him (the Amir) whenever practicable from time to time.

Then as regards B. It was the phrase used in the case of Canada when war was by no means proximate, & when we had no war on our hands. Is it desirable to erect such a phrase into a formula? May not the meaning, which is war, be quite well conveyed in other words without so high sounding a phrase? (I do not know that the words I have suggested are very good ones).

I should think the telegrams ought to be circulated—and I presume they will go to the Queen.

W. E. Gladstone to Kimberley
22 March 1885

Telegram to the Viceroy [Draft]
Secret—

Your Excellency should in your approaching conference with the Amir use every effort to ascertain in the most distinct manner possible

how far the Amir is prepared to
proceed in confidential relations with
us and in execution of the agreement-
entered into with him in 1880.

*It was declared by us in
1880 but did it not exist
before?* W.E.G.

Nothing would be worse than that
we should proceed upon an
equivocal and half explained
understanding with him, the
consequence of which might be his
abandonment of our alliance for that
of Russia when we (were) actually
committed to serious steps.

had already become?
I agree K

You should endeavour to induce
him to place himself unreservedly
in our hands as regards the
settlement of his frontier
by negotiation.

(A) *It is also of vital importance that he should*
I agree

We shall act for him as we
should act for ourselves if the
frontier were our own, and we
shall do our utmost to obtain
recognition of all his just rights,
but it is very important that he
should not take an extreme view
of his claims, as it may appear to
us that it may be better to make
some concession from his full
claim rather than fail to bring
the matter to a peaceful conclusion,
or that it is necessary that
some territory should be
relinquished to prevent
obligations being placed on him
as regards the maintenance of
order on his frontier which he
cannot be expected to adequately
discharge.

*Could this sentence be
broken up*

on the other hand it is
manifestly not for his
interest that obligations
should be placed on him as
regards the maintenance of
order on his frontier which
he cannot adequately
discharge and it may
in our opinion be advis-
able to make certain
concessions rather than
fail to bring the matter
to a peaceful conclusion

You should therefore
endeavour to persuade
him not to take an
extreme view of his claims

Assuming that the Amir
will be ready to defend Herat to
the utmost of his power you should
offer him any assistance he may
require for this purpose and which

you may judge to be expedient,
~~either~~ in money, arms,
~~or~~ and officers.

If the Russians should
~~cross the acknowledged~~
~~Afghan frontier for the~~
~~purpose of invasion, and~~   invade the undisputed
seizing Herat, Her Majesty's   Afghan territory with
Government will be prepared   the object of
to support the Amir
~~with the whole strength~~   (B) *by* ~~military mea~~ *the*
~~of the Empire,~~   *forces of Her Majesty?*
and they will concert with
him as to the best mode of
supporting the Afghan forces,
but they must reserve to themselves
full liberty as to the particular
measures which it may be
advisable to take for prosecuting
the war to a successful issue.

From Secretary of State to Viceroy, 25 March 1885
Private. Yours. 21st.

We are not in favour of such an expedition, at the present time, to Herat, as you describe. Such a demonstration as the despatch of 25,800 men from this country as soon as they can be got ready would render continuation of negotiation extremely doubtful; and, apart from this, would not the Russians be sure to advance at once when they saw us preparing to move forward with so great an army? If so, how could we be in time? The Amir should, if attacked, make best defence he can at Herat, and we shall be ready if war breaks out to give him military support in such manner as may appear best, but we do not think you should pledge yourself now to undertaking an operation at so great a distance as Herat, or that you should, at the present time, extend your preparations beyond what may be necessary to take up a military position nearer our own frontier, such as you mention under the head of your second question. An attack on Herat will mean war between us and Russia everywhere, and the Amir must leave us to fight the battle in the way we think most likely to secure success. Subject to these considerations, what reinforcements do you require? We have determined to take at once authority to call out our reserves, but do not mention this until it is announced here. I am sending you also a secret telegram on this subject.

II

Sir Philip Currie's Negotiations with Count Herbert and Prince Otto von Bismarck in the Autumn of 1885

Homburg, 4 August 1885

Dear Lord Salisbury

I am staying here to drink the waters and have fallen in with Herbert Bismarck, who is at Königstein, a few miles from this place. Being aware, from recent conversations, of your views as to the possibility of arriving at a settlement of the Zulficar difficulty through the intervention of Prince Bismarck, I thought it might be useful if I spoke to his son in that sense. I accordingly explained to him how matters stand, & how the discussion is now narrowed to the single point of the Zulficar Pass: I pointed out the danger to the peace of the world of leaving things in a state which may at any moment produce a rupture between England & Russia, and asked him whether it would be possible to induce the Prince to arbitrate upon the interpretation to be given to the words of M. de Giers's Telegram of April 16 in wh[ich] he agreed to the exchange of Zulficar for Penjdeh. I referred to the position of Prince Bismarck, which made him practically the arbiter of the destinies of Europe, and to the certainty that any assistance he might give us in coming to a settlement, would establish a claim on the gratitude of the English nation and would lead in the future to a closer union between Germany & England.

Count Herbert listened to what I said with much attention, but expressed unwillingness to make any commu[nicatio]n to his father on the subject, at a time when he was holiday making, and had been for some weeks absent from Berlin. He did not think the Prince would approve of his doing so. He asked why a communication could

not be made through Malet who is on the point of returning to
Germany. I said that I thought you would be very glad to know
privately in the first instance how such a commu[nicatio]n would be
received; that if made thru' our Ambassador, however confidentially,
it would assume to a certain extent, an official form, and that therefore I ventured to ask him to write to the Chancellor & sound him
on the subject.

After some discussion he agreed to do so, but said he must warn
me that the answer would probably be that the proposal must come
through the ordinary channels. According to his experience of his
father, he would not enter into the question on any other footing. I
asked him to use his influence, and to try & get at any rate some
indication as to the reception the proposal would meet if made confidentially through the Ambassador.

Count Herbert then spoke generally of the question. He did not
believe in the probability of a rupture, thought the Russians had no
present intention of advancing on Herat, & that the Afghans were
in much greater force on the frontier than they were. He doubted
Russia agreeing to arbitration as to Zulficar. It was a question of
prestige. The Emp[eror] had taken the matter into his own hands &
for the first time had gained some popularity by being supposed to
have shewn more firmness than his Ministers. He would wish to confirm this reputation & was vain of his diplomatic triumph.

Count Herbert entirely concurred as to the value of a close
alliance between England & Germany. He said the German
Gov[ernment] had always held the same view, but that the irritating policy of the late Cabinet had been impossible to understand.
He referred to his last visit to England when he had reminded Lord
Granville of the proposals he had made on a former occasion for an
agreement as to Colonial questions. Lord Granville had at first
denied that they had ever been made, but on C[oun]t Herbert
repeating the words he had used, admitted that something had been
said, but that he had not fully understood it. He had added that he
was not conversant with Colonial questions, and had suggested that
Count Herbert should have conversations with L[or]d Kimberley
& L[or]d Derby. Count Herbert replied that he had not come to
hold conferences, but to discuss the matter with the foreign minister.
There was no danger, he said, of such misunderstandings under the
present Gov[ernmen]t. Your thorough knowledge of foreign questions would prevent them, and if difficulties arose, you would look
into them yourself.

In the course of the conversation as to the suggested arbitration,

Count Herbert said that his father might be unwilling to undertake the task from fear of irritating public opinion in England if the decision were unfavorable. In Russia, if the Emp[eror] was satisfied, there was nothing more to be thought of, but in England with our parliament & free press, a solution might satisfy the Cabinet & yet be badly received by the Country. Lord Rosebery, who is staying here, had told him that the question was one about which there was a very strong feeling in England. Count Münster had reported that Sir C[harles] Dilke had used similar language at a dinner at which you were present. I said that the feeling against further concessions to Russia was no doubt very strong, but there was also a great desire for the settlement of the question, and I did not believe that a decision fairly & impartially given, even if it proved adverse, would cause any irritation in England against the Arbitrator.

Count Herbert mentioned incidentally that if arbitration were to take place, the Emperor as Head of the State would have to be the nominal arbitrator.

He believed his father's view was that it was better that the sovereigns of the smaller states should arbitrate between the Great Powers, as the latter had common or conflicting interests on so many points that it was difficult for them to appear quite impartial judges between two of their own number.

Ever dear Lord Salisbury
Yours very truly,
Philip W. Currie

ps. I enclose a copy of a short résumé, which I had prepared before seeing Count Herbert, of what I proposed saying to him, and which I gave him to read.

Copy of Paper shewn to C[oun]t Herbert Bismarck at
Königstein. 3 August 1885

The Affghan boundary negot[iatio]ns have come to a deadlock on the question as to how much of Zulficar Pass is to be given to Afghanistan. The Russian Gov[ernment] undertook, before Lord Salisbury came into office, to exchange Zulficar for Penjdeh. The Ameer was formally promised that he would have the Zulficar Pass and agreed to a boundary traced on that basis.

Our officers are unanimously of opinion that the pass extends to a point 9 or 10 versts from the Heri Rud marked C upon the map. The Russians will only give the first portion of the pass (about 3 versts of it) and object to ceding the remainder on the ground that it would interfere with the communications on their side of the frontier.

The position is critical and, if a settlement is not arrived at within the next few months, is very likely to lead to war. The Russian Commanders are enterprising and are eager for a dash at Herat. The Afghans are rash, and another Penjdeh affair may occur at any moment. Either of these contingencies would inevitably produce a rupture between England & Russia, which would lead to hostilities, not only in Central Asia, but in every part of the world where England could deal a blow at her antagonist. The point on which we should concentrate the greatest part of our energies would be the cutting of the communications between Russia and her Central Asian possessions. For this it would be an absolute necessity for us to obtain an entrance to the Black Sea for our ships, and this we should unquestionably do by some means or other, whatever view Europe might hold as to the localisation of the war.

In order to avert this calamity, the only plan seems to be to make an appeal to Prince Bismarck to mediate between the 2 Countries. The questions at issue being now reduced to the one point of Zulficar, all that would be required to bring about a settlement, would be that H[is] H[ighness] should adjudicate upon the interpretation of the words of M. de Giers's Telegram of April 16 agreeing to cede Zulficar in exchange for Penjdeh. We could lay before him the evidence of our officers as to what is included in the Zulficar Pass. The Russians might do the same. Or if the Prince thought it necessary, he might send a German officer to the spot to decide the question. In making this appeal to the Prince, stress might be laid upon the unprecedented position which he occupies in Europe, which has made him practically the arbiter of the destinies of other nations. The constant & unswerving desire for the maintenance of Peace which he has shown, his moderation and justice towards other Countries, inspire confidence that his intervention (if he would give it) would be exercised with perfect fairness. The English people trust him and would be satisfied with his verdict. It is not likely that in Russia, where it is believed that (outside the ranks of the military party) a sincere desire exists for peace, his judgment would be questioned. The Prince would be adding lustre to his renown, and it would not be the least of his great achievements that his moderating & pacific influence should have secured peace between two of the great Powers of Europe, when all other hopes of agreement had failed.

If he were to effect this, he would secure for himself and his Country the lasting gratitude of England, and he would be laying the foundations of a closer and more intimate alliance between the two Countries.

The present Prime Minister of England is known to be favorable
to such an alliance in the fullest sense of the terms, and once established, the English people, who have the strongest leaning towards
their old Protestant ally, would not allow their Government (from
whatever party it might be taken) to swerve from it. A close union
between the greatest military power and the greatest naval power
would produce a combination that would not only secure the peace
of the world, but would also be in the highest degree advantageous to
the interests of the two Countries. It would put Germany at ease as
regards the safety of her Colonial possessions in the event of European complications, and it would leave England free to defend her
interests in the event of unprovoked aggression on the part of Russia
against her Indian Empire, without fear of hostile neutrality on the
part of the European Powers.

P[hilip] C[urrie]

Homburg, 7 August 1885
Private

Dear Lord Salisbury

Jocelyn was away from Darmstadt for a few days so I was not able
to send you a telegram: but forwarded the figures to Arlington Street
by post. I now take advantage of the monthly messenger who leaves
on the 9th to send you a written report of my interview with Herbert
Bismarck. He was very cordial & friendly, spoke of his respect &
regard for you in the warmest terms, and said he felt flattered
at your wishing to make the commu[nicatio]n through him.

But he was evidently afraid of a snub from his father. When I
asked him to use his influence, he said 'no one has any influence with
my father——' The only point that seemed rather to surprise him
in the paper I showed him was the declaration that we must &
should go into the Black Sea in case of war with Russia. He said 'but
it is closed by a Treaty to which all the Powers of Europe are parties.'
I said 'not if the Porte invited us in' and that they could not expect
us to make war with one arm tied behind our backs. He read the
paper carefully through 3 or 4 times. Our conversation lasted for
some hours & I argued thru every point with him at length, but I
think I have given you the gist of all that he said of importance. A
telegram to Jocelyn Darmstadt would reach me at once, as he is now
here and it would be forwarded. I propose to stay here till next
Thursday evening the 13th by which time an answer will I hope

have arrived. I then return to England & take a week's holiday
before returning to work at the F[oreign] O[ffice].

Yours very truly,

Philip W. Currie

Homburg, 9 August 1885

Private and Confidential

Dear Lord Salisbury

With reference to what Herbert Bismarck said as to the Prince's
readiness to state his views to one of your colleagues or a person in
your confidence, I asked him if he thought it would be well for me to
go to Varzin at once & see the Prince. He said that he thought there
would be a better opportunity of doing so a month hence when the
Prince would move to Friedrichsruh, which was more accessible,
being on the railway between Homburg and Berlin, and where the
visit of an Englishman would excite less observation. It was there he
said that C[oun]t Schouvaloff had twice visited his father before the
Berlin Congress, and a Cardinal had once been entertained there
and had come down to dinner in a red suit, without the fact becoming known.

Nothing could be more friendly than Herbert's manner and he
seems really fond of his English friends of whom there are many
here.

I propose to leave on Thursday morning unless I hear from you
to the contrary. I have sent off a telegram, containing the substance
of my letters, this morning.

Yours very truly,

P. W. Currie

10 August 1885

Private

Dear Lord Salisbury

Herbert Bismarck came over yesterday from Königstein & brought
an English translation which he had made of his father's answer, and
which he allowed me to read. I regret to say that it was unfavorable,
though couched in the most friendly terms. It had been dictated by
the Prince to his son in law M. de Rantzau, and was a lengthy
document filling nearly two sheets of foolscap.

It began by stating that the Prince was flattered at your having
made the communication to him, and that he would have been very

glad to do what he could to promote good relations and peace
between England & Russia, but doubted whether the course suggested would have that effect. He could not undertake arbitration
unless it was also proposed by Russia in concert with England; and
this was unlikely as Russia had already shewn her dislike to German
arbitration when the Penjdeh affair was under discussion.

The Prince was of opinion that the object of Russia in protracting
the negotiations was to gain time until she was better prepared and
her railroads completed. He was more inclined, than Lord Salisbury
seemed to be, to think that Russia intended a further advance, and
if this was the case, she would be unwilling to agree to German
arbitration, which might have the effect of depriving her of the
further acquisitions to which she was looking forward.

The Prince had at one time thought that the object of Mr. Gladstone's Government was to engage in war with Russia in order to
conciliate the public opinion of England which had been alienated
by the blunders of his foreign policy. His Highness now believed that
the Russian Gov[ernment] might be inclined to push matters on
with a view of combating the Nihilism which was on the increase
in the Russian army.

Any declaration made by the Prince of his willingness to arbitrate between England & Russia would be construed as pressure on
the part of Germany on Russia. The Prince thought that arbitra-
tions between the Great Powers should be conducted by the
Sovereigns of the smaller States. Otherwise they tended to produce
bad blood between the arbitrary state & the disputants. It was the
interest of Germany to be on good & friendly terms both with
England & Russia, & arbitration would be sure to alienate one if
not both of them. The two parties to a law suit were invariably each
convinced of the justice of their respective claims; & the one against
which judgment was given always thought that an unfair view had
been taken of his case. It was the same in disputes between nations.
The arbitrator would suffer from the annoyance felt by the defeated
party.

The Prince thought that the question might be examined by
experts (This was not clearly explained, but I understood that he
meant English and Russian experts, which would agree with M. de
Staal's last suggestion).

If Germany he undertook arbitration and decided against Russia,
the Russian press would at once commence a crusade against Germany, and it was not sure that it would not provoke Russian hostility, even if he decided in their favor. He referred to the Berlin

Congress as a case in point, when he had supported all that he understood Russia to want, and had then been violently attacked for preventing Russia from continuing the war & depriving her of the advantages which, it was pretended, she might have gained in a further campaign, although she would have had (as Herbert Bismarck added) England & Austria against her as well as Turkey.

The Prince added that if he decided against England, public opinion there would probably resent it, and his arbitration might then do the present Government more harm than good. He believed that Mr. Gladstone's Gov[ernment] had been upset in consequence of the failure of their foreign policy, and a defeat on the Zulficar question might lead to a downfall of the present administration.

The Prince concluded by saying that he was most anxious to please Lord Salisbury personally and that he desired strongly to comply with his request, but that the interests of Germany did not allow him to do so, and that Lord Salisbury as a patriotic statesman, would understand that they must be his first care.

After I had read the letter of which the above is a summary, Count Herbert said that M. Rantzau, who was acting as his father's secretary at Varzin, had written him a private letter containing in still stronger terms the friendly feeling of Prince Bismarck towards Lord Salisbury's Gov[ernment] & stating his readiness to assist them as much as he could in Turkey, Egypt & elsewhere abroad, and his wish that he was able to do so equally at home (i.e. in England). The Prince was pleased at the communication having been made through a strictly private channel as it enabled him to answer without reserve, and dispensed him from communicating with the Emperor. The fact of its having been made would be known only to the Prince, his son in law and Count Herbert. The Count said that in writing to his father he had mentioned that I had expressed a hope that his answer would give some indication of the reception his view of the suggested arbitration, in the event of his refer saying that it must come through the usual channel (see my letter of Aug[ust] 4). Prince Bismarck appears to have understood this as a request for an expression of his views generally on the question, and M. de Rantzau wrote that although the Prince would not like to put them on paper, he would be willing to state them 'between 4 eyes' if he saw a colleague or confidential agent of Lord Salisbury.

In the course of our conversation Herbert Bismarck repeated still more emphatically what he had said at our previous interview as to the difficulty of a settlement being increased by the fact that the

Emperor of Russia was dealing with the boundary question himself,
& having been lauded up to the skies by his courtiers for his supposed diplomatic triumph, was now persuaded that he was the first
diplomatist of the age. He also said that according to the reports
received from Russia at Berlin, Nihilism was much on the increase
in the navy, line regiments & artillery. In the two last named services it was especially due to the partiality shewn to the officers of
the Imperial guard, to whom the commands of all regiments were
given, while the line officers never rose above the command of a
battalion. Herbert Bismarck's line towards Russia was one of bitter-
ness & dislike. I suspect that in this as in other things he shares his
father's opinions, but (as he said) 'what we have to think of is the
danger of a coalition against us of Russia and France,' and it is the
fear of such an eventuality which determines the Prince to do
nothing that might fan into a flame the smouldering hatred of the
Russian nation against Germany. He is convinced that his interference in the Afghan quarrel would have this effect and for the
present I do not believe that anything would turn him from his
resolution to stand aloof from it.

  'The water' said Herbert 'is too hot for us to put our finger in.'
                                        Yours very truly,
                                              Philip W. Currie

                                            21 September 1885
Dear Lord Salisbury
  I have received the inclosed today from H[erbert] Bis[marc]k proposing that I should go to Friedrichsruh on Saturday next, & giving
me all directions viâ Flushing. If you would like to see me first, I
ought, I suppose, to start for Dieppe on Friday morning & after
seeing you, go on to Paris by an evening train so as to be in time to
go from Paris on Saturday. I have failed in discovering in a foreign
Bradshaw when the trains go from Paris to Homburg or how long
they take. Perhaps you could kindly have this looked out in an
indicateur as I ought to let H[erbert] B[ismarck] know at once by at
what hour I should arrive at Friedrichsruh—The boat leaves New-
haven at 9 on Friday morning so that I should be with you in
good time. Will you write me a letter desiring me to come over to
Dieppe for a few days on business which will serve as my reason for
going away. I think it might be best to ask Pauncefote to come.
Lister will have to remain in sole charge, unless you think it

R

w[oul]d be worth while asking Pauncefote to come up for a few days from Christchurch.

Ever yours truly,
Philip W. Currie

Notes of conversations with Prince Bismarck at Friedrichsruh.
28 September 1885

For Lord Salisbury

Notes of my visit to Friedrichsruh. September 1885. Secret.

In the morning I walked with the Prince alone.

He said that he was glad to have an opportunity of talking openly with a person in the confidence of Lord Salisbury though he regretted that this conversation did not follow the elections instead of preceding them. Though he hoped that the present Gov[ernment] would remain in office it was possible that Mr. Gladstone might become Prime Minister again & he was a man who had no knowledge of foreign affairs & with whom it was impossible to do business.

But what he was about to say had reference to England as a nation.

Friendship with England had been the traditional policy of Prussia. The first thing that had interrupted it was the conduct of England during the Franco German War—Her neutrality had a leaning on the French side, and this the German nation had not forgiven. Later had come the Colonial questions. But the policy which he had pursued and which had been considered as unfriendly to England was not inspired by any feeling against her or wish to injure her. It related only to questions where England & France were at variance and he had sided with France in order to try and extinguish the animosity of that country against Germany. He had thought, (mistakenly, as he now saw) that in time it would be possible for France to be so far reconciled to Germany that ~~the French~~ she would give up seeking constantly for an opportunity of revenge— Such had been the case after Waterloo, & France which had been on the most hostile terms with England in 1840 had been close friends with her 10 years later.

With this view he had humored and made love to the French. He had helped them in Egypt & Madagascar and had indulged them in the Congo affair. He had persevered in this policy for 15 years, but it had entirely failed and he had now finally made up his mind that he had been following a wild goose chase. The game was beyond his power to catch. All his efforts had been thrown away &

France was as ready to seize any opportunity of attacking Germany as ever. The Spanish affair had been the last drop in the balance which had decided him. He now washed his hands of France and was prepared to side with England in questions between the 2 Countries. There were now no points of difference between England & Germany. As far as the Colonies went, he had got all he wanted, and more than he believed Germany could digest. He had never favored the Colonial idea himself, but opinion in Germany ran so strongly in favor of Colonial enterprise that he could not resist it, or rather that he could not refrain from turning the Colonial stream into the main channel of his Parliamentary policy. He would support England against France, and if ever the differences between the two Countries were pushed to the brink of war, he would not allow the war to take place. It was impossible for the French to engage in war with a power like England without being secured on her Eastern frontier and that security he would not give her. A war between England & France would in no case be favorable to German interests. If England was victorious, it would leave things no better than they were at present. If France conquered by invading England, the balance of Power in Europe would be permanently disturbed, and France might ally herself with Russia against Germany.

The only other Power with which we were likely to come in conflict was Russia and in that case he could only promise us neutrality. He considered that for Germany a war with Russia was much more serious than with France. ~~Even~~ However victorious the German armies might be it would take a very long time to bring Russia to terms. The Country would not support an invading army, the villages were mere wood shacks, unfit to lodge troops and the experience of Charles XII and Napoleon showed the difficulties to be contended with. He wished ~~France~~ Russia and England to remain at peace, as a quarrel between two of one's friends was always disagreeable, but his chief preoccupation must be to prevent a quarrel between Russia & Austria. The dam which he had built up between them burst on the average once a year, and then he had, like a bricklayer, to patch it up.

If Russia & Austria went to war & Germany remained neutral, the losing Power would have an undying hatred for her, and would look out for opportunities of revenge. He could not say which side would win, 'perhaps Russia,' but the result, if Austria lost, would be her total annihilation or her falling under the influence of Russia who might purchase her alliance by territorial concessions. Neither alternative would suit him. He would not annex the German provinces of Austria—there were too many discordant nationalities in them & too many Catholics and the unity of Germany would be impaired by such an accession of hostile elements. On the other hand, he could not have Russia at Vienna.

With reference to his promise of neutrality between Russia & England, I asked if the assurance given to the former that German & Austrian influence would be exerted to prevent Turkey opening the Straits to us was not a departure from strict neutrality and an encouragement to Russia to persevere in an aggressive policy against us.

The Prince defended himself rather lamely: said that Russia had asked his opinion whether Turkey would be justified in admitting the English fleet, and he had been obliged to answer that he considered that she had no right to do so unless herself a belligerent. It was a question he said of existing treaties.

The Prince expressed pleasure at our having come to an arrangement with Russia and hoped that it would be lasting. I said that even if it were not it had given us time to prepare and that Lord Salisbury believed that in a few months we should be in such a position that we need not fear a Russian advance.

At 11 o clock we sat down to a repast of peaches & grapes which is part of the 'régime' which the Prince is following——

He talked about the Bulgarian question: He observed that in ordinary times Russia desired the union & Austria opposed it: but now the case was reversed. The Russians would like to undo it, if by this means Prince Alexander whom they hated could be got rid of. The Austrians on the other hand seemed disposed to agree to it, and to look upon it as the best means of maintaining tranquillity in the Balkan peninsula.

The Prince said that his principal object must be to prevent the affair from leading to a quarrel between Austria & Russia, but that he had not made up his mind what would be the best arrangement. The Turks had lost the favorable moment for intervening. (I understood from Count Herbert Bismarck that the Prince had advised the Sultan through the Turkish Ambassador at Berlin to take this course but that the Sultan had telegraphed a second time for a confirmation of the advice and that the Prince had then declined to renew it).

The Prince said he did not know Lord Salisbury's views. I said that your view was that as the Turks had not taken action and did not appear disposed to do so, the union could not be undone. But you attached importance to the maintenance of distinct constitu-

tions in Bulgaria & Eastern Roumelia. You thought the Bulgarian
Constitution unworkable & considered that the existence of the two
different constitutions might enable the Prince to play off one part
of his dominions against another and would thus give ~~him gre~~ more
security to his position. You also thought that Austria should declare
her intention of not allowing the movement to spread to Macedonia.
The Prince appeared to agree in these views & said that Austria had
already done what she could in regard to Macedonia.

At 1 we met at luncheon. Count Rantzau, the Prince's son in law
& secretary being present. The Prince talked again of the Bulgarian
question. He thought a solution might perhaps be found if the Porte
nominated Prince Alexander Governor General of E[astern]
Roumelia. He did not know if Russia would consent on account of
her dislike of the Prince. I asked how the Bulgarians would be
induced to agree. Would they do so merely out of deference to the
will of Europe? He suggested that the Servians, who were burning
for the fray, might be used as an instrument of pressure. The Servian
army he said was much better than the Bulgarian and the threat of
letting them loose ~~on them~~ might bring the Bulgarians to reason. With
regard to Macedonia he observed that not more than 1/3 of the population were Bulgarian. In the South they were Greeks, in the west
~~Bulgarians~~ Albanians. Austria was uneasy about Servia and felt
obliged to give her her head to a certain extent, from fear that King
Milan might lose his throne if he did not comply with the wishes of
his subjects, or that the Servians might throw themselves into the
arms of Russia.

He then referred to the suggestion he made to Malet as to sending
the English fleet to Athens. I said you objected to do this as an
isolated act which might be misconstrued, but that I believed you
would be willing, if a general plan of proceeding was concerted, to
put pressure upon Greece in the interests of general peace: but,
nationality for nationality, you were on the side of the Greeks. The
Prince explained that he had thought that the presence of one or
two English ships at Piraeus would be a visible sign to the excited
populations that Europe had its eye on their proceedings. He did
not however press the point. He alluded again to the hatred felt
against Prince Alexander by the Russians who went so far as to
bring disgraceful charges against him.

At dinner the conversation did not turn on politics, but after it was
over the Prince sat down to a large China pipe of which four were
ready filled for him & which he smoked in succession.

He observed that there were some people in Austria who wished to substitute for the treaty between Austria & Germany a law to be passed in each Country, by which their alliance would become an essential part of the Constitution of both states. He explained that the object would be that the union of the two Countries would not terminate with the expiration of the Treaty and would not be dependent on the will of the Sovereigns, but would continue until the law was repealed by the respective Parliaments. He went on to say that a Treaty with England was an uncertain thing, as with a change of Ministry it might no longer be considered binding. I said that in England Treaties concluded under one Government were equally binding on their successor and asked if he thought England less faithful to Treaties than other nations.

He answered that he would not say that, but there was the Luxemburg Treaty which was no sooner signed than it was explained away by the Minister of the day. Would England fight if Belgium were attacked?

I said, no doubt, if she had an ally and reminded him of the steps taken by Mr. Gladstone's Gov[ernment] to secure the neutrality of Belgium in 1870. He said 'Yes but new Treaties were thought necessary'.

I said that ever since I had been in the Foreign Office Belgium and Constantinople had been looked upon as questions about which England would fight, and though she might not now be prepared to engage in a war with Russia for the latter object unsupported, she would no doubt do so if other Powers would join her.

He said the feeling in Austria was that she could not count no reliance could be placed on the support of England. Mr. Gladstone had denounced the Austrian Government & thrown over their Austrian alliance & this might happen again. I said I was not going to defend Mr. Gladstone's declaration against Austria, but it was made when he was out of office, and did not apply to the question of a Russian attack on Cons[tantino]ple but to the supposed intention of Austria to interfere with the emancipation of the Christians in the Balkan States from Turkish rule. I thought that even Mr. Gladstone would act with Austria in opposing the Russian occupation of Cons[tantino]ple. The Prince referred to Mr. Gladstone's visit to the Emperor of Russia at Copenhagen as having increased the distrust of his intentions felt in Austria.

We then had a long discussion as to the result of Russia obtaining possession of Cons[tantino]ple. He maintained that it would do no harm to any one except Russia herself, who would be weakened by the extension of her line of defence and would become more vulnerable. The strength of Russia, he said, consisted entirely in the millions of peasants inhabiting Russia proper and in their devotion to the Czar who lived in the midst of them. If he moved his residence from Petersburg & Moscow the whole thing would fall to pieces. Cons[tantino]ple could therefore only be an outpost of the Empire. Even if the Emperor went too often to Copenhagen, he might hear one day that a catastrophe like the one in E[astern] Roumelia had happened during his absence. The Country was full of secret societies: there were many nihilists in the army: the peasants were discontented on account of the unfair way in which their lands were redistributed every 2 or 3 years under the Communal system: enormous corruption prevailed everywhere. He did not believe that the present Government in Russia had as much stability as even the French Republic. If Russia was not on the frontiers of his Country, he should not trouble himself about her at all. But he dreaded a war with her, not because he doubted the success of the German arms, but because it would be impossible to bring the war to a speedy termination, owing to the nature of the Country. In attack, Russia was despicable: She would have been beaten by the Turks in the last war if she had not bribed the Turkish Generals, and Osman Pasha, ~~who had been overlooked~~ whom by inadvertence they had omitted to buy, had repeatedly defeated them at Plevna.

But she was not vulnerable to attack. He admitted that he could not get the Austrians to agree with him as to the unimportance of the acquisition of Cons[tantino]ple by Russia, but said that people in Germany who had thoroughly studied the question took his view.

Austria would no doubt be disposed to resist the advance of Russia if she could count on the alliance of England. I said it was difficult for any one who had been brought up in the English view of foreign policy to admit that the possession of Cons[tantino]ple by Russia would not be a misfortune for the rest of Europe. Surely her increase of prestige and the stimulus it would give to her energies would alone be a menace to Germany and still more to Austria, while it would inevitably bring the Slav populations of the Balkan peninsula under her rule. As far as England was concerned the evil result was perhaps confined to the loss of the only vulnerable point where we could strike at Russia in the event of her attacking India and by occupying the Black Sea with our fleet could cut her communication in the Caucasus.

He would not admit that it would strengthen Russia in any way. She had already more population than she could manage. She was obligated to keep up enormous forces in her provinces and in Poland, and if she held Constantinople, would have to keep at least 200,000 men there. Russia could never become a formidable naval power. He had said this to the Emp[eror] of the French who had observed to him (I think in 1867) that if Russia held Cons[tantino]ple the preponderance of France in the Mediterranean would be in danger, as Russia would acquire a Greek maritime population to man her navy. Russia therefore would not, owing to her possession of the Dardanelles, become dangerous to England as a rival Naval Power. As to the Black Sea being a vulnerable point, that was all a mistake. Nothing could be done in the Caucasus. The independence of the Country had been entirely destroyed and the tribes broken up and defeated. The road to Central Asia was down the Volga and across the Caspian, not through the Caucasus. It would be easier to stir up an insurrection in Poland than in Circassia. The Baltic was more vulnerable than the Black Sea. Our fleet could do nothing more than bombard Odessa & clear the Sea of Russian shipping, neither of which measures would injure Russian trade, which (as he knew to his cost) took the inland route, the railways flooding Germany with cheap corn.

I pressed him on this question of the Russian possession of Cons[tantino]ple in the hope of discovering what his real intentions are in the matter. He gave me the impression of having labored, with only partial success, to convince himself that Germany could stand aside and leave Cons[tantino]ple either to fall into Russian hands, or to be kept out of them by an Anglo-Austrian alliance.

His language occasionally betrays distrust of Austria. Towards Russia his tone is one of dislike & contempt & he dwells with pleasure on stories of Russian corruption, and dishonesty.

The conversation then turned to Egypt. He said the existence of the Canal made it essential for England to hold the Country. I asked if our naval superiority would not enable us to secure the use of the Canal in time of war. He said that was not enough as the banks might be occupied & the canal blocked ~~by the explosion.~~

I said that your view was that our occupation should not be permanent, but that you could not fix a date for evacuation, and that you considered that we ought to retain a privileged position, and that the task of sending troops if necessary to restore order should be confined to us. Did he think that the Powers would agree to our having such a position? He said he saw no reason why the German Powers should object. Russia or France might do so, and our danger would be that Turkish troops supported by Russia, or the

French fleet might arrive before us—I said your idea was that we might have troops in Cyprus for the purpose. He said that our principal difficulty would no doubt be with France, but we need not so much mind her, as she could not go to war with us, without security on her Eastern frontier which he did not intend to give her. I spoke of the efforts we had made and were making to improve the condition of the people. He seemed to look upon this rather as an amiable weakness on our part, and said that in Egypt they complained that we had abolished the courbash & that the peasants would not work.

September 29

The Prince came to my room in the morning & mentioned that C[oun]t Münster would be recalled & would be succeeded by Count Hatzfeldt. The latter was the diplomatist he had most confidence in and his selection for the post was due to the Prince's wish to establish real & intimate relations with England. C[oun]t Münster he said was a worthy honest man but was always riding & driving & did not attend properly to business. In mentioning that C[oun]t Münster was appointed to Paris he said that it did not much matter who the German Rep[resentative] there was, now that he had given up any idea of improving the relations of Germany with ~~washed his hands of France the attempt~~ France.

The Prince then read me the telegrams he had received on the E[astern] Roumelian question.

M. de Giers arrived at 11 o clock to spend the day and in consequence I did not see the Prince alone again except for a short time in his room. When I said that as I might not have another opportunity I wished to tell him that you had charged me to say that if he would state his views on the Bulgarian question you would act with him as far as your position allowed, the difficulties of which he would understand. Italy professed her desire to act entirely with us and you were anxious that as far as possible the 4 Powers should act together. He concurred and said that now that he had broken with France he should find his relations with Italy much more easy.

In the course of conversation the Prince refering [sic] to the dispute with Spain about the Caroline Is[lands] said Germany could afford to take no notice of Spanish violence. Her military reputation was not at stake. Once on a time she had been 'Fighting Bob,' but that was when it was necessary by blood & iron to emerge from the impossible position in which she was placed. She had been hemmed in on all sides & had not room to breathe: but that was all changed now. Germany did not require any more glory & had got all she wanted. She would be foolish to engage in further quarrels.

The Prince said that he was much obliged to you for the assistance you had given him in the question of the Caroline Is[lands]. If an arrang[emen]t was come to with Spain through the arbitration of the Pope, which he had proposed, or in any other way, he should stipulate for the same advantage for English commerce as for German commerce. He also intended to invite the United States Gov[ernment] to become a party to the convention on account of their missionary interests in the Islands. He had sounded the U[nited] S[tates] Minister on the subject.

September 30

I spent the day at Friedrichsruh but did not have much political conversation with the Chancellor. In the morning he was at work & during the rest of the day he talked principally on other topics.

With regard to the Bulgarian Question, he was waiting to hear from M. de Giers the result of his interview with the Emp[eror] of Russia at Copenhagen.

When I took leave of the Prince, he spoke very kindly of the pleasure he had felt in seeing me at Friedrichsruh, desired me to convey his best regards to you & said he hoped there would now be the best possible understanding between the 2 Countries. I said I hoped he would not forget to instruct his agents in Egypt to support our Rep[resentative]. He said that they would certainly do so.

P[hilip] Currie

These documents were in a separate bundle entitled 'P. Currie's negotiations with Bismarck. 1885.' Loose papers, Pte. Salisbury Papers.

III

Extract from: Memorandum respecting the Boundary between Persia and Russia; and the Understanding between Great Britain and Russia as to the Maintenance of the Independence and Integrity of Persia. F.O. 251/57.

The following is the 'Understanding' between this country and Russia as to the maintenance of the integrity and independence of Persia.

No formal Treaty or agreement exists by which England and Russia mutually agree to respect the integrity of the Persian territory; but in 1834, on the occasion of the nomination by the Shah of Persia of Mahommed Meerza as his successor, an 'Understanding' was come to between the British and Russian Governments on the subject of Persia.

In a despatch to Mr. Bligh, dated 5th September, 1834, Lord Palmerston said:—

'You will also say that Her Majesty's Government are gratified to find that the Governments of Great Britain and Russia are acting, with regard to the affairs of Persia, in the same spirit, and are equally animated by a sincere desire to maintain, not only the internal tranquillity, but also the independence and integrity of Persia.'

In November 1838 Russia alluded to the 'happy agreement of views and actions' which the two governments had so much at heart to form in 1834, and a copy of the foregoing despatch, written by Lord Palmerston to Mr. Bligh in September 1834, was forwarded from St. Petersburgh to the Russian Ambassador in London, in order that he might show it to Lord Palmerston, with an assurance that the same desire which then influenced the Russian Government to have a friendly understanding with England upon the affairs of Persia still existed, and an expression of regret on the part of Russia that the good understanding which had existed between the Court of London and that of Tehran was disturbed for the time.

Lord Palmerston expressed his entire satisfaction at receiving this declaration that the Russian policy with regard to Persia remained unchanged, and that it was the same which the two Powers had agreed to adopt in 1834.

The correspondence of 1834 and 1838 was laid before Parliament in 1839, with other papers relating to the affairs of Persia and Afghanistan, and the passages quoted above are to be found at pages 3, and 191, 192.

This correspondence is also printed in a separate volume in octavo.

In June 1873 the Persian Government inquired what understanding existed between Great Britain and Russia respecting the maintenance of the integrity of Persia, when it was informed of what had passed in 1834 and 1838.

Count Brunnow was also told of the communication which had been made to the Persian Government, at which he expressed his satisfaction.

E. Hertslet,
Foreign Office
22 April 1874

IV

The Marquis of Salisbury to
Sir Henry Drummond Wolff
No. 14, Very Confidential, 29 February 1888

From: F.O. 60/491

On your departure from England to take up the appointment of Her Majesty's Envoy at Tehran, it may be convenient that you should be furnished with a brief statement of the principal questions with which you have to deal.

The inclosed copies of correspondence which has passed between this Department and the India Office will place you in possession of the views of Her Majesty's Government as to the leading features of the policy to be pursued by Great Britain towards Persia.

It is to the interest of this country that the integrity of Persia should be maintained, that its resources should be developed, and that its Government should be strong, independent, and friendly. It is to the promotion of these objects that your attention should be directed, and so long, at least, as there is any reasonable hope of their being realized, the efforts of Her Majesty's Government would be directed to frustrate any policy incompatible with them.

An understanding exists between this country and Russia as to the maintenance of the integrity and independence of Persia, but it is of a somewhat informal and indefinite nature, consisting mainly of an exchange of assurances in 1834 and 1838 as to the identity of the policy of the two countries in this respect.

The correspondence has been laid before Parliament, and in 1873 the Persian Government, in reply to an inquiry as to the nature of the understanding, was officially informed of it by Her Majesty's Government, and the Russian Ambassador in London expressed his satisfaction at the communication.

It is to be noticed that when, in 1865, Lord Russell proposed an exchange of declarations with the Russian Government containing an Agreement not to disturb the then state of possession in Central Asia, and also to respect the independence of the Persian Monarchy, to abstain from encroachments upon the territory of Persia, and to act in such a manner as might best support and strengthen the Sovereignty of the Shah, Prince Gortchakoff declined to make a corresponding declaration, alleging the behaviour of the Khan of Bokhara as a ground for not entering into the engagement respecting Central Asia, and remarking that he could not understand the connection between Central Asia and the Persian Monarchy. Lord Russell's declaration, as regards the latter country, Prince Gortchakoff described as very satisfactory and quite in accordance with the views of the Imperial Government, but he added that he had never suspected Her Majesty's Government of any intention of encroaching upon the territory of the Shah.

The assurances, however, of the desire of the Russian Government to respect the integrity and promote the independence and prosperity of Persia were renewed in the correspondence which took place on this occasion.

The northern frontier between Russia and Persia, to the west of the Caspian Sea, was laid down in the Treaty of Gulistan of the 12th October, 1813, and subsequently modified by the Treaty of Tourkmantchai of 10th (22nd) February, 1828.

The frontier to the east of the Caspian for a long time remained undefined, and was the subject of protracted discussions, which it is not necessary here to recapitulate.

On the 21st December, 1881, a Treaty was signed between Russia and Persia at Tehran, which made the course of the Attrek the boundary between the possessions of the two countries from the Caspian Sea to Chat, and laid down the frontier from the latter place as far as Baba-Dormuz. This Treaty was made public, and was laid before Parliament at the time.

But on the same occasion a further Secret Treaty was signed, defining the frontier as far as the neighbourhood of Sarakhs, and containing some further arrangements respecting the administration of the districts on either side of the line. The existence of this Agreement was for a long time denied, but the Shah, in January of last year, gave a copy of it secretly to Mr. Nicolson, with a Map showing the direction of the frontier-line. This Map cannot, however, be relied upon for accuracy, and we are not at present in possession of surveys of the country which would enable the frontier to be fully identified.

There have for some time been reports of further negotiations having been entered upon, and of fresh demands on the part of Russia being in contemplation, if not actually advanced, but the information on the subject is vague and doubtful. I inclose herewith an interesting collection of very confidential papers bearing on the subject which includes a Report on the Russian administration of the frontier districts, an abstract of a supposed plan for a future possible advance by Russia on India, and the bases of a Convention to be proposed to the Persian Government.

You will perceive that, even supposing the Russian Government to abide by the frontier-line laid down in the Secret Convention of 1881 as far as Sarakhs, there will still remain a tract of some 70 miles of frontier to be defined between that place and the extreme north-western point of the Afghan frontier at Zulfikar. Some indication of the claims which the Russian negotiators may possibly put forward in regard to this part of the frontier, as well as of the modifications which they may desire in other parts, is furnished by a remarkable pamphlet published in 1881 by General Petruscevitch, of which a copy is herewith inclosed, with a Memorandum on it by Colonel Napier.

[Marginal Note. In India Office Letter of 7 December 1881. No copies of pamphlet obtainable. Copy of map only sent herewith. Copy sent to Tehran in F.O. Desp. No. 121, 16 December 1881.]

In connection with this subject, and as illustrative both of the interest which Her Majesty's Government have taken in it, and of the difficulty of obtaining the entire confidence of the Shah and his Ministers in any transactions which affect their attitude towards Russia, it may be useful to mention some episodes in the history of the transactions which took place during the Russian progress towards Merv and before the eventual occupation of that place by the Russian forces.

In October 1879, after the massacre of the British Mission at Cabul had led to a renewal of the war with Afghanistan, and to the deposition of the Ameer Yakoub Khan, it was proposed by Sir

R[onald] Thomson that Persia should be placed in temporary possession of Herat on certain conditions, on the proper fulfilment of which her continued occupation would depend. The idea was approved by Her Majesty's Government, and a long negotiation followed with the Persian Government as to the terms of the Convention. The principal conditions will be found in the inclosed drafts of a Convention, and of notes to be signed by the Persian Minister for Foreign Affairs. They included the right to appoint a British Resident at Herat with a sufficient escort, and to occupy the city and territory with British troops in the event of its security being threatened, the exclusion of foreign officers or agents other than British, the conclusion of a Commercial Treaty between Persia and Great Britain favourable to British commerce, and the opening of the Karun River to steam navigation for foreign mercantile ships. The Persian Government were to do what they could to prevent the advance of Russia in the Turkoman country, or a Russian occupation of Merv.

These conditions had, at an early stage, been accepted by the Shah, but after an almost interminable series of discussions on points of detail and changes of wording, and when matters appeared almost ripe for the signature of the Convention, the Persian Government announced suddenly, in February 1880, that they were not prepared to proceed further unless the arrangement were made permanent.

The matter was consequently dropped. A change of Administration in this country occurred shortly afterwards, and an offer on the part of the Persian Government in the following May to renew the negotiation was declined.

The Treaty between Russia and Persia of December 1881, defining the frontier as far as Baba-Dormuz, having been made public, and the Persian Government having positively denied the existence of any Agreement as to the frontier beyond that place, Lord Granville, in February 1882, proposed to the Russian Government that an Agreement should be come to between England and Russia and Persia for the settlement of this frontier as far as the point where it met that of Afghanistan in the neighbourhood of the Heri-Rud, and for its subsequent demarcation by English, Russian, and Persian officers.

The Russian Government declined this proposal, on the ground that the question concerned Russia and Persia alone, but expressed their readiness to come to an agreement as to the frontier of Afghanistan.

At the same time, the Government of India, with a view of preventing a Persian cession of the Atak and of Sarakhs to Russia, and
of strengthening Persia's hold over those districts by making her
occupation of them effective, agreed, if necessary, to grant an annual
subsidy of 5 lacs of rupees to the Persian Government for a limited
period.

Sir R[onald] Thomson, in March 1882 and again in May 1883,
made it understood to the Shah and his Ministers, in guarded
language, that Her Majesty's Government were prepared to offer
such a subsidy. But on neither occasion was the offer taken up in any
way.

The subsequent occupation of Merv by Russia, which it had been
the object of Her Majesty's Government at the time to prevent, and
the settlement of the north-western frontier of Afghanistan, have
greatly changed the situation; but it is obvious that the security of
Herat may still be seriously affected by the acquisition of territory
by Russia in Khorassan to the immediate north-west, or *a fortiori* to
the west or south-west of the Afghan frontier near Zulfikar, as suggested by General Petruscevitch.

The matter is one which should be closely and carefully watched.
It has not been lost sight of by the War Office, and attention was
called in a Memorandum forwarded by that Department in July
1886, of which copy is herewith inclosed, to the importance of
settling the frontier between Persia and Afghanistan, with a view to
preventing such encroachments as far as possible, by a previous
definition of the territory acknowledged to be Persian. The suggestion was considered, but the Secretary of State for India was
disposed to doubt the expediency of raising the question at that time,
more especially as the arbitral decision given by Her Majesty's
Government in 1873 in regard to the Seistan portion of the frontier
had been received with dissatisfaction by both Persia and Afghanistan, and has ever since been the subject of repeated complaints.

As lately as May 1885, a fresh difference has arisen between
Persia and Afghanistan as to the possession of a district named
Hashtadan, in the neighbourhood of Kafir Kaleh, which the Afghans
claim on the ground of ancient pasturage rights. It was agreed last
summer by the two parties that the question should be investigated
and decided by Brigadier-General Maclean, an officer of the
Government of India, who is stationed on the Perso-Afghan border
for purposes of observation, and for the settlement of any matters
which may arise between the Persian and Afghan officials. It does
not appear that the inquiry has yet taken place. Should the dispute

be settled fairly to the satisfaction of both parties, which, perhaps, is too sanguine an expectation, an opportunity might be afforded to propose a definition of the whole frontier. But the question is one of much delicacy, and should not be entered upon without careful consideration and full consultation between Her Majesty's Government and the Government of India.

In the meanwhile, the Persian Government should be encouraged and warned to do their utmost in strengthening the administration and police of the frontier districts. Measures for this purpose, while materially useful for the establishment of their territorial claims, cannot be interpreted as having any unfriendly signification towards the Russian authorities.

Copies of the correspondence respecting Brigadier-General Maclean's appointment, and the instructions under which he is acting, are inclosed herewith for your information. It will be seen that he is under the orders of the Government of India, but you will receive copies of his reports, and there are many subjects on which he will require your advice, and possibly a reference by you to this Department. In such cases care must be taken that the Government of India should be kept fully informed of what passes, so that there may be no chance of confusion or contradictory directions.

On the side of Turkey the frontier of Persia is still in parts not accurately defined.

An attempt was made in 1844 to settle the differences which had arisen between Turkey and Persia on this and other subjects by a Commission, which met at Erzeroum, composed of Plenipotentiaries of those two Powers, and of Commissioners nominated by England and Russia.

These negotiations resulted in the Treaty of Erzeroum of the 31st May, 1847, which stipulated that the frontier should be laid down by Commissioners and engineers appointed for the purpose by the Contracting Parties.

Subsequent meetings of the Commission were held in 1849, 1850, and 1851 in Bagdad and Mohammerah, but it became evident that no immediate agreement could be hoped for between the two parties directly interested, and in accordance with a proposal made by Lord Palmerston in 1851 surveys were made and Maps prepared at great expense, by the British and Russian Commissioners, of the districts through which the mediating Powers considered that the frontier ran.

The preparation of the Map, which embraced territory 700 miles in length by from 20 to 40 miles broad, was not completed till 1865.

s

In May of that year the Porte was informed that, in the opinion of the mediatory Powers, the future line of boundary between the respective dominions of the Sultan and the Shah was to be found within the limits traced on the Map; that the two Mahommedan Governments should themselves mark out the line; and that, in the event of any difference arising between them in regard to any particular locality, the points in dispute should be referred to the decision of the Governments of England and Russia. A similar communication was made to the Persian Government. A further delay of several years, however, occurred before the Map was actually presented in its final shape, as it was found necessary to compare and correct the English and Russian versions, and to reproduce it in an amended form.

On the 3rd August, 1869, a Convention was signed at Constantinople between the Grand Vizier and the Persian Ambassador, by which it was agreed that, pending the settlement of the disputed boundary, the *status quo* should be maintained, and no new buildings should be erected upon the disputed territories.

Shortly afterwards, the British and Russian Representatives at Constantinople each presented the Ottoman Government with a copy of the Map; copies were similarly presented by the British and Russian Representatives at Tehran in February 1870.

Both the Persian and Turkish Governments are therefore in possession of two copies of the Map, the intention being that one copy should be retained by each Government, and that the other two copies should be intrusted to any Commission which should be formed for the purpose of marking out the actual frontier-line. Copies of the Map also exist in the British and Russian Missions at Constantinople and Tehran, in this office, and in the Government archives at St. Petersburgh.

No Commission, however, has ever been appointed to lay down the frontier, and from time to time disputes arise as to certain districts.

One source of difference has been removed by the provision contained in Article LX of the Treaty of Berlin, by which the town and territory of Khotur were ceded by Turkey to Persia.

But this has not prevented the occurrence of questions regarding other parts of the frontier. The latest of these arose in 1884, and was the revival of an old dispute respecting certain districts on the slope of the Pusht-i-kuh range, near the Tigris. An attempt was made to settle the points at issue under the mediation of Great Britain and Russia, and it was arranged that the *status quo* should, in the meantime, be observed. But, although the Shah pressed in July last for some steps to arrange definitely this and other unsettled points, it has been found impossible to induce the Porte to move further.

The districts traversed by the frontier are still so wild and sparsely populated that the absence of a defined boundary, which would in more civilized countries be intolerable, is probably not very severely felt. It is, in any case, a question which can only be satisfactorily settled with the good-will of the two parties principally concerned, and Her Majesty's Government can do no more than use their good offices to produce such a favourable disposition on either side.

You will find in the archives of Her Majesty's Legation some recent correspondence respecting the erection by the Turkish authorities of a fort at Fao, near the mouth of the Shat-el-Arab. This proceeding is in contravention of the agreement come to at the time of the signature of the Treaty of 1847, that the two parties should abstain from erecting fortifications on their respective sides of the river between Mohammerah and the sea. Her Majesty's Government are interested in the trade and navigation of the river which is to a large extent in British hands, and have remonstrated against the completion of the fort. But the Porte has contended that the point is one to be discussed between Turkey and Persia and, although the course of negotiations in 1846–47 afforded good grounds for a contention to the contrary, it has been thought better that the subject should be dropped, unless strongly taken up by the Persian Government.

As regards the internal condition of the country, the inclosed Report by Mr. Herbert, then Second Secretary in Her Majesty's Legation at Tehran, would go far to confirm the gloomy account given by Malcom Khan to Viscount Cross; but it is in some respects corrected by the observations, also inclosed, of Colonel Sir Murdoch Smith, whose long experience as Director of the Indo-European Telegraph in Persia entitles him to speak with authority.

The efforts of Her Majesty's Government for the promotion of internal progress have been principally directed of late years towards opening the South of Persia to British and other foreign commerce by improved means of communication. They have constantly urged upon the Shah and his Ministers that the Karun should be thrown open to steam navigation, but, owing in great part it is believed to Russian opposition, their representations have been unsuccessful. They have also at intervals advocated the construction of railways and waggon-roads.

In 1872, some months before his visit to Europe, the Shah granted to Baron Reuter a Concession for seventy years for the construction of a railway from Resht through Tehran to the Persian Gulf, with an exclusive right to the working of all mines, except gold and silver mines, the execution of irrigation works, the management of the State forests and uncultivated lands, and the *régie* of the Customs for twenty years. The Concession was of an extravagant character, amounting to a virtual monopoly of the industrial and natural resources of the country. Consequently, when, on the failure of Baron Reuter to perform certain conditions of the Contract, the Persian Government took advantage of the circumstance to cancel the whole concession, Her Majesty's Government did not consider that they had acted otherwise than judiciously in their own interests.

But, in view of the considerable expense to which Baron Reuter had been put, and of his assertions that his failure to fulfil the Contract was due to the negligence or obstruction of the Persian officials, Her Majesty's Government have urged that he is entitled to some compensation, or to a Concession of a more limited character. And, whenever endeavours have been made at Tehran to obtain railway Concessions for other parties, Her Majesty's Government have supported Baron Reuter's protests against the grant of such Concessions until his claims have in some way been satisfied.

As the railway schemes which have hitherto been brought forward in this manner have scarcely been of a substantial or serious nature, this action of Her Majesty's Government cannot be said to have really operated to the discouragement of enterprise in Persia. But their attitude in this respect could not be indefinitely maintained without inconvenience and an apparent want of friendship towards Persia.

In 1885, a proposal was made by Baron Reuter to make use of his Concession for the formation of an International Company under the protection of such of the Great Powers as might be willing to join in it, and an attempt was made by Her Majesty's Government to obtain the co-operation of the Government of Germany in supporting it. But their overtures were not favourably received, and the project was dropped.

Her Majesty's Government did not, however, desist from urging on the Shah, at every favourable opportunity, the desirability of improving the means of communication between the capital and the south of Persia, and in May 1886 His Majesty informed Mr. Nicolson that he was desirous of seeing a railway from the south, undertaken by a European, or mixed Persian and European Company; that, if a railway were impracticable, he would fall back upon a

road; that he had also decided to throw open the Karun to navigation, but thought this had better wait till the railway or road were
open, when it would follow as a natural consequence, and that he
would like the navigation to be under a Persian Company.

A reply was sent expressing the gratification of Her Majesty's
Government at this decision, and, in deference to the Shah's wish to
be furnished with a complete scheme, consultations were held with
the competent authorities of the India Office, with Mr. Mackinnon,
and with Mr. Mackenzie, of the firm of Gray, Dawes, and Co. (who
have the principal share of the steam navigation of the Tigris and
Euphrates). A draft Concession was drawn up, framed on the model
of those granted by the Government of India, with such modifications as the different circumstances of the case suggested, which it
was believed might be accepted, and put forward with fair chances
of success, by English financiers. Steps were also taken to make
Baron Reuter a party to the scheme, and he professed his willingness to accept a share in it, as a recognition of his claims under his
former Concession. The draft Concession was submitted to the
Persian Government for their examination. The latter at first
required certain modifications in the draft, some of which were
agreed to, but they have now presented a Counter-Project, which,
in its present shape, would certainly not be acceptable to European
capitalists.

The principal points of divergence between the views of the two
Governments are as follows:—

Her Majesty's Government, and the authorities they have consulted, look naturally to the necessity of offering to the public a fair
prospect of sufficient return for the money invested. For this purpose
it is important to keep the scheme within moderate limits, to make
use of the river navigation as far as the Karun is open for vessels of
proper draught, that is to say, up to the neighbourhood of Ahwaz, to
commence the railway from that point only, and not to extend it
further in the first instance than is necessary to give access to the
rich wheat-growing plateau which lies to the north and north-west
of Dizful.

The line so far does not present any great engineering difficulties,
would, therefore, be comparatively inexpensive, and promises a
speedy return of remunerative traffic. The estimated cost of a railway from the starting point, 6 miles below Ahwaz, to a point on the
Kerkha River, 12 miles north of Dizful (in all, about 100 miles), is
less than 500,000*l*, to which would be added the cost of establishing

steam navigation up the Karun from Mohammerah. The further sections of the railway from the Kerkha River to Khoramabad, and from thence to Kum and Tehran (a distance of 400 miles, in the latter part over mountainous country, and estimated to cost not less than 4,000,000*l*), would be left to be completed gradually, at first by waggon-roads, and subsequently by railways, as circumstances and the success of the first part of the undertaking might permit.

The wish of the Shah, on the other hand, is avowedly for a complete railway between Mohammerah and Tehran, a distance in all of 622 miles, estimated to cost not less than 5,500,000*l*. His Majesty shows a rooted aversion to opening the Karun to a British Steam Navigation Company, and maintains that any Company founded for the purpose must be purely Persian, and under Persian control. Messrs. Gray, Dawes, and Co., would not object to the company being nominally Persian, and to the vessels flying the Persian flag. But Mr. Mackenzie has pointed out that, in order to have any security for its proper working, it is essential that the management should be in English hands. In a confidential message sent to Mr. Nicolson by the Shah in October 1886 His Majesty explained that his reluctance to open the Karun was caused by a threat of the Russian Government to enter the Gulf of Enzeli, on the Caspian, if this concession were made. It is difficult to understand the exact meaning and purport of this threat, if indeed it has any existence in fact; but no further explanations have been obtained on the subject. The objections of the Persian Government to opening the Karun to foreign navigation seem, however, from the language of their Counter-Draft of Concession, to be still undiminished.

Finally, a most serious obstacle to the successful initiation of the scheme consists in the difficulty of finding sufficient security for the payment of a certain and moderate interest on the capital during the first stages of the undertaking, and at any subsequent period when the working profits may prove insufficient. Without some such security it is not to be hoped that British capitalists will be ready to invest their money in an enterprise, which contains so many elements of risk. It will be seen from the inclosed copy of a letter from the India Office that the Government of India are not prepared to guarantee a rate of interest on the railway, though they might possibly be induced to entertain a proposal to share such a guarantee with the Imperial Government. I am not of opinion, however, that a proposal for such a guarantee could under present circumstances be submitted to Parliament with any hope of a favourable reception. The efforts of Her Majesty's Government have therefore been directed to obtaining a promise of a lien on the Persian Customs for the amount required to make up a certain rate of interest on the capital that may be subscribed. The Persian Government have hitherto shown considerable reluctance to grant the powers of supervision that would be necessary to make such a lien effective. This reluctance is perhaps not unnatural, but there is little doubt that under European supervision the Customs would become much more remunerative, and without it the security for a fixed contribution would be little more than nominal.

Such are the principal points at issue, and it will be for you to consider on your arrival at Tehran whether and in what manner you should continue to urge the scheme, or whether for a time it should be left in abeyance. It has the support of the Zil-es-Sultan, who has recently received the distinction of the G.C.S.I., and who is alive to the benefits which the southern provinces under his rule would derive from the railway. And there are not wanting arguments which should strongly dispose the Shah in favour. Irrespective of the increased prosperity which it promises to bring (a consideration which perhaps weighs little with an Oriental Ruler, except in so far as it involves increased revenue), there can be no question that the improved communication with the south would increase the hold of the Central Government over that portion of the kingdom, and that, while scarcely available for purposes of hostile invasion, it would render it much easier for England in case of need to assist the Shah against foreign aggression or pressure.

The financial aspect of the question is, however, the most difficult one from a practical point of view. Her Majesty's Government in this respect are working at some disadvantage, inasmuch as they are not at present proposing conditions on behalf of any actual or even prospective Company, but have been endeavouring to frame a basis on which such a Company might be formed. The negotiation would perhaps be on a more satisfactory, and certainly on a more regular, footing, if it were in the hands of some financial Association, supposing that such could be found, who would be willing to treat with the Persian Government with your assistance and support.

In this and in all other questions of progress and reform, such as the employment of Europeans in the administration (as often recommended by the Persian Minister in this country), you will probably find it necessary to proceed with great caution, and to bear constantly in mind the fact that, leaving out of the question any personal feelings of timidity or indolence, the Sovereign of Persia is at the head of a very loosely organized system of government, largely

tainted by corruption, and that he has to deal with a public opinion
still highly fanatical and exclusive, not easily controlled or informed,
and not the less dangerous when roused because it has few legitimate
means of expression.

LIST OF ENCLOSURES

1. Correspondence with India Office. [I.O. March 5, June 24. to I.O.
   March 9. July 2.]
2. Memo. resp. Perso-Russian boundary, & understanding between Great
   Britain & Russia as to Maintenance of Persian integrity. (F.O. Ap.
   24, 1874.)
3. Analysis by Lord Tenterden of Parl. Papers resp. C. Asia, 1838–78,
   (with continuation). [3785]
4. Memo: on Attrek frontier. Sept. 1877.
5. Central Asia No. 1. 1882.
6. Mr. Nicolson. No. 13. Jan. 25. 87.
7. Mr. Nicolson. Sep. & Secret, April 29, 1886. [Sec. & Conf. 3024]
8. Col. Karaview's Memo: (Sec. 5363).
[9. Col. Petruscevitch's Pamphlet. With Map. Sent to F.O. Nov. 29. 1881.[1]]
10. Draft of Convention & Notes. Jan. 6. 1880.
11. War Office—July 27. 1886.
12. Enclosures in India Office, May 20. 1886. & Feb. 23 1887.
13. Memo (E.H.) on Turco-Persian boundary question. Jan. 10. 1873.
14. Mr. Herbert's Report on Internal Condition of Persia. (In Mr. Nicol-
    son's 149, Dec. 8. 1886.) Conf. No. 5392.
15. India Office. March 24. 1887. (Mem. by Col. Murdoch Smith.)
16. Abstract of Correspondence relative to Reuter Concession. [Conf. Nos.
    5120, 5232, & continuation]
17. India Office. June 27. 1887.
18. India Office Memoranda.
    (1) Russian movements in C. Asia. (1 & 2)
    (2) Demarcation of Afghan Boundary. (1, 2, 4, 5.) No copies of part 3
        available.

[1] See marginal note, p. 258.

V

Assurance given by British Minister to Shah respecting maintenance of Integrity of Persia Tehran, 24 October 1888

Assurance given to the Amin-es-Sultan by Sir Henry Drummond Wolff

From: Treaty series 14B. Persia. F.O. 93/75/14B.

In the event of any Power making an attack without just cause or provocation on Persia, or attempting to take possession of Persian territory against the will of the Persian Gov[ernmen]t, H[er] M[ajesty's] Gov[ernmen]t engage to make earnest representations against such proceedings & to take such steps as may in their judgment be best calculated to prevent any infringement of the integrity of Persia.

It is understood that, in order to enable H[er] M[ajesty's] Gov[ernmen]t to carry out this engagement, the Persian Gov[ernmen]t will give H[er] M[ajesty's] Gov[ernmen]t immediate notice of any demands threatening to the integrity of Persia which may be made upon them by any foreign Power.

VI

The Marquis of Salisbury to Sir Henry Drummond Wolff Unnumbered Telegram, Secret and Confidential, 19 May 1890

From: F.O. 60/513.

Your secret & confidential despatch of April 21.

First as to railways. There are three possible cases. The Russians may try to make a line through Khorassan towards Herat. I fear this is very likely & that for this they may spend Treasury money. The only instructions I can give are that you should resist it to the utmost of your power, though I am doubtful of your success.

The second case is that the Russians may wish to make a line from their frontier to Teheran. I should not resist this, but only insist that we should have a corresponding concession in the South for a line of similar value & importance, to be selected in consultation with the Legation. I do not think that the Russians will pay for this line with Treasury money, & their power of raising it from capitalists is very doubtful.

The third case is the one of which you speak, that they should desire to make a line through to Bunder Abbas. I am quite sure they will not try to do this with Treasury money: they will go into the market; & if they go into the market we should have them at our mercy. By announcing that we should look upon the construction of the line as a hostile act, & that we would not undertake, in the case of any future disturbance, to respect the property of any shareholder or other person in the line, or any obligations upon it, we should effectually prevent money being raised on any Bourse in Europe.

I think it is better, at all events for the moment, to deal with the railway question entirely on the defensive. I do not myself believe that the question of Anglo-Persian railways will be solved till a railway has been made through Beloochistan from Chaman to Seistan. I understand that in the councils of the Government of India there is much division of opinion on this question; but I believe that when once they have got railway trains running to Chaman, the absurdity of stopping there will force the Indian Gov[ernmen]t to go on, whatever they may say now.

I cannot think that a railway made by English capital on any terms whatever from the sea-coast to Teheran is a very probable contingency.

Secondly as to the Veliahd. I am against the policy of trying to make a partisan of one of the possible successors to the throne. We did it in the case of the Zil, & egregiously failed. Without prejudging the action which may be necessary when the crisis approaches, I think that any attempt, most of all any conspicuous attempt, to make a party among Persian princes & Persian statesmen will only injure our own position, & fatally damage those whom we patronise.

My long telegram to Wolff this week has not been printed has it! If so—why?

S

It has not been printed, as many of Wolff's telegrams are not.

It has only gone to the Queen & the Under Secretaries and I am still not sure from your two minutes whether it is to be treated as an ordinary telegram or not.

E B

Certainly print. It should always be printed unless marked private. In this case it is important because it is the only means my Colleagues have of knowing what I am doing.

S

BIBLIOGRAPHY

I. MANUSCRIPT SOURCES

A. OFFICIAL DOCUMENTS

Great Britain

(a) Public Record Office.

The Foreign Office Archives of particular relevance are in the following series: F.O. 60 (Persia); F.O. 64 (Prussia, Germany); F.O. 65 (Russia). Additional material is to be found in F.O. 93, F.O. 97, F.O. 248 and F.O. 251.

The Archives of the War Office and the Admiralty are also important, cf. especially W.O. 32, 33, and 106, and Admiralty 1 and 116.

(b) Commonwealth Relations Office: India Office Records.

The main series are: Despatches to India, Political and Secret Department, 1885–1892; Home Correspondence, Political and Secret Department, 1875–1892; Letters from India, Political and Secret Department, 1885–1892; Persian Correspondence, 1885–1888.

United States of America

Archives of the United States, Washington, D.C. State Department Records.

Persia. Diplomatic Dispatches: 1883–1906; Teheran. Consular Letters: 1883–1906.

Austria

Vienna State Archives.

Transcripts in the possession of Dame Lillian Penson. These transcripts are from volumes of correspondence between Austria-Hungary and Great Britain. This collection contained a number of useful dispatches relating to the affairs of Central Asia.

B. PRIVATE PAPERS

(a) *Public Record Office*

The Papers of Sir John Charles Ardagh. P.R.O. 30/40/—.

In India Major-General Ardagh was Private Secretary to the Marquis of Lansdowne, Governor-General and Viceroy, from 1888 until the end of 1893. Ardagh's memoranda and rough notes written for the use of the Viceroy are of value to this study.

The Papers of George Leveson-Gower, second Earl of Granville. P.R.O. 30/29/—.

The Correspondence of Lord Granville when he was Secretary of State for Foreign Affairs, 1880–5, contains a considerable body of relevant material. Of particular interest is his correspondence with Mr. Gladstone, the Marquis of Hartington, the Earl of Kimberley, the Earl of Northbrook, and the Queen. The 'cabinet opinions' throw light on the Penjdeh crisis.

The Papers of Stafford Henry Northcote, first Earl of Iddesleigh.

This collection, deposited temporarily in the Public Record Office, is large and full for earlier years, but few documents for the period of Lord Iddesleigh's Foreign Secretaryship, August 1886 to January 1887, seem to be extant.

The Papers of Sir William Arthur White. F.O. 364/1 and 2.

This collection consists of two volumes of diplomatic correspondence, 1857–90, in which some very useful items were found.

(b) *British Museum*

The Papers of William Ewart Gladstone. B.M. Add. MSS. 44086–44835.

Of particular interest are the letters exchanged with Lord Granville, Lord Hartington, Lord Kimberley, and Lord Rosebery.

Volumes pertaining to the present study are:

1882–1886—B.M. Add. MSS. 44228. Vol. cxliii. Correspondence Lord Kimberley.

1884–1885—B.M. Add. MSS. 44147. Vol. lxii. Correspondence Lord Hartington.

1885—B.M. Add. MSS. 44769. Vol. dclxxxiv. Miscellaneous Memoranda.

1885—B.M. Add. MSS. 44178. Vol. xciii. Correspondence Lord Granville.

1886—B.M. Add. MSS. 44179. Vol. xciv. Correspondence Lord Granville.

1886–1892—B.M. Add. MSS. 44289. Vol. cciv. Correspondence Lord Rosebery.

The Papers of Sir Austen Henry Layard, B.M. Add. MSS. 38931–39164.

The volume pertaining to the present study is:

1877–1879—B.M. Add. MSS. 39164. Vol. ccxxxiv. Confidentia Print, etc., India.

This volume contains some letters exchanged between Lord Salisbury and Lord Lytton.

(c) *India Office Library*

The Papers of Lord George Francis Hamilton.

This collection contains thirty-five bound volumes of private and semi-private correspondence between Lord George Hamilton, Secretary of State for India from 1895 to 1903, and the Viceroys of India, Lord Elgin and Lord Curzon.

(d) *Christ Church, Oxford*

The Papers of Robert Arthur Talbot Gascoyne Cecil, third Marquis of Salisbury.

The papers of Lord Salisbury are now deposited in Christ Church, Oxford. Considerable, and vital, material for this study came from this collection. The bound volumes of the private Foreign Office correspondence are rewarding. Much of the material is not bound, but is arranged in bundles.

(e) *In Private Houses*

The Papers of Sir Michael Hicks Beach, first Earl St. Aldwyn.

These papers are in the possession of the family at Coln St. Aldwyn. Work in the collection was useful from the general point of view, but few documents bear directly on Persia.

The Papers of Edward Robert Bulwer, first Earl of Lytton.

Robert, Earl of Lytton, was Viceroy and Governor-General of India from 1876 to 1880. His papers at Knebworth are in the possession of his granddaughter, Lady Hermione Cobbold. The collection of documents relating to India is impressive—both in bulk and in the quality of the material. The originals of Lord Salisbury's letters to Lord Lytton are here.

The Papers of John Wodehouse, first Earl of Kimberley.

These papers, still in the possession of the family, are in Kimberley House. The collection, very large, is still in the process of being sorted and catalogued. Many documents related directly to this study, and work in this collection proved most rewarding. The correspondence of Lord Kimberley with the Viceroys—Lord Ripon, Lord Dufferin, and Lord Lansdowne—was invaluable.

II. PUBLISHED DOCUMENTS

AITCHISON, CHARLES U. (compiler). *A Collection of Treaties, Engagements and Sanads Relating to India and Neighbouring Countries.* 14 vols. Revised and continued up to the end of 1930 under the authority of the Government of India. Calcutta: Government of India, Central Publication Branch, 1933.

'A.M.' 'Russo-British Relations in the Eighties', *Slavonic Review*, iii (1924), 179–86.

British and Foreign State Papers, 1812–. London: His Majesty's Stationery Office, 1841–. Covered for the years 1812 to 1914, 108 vols.

GOOCH, GEORGE P., and TEMPERLEY, HAROLD (editors). *British Documents on the Origins of the War, 1898–1914.* 11 vols. London: His Majesty's Stationery Office, 1926–30.

Great Britain. Sessional Papers.

Vol. lxxv (1873)
Correspondence with Russia respecting Central Asia, October 1872– January 1873, pp. 693–711. [C. 699]

Vol. lvi (1878–9)
Correspondence respecting the relations between the British Government and that of Afghanistan since the Accession of the Ameer Shere Ali Khan. [Afghanistan No. 1 (1878)], pp. 369–640. [C. 2190]

Vol. lxxvii (1878–9)
Despatches from the Governor General of India in Council to the Secretary of State in 1867, with Minutes enclosed, on Central Asia and Quetta, and Reply, pp. 109–66 (H.C. 73).

Vol. lxxxvii (1884)
Correspondence respecting the Affairs of Asia. [Central Asia No. 1 (1884)], pp. 57–184. [C. 3930]

Vol. lxxxvii (1884–5)
Telegram from Lieutenant-General Sir Peter Lumsden relative to the Fight between the Russians and the Afghans at Ak Tépé. [Central Asia No. 1 (1885)], pp. 21–3. [C. 4363]
Further Correspondence respecting Central Asia. [Central Asia No. 2 (1885)], pp. 25–231. [C. 4387]
Maps. [Central Asia No. 3 (1885)], pp. 323–34. [C. 4388]
Further Correspondence respecting Central Asia. [Central Asia No. 4 (1885)], pp. 233–315. [C. 4389]
Further Correspondence respecting Central Asia. [Central Asia No. 5 (1885)], pp. 335–79. [C. 4418]

Vol. lxxvii (1888)
Further Correspondence respecting the Affairs of Central Asia. [Central Asia No. 1 (1888)], pp. 729–55. [C. 5254]
Further Correspondence respecting the Affairs of Asia. [Central Asia No. 2 (1888)], pp. 757–79. [C. 5518]

Vol. lxxix (1892)
Correspondence respecting the Persian Tobacco Concession. [Persia No. 1 (1892). Despatches, dated March 1890–May 1892, pp. 205–97. [C. 6707]

HERTSLET, EDWARD (compiler). *Treaties, etc.*, *Concluded between Great Britain and Persia, and between Persia and other Foreign Powers, Wholly or Partially in Force on the 1 April 1891.* London: Butterworth's, 1891.

Krasny Arkhiv, vol. liii. Moscow: 'Obraztsovaya', 1932.

LEPSIUS, JOHANNES, BARTHOLDY, ALBRECHT MENDELSSOHN, and THIMME, FRIEDRICH (editors). *Die Grosse Politik der europäischen Kabinette, 1871–1917.* 40 vols. Berlin: Deutsche Verlagsgesellschaft für Politik und Geschichte, 1922–7.

MEYENDORFF, BARON ALEXANDRE. *Correspondance diplomatique de M. de Staal, 1884–1900.* 2 vols. Paris, 1929.

Ministère des Affairs Étrangères. *Documents diplomatiques français, 1871–1914.* First Series, 1871–1900, 11 vols. Paris: Commission de Publication des Documents Relatifs aux Origines de la Guerre de 1914, 1929–.

Reports and Papers, Political, Geographical, and Commercial, Submitted to Government by Sir Alexander Burnes, Lieutenant Leech, Doctor Lord, and Lieutenant Wood, Employed on Missions in the Years 1835–1836–1837 in Sinde, Affghanisthan, and Adjacent Countries. Printed by Order of Government. Calcutta: G. H. Huttman, Bengal Military Orphan Press, 1839.

Selections from the Records of the Government of India. Foreign Department. 16 vols. Calcutta: Published by Authority, 1876–93. 'Report on the Administration of the Persian Gulf Political Residency and Muscat Political Agency.' Title slightly changed in 1887.

TEMPERLEY, HAROLD, and PENSON, LILLIAN M. (editors). *Foundations of British Foreign Policy from Pitt (1792) to Salisbury (1902).* Cambridge University Press, 1938.

TEMPERLEY, HAROLD, and PENSON, LILLIAN M. (editors). *A Century of Diplomatic Blue Books, 1814–1914.* Cambridge University Press, 1938.

III. CONTEMPORARY WRITINGS, MEMOIRS AND DIARIES

ABBOTT, JAMES. *Narrative of a Journey from Heraut to Khiva, Moscow, and St. Petersburg, during the late Russian Invasion of Khiva.* 2 vols. London: W. H. Allen and Co., 1884.

AINSWORTH, WILLIAM FRANCIS. *The River Karun: An Opening to British Commerce.* London: W. H. Allen and Co., 1890.

ANDERSON, T. S. *My Wanderings in Persia.* London: James Blackwood and Co., 1880.

'AN INDIAN OFFICER.' *Russia's March towards India*. 2 vols. London: Sampson Low, Marston, and Co., 1894.

BALFOUR, LADY BETTY. *Personal and Literary Letters of Robert First Earl of Lytton*. 2 vols. London: Longmans, Green and Co., 1906.

BELL, MARK S. 'A Visit to the Kárún River and Kúm', *Blackwood's Edinburgh Magazine*, cxlv (April 1889), 453–81.

— 'Kúm to Isfahán', *Blackwood's Edinburgh Magazine*, cxlv (June 1889), 843–64.

BELLEW, HENRY W. 'Our Relations with Afghanistan', *Asiatic Quarterly Review*, Second Series, ii (January 1891), 28–62; (April 1891), 283–318.

BENJAMIN, SAMUEL G. W. *Persia and the Persians*. Boston: Ticknor and Co., 1887.

BIDDULPH, CUTHBERT EDWARD. *Four Months in Persia and a Visit to Transcaspia*. London: Kegan Paul, Trench, Trübner and Co., 1892.

— 'A March through the Great Persian Desert', *Asiatic Quarterly Review*, Second Series, ii (October 1891), 234–42.

BIRD, ISABELLA LUCY (Mrs. J. F. Bishop). *Journeys in Persia and Kurdistan*. 2 vols. London: John Murray, 1891.

BOULGER, DEMETRIUS CHARLES. 'England and Persia', *Asiatic Quarterly Review*, First Series, vii (January 1889), 190–201.

— *England and Russia in Central Asia*. 2 vols. London: W. H. Allen and Co., 1879.

BRACKENBURY, HENRY. *Some Memories of My Spare Time*. Edinburgh: William Blackwood and Sons, 1909.

BROWNE, EDWARD GRANVILLE. *A Year amongst the Persians*. Cambridge: University Press, 1926; n.e. Adam and Charles Black, 1950.

BUCKLE, GEORGE EARLE (editor). *The Letters of Queen Victoria. A Selection from Her Majesty's Correspondence and Journal between the Years 1886 and 1901*, Third Series, 1886–1901. 3 vols. London: John Murray, 1930–2.

BURNE, OWEN TUDOR. *Memories*. London: Edward Arnold, 1907.

BURNES, ALEXANDER. *Travels into Bokhara; containing the Narrative of a Voyage on the Indus from the sea to Lahore, and an account of a Journey from India to Cabool, Tartary, and Persia*. 3 vols. London: John Murray, 1839.

CAMPBELL, GEORGE D. (The Duke of Argyll). *The Eastern Question from the Treaty of Paris 1856 to the Treaty of Berlin 1878, and the Second Afghan War*. 2 vols. London: Strahan and Co., 1879.

'Career of an Indian General', *Blackwood's Edinburgh Magazine*, cxliv (November, 1888), 664–80.

T

CECIL, LORD ROBERT. 'Foreign Policy of England', *Quarterly Review*, cxv (April 1864), 481–529.

CECIL, ROBERT, Third Marquess of Salisbury. *Essays—Biographical.* London: John Murray, 1905.

CHAMPAIN, J. U. BATEMAN. 'On the Various Means of Communication between Central Persia and the Sea', *Proceedings of the Royal Geographical Society*, v (March 1883), 121–38.

CHIROL, VALENTINE. *Fifty Years in a Changing World.* London: Jonathan Cape, 1927.

COLLINS, EDWARD TREACHER. *In the Kingdom of the Shah.* London: T. Fisher Unwin, 1896.

CONOLLY, ARTHUR. *Journey to the North of India, overland from England, through Russia, Persia, and Affghaunistaun.* 2 vols. London: Richard Bentley, 1834.

CURZON, GEORGE NATHANIEL. 'The Fluctuating Frontier of Russia in Asia', *Nineteenth Century*, xxv (February 1889), 267–83.

— 'The Karun River and the Commercial Geography of Southwest Persia', *Proceedings of the Royal Geographical Society*, xii (September 1890), 509–32.

— 'Memorandum on the Society's New Map of Persia', *Proceedings of the Royal Geographical Society*, xiv (February 1892), 69–78. Map, p. 140.

— *Persia and the Persian Question.* 2 vols. London: Longmans, Green and Co., 1892.

— *Russia in Central Asia in 1889 and the Anglo-Russian Question.* London: Longmans, Green and Co., 1889.

— 'The Transcaspian Railway', *Proceedings of the Royal Geographical Society*, xi (May 1889), 273–95.

DE WINDT, HARRY. *A Ride to India across Persia and Baluchistan.* London: Chapman and Hall, 1891.

'DIPLOMATICUS.' 'The Imperial Bank of Persia', *Asiatic Quarterly Review*, First Series, viii (October 1889), 241–56.

DOBSON, GEORGE. *Russia's Railway Advance into Central Asia.* London: W. H. Allen and Co., 1890.

EDWARDS, HENRY SUTHERLAND. *Russian Projects against India: From the Czar Peter to General Skobeleff.* London: Remington and Co., 1885.

FEUVRIER, JEAN BAPTISTE. *Trois ans à la cour de Perse.* Paris, 1906.

GOLDSMID, FREDERIC JOHN. *Central Asia, and its Question.* London: Edward Stanford, 1873.

— (editor). *Eastern Persia, an Account of the Journeys of the Persian Boundary Commission, 1870–71–72,* 2 vols. London: Macmillan and Co., 1876.

— 'Lieutenant H. B. Vaughan's Recent Journey in Eastern Persia', *Proceedings of the Royal Geographical Society*, xii (October 1890), 577–96.

— 'A Railway through Southern Persia', *Scottish Geographical Magazine*, vi (December 1890), 617–32.

GORDON, THOMAS EDWARD. *Persia Revisited, 1895.* London: E. Arnold, 1896.

— *A Varied Life: A Record of Military and Civil Service, of Sport and of Travel in India, Central Asia and Persia, 1849–1902.* London: John Murray, 1906.

GRANT DUFF, MOUNTSTUART ELPHINSTONE. *Notes from a Diary 1889–1891.* 2 vols. London: John Murray, 1901.

GREY, EDWARD (Viscount Grey of Fallodon). *Twenty-five Years, 1892–1916.* 2 vols. London: Hodder and Stoughton, 1925.

GRIFFIN, LEPEL. 'Russia, Persia, and England', *Nineteenth Century*, xl (July 1896), 1–18.

GWYNN, STEPHEN (editor). *The Letters and Friendships of Sir Cecil Spring-Rice. A Record.* 2 vols. Boston: Houghton-Mifflin Co., 1929.

HARDINGE, ARTHUR HENRY. *A Diplomatist in the East.* London: Jonathan Cape, 1928.

HERTSLET, EDWARD. *Recollections of the Old Foreign Office.* London: John Murray, 1901.

HOLDICH, THOMAS HUNGERFORD. 'The Geographical Position of Mashhad (Meshed)', *Proceedings of the Royal Geographical Society*, vii (November 1885), 735–7.

LANG, ANDREW. *Life, Letters, and Diaries of Sir Stafford Northcote, First Earl of Iddesleigh.* 2 vols. Edinburgh: William Blackwood and Sons, 1890.

LANSDELL, HENRY. *Russian Central Asia, including Kuldja, Bokhara, Khiva, and Merv.* 2 vols. London: Sampson Low, Marston, Searle and Rivington, 1885.

LAW, EDWARD FITZGERALD. 'The Awakening of Persia', *Nineteenth Century*, xxvi (December 1889), 1001–13.

LE MESSURIER, AUGUSTUS. *From London to Bokhara, and a Ride through Persia.* London: R. Bentley and Son, 1889.

LUCY, HENRY W. (editor). *Speeches of the Marquis of Salisbury.* London: Routledge and Sons, 1885.

LYNCH, HENRY FINNIS BLOSSE. 'Across Luristan to Ispahan', *Proceedings of the Royal Geographical Society*, xii (September 1890), 533–53.

— 'Notes on the Present State of the Karun River, between Shushter and the Shat-el-Arab', *Proceedings of the Royal Geographical Society*, xiii (October 1891), 592–5.

MacGregor, Charles Metcalfe. *The Defence of India: A Strategical Study*. Simla: Government Central Branch Press, 1884.

Malcom Khan. 'Persian Civilization', *Contemporary Review*, lix (February 1891), 238–44.

Malleson, George Bruce. *Herat: The Granary and Garden of Central Asia*. London: W. H. Allen and Co., 1880.

Marvin, Charles. *Reconnoitring Central Asia*. London: W. Swan Sonnenschein, 1884.

—— *The Russians at Merv and Herat, and their Power of Invading India*. London: W. H. Allen and Co., 1883.

Mauley, Lord de. 'The Wellesleys in India', *Asiatic Quarterly Review*, First Series, iii (January 1887), 178–205.

'Military Balance of Power in Asia', *Blackwood's Edinburgh Magazine*, cxliii (June 1888), 877–92.

Millspaugh, A. C. *Americans in Persia*. Washington: Brookings Institution, 1946.

Mir Munshi, Sultan Mahomed Khan (editor). *The Life of Abdur Rahman Amir of Afghanistan*. 2 vols. London: John Murray, 1900.

Morier, James. *A Second Journey through Persia, Armenia, and Asia Minor to Constantinople, Between the years 1810 and 1816*. London: Longman, Hurst, Rees, Orme, and Brown, 1818.

O'Donovan, Edmond. *The Merv Oasis*. 2 vols. London: Smith, Elder and Co., 1882.

Owen, Sidney J. *A Selection from the Despatches, Treaties, and Other Papers of the Marquess of Wellesley, during his Government of India*. Oxford: Clarendon Press, 1877.

Parliamentary Debates, Third Series (Hansard). Vols. 294–356 (1884–1892); Fourth Series (authorized edition), vols. 1–127 (1893–1903). London: H.M. Stationery Office, 1884–1903.

'Persicus.' 'The Regeneration of Persia', *Asiatic Quarterly Review*, First Series, x (July 1890), 1–17; Second Series, ii (January 1891), 1–12.

Pulling, F. S. *The Life and Speeches of the Marquis of Salisbury*. 2 vols. London: Sampson Low, Marston, Searle, and Rivington, 1885.

Raverty, H. G. *Muscovite Proceedings on the Afghan Frontier*. Reprinted from the *United Service Gazette* (7 and 14 February 1885).

—— *Notes on Afghánistán and Part of Balúchistán, Geographical, Ethnological, and Historical*. London: Eyre and Spottiswoode, 1880.

Rawlinson, Henry Creswicke. *England and Russia in the East. A Series of Papers on the Political and Geographical Condition of Central Asia*. London: John Murray, 1875.

RIDGEWAY, WEST. 'The New Afghan Frontier', *Nineteenth Century*, xxii (October 1887), 470–82.

ROBERTS, LORD (Frederick Sleigh Roberts, Field-Marshal Lord Roberts of Kandahar). *Forty-one Years in India*. London: Macmillan and Co., 1898.

RONALDSHAY, EARL OF (Lawrence John Lumley Dundas, second Marquis of Zetland). *On the Outskirts of Empire in Asia*. Edinburgh: William Blackwood and Sons, 1904.

SCHUYLER, EUGENE. *Turkistan: Notes of a Journey in Russian Turkistan, Khokand, Bukhara, and Kuldja*. 2 vols. New York: Scribner, Armstrong and Co., 1877.

SMITH, R. MURDOCK. 'The Karun River as a Trade Route', *Journal of the Society of Arts*, xxxvii (10 May 1889), 561–71.

STEWART, CHARLES EDWARD. 'The Herat Valley and the Persian Border, from Hari-Rud to Sistan', *Proceedings of the Royal Geographical Society*, viii (March 1886), 137–56.

SYKES, PERCY MOLESWORTH. *Ten Thousand Miles in Persia or Eight Years in Iran*. London: John Murray, 1902.

The Times, 1884–1903.
    Reading the daily summaries of war preparations and the leading articles about Russia and the Afghan crisis gives a vivid picture of the nearness to war in 1885. The series of special articles written by Curzon (1889–90) and by Valentine Chirol (1902–3) were most informative. Both used their articles as the basis for a book: Curzon, *Persia and the Persian Question*; and Chirol, *The Middle Eastern Question*,

VAMBERY, ARMENIUS. *The Coming Struggle for India*. London: Cassell and Co., 1885.

— 'The Russian Advance in the Pamirs', *New Review*, vii (September 1892), 262–70.

— 'Will Russia Conquer India?', *Nineteenth Century*, xvii (January 1885), 25–42; (February 1885), 297–311.

WARBURTON, ROBERT. *Eighteen Years in the Khyber, 1879–1898*. London: John Murray, 1900.

WILLS, CHARLES JAMES. *In the Land of the Lion and the Sun, or Modern Persia*. London: Macmillan and Co., 1883.

WISHARD, JOHN G. *Twenty Years in Persia: A Narrative of Life under the Last Three Shahs*. New York: Fleming H. Revell Co., 1908.

WOLFF, H. D. *Rambling Recollections*. 2 vols. London: Macmillan and Co., 1908.

WOLFF, JOSEPH. *Narrative of a Mission to Bokhara in the Years 1843–1845, to ascertain the fate of Colonel Stoddart and Captain Conolly*. London: John W. Parker, 1845.

WYLLIE, J. W. S. 'Foreign Policy of Sir John Lawrence', *Edinburgh Review*, cxxv (January 1867), 1–47.

— 'Masterly Inactivity', *Fortnightly Review*, new series, vi (December 1869), 585–615.

— 'Mischievous Activity', *Fortnightly Review*, new series, vii (March 1870), 278–308.

YATE, ARTHUR C. *England and Russia Face to Face in Asia: Travels with the Afghan Boundary Commission*. Edinburgh: William Blackwood and Sons, 1887.

YATE, CHARLES E. *Northern Afghanistan or Letters from the Afghan Boundary Commission*. Edinburgh: William Blackwood and Sons,1888.

YOUNGHUSBAND, F. E. 'Journeys in the Pamirs and Adjacent Countries', *Proceedings of the Royal Geographical Society*, xiv (April 1892), 205–34.

YOUNGHUSBAND, G. J. 'The Invasion of India by Russia', *Nineteenth Century*, xxxiii (May 1893), 727–48.

IV. SECONDARY WORKS

ALLAN, JAMES G. *The Strategic Principles of Lord Lytton's Afghan Policy*. London: Central Asian Society, 1937.

BALFOUR, LADY BETTY. *The History of Lord Lytton's Indian Administration, 1876 to 1880: Compiled from Letters and Official Papers*. London: Longmans, Green and Co., 1899.

BENNETT, THOMAS JEWELL. 'The Past and Present Connection of England with the Persian Gulf', *Journal, Royal Society of Arts*, l (13 June 1902), 634–52.

BLACK, CHARLES EDWARD DRUMMOND. 'A Short History of the Reform Movement in Persia', *Journal of the United Service Institution of India*, xxxviii (October 1909), 505–12.

BOULGER, DEMETRIUS CHARLES. 'Cabul and Herat', *Contemporary Review*, lxxvii (January 1900), 40–9.

BROCKWAY, THOMAS P. 'Britain and the Persian Bubble, 1888–1892', *Journal of Modern History*, xiii (March 1941), 36–47.

BROWNE, EDWARD GRANVILLE. *A Literary History of Persia*. 4 vols. London: T. F. Unwin, 1902–28.

— *The Persian Revolution of 1905–1909*. Cambridge University Press, 1910.

— *The Press and Poetry of Modern Persia*. Cambridge University Press, 1914.

BRUCE, C. E. 'The Indian Frontier Problem', *The Asiatic Review*, xxxv (July 1939), 492–514.

BRUCE, RICHARD ISAAC. *The Forward Policy and its Results or Thirty-five Years' Work amongst the Tribes on our North-Western Frontier of India*. New York: Longmans, Green and Co., 1900.

BULLARD, READER. *Britain and the Middle East from the Earliest Times to 1950*. London: Hutchinson's University Library, 1951.

CAPENNY, S. H. F. 'An Indo-European Highway: An Account of Colonel Mark Bell's Views', *Scottish Geographical Magazine*, xvi (September 1900), 523–34.

CECIL, LADY GWENDOLEN. *Life of Robert, Marquis of Salisbury*. 4 vols. London: Hodder and Stoughton, 1921–32.

CHAPMAN, E. F. *Our Commercial Policy in the East*. London: Central Asian Society, 1904.

CHIROL, VALENTINE. *The Middle Eastern Question; or, Some Political Problems of Indian Defence*. London: John Murray, 1903.

CHURCHILL, WINSTON LEONARD SPENCER. *Lord Randolph Churchill*. 2 vols. London: Macmillan and Co., 1906.

CODRINGTON, K. DE B. 'A Geographical Introduction to the History of Central Asia', *Geographical Journal*, civ (July–August 1944), 27–40; (September–October 1944), 73–91.

COVILLE, A., and TEMPERLEY, HAROLD. *Studies in Anglo-French History*. 'The Foreign Policy of Lord Salisbury, 1878–80. The Problem of the Ottoman Empire.' By Lillian M. Penson. Cambridge University Press, 1935.

CREWE, MARQUESS OF (Robert Offley Ashburton Crewe-Milnes). *Lord Rosebery*. 2 vols. London: John Murray, 1931.

CURZON, GEORGE NATHANIEL (Lord Curzon of Kedleston). *Frontiers*. Oxford: Clarendon Press, 1907.

DAVIES, C. COLLIN. *The Problem of the North-West Frontier, 1890–1908*. Cambridge University Press, 1932.

— 'Pandjdih', in *Encyclopedia of Islam*. Edited by M. Th. Houtsma et al. Vol. iii, 1023–4. London: Luzac and Co., 1936.

DAVIS, HENRY WILLIAM CARLESS. *The Great Game in Asia* (1800–1844). Oxford University Press, 1927.

DICKSON, WILLIAM KIRK. *The Life of Major-General Sir Robert Murdoch Smith*. Edinburgh: William Blackwood and Sons, 1901.

DURAND, H. MORTIMER. *Life of Right Honourable Sir Alfred Comyn Lyall*. Edinburgh: William Blackwood and Sons, 1913.

EDMONDS, C. J. 'Luristan', *Geographical Journal*, lix (January 1922), 335–56.

ELSMIE, G. R. *Field Marshal Sir Donald Stewart: An Account of His Life Mainly in His Own Words*. London: John Murray, 1903.

Encyclopedia Britannica. 11th ed.

FISHER, B. 'Irrigation Systems of Persia', *The Geographical Review*, xviii (May 1928), 302–6.

FISHER, WILLIAM B. *The Middle East*. London: Methuen and Co., 1950.

FITZMAURICE, LORD EDMOND. *The Life of Granville George Leveson Gower, Second Earl of Granville, 1815–1891*. 2 vols. London: Longmans, Green and Co., 1905.

FORTESCUE, L. S. 'The Western Elburz and Persian Azerbaijan', *Geographical Journal*, lxiii (April 1924), 301–18.

FRASER-TYTLER, WILLIAM KERR. *Afghanistan: A Study of Political Developments in Central Asia*. Oxford University Press, 1950.

FRECHTLING, L. E. 'The Reuter Concession in Persia', *The Asiatic Review*, xxxiv (July 1938), 518–33.

FRYE, RICHARD N. *Iran*. London: George Allen and Unwin, 1954.

FURON, RAYMOND. *La Perse*. Paris: Payot, 1938.

GATHORNE-HARDY, First Earl of Cranbrook. *A Memoir, with Extracts from his Diary and Correspondence*. 2 vols. London: Longmans, Green and Co., 1910.

GOLDSMID, FREDERIC JOHN. 'Major General Sir Henry Creswicke Rawlinson', *Geographical Journal*, v (May 1895), 490–7.

GOPAL, S. *The Viceroyalty of Lord Ripon, 1880–1884*. Oxford University Press, 1953.

GORDON, THOMAS EDWARD. 'The Problem of the Middle East', *Nineteenth Century*, xlvii (March 1900), 413–24.

— *The Reform Movement in Persia*. London: Central Asian Society, 1907.

GRENVILLE, J. A. S. *British Foreign Policy, 1899–1902*. London: Unpublished doctoral dissertation, 1954.

GRIFFIN, LEPEL. 'Persia', *Imperial and Asiatic Quarterly Review*, Third Series, ix (April 1900), 225–41.

GROSECLOSE, ELGIN. *Introduction to Iran*. New York: Oxford University Press, 1947.

HAAS, W. S. *Iran*. New York: Columbia University Press, 1946.

HAMILTON, LORD GEORGE. *Parliamentary Reminiscences and Reflections, 1868–1906*. 2 vols. London: John Murray, 1917–22.

HARDINGE, ARTHUR HENRY. *A Diplomatist in the East*. London: Jonathan Cape, 1928.

HARRISON, J. V. 'The Bakhtiari Country, South-Western Persia', *Geographical Journal*, lxxx (September 1932), 193–210.

HEDIN, SVEN. *Overland to India*. 2 vols. London: Macmillan and Co., 1910.

HICKS BEACH, LADY VICTORIA ALEXANDRINA. *Life of Sir Michael*

Hicks Beach, Earl St. Aldwyn. 2 vols. London: Macmillan and Co., 1932.

HOGARTH, DAVID GEORGE. *George Nathaniel Curzon, Marquess Curzon of Kedleston, 1859–1925.* British Academy Lecture, 1926.

— *The Nearer East.* London: Henry Frowde, 1905.

HOLDICH, THOMAS HUNGERFORD. 'Between the Tigris and the Indus', *Geographical Review*, iv (September 1917), 161–70.

— *England's Strength in Asia.* London: Central Asian Society, 1905.

— *The Gates of India, Being an Historical Narrative.* London: Macmillan and Co., 1910.

— *The Indian Borderland, 1880–1900.* London: Methuen and Co., 1901.

HOLLAND, BERNARD HENRY. *The Life of Spencer Compton, Eighth Duke of Devonshire.* 2 vols. London: Longmans, Green and Co., 1911.

HOTZ, A. 'Persian Trade Route', *Journal of the Society of Arts*, xlvii (March 1899), 341–59.

HUNTER, WILLIAM WILSON (editor). *India and Modern Persia.* New York: P. F. Collier and Son Corp., 1939.

HUNTINGTON, ELLSWORTH. 'The Depression of Sistan in Eastern Persia', *Bulletin of the American Geographical Society*, xxxvii (No. 5, 1905), 271–81.

— *The Pulse of Asia.* London: Archibald Constable and Co., 1907.

HUTTON, WILLIAM H. *The Marquess Wellesley, K.G.* Oxford: Clarendon Press, 1893.

JACKSON, ABRAHAM VALENTINE WILLIAMS. *Persia Past and Present: A Book of Travel and Research.* New York: Macmillan Co., 1906.

JAMES, DAVID. *Lord Roberts.* London: Hollis and Carter, 1954.

JEYES, S. H. *The Life and Times of the Right Honourable The Marquis of Salisbury: A History of the Conservative Party during the Last Forty Years.* 4 vols. London: J. S. Virtue and Co., no date.

KAYE, JOHN WILLIAM. *History of the War in Afghanistan.* 3 vols. London: William H. Allen and Co., 1878.

KENNEDY, AUBREY LEO. *Salisbury, 1830–1903: Portrait of a Statesman.* London: John Murray, 1953.

LAMBTON, A. K. S. *Landlord and Peasant in Persia.* London: Oxford University Press, 1953.

LEE, SIDNEY. *King Edward VII: A Biography.* 2 vols. New York: Macmillan Co., 1925–7.

LE STRANGE, GUY. *The Lands of the Eastern Caliphate, Mesopotamia, Persia and Central Asia, from the Moslem Conquest to the Time of Timur.* Cambridge University Press, 1905.

LITTEN, WILHELM. *Persien: Von der 'pénétration pacifique' zum 'Protektorat'. Urkunden und Tatsachen zur Geschichte der europaischen* '*pénétration pacifique*' *in Persien, 1860–1919*. Berlin: Walter de Gruyter and Co., 1920.

LOCKHART, LAURENCE. 'The "Political Testament" of Peter the Great', *Slavonic Review*, xiv (1936), 438–41.

LYALL, ALFRED. *The Life of the Marquis of Dufferin and Ava*. 2 vols. London: John Murray, 1905.

— *The Rise and Expansion of the British Dominion in India*. London: John Murray, 1910.

LYDE, LIONEL. *The Continent of Asia*. London: Macmillan and Co., 1933.

MACAULAY, D. I. *India in Imperial Defence*. London: Central Asian Society, 1910.

MAHAN, ALFRED T. *The Problem of Asia and its Effect upon International Policies*. Boston: Little, Brown and Co., 1900.

MARDER, A. J. *British Naval Policy 1880–1905*. London: Putnam and Co., 1940.

MAURICE, FREDERICK BARTON (editor). *The Life of General Lord Rawlinson of Trent: From his Journals and Letters*. London: Cassell and Co., 1928.

MINTO, MARY COUNTESS OF. *India, Minto and Morley 1905–1910*. London: Macmillan and Co., 1934.

MORISON, JOHN LYLE. *From Alexander Burnes to Frederick Roberts: A Survey of Imperial Frontier Policy*. Raleigh Lecture on History. Reprinted from the *Proceedings of the British Academy*, 1936.

MORLEY, JOHN. *The Life of William Ewart Gladstone*. 3 vols. London: Macmillan and Co., 1903.

— *Recollections*. 2 vols. London: Macmillan and Co., 1917.

NEWTON, LORD (Thomas Wodehouse Legh). *Lord Lansdowne: A Biography*. London: Macmillan and Co., 1929.

NICOLSON, HAROLD. *Sir Arthur Nicolson, Bart. First Lord Carnock. A Study in the Old Diplomacy*. London: Constable and Co., 1930.

NOEL, J. B. L. 'A Reconnaissance in the Caspian Provinces of Persia', *Geographical Journal*, lvii (June 1921), 401–18.

PENSON, LILLIAN M. 'The Principles and Methods of Lord Salisbury's Foreign Policy', *Cambridge Historical Journal*, v (No. 5, 1935–7), 87–106.

PENTON, EDWARD. 'The New Trade Route to Persia by Nushki and Sistàn', *Journal of the Society of Arts*, l (22 December 1901), 65–78.

PEROWNE, JOHN THOMAS WOOLRYCH. *Russian Hosts and English Guests in Central Asia*. London: Scientific Press, 1898.

POPOWSKI, JOSEF. *The Rival Powers in Central Asia; or, the Struggle between England and Russia in the East.* Westminster: Archibald Constable and Co., 1893.

PRATT, IDA (directed by Dr. Richard Gottheil). *List of Works in the New York Public Library relating to Persia.* New York: Bulletin of the New York Public Library, 1915.

RAWLINSON, GEORGE. *A Memoir of Major General Sir Henry Creswicke Rawlinson.* New York: Longmans, Green and Co., 1898.

RONALDSHAY, EARL OF (Lawrence John Lumley Dundas, 2nd Marquis of Zetland). *The Life of Lord Curzon: Being the Authorized Biography of George Nathaniel, Marquess Curzon of Kedleston.* 3 vols. London: Ernest Benn, 1928.

ROSS, EDWARD DENISON. *The Persians.* Oxford: Clarendon Press, 1942.

SKRINE, FRANCIS HENRY. *The Expansion of Russia, 1815–1900.* Cambridge University Press, 1915.

— and ROSS, EDWARD DENISON. *The Heart of Asia.* London: Methuen and Co., 1899.

SMITH, COLIN L. *The Embassy of Sir William White at Constantinople.* Oxford University Press, 1957.

SPARROY, WILFRID. 'Elder Brother of the Shah', *Blackwood's Edinburgh Magazine*, clxviii (August 1900), 264–77.

STAMP, LAURENCE DUDLEY. *Asia: A Regional and Economic Geography.* London: Methuen and Co., 1952.

STEIN, AUREL. 'Early Relations between India and Īrān', *The Asiatic Review*, xxxiv (January 1938), 38–64.

SUMNER, B. H. *Tsardom and Imperialism in the Far East and Middle East, 1880–1914.* London: H. Milford, 1942.

— *Russia and the Balkans, 1870–1880.* Oxford: Clarendon Press, 1937.

SYKES, ELLA CONSTANCE. *Persia and its People.* London: Methuen and Co., 1910.

SYKES, PERCY MOLESWORTH. 'A Fourth Journey in Persia, 1897–1901', *Geographical Journal*, xix (February 1902), 121–73.

— 'A Fifth Journey in Persia', *Geographical Journal*, xxviii (November 1906), 425–53; (December 1906), 560–92.

— 'Geography of Southern Persia as Affecting its History', *Scottish Geographical Magazine*, xviii (December 1902), 617–26.

— *A History of Afghanistan.* 2 vols. London: Macmillan and Co., 1940.

— *A History of Persia.* 2 vols. London: Macmillan and Co., 1930.

— 'Recent Journeys in Persia', *Geographical Journal*, x (December 1897), 568–97.

— *The Right Honourable Sir Mortimer Durand*. London: Cassell and Co., 1926.

— 'A Sixth Journey in Persia', *Geographical Journal*, xxxvii (January 1911), 1–19; (February 1911), 149–65.

TERENZIO, PIO-CARLO. *La rivalité Anglo-Russe en Perse et en Afghanistan jusqu'aux accords de 1907*. Paris, 1947.

THORNTON, A. P. 'British Policy in Persia, 1858–1890', *English Historical Review*, lxix (October 1954), pp. 554–79; (January 1955), pp. 55–71.

THORNTON, THOMAS HENRY. *Colonel Sir Robert Sandeman: His Life and Work on our Indian Frontier*. London: John Murray, 1895.

TUCKER, ALEXANDER LAUZAN PENDOCK. *Sir Robert G. Sandeman*. New York: Macmillan Co., 1921.

VALIKHANOF, CAPTAIN, *et al*. *The Russians in Central Asia: Their Occupation of the Kirghiz Steppe and the Line of the Syr-Daria: Their Political Relations with Khiva, Bokhara, and Kokan*. London: Edward Stanford, 1865.

VAMBERY, ARMENIUS. *Western Culture in Eastern Lands: A Comparison of the Methods Adopted by England and Russia in the Middle East*. London: John Murray, 1906.

WATSON, ROBERT GRANT. *A History of Persia from the Beginning of the 19th Century to the Year 1858*. London: Smith Elder and Co., 1866.

WHIGHAM, HENRY JAMES. *The Persian Problem: An Examination of the Rival Positions of Russia and Great Britain in Persia with some Account of the Persian Gulf and the Bagdad Railway*. London: Isbister and Co., 1903.

WILSON, ARNOLD TALBOT. *A Bibliography of Persia*. Oxford: Clarendon Press, 1930.

— *The Persian Gulf, An Historical Sketch*. Oxford: Clarendon Press, 1928.

WILSON, CHARLES. *Major General Sir Robert Murdoch Smith*. Chatham: W. and J. Mackay and Co., 1900.

WOLF, LUCIEN. *Life of the First Marquess of Ripon*. 2 vols. London: John Murray, 1921.

YATE, ARTHUR C. 'The Reform of Persia', *Imperial and Asiatic Quarterly Review*, Third Series, xxxiv (October 1912), 225–35.

— 'Through Persia from the Gulf to the Caspian', *Imperial and Asiatic Quarterly Review*, Third Series, xxix (April 1910), 370–8.

— 'The Zill-es-Sultan', *Imperial and Asiatic Quarterly Review*, Third Series, xxiv (July 1907), 108–11.

YATE, CHARLES E. *Khurasan and Sistan*. Edinburgh: William Blackwood and Sons, 1900.
— 'Russia and England in Persia', *Nineteenth Century*, lix (June
1906), 899–905.

Index

'Abd-ar-Rahman, 80
Admiralty, 72, 83, 97, 215–19
Afghanistan, 193, 255; Russian advance towards and effect upon British policy in India, 2–4, 13–16, 23, 28, 40, 46, 57, 62, 64–5, 89, 101, 144, 172, 179, 194, 205–7, 209, 214, 221, 224; and Persia, 18, 21, 90, 98–9, 128; British position in, 20, 65, 90, 98–9, 206–7, 214; boundary delimitations, 38, 67–85, 104, 110 n. 2, 128, 237 ff.; condition of (1878–9), 49–50, 258 ff.; and Penjdeh, 70 ff.; Cabinet opinions on policy in 1885, 227 ff.; Amir of, mentioned, 4, 14, 18, 22, 49, 70, 74, 76, 79–81, 101, 109, 210, 227 ff.; *see also* 'Abd-ar-Rahman, Sher 'Ali, Yaqub Khan, Zaman Shah
Ahwaz, 146, 164, 178, 265
Aitchison, Sir Charles U., 200
Ak Masjid (Perovski), 55
Akhal territory, 85
Alexander the Great, 23, 61
Alexander II, Emperor of Russia (1855–81), 49, 55–6, 151
Alexander III, Emperor of Russia (1881–94), 5, 31, 109–10, 114–15, 118, 139, 149, 156, 172; and Merv, 64; and Penjdeh crisis, 71–2, 76, 81, 238–9, 245; and military party, 103, 111, 118, 135, 138, 187; and Wolff, 129–34; and opening of Karun river, 167–9; and Pamirs, 190–1; Bismarck on, 250–1
Alexander of Battenberg, Prince of the Bulgarians, 151, 248–9
Alikhanoff, Colonel, 64, 80, 118
Altham, Lt.-Col. E. A., 220–2
American ministers in Persia, 4, 21, 101, 145, 165, 177, 185
Amin as-Sultan (Mirza Ali Asghar Khan), 140, 151 n. 2, 154, 159–60, 163–4, 173–4, 183–5

Amu Darya, *see* Oxus
Anglo-Asiatic Syndicate, 173
Anglo-Japanese Alliance, 222
Anglo-Russian agreements over Persia, 68, 102, 112, 115, 118, 210–11, 255–7
Anglo-Russian Convention (1907), 43, 120, 135, 138, 193, 223
Annenkoff, General M., 59
Aral Sea, 54–5, 66
Aras river, 5, 8
Ardagh, General Sir John, 218 n. 2
Argyll, George Douglas Campbell, 8th Duke of, 42, 66, 75, 96–7, 224
Arys river, 55
Ashkabad, 59–61, 85, 168
Ashurada, 58
Astrabad, 171, 188
Atrek, 5, 58, 85–6, 182, 259
Auckland, George Eden, Earl of, 47
Auliata, 55
Austria, 1, 89, 91, 99, 109, 126, 244, 247 ff.
Azerbaijan, 8–10, 139, 150, 184

Baba-Dormuz, 257–8
Baghdad, 261
Bakhtiaris, 7, 9–10, 161
Baku, 61
Balkans, 84–5, 109–11, 250–1
Balkh, 17, 106
Baluchistan, 18, 21, 27–8, 45, 178, 195, 208, 270; British control over, 4, 13–14, 20, 200–4
Bandar 'Abbas, 89, 270
Batum, 37, 61
Beaconsfield, Lord, *see* Disraeli
Belgium, 215, 250
Bell, Colonel Mark, 177
Belyavsky, Colonel, 54–5
Benjamin, S. G. W., 4–5, 101 n. 1
Beresford, Lord Charles, 16
Berlin, Congress of (1878), 242–4
Berlin, Treaty of (1878), 128, 262

U